AMERICA'S
Wonderful
LITTLE
HOTELS
& INNS
Fourteenth Edition

The South

States Covered in this Edition

Alabama	Louisiana
Arkansas	Mississippi
Florida	North Carolina
Georgia	South Carolina
Kentucky	Tennessee

Also in this Series

America's Wonderful Little Hotels & Inns, U.S.A. and Canada
America's Wonderful Little Hotels & Inns, New England
America's Wonderful Little Hotels & Inns, The Middle Atlantic
America's Wonderful Little Hotels & Inns, The Midwest
America's Wonderful Little Hotels & Inns, The Rocky Mountains and The Southwest
America's Wonderful Little Hotels & Inns, The West Coast
Europe's Wonderful Little Hotels & Inns, Great Britain & Ireland
Europe's Wonderful Little Hotels & Inns, The Continent

AMERICA'S
Wonderful
LITTLE
HOTELS
& INNS
Fourteenth Edition

The South

Edited by Sandra W. Soule

Associate Editors:
Nancy P. Barker, June C. Horn,
Alexandra Brady, Meg Cassidy, Abby Humphrey,
Betsy Sandberg

Contributing Editors:
Suzanne Carmichael, Susan Waller Schwemm, Diane Wolf,
Mary Ann Boyle

Editorial Assistant:
Jeffrey Soule

St. Martin's Press
New York

This book is dedicated to the people who take the time and trouble to write about the hotels and inns they've visited, and to my children—Hilary and Jeffrey—my husband, and my parents.

ISBN 0-312-11484-2

First Edition: December 1994

10   9   8   7   6   5   4   3   2   1

Maps by David Lindroth © 1994, 1992, 1991, 1990, 1989, 1988, 1987 by St. Martin's Press

Contents

Acknowledgments

I would like again to thank all the people who wrote in such helpful detail about the inns and hotels they visited. To them belong both the dedication and the acknowledgments, for without their support, this guide would not exist. If I have inadvertently misspelled or omitted anyone's name, please accept my sincerest apologies.

I would also like to thank Hilary Rubinstein, who originated the concept for this series. Also thanks to my helpful and supportive editors Anne Savarese and Helen Packard; to my wonderful colleagues Nancy Barker, June Horn, Alex Brady, Meg Cassidy, Betsy Sandberg, Mary Ann Boyle, Suzanne Carmichael, Susan Schwemm, Nancy Debevoise, Gail Davis, Linda Goldberg, Tina Kirkpatrick, and Diane Wolf; and to faithful respondents Peg Bedini, Robert Boas, Donna Bocks, Pat Borysiewicz, James Burr, John Chiles, Ann Christofferson, Marjorie Cohen, Happy and Ernie Copley, Dianne Crawford, Brian Donaldson, Sally Ducot, Ellie & Robert Freidus, BJ Hensley, Stephen Holman, William Hussey, Linda Intaschi, Keith Jurgens, Al and Lauren Kenney, Zita Knific, Bill MacGowan, Carolyn Mathiasen, Celia McCullough, Mark Mendenhall, Carolyn Myles, Betty Norman, Bill Novack, Pam Phillips, Adam Platt, Mary Louise Rogers, Duane Roller, Marion Ruben, Joe and Sheila Schmidt, Fritz Shantz and Tara O'Neal, Mary Jane Skala, Jeanne Smith, Ruth Tilsey, Lee Todd, Wendi Van Exan, Hopie Welliver, Rose Wolf, Karl Wiegers and Chris Zambito, and the many others who went far beyond the call of duty in their assistance and support.

Introduction

Reading the Entries

Each entry generally has three parts: a description of the inn or hotel, quotes from guests who have stayed there, and relevant details about rooms, rates, location, and facilities. Occasionally you may find that no general description is given or that the factual data are incomplete. There are two reasons for this: Either the descriptions supplied by guests made this unnecessary, or the facility failed to supply us with adequate information. Please remember that the length of an entry is in no way a reflection of that inn or hotel's quality. Rather, it is an indication of the type of feedback we've received both from guests and from the innkeepers themselves. Some hotel owners are totally un-aware of this guide; others take an active role in encouraging their guests to write.

Wherever a location is of particular tourist interest, we've tried to include some information about its attractions. If we have only one listing for a town, this description usually falls within the body of the entry. If there is more than one inn or hotel listed for a town, the description of the town and information about its location precede the individual entries.

In some areas the magnet is not a particular town but rather a compact, distinct region. Travelers choose one place to stay and use it as a base from which to explore the area. But because this guide is organized by town, not by region, the entries are scattered throughout the chapter. When this applies, you will see the name of the region noted under the "Location" heading; check back to the introduction for a description of the region involved. When an inn is located in a small village close to a better-known town, cross-references are provided to make the process easier.

The names at the end of the quotations are those who have recom-mended the hotel or inn. Some entries are entirely or largely quoted from one report; if several names follow the quotation, we have distinguished the writers of the quoted material by putting their names first. Some writers have requested that we not use their names; you will see initials noted instead. *We never print the names of those who have sent us adverse reports, although their contributions are invaluable indeed.*

Although we have tried to make the listings as accurate and com-plete as possible, mistakes and inaccuracies invariably creep in. The most significant area of inaccuracy applies to the rates charged by each establishment. In preparing this guide, we asked all the hotels and inns to give us their 1995–1996 rates, ranging from the least expensive room in the off-season to the most expensive peak-season price. Some did so, while others just noted the 1994 rate.

Some of the shorter entries are marked "**Information please:**" or "**Also recommended:**" The former usually refer to establishments which have just come to our attention, as well as those that were listed in past editions. The latter are sometimes too big or small for a full entry, or those that have been recommended just as we were going to press.

Please remember that the process of writing and publishing a book takes nearly a year. *You should always double-check the rates when you make your reservations; please don't blame the hotel or this guide if the prices are wrong.* On the other hand, given the current level of inflation, you should not encounter anything more than a 5% increase, unless there has been a substantial improvement in the amenities offered or a change of ownership. Please let us know immediately if you find anything more than that!

If you find any errors of omission or commission in any part of the entries, we urgently request your help in correcting them. We recognize that it takes extra time and effort for readers to write us letters or fill in report forms, but this feedback is essential in keeping this publication totally responsive to consumer needs.

The Fifteen Commandments of Vacation Travel

We all know people who come back from a vacation feeling on top of the world, and others who seem vaguely disappointed. Here's how to put yourself in the first category, not the second.

1. Know yourself. A successful vacation is one that works for the person you are, not the person you think you should be. Confirmed couch potatoes who resent having to walk from the far end of the parking lot will not find true fulfillment on a trek through the Himalayas. If privacy is a top priority, a group tour or communal lodge will turn fantasy into frustration. Acknowledge your own comfort levels. How important is it for you to be independent and flexible? Structured and secure? How essential are the creature comforts when it comes to sleeping, eating, and bathing? Would you rather have one week of luxury travel or two weeks of budget food and accommodation? And remember that while your personality doesn't change, your needs do. The type of vacation you plan for a romantic getaway is totally different from a family reunion.

2. Know your travel companions. Adjust your plans to accommodate your travel partners. Whether you are traveling with friends, spouse, children, and/or parents, you'll need to take their age, attention span, agility, and interests into account. If you're traveling with the kids, balance a morning at an art museum with an afternoon at the zoo; if you're spending time with elderly parents, make sure that they can stroll a country lane while you go rock-climbing; if your group includes skiers and non-skiers, pick a resort that has appealing shops and other activities.

3. Plan ahead: anticipation is half the fun. Enjoy the process. The more you know about an area you're going to visit, the more fun you'll have.

Skim a guidebook; get a calendar of events; write to the local chambers of commerce and tourist offices; read a novel set in the region; talk to friends (or friends of friends) who have been there recently.

4. Don't bite off more than you can chew. Keep your itinerary in line with the amount of time and money available. Focus on seeing a smaller area well, rather than trying to cover too much ground and seeing nothing but interstate highways. Don't overprogram; allow yourself the luxury of doing nothing.

5. Avoid one-night stands. Plan to stay a minimum of two nights everywhere you go. A vacation made up of one-nighters is a prescription for exhaustion. You will sleep poorly, spend most of your time in transit, and will get only the smallest glimpse of the place you're visiting. If it's worth seeing, it's worth spending a full day in one place.

6. Travel off season. Unless your vacation dates are dictated by the school calendar, off-season travel offers many advantages: fewer crowds, greater flexibility, and a more relaxed atmosphere. Learn to pick the best dates for off-season travel; typically these are the weeks just before and after the rates change. Off-season travel offers big savings, too; for example, most ski areas are delightful places to visit in summer, and offer savings of 50% or more on accommodations.

7. Book well ahead for peak season travel. If you must travel during peak periods to popular destinations, make reservations well in advance for the key sites to avoid aggravation, extra phone calls, and additional driving time.

8. Take the road less traveled by. Get off the beaten path to leave the crowds behind. Instead of booking a room in the heart of the action, find a quiet inn tucked in the hills or in a neighboring village. If you visit the Grand Canyon in August, at the height of the tourist season, stay at the North Rim, which attracts 90% fewer visitors than the South Rim.

9. Ditch the car. Sure you need a car to get where you're going. But once you're there, get out and walk. You'll see more, learn more, experience more at every level, while avoiding crowds even at the most popular destinations. We promise. Car travel is an isolating experience, even when you're in bumper-to-bumper traffic.

10. Hang loose. The unexpected is inevitable in travel, as in the rest of life. When your plans go astray (and they will), relax and let serendipity surprise you. And keep your sense of humor in good working order. If possible, travel without reservations or a set itinerary.

11. Carpe diem—seize the day. Don't be afraid to follow your impulses. If a special souvenir catches your eye, buy it; don't wait to see if you'll find it again later. If a hiking trail looks too inviting to pass up, don't; that museum will wait for a rainy day.

12. Don't suffer in silence. When things go wrong—an incompetent guide, car troubles, a noisy hotel room—speak up. Politely but firmly express your concern then and there; get your room changed, ask for a refund or discount, whatever. Most people in the travel business would rather have you go away happy than to leave grumbling.

13. Remember—being there is more than seeing there. People travel to see the sights—museums and mountains, shops and scenery—but it is making new friends that can make a trip memorable. Leave a door open to the people-to-people experiences that enrich travel immeasurably.

14. Don't leave home to find home. The quickest way to take the wind out of the sails of your trip is to compare things to the way they are at home. Enjoy different styles and cultures for what they are and avoid comparisons and snap judgments.

15. Give yourself permission to disregard all of the above. Nothing is immutable. If you find a pattern that works for you, enjoy it!

Inngoer's Bill of Rights

We've read through a lot more brochures for inns and hotels than the average bear, and can attest to the fact that not one makes mention of its possible drawbacks, however slight. Furthermore, unlike this guidebook, *which accepts no fee of any kind for an entry*, many inn guidebooks charge a listing or membership fee of some kind, making them basically paid advertisements. Despite brochure promises and glowing listings in other books, we all know that perfection isn't possible in this world, but we feel that (despite the irate reactions of some innkeepers) complete and honest reporting will give readers *reasonable* expectations, ones that are often surpassed in the best of hostelries.

On the other hand, travelers have the right to expect certain minimum standards. These rights are especially important in hotels and inns at the top end of the rate scale; we don't expect as much from more modestly priced places, although it certainly is often received.

So, please use this Bill of Rights as a kind of checklist in deciding how you think a place stacks up on your own personal rating scale. And, whether an establishment fails, reaches, or exceeds these levels, be sure to let us know. We would also hope that innkeepers will use this list to help evaluate both the strong points and shortcomings of their own establishments, and are grateful to those who have already done so.

The right to suitable cleanliness: An establishment that looks, feels, and smells immaculate, with no musty, smoky, or animal odors.

The right to suitable room furnishings: A firm mattress, soft pillows, fresh linens, and ample blankets; bright lamps and night tables on each side of the bed; comfortable chairs with good reading lights; and adequate storage space.

The right to comfortable, attractive rooms: Guest rooms and common rooms that are as livable as they are attractive. Appealing places where you'd like to read, chat, relax.

The right to a decent bathroom: Cleanliness is essential, along with reliable plumbing, ample hot water, good lighting, an accessible electric outlet, space for toiletries, and thirsty towels.

The right to privacy and discretion: Privacy must be respected by the innkeeper and ensured by adequate sound-proofing. The right to discretion precludes questions about marital status or sexual preference. No display of proselytizing religious materials.

The right to good, healthful food: Fresh nutritious food, ample in quantity, high in quality, attractively presented, and graciously served in smoke-free surroundings.

The right to comfortable temperatures and noise levels: Rooms should be cool in summer and warm in winter, with windows that open, and quiet, efficient air conditioning and heating. Double windows, drapes, and landscaping are essential if traffic noise is an issue.

The right to fair value: Prices should in reasonable relation to the facilities offered and to the cost of equivalent local accommodation.

The right to genuine hospitality: Innkeepers who are glad you've come and who make it their business to make your stay pleasant and memorable; who are readily available without being intrusive.

The right to a caring environment: Welcoming arrivals with refreshments, making dinner reservations, providing information on activities, asking about pet allergies and dietary restrictions, and so on.

The right to personal safety: A location in a reasonably safe neighborhood, with adequate care given to building and parking security.

The right to professionalism: Brochure requests, room reservations, check-ins and outs handled efficiently and responsibly.

The right to adequate common areas: At least one common room where guests can gather to read, chat, or relax, free of the obligation to buy anything.

The right of people traveling alone to have all the above rights: Singles usually pay just a few dollars less than couples, yet the welcome, services, and rooms they receive can be inferior.

The right to a reasonable cancellation policy: Penalties for a cancellation made fewer than 7-14 days before arrival are relatively standard. Most inns will refund deposits (minus a processing fee) after the deadline only if the room is rebooked.

The right to efficient maintenance: Burnt-out bulbs and worn-out smoke detector batteries are the responsibility of the innkeeper—not the guest. When things go wrong, guests have the right to an apology, a discount, or a refund.

Of course, there is no "perfect" inn or hotel, because people's tastes and needs vary so greatly. But one key phrase does pop up over and over again: "I felt right at home." This is not written in the literal sense—a commercial lodging, no matter how cozy or charming, is never the same as one's home. What is really meant is that guests felt as welcome, as relaxed, as comfortable, as they would in their own home.

What makes for a wonderful stay?

We've tried our best to make sure that all the hotels and inns listed in this guide are as wonderful as our title promises. Inevitably, there will be some disappointments. Sometimes these will be caused by a change in ownership or management that has resulted in lowered standards. Other times unusual circumstances will lead to problems. Quite often, though, problems will occur because there's not a good "fit" between the inn or hotel and the guest. Decide what you're looking for, then find the inn that suits your needs, whether you're looking for a casual environment or a dressy one, a romantic setting or a family-oriented one, a vacation spot or a business person's environment, an isolated country retreat or a convenient in-town location.

We've tried to give you as much information as possible on each hotel or inn listed, and have taken care to indicate the atmosphere each inn-keeper is trying to create. After you've read the listing, write, if there is time, for a copy of the establishment's brochure, which will give you more information. Finally, feel free to call any inn or hotel where you're plan-ning to stay, and ask as many questions as necessary.

Inn etiquette

A first-rate inn is a joy indeed, but as guests we need to do our part to respect its special qualities. For starters, you'll need to maintain a higher level of consideration for your fellow guests. Century-old Victorians are noted for their nostalgic charms, not their sound-proofing; if you come in late or get up early, remember that voices and footsteps echo off all those gleaming hardwood floors and doors. If you're going to pick a fight with your roommate, pull the covers up over your head or go out for a walk. If you're sharing a bath, don't dawdle, tidy up after yourself, and dry your hair back in your room. If you've admired the Oriental carpets, antique decor, handmade quilts, and the thick fluffy towels, don't leave wet glasses on the furniture, put suitcases on the bed, or use the towels for removing make-up or wiping the snow off your car. After all, innkeepers have rights too!

Hotels, inns . . . resorts and motels

As the title indicates, this is a guide to exceptional inns and hotels. Generally, the inns have 5 to 25 rooms, although a few have only 2 rooms and some have over 100. The hotels are more often found in the cities and range in size from about 50 to 200 rooms.

The line between an inn or hotel and a resort is often a fine one. There are times when we all want the extra facilities a resort provides, so we've added a number of reader-recommended facilities. We've also listed a handful of motels. Although they don't strictly fall within the context of this book, we've included them because readers felt they were the best option in a specific situation. Some entries are members of the Best Western chain. Please don't be put off by this; Best Western is a franchise operation, with no architectural unity from one property to the next. Those listed in this guide have substantial architectural or historical ap-peal, and concerned, professional management.

Although we do not provide full coverage of hotel chains, we do want to point out that the Four Seasons and Ritz-Carlton hotels are almost impossible to beat at the luxury end of the spectrum. Readers consistently rave about their unbeatable combination of unparalleled service and plush accommodation; weekend rates make them an exceptional value.

What is a B&B anyway?

There are basically two kinds of B&Bs—the B&B homestay and the B&B inn. The homestay is typically the home of an empty nester, who has a few empty bedrooms to fill, gaining some extra income and pleasant company. B&B inns are run on a more professional basis, independently marketed and subject to state and local licensing. Guests typically have dedicated common areas for their use, and do not share the hosts' living quarters, as in a homestay. We list very few homestays in this guide. Full-service or country inns and lodges are similar to the B&B inn, except that they serve breakfast and dinner on a regular basis, and may be somewhat larger in size; dinner is often offered to the public as well as to house guests. The best of all of these are made special by resident owners bringing the warmth of their personalities to the total experience. A B&B is *not* a motel that serves breakfast.

Rooms

All hotel and inn rooms are not created equal. Although the rooms at a typical chain motel or hotel may be identical, the owners of most of the establishments described in this book pride themselves on the individual-ity of each guest room. Some, although not all, of these differences are reflected in the rates charged.

More importantly, it means that travelers need to express their needs clearly to the innkeepers when making reservations and again when checking in. Some rooms may be quite spacious but may have extremely small private baths or limited closet space. Some antique double beds have rather high footboards—beautiful to look at but torture for six-footers. Many inns are trading their double beds in for queens and kings; if you prefer an oversize bed, say so. If you want twin beds, be sure to specify this when making reservations and again when you check in; many smaller inns have only one twin-bedded rooms.

Some rooms may have gorgeous old bathrooms, with tubs the size of small swimming pools, but if you are a hard-core shower person, that room won't be right for you. Many others have showers but no baths, which may be disappointing if you love a long, luxurious soak in the tub. If you are traveling on business and simply must have a working-size desk with good lighting, speak up. Some rooms look terrific inside but don't look out at anything much; others may have the view but not quite as special a decor. Sometimes the largest rooms are at the front of the house, facing a busy highway. Decide what's important to you. Although the owners and staff of the hotels and inns listed here are incredibly hard-working and dedicated people, they can't read your mind. Let your needs be known, and, within the limits of availability, they will try to accommo-date you.

Our most frequent complaints center around beds that are too soft and inadequate reading lights. If these are priorities for you (as they are for us), don't be shy about requesting bedboards or additional lamps to remedy the situation. Similarly, if there are other amenities your room is lacking—extra pillows, blankets, or even an easy chair—speak up. Most innkeepers would rather put in an extra five minutes of work than have an unhappy guest.

If your reservation is contingent upon obtaining a particular room, make this very clear to the innkeeper. Some inns will not accept such reservations, feeling that they are too difficult to guarantee. Those that do accept them have an obligation to meet their guarantee; if circumstances prevent them from following through on the promised room, make it clear that you expect some sort of remuneration—either the return of your deposit or a reduction in the price of another room.

If you really don't like your room, ask for another as soon as possible, preferably before you've unpacked your bags. The sooner you voice your dissatisfaction, the sooner something can be done to improve the situation. If you don't like the food, ask for something else—in other words, you're the guest, make sure you get treated like one. If things go terribly wrong, don't be shy about asking for your money back, and be *sure* to write us about any problems.

What is a single? A double? A suite? A cottage or cabin?

Unlike the proverbial rose, a single is not a single is not a single. Sometimes it is a room with one twin bed, which really can accommodate only one person. Quite often it is described as a room with a standard-size double bed, in contrast to a double, which has two twin beds. Other hotels call both of the preceding doubles, although doubles often have queen- or even king-size beds instead. Many times the only distinction is made by the number of guests occupying the room; a single will pay slightly less, but there's no difference in the room.

There's almost as much variation when it comes to suites. We define a suite as a bedroom with a separate living room area and often a small kitchen, as well. Unfortunately, the word has been stretched to cover other setups, too. Some so-called suites are only one large room, accommodating a table and separate seating area in addition to the bed, while others are two adjacent bedrooms which share a bath. If you require a suite that has two separate rooms with a door between them, specify this when you make reservations.

Quite a few of our entries have cabins or cottages in addition to rooms in the main building. In general, a cabin is understood to be a somewhat more rustic residence than a cottage, although there's no hard-and-fast rule. Be sure to inquire for details when making reservations.

Making reservations

Unless you are inquiring many months in advance of your visit, it's best to telephone when making reservations. This offers a number of advantages: You will know immediately if space is available on your requested dates; you can find out if that space is suitable to your specific needs. You will have a chance to discuss the pros and cons of the available rooms and will be able to find out about any changes made in recent months—new facilities, recently redecorated rooms, nonsmoking policies, even a change of ownership. It's also a good time to ask the innkeeper about other concerns—Is the neighborhood safe at night? Is there any renovation or construction in progress that might be disturbing? Will a wedding reception or bicycle touring group affect use of the common areas during your visit? If you're reserving a room at a plantation home that is available for public tours, get specifics about the check-in/out times; in many, rooms are not available before 5 P.M. and must be vacated by 9 A.M. sharp. The savvy traveler will always get the best value for his accommodation dollar.

If you expect to be checking in late at night, *be sure to say so;* many inns give doorkeys to their guests, then lock up by 10 P.M.

We're often asked about the need for making advance reservations. If you'll be traveling in peak periods, in prime tourist areas, and want to be sure of getting a first-rate room at the best-known inns, reserve at least three to six months ahead. This is especially true if you're traveling with friends or family and will need more than one room. On the other hand, if you like a bit of adventure, and don't want to be stuck with cancellation fees when you change your mind, by all means stick our books in the glove compartment and hit the road. If you're traveling in the off-season, or even midweek in season, you'll have a grand time. But look for a room by late afternoon; never wait until after dinner and expect to find something decent. Some inns offer a discount after 4:00 P.M. for last-minute bookings; it never hurts to ask.

Payment

The vast majority of inns now accept credit cards. A few accept credit cards for the initial deposit but prefer cash, traveler's checks, or personal checks for the balance; others offer the reverse policy. When no credit cards are accepted at all, you can settle your bill with a personal check, traveler's check, or even cash.

When using your credit card to guarantee a reservation, be aware that most inns will charge your card for the amount of the deposit, unlike motels and hotels which don't put through the charge until you've checked in. A few will put a "hold" on your card for the full amount of your entire stay, plus the cost of meals and incidentals that you may (or may not) spend. If you're using your card to reserve a fairly extended trip, you may find that you're well over your credit limit without actually having spent a nickel. We'd suggest inquiring; if the latter is the procedure, either send a check for the deposit or go elsewhere. If you have used American Express, Diners Club, Mastercard, or Visa to guarantee your reservation, these companies guarantee if a room is not available, the hotel is supposed to find you a free room in a comparable hotel, plus transportation and a free phone call.

Rates

All rates quoted are per room, unless otherwise noted as being per person. Rates quoted per person are usually based on double occupancy, unless otherwise stated.

"Room only" rates do not include any meals. In most cases two or three meals a day are served by the hotel restaurant, but are charged separately. Average meal prices are noted when available. In a very few cases no meals are served on the premises at all; rooms in these facilities are usually equipped with kitchenettes.

B&B rates include bed and breakfast. Breakfast, though, can vary from a simple continental breakfast to an expanded continental breakfast to a full breakfast. Afternoon tea and evening refreshments are sometimes included as well.

MAP (Modified American Plan) rates are often listed per person and include breakfast and dinner. Only a few of the inns listed serve lunch, although many will prepare a picnic on request for an additional charge. Full board rates include three squares a day, and are usually found only at old-fashioned resorts and isolated ranches.

State and local sales taxes are not included in the rates unless otherwise indicated; the percentage varies from state to state, city to city, and can reach 20% in a few urban centers, although 10–15% is more typical.

When inquiring about rates, always ask if any off-season or special package rates are available. Sometimes discounted rates are available *only* on request; seniors and AAA members often qualify for substantial discounts. During the week, when making reservations at city hotels or country inns, it's important to ask if any corporate rates are available. Depending on the establishment, you may or may not be asked for some proof of corporate affiliation (a business card is usually all that's needed), but it's well worth inquiring, since the effort can result in a saving of 15–20%, plus an upgrade to a substantially better room.

A number of companies specialize in booking hotel rooms in major cities at substantial discounts. Although you can ask for specific hotels by name, the largest savings are realized by letting the agency make the selection; they may be able to get you a discount of up to 65 percent. **Hotel Reservations Network** (8140 Walnut Hill Lane, Dallas, Texas 75231; 800–96–HOTEL) offers discount rates in over 20 U.S. cities plus London and Paris; **Quikbook** (381 Park Avenue South, New York, New York 10016; 800–789–9887) is a similar service with competitive rates.

Another money-saving trick can be to look for inns in towns a bit off the beaten path. If you stay in a town that neighbors a famous resort or historic community, you will often find that rates are anywhere from $20 to $50 less per night for equivalent accommodation. If you're travelling without reservations, and arrive at a half-empty inn in late afternoon, don't hesitate to ask for a price reduction or free room upgrade. And of course, watch for our ¢ symbol, which indicates places which are a particularly good value.

If an establishment has a specific tipping policy, whether it is "no tipping" or the addition of a set service charge, it is noted under "Rates." When both breakfast and dinner are included in the rates, a 15% service charge against the total bill—not just the room—is standard; some inns are charging 18–20%. A number of B&Bs are also adding on a service charge, a practice which also sits poorly with us. If you feel—as many of our readers do—that these fees are a sneaky way of making rates seem lower than they really are, let the innkeeper (and us) know how you feel. When no notation is made, it's generally expected that guests will leave $1–3 a night for the housekeeping staff and 15% for meal service. A number of inns have taken to leaving little cards or envelopes to remind guests to leave a tip for the housekeepers; most readers find this practice objectionable. If you welcome a no-tipping policy and object to solicitation, speak up.

While the vast majority of inns are fairly priced, there are a few whose rates have become exorbitant. Others fail to stay competitive, charging top weekend rates when a nearby luxury hotel is offering a beautiful suite at a lower price. No matter how lovely the breakfast, how thoughtful the innkeepers, there's a limit to the amount one will pay for a room without an in-room telephone, TV, or a full-size private bathroom. We recently learned about a B&B that has the nerve to charge $125 for a room with shared bath, and asks you to bring your own pool towels during the summer!

Deposits and cancellations

Nearly all innkeepers print their deposit and cancellation policies clearly on their brochures. Deposits generally range from payment of the first night's stay to 50% of the cost of the entire stay. Some inns repeat the cancellation policy when confirming reservations. In general, guests canceling well in advance of the planned arrival (two to four weeks is typical) receive a full refund minus a cancellation fee. After that date, no refunds are offered unless the room is resold to someone else. A few will not refund *even if the room is resold,* so take careful note. If you're making a credit card booking over the phone, be sure to find out what the cancellation policy is.

We would like to applaud the inns which require only two to seven days' notice of cancellation, and would love to see other areas follow suit. We also feel strongly that even if you cancel on short notice, you should be given the opportunity to rebook within a reasonable time period rather than losing your entire deposit.

Sometimes the shoe may be on the other foot. Even if you were told earlier that the inn at which you really wanted to stay was full, it may be worthwhile to make a call to see if cancellations have opened up any last-minute vacancies.

Minimum stays

Two- and three-night minimum weekend and holiday stays are the rule at many inns during peak periods. We have noted these when possible, although we suspect that the policy may be more common than is always indicated in print. On the other hand, you may just be hitting a slow period, so it never hurts to call at the last minute to see if a one-night reservation would be accepted. Again, cancellations are always a possibility; you can try calling on a Friday or Saturday morning to see if something is available for that night.

Pets

Very few of the inns and hotels listed accept pets. When they do we've noted it under "Extras." On the other hand, most of the inns listed in this book have at least one dog or cat, sometimes more. These pets are usually found in the common areas, sometimes in guest rooms as well. If you are highly allergic to animals, *we strongly urge that you inquire for details before making reservations.*

Children

Some inns are family-style places and welcome children of all ages; we've marked them with our ⚲ symbol. Others do not feel that they have facilities for the very young and only allow children over a certain age. Still others cultivate an "adults only" atmosphere and don't even welcome children at dinner. When inns and hotels do not encourage all children, we've noted the age requirement under the heading "Restrictions." If special facilities are available to children, these are noted under "Facilities" and "Extras." If an inn does not exclude children yet does not offer any special amenities or rate reductions for them, we would suggest it only for the best-behaved youngsters.

Whatever the policy, you may want to remind your children to follow the same rules of courtesy toward others that we expect of adults. Be aware that the pitter-patter of little feet on an uncarpeted hardwood floor can sound like a herd of stampeding buffalo to those on the floor below. Children used to the indestructible plastics of contemporary homes will need to be reminded (more than once) to be gentle with antique furnishings.

State laws governing discrimination by age are affecting policies at some inns. To our knowledge, both California and Michigan now have such laws on the books, although this was rarely reflected in the brochures sent to us by inns in those states. Some inns get around age discrimination by limiting room occupancy to two adults. This discourages families by forcing them to pay for two rooms instead of one. Our own children are very clear on their preferences: although they've been to many inns that don't encourage guests under the age of 12, they find them "really boring"; on the other hand, they've loved every family-oriented place we've ever visited.

Porterage and packing

Only the largest of our listings will have personnel whose sole job is to assist guests with baggage. In the casual atmosphere associated with many inns, it is simply assumed that guests will carry their own bags. If you do need assistance with your luggage, don't hesitate to ask.

If you're planning an extended trip to a number of small inns, we'd suggest packing as lightly as possible, using two small bags rather than one large suitcase. You'll know why if you've ever tried hauling a 50-pound oversize suitcase up a steep and narrow 18th-century staircase. On the other hand, don't forget about the local climate when assembling your wardrobe. In mountainous and desert regions, day- and nighttime temperatures can vary by as much as 40 degrees. Also, bear in mind that Easterners tend to dress more formally than Westerners, so pack accordingly.

Meals

If you have particular dietary restrictions—low-salt, vegetarian, or religious—or allergies—to caffeine, nuts, whatever—be sure to mention these when making reservations and *again* at check-in. If you're allergic to a common breakfast food or beverage, an evening reminder will ensure that you'll be able to enjoy the breakfast that's been prepared for you. Most innkeepers will do their best to accommodate your special needs, although, as one innkeeper noted tartly, "we're not operating a hospital."

In preparing each listing, we asked the owners to give us the cost of prix fixe and à la carte meals when available. An "alc dinner" price at the end of the "Rates" section is the figure we were given when we requested the average cost, of a three-course dinner with a half bottle of house wine, including tax and tip. Prices listed for prix fixe meals do not include wine and service. Lunch prices, where noted, do not include the cost of any alcoholic beverage. Hotels and inns which serve meals to the public are noted with the ✕ symbol.

Dinner and lunch reservations are always a courtesy and are often essential. Most B&B owners will offer to make reservations for you; this can be especially helpful in getting you a table at a popular restaurant in peak season and/or on weekends. Some of the establishments we list operate restaurants fully open to the public. Others serve dinner primarily to their overnight guests, but they also will serve meals to outsiders; reservations are essential at such inns, usually eight or more hours in advance.

A few restaurants require jackets and ties for men at dinner, even in rather isolated areas. Of course, this is more often the case in traditional New England and the Old South than in the West. Unless you're going only to a very casual country lodge, we recommend that men bring them along and that women have corresponding attire.

Breakfast: Breakfast is served at nearly every inn or hotel listed in this guide. Those that do not, should. No inn is truly "wonderful" if you have to get in your car and drive somewhere for a morning meal. Nor do we consider the availability of coffee and tea alone an appropriate substitute. The vast majority of lodgings listed include breakfast in their rates. Whenever possible we describe a typical breakfast, rather than using the terms "continental" or "full" breakfast.

Continental breakfast ranges from coffee and store-bought pastry to a lavish offering of fresh fruit and juices, yogurt and granola, cereals, even cheese and cold meats, homemade muffins and breads, and a choice of decaffeinated or regular coffee, herbal and regular tea. There's almost as much variety in the full breakfasts, which range from the traditional eggs, bacon, and toast, plus juice and coffee, to three-course gourmet extravaganzas.

We've received occasional complaints about breakfasts being too rich in eggs and cream, and too sweet, with no plain rolls or bread. A dietary splurge is fun for a weekend escape, but on a longer trip we'd advise requesting a "healthy breakfast" from your innkeeper. You can be sure

13

that they don't eat their own breakfasts every day! Equally important to many guests are the timing and seating arrangements at breakfast. As one reader put it: "We stayed at a B&B where breakfast is served at one large table, promptly at 8:30 A.M. This is a mixed blessing. The breakfast was lovely and fresh, and the setting encouraged a convivial meal with the other guests. But there are those who consider any conversation prior to a second cup of coffee to be barbaric. More importantly, this doesn't allow for different time schedules." *(William Hussey)*

Lunch: Very few of the inns and hotels listed here serve lunch. Those that do generally operate a full-service restaurant or are located in isolated mountain settings with no restaurants nearby. Quite a number of B&B inns are happy to make up picnic lunches for an additional fee.

Dinner: Meals served at the inns listed here vary widely from simple home-style family cooking to gourmet cuisine. We are looking for food that is a good, honest example of the type of cooking involved. Ingredients should be fresh and homemade as far as is possible; service and presentation should be pleasant and straightforward. We have no interest in the school of "haute pretentious" where the hyperbolic descriptions found on the menu far exceed the chef's ability.

Drinks

With a very few exceptions (noted under "Restrictions" in each listing), alcoholic beverages may be enjoyed in moderation at all of the inns and hotels listed. Most establishments with a full-service restaurant serving the public as well as overnight guests are licensed to serve beer, wine, and liquor to their customers, although "brown-bagging" or BYOB (bring your own bottle) is occasionally permitted, especially in dry counties. Bed & breakfasts, and inns serving meals primarily to overnight guests, do not typically have liquor licenses, although most will provide guests with setups, i.e., glasses, ice, and mixers, at what is often called a BYO (bring your own) bar.

Overseas visitors will be amazed at the hodgepodge of regulations around the country. Liquor laws are determined in general by each state, but individual counties, or even towns, can prohibit or restrict the sale of alcoholic beverages, even beer.

Smoking

The majority of B&Bs and inns prohibit indoor smoking entirely, allowing it only on porches and verandas; a few don't allow smoking anywhere on the grounds. Larger inns and hotels usually do permit smoking, prohibiting it only in some guest rooms, and dining areas. Where prohibitions apply we have noted this under "Restrictions." We suggest that confirmed smokers be courteous or make reservations elsewhere. If there is no comment about smoking under "Restrictions," non-smokers should ask if smokers will be in residence.

Physical limitations and wheelchair accessibility

We've used the well-known symbol ♿ to denote hotels and inns that are wheelchair accessible. Where available, additional information is noted under the "Extras" heading. Unfortunately, what is meant by this symbol varies dramatically. In the case of larger hotels and newer inns, it usually means full access; in historic buildings, access may be limited to the restaurant and public rest rooms only, or to a specific guest room but not the common areas. *Call the inn/hotel directly for full details and to discuss your needs.*

If you do not need a wheelchair but have difficulty with stairs, we urge you to mention this when making reservations; many inns and small hotels have one or two rooms on the ground floor, but very few have elevators. Similarly, if you are visually handicapped, do share this information so that you may be given a room with good lighting and no unexpected steps.

Air-conditioning

Heat is a relative condition, and the perceived need for air-conditioning varies tremendously from one individual to the next. If an inn or hotel has air-conditioning, you'll see this listed under "Rooms." If it's important to you, be sure to ask when making reservations. If air-conditioning is not available, check to see if fans are provided. Remember that top-floor rooms in most inns (usually a converted attic) can be uncomfortably warm even in relatively cool climates.

Transportation

A car is more or less essential for visiting most of the inns and hotels listed here, as well as the surrounding sights of interest. Exceptions are those located in the major cities. In some historic towns, a car is the easiest way to get there, but once you've arrived, you'll want to find a place to park the car and forget about it.

If you are traveling by public transportation, check the "Extras" section at the end of each write-up. If the innkeepers are willing to pick you up from the nearest airport, bus, or train station, you'll see it noted here. This service is usually free or available at modest cost. If it's not listed, the innkeeper will direct you to a commercial facility that can help.

Parking

Although not a concern in most cases, parking is a problem in many cities, beach resorts, and historic towns. If you'll be traveling by car, ask the innkeeper for advice when making reservations. If parking is not on-site, stop at the hotel first to drop off your bags, then go park the car. In big cities, if "free parking" is included in the rates, this usually covers only one arrival and departure. Additional "ins and outs" incur substantial extra charges. Be sure to ask.

If on-site parking is available in areas where parking can be a problem, we've noted it under "Facilities." Since it's so rarely a problem in country inns, we haven't included that information in those listings. Regrettably, security has become an issue in most cities. Never leave anything visible inside the car; it's an invitation for break-in and theft.

Christmas travel

Many people love to travel to a country inn or hotel at Christmas. Quite a number of places do stay open through the holidays, but the extent to which the occasion is celebrated varies widely indeed. We know of many inns that decorate beautifully, serve a fabulous meal, and organize all kinds of traditional Christmas activities. But we also know of others, especially in ski areas, that do nothing more than throw a few token ornaments on a tree. Be sure to inquire.

Is innkeeping for me?

Many of our readers fantasize about running their own inn; for some the fantasy may soon become a reality. Before taking the big plunge, it's vital to find out as much as you can about this demanding business. Begin by reading *How to Start and Run Your Own Bed & Breakfast Inn* by long-time innkeepers Ripley Hotch and Carl Glassman, covering everything from financing to marketing to day-to-day innkeeping responsibilities. ($14.95; Stackpole Books, P.O. Box 1831, Harrisburg, PA 17105; 800–732–3669). The two best sources for in-depth information are the Professional Association of Innkeepers, International (PAII—pronounced "pie") and Oates and Bredfeldt Consultants. PAII co-directors Pat Hardy and Jo Ann Bell publish *Innkeeping Newsletter*, various books for would-be innkeepers, and coordinate workshops for aspiring innkeepers. For details contact them at PAII, P.O. Box 90710, Santa Barbara, CA 93190; 805–567–1853. An equally good source, especially in the East, are consultants Bill Oates and Heide Bredfeldt. Contact them at P.O. Box 1162, Brattleboro, VT 05301; 802–254–5931 to find out when and where they'll be offering their next seminar entitled "How to Purchase and Operate a Country Inn." Bill and Heide are highly respected pros in this field and have worked with innkeepers facing a wide range of needs and problems; his newsletter, *Innquest*, is written for prospective innkeepers looking to buy property.

For more information

The best sources of travel information in this country and in Canada are absolutely free; in many cases, you don't even have to supply the cost of a stamp or telephone call. They are the state and provincial tourist offices.

For each state you'll be visiting, request a copy of the official state map, which will show you every little highway and byway and will make exploring much more fun; it will also have information on state parks and major attractions in concise form. Ask also for a calendar of events and for information on topics of particular interest, such as fishing or antiquing, vineyards or crafts; many states have published B&B directories, and some are quite informative. If you're going to an area of particular tourist interest, you might also want to ask the state office to give you the name of the regional tourist board for more detailed information. You'll find the addresses and telephone numbers for all the states and provinces covered in the Appendix at the back of this book.

You may also want to contact the local chamber of commerce for information on local sights and events of interest or even an area map. You can get the necessary addresses and telephone numbers from the inn or hotel where you'll be staying or from the state tourist office.

If you are one of those people who never travel with fewer than three guidebooks (which includes us), you will find the AAA and Mobil regional guides to be helpful references. The Mobil guides can be found in any bookstore, while the AAA guides are distributed free on request to members. Both series cover hotels, restaurants, and sightseeing information, although we find the AAA guides to offer wider coverage and more details. If you're not already an AAA member, *we'd strongly urge you join before your next trip;* in addition to their road service, they offer quality guidebooks and maps, and an excellent discount program at many hotels (including a number listed here).

Guidebooks are published only once every year or two; if you'd like to have a more frequent update, we'd suggest one of the following:

Country Inns/Bed & Breakfasts (P.O. Box 182, South Orange, NJ 07079; 201–762–7090), $18, 6 issues annually. You know what they say about a picture being worth a 1000 words. A must for inngoers.

The Discerning Traveler (504 West Mermaid Lane, Philadelphia, PA 19118; 800–673–7834 or 215–247–5578), $50, 6 issues annually, $8 single copy. Picks a single destination in the New England, Mid-Atlantic, or Southern states and covers it in real depth—sights, restaurants, lodging, and more. The authors have published three delightful books on the subject as well.

Where is my favorite inn?

In reading through this book, you may find that your favorite inn is not listed, or that a well-known inn has been omitted from this edition. Why? Two reasons, basically: In several cases, establishments have been dropped because our readers had unsatisfactory experiences. Feel free to contact us for details. Other establishments have been omitted because we've had no reader feedback at all. This may mean that readers visiting these hotels and inns had satisfactory experiences but were not sufficiently impressed to write about them, or that readers were pleased but just assumed that someone else would take the trouble. If the latter applies, please, please, do write and let us know of your experiences. We try to visit as many inns as possible ourselves, but it is impossible to visit every place, every year. So please, keep those cards, letters, and telephone calls coming! As an added incentive, we will be sending free copies of the next edition of this book to our most helpful respondents.

Little Inns of Horror

We try awfully hard to list only the most worthy establishments, but sometimes the best-laid plans of mice and travel writers do go astray. Please understand that whenever we receive a complaint about an entry in our guide we feel terrible, and do our best to investigate the situation. Readers occasionally send us complaints about establishments listed in *other* guidebooks; these are quite helpful as warning signals.

The most common complaints we receive—and the least forgivable—are on the issue of dirt. Scummy sinks and bathtubs, cobwebbed windows, littered porches, mildewed carpeting, water-stained ceilings, and grimy linens are all stars of this horror show.

Next in line are problems dealing with the lack of maintenance: peeling paint and wallpaper; sagging, soft, lumpy mattresses; radiators that don't get hot and those that make strange noises; windows that won't open, windows that won't close, windows with no screens, decayed or inoperable window shades; moldy shower curtains, rusty shower stalls, worn-out towels, fluctuating water temperatures, dripping faucets, and showers that only dribble, top the list.

Food complaints come next on this disaster lineup: poorly prepared canned or frozen food when fresh is readily available; meals served on paper, plastic, or worst of all, styrofoam; and insensitivity to dietary needs. Some complaints are received about unhelpful, abrasive, or abusive innkeepers, with a few more about uncaring, inept, or invisible staff. Complaints are most common in full-service inns when the restaurant business preoccupies the owners' attention, leaving overnight guests to suffer.

Last but not least are noise headaches: trucks and trains that sound like they're heading for your pillow, and being awakened by the sound of someone snoring—in the next room. More tricky are questions of taste—high Victorian might look elegant to you, funereal to me; my collectibles could be your Salvation Army thriftshop donation. In short, there are more than a few inns and hotels that give new meaning to the phrase "having reservations"; fortunately they're many times outnumbered by the many wonderful places listed in this guide.

Pet peeves

Although we may genuinely like an inn, minor failings can keep it from being truly wonderful. Heading our list of pet peeves is inadequate bedside reading lights and tables. We know that there is not always room for a second table, but a light can always be attached to the wall. For reasons of both safety and comfort, a lamp should be at every bedside. Another reader is irked by inadequate bathroom lighting: "I think it must be an innkeepers' conspiracy to keep me from ever getting my makeup on properly." (SU) Equally annoying is the addition of fancy amenities when the basics are inadequate. As one reader put it: "Brandy by the bed and chocolates on the pillow are no excuse to overlook all other aspects of an enjoyable stay. When everything else is perfect, the small touches make a hotel magical, but in the absence of solid comfort the extras are mostly jarring." *(Robert Freidus)* Other readers object to overly friendly innkeepers: "The innkeeper chatted with us all during breakfast, and was disappointed that we didn't plan to go in to say goodbye after we loaded up the car. Innkeepers should remember that the guests are customers, not long-lost relatives." *(Karl Weigers & Chris Zambito)* Another common gripe concerns clutter: "Although pretty and interesting, the many collectibles left us no space for our personal belongings." And: "Instructions were posted everywhere—how to operate door locks, showers, heat, air-conditioning, and more." Anything you'd like to add?

Glossary of Architectural and Decorating Terms

We are not architectural experts, and when we started writing *America's Wonderful Little Hotels & Inns*, we didn't know a dentil from a dependency, a tester from a transom. We've learned a bit more since then, and hope that our primer of terms, prepared by associate editor Nancy Barker, will also be helpful to you.

Adam: building style (1780–1840) featuring a classic box design with a dominant front door and fanlight, accented by an elaborate surround or an entry porch; cornice with decorative moldings incorporating dentil, swag, garland, or stylized geometric design. Three-part Palladian-style windows are common.

antebellum: existing prior to the U.S. Civil War (1861–1865).

Arts and Craft movement: considered the first phase of the Modern movement that led to the Prairie style (1900–20) of Frank Lloyd Wright in Chicago, and the Craftsman style (1905–30) of the Greene brothers in Southern California. In the Arts and Craft style, historical precedent for decoration and design was rejected and ornamentation was "modernized" to remove traces of its historic origins. It features low-pitched roofs, wide eave overhangs, and both symmetrical and asymmetrical front façades.

beaded board: simple ornamented board, with a smooth, flat surface alternating with a half-round, rod-like carving (bead) running the length of the board. Common wainscoting or panelling in Victorian-era homes.

carpenter Gothic: *see* country, folk Victorian.

chinoiserie: imitation of Chinese decorative motifs; i.e., simulated Oriental lacquer covering pine or maple furniture. *See* also Chippendale below.

Chippendale: named for English furniture designer, Thomas Chippendale, of the Queen Anne period (1750–1790); the style varies from the Queen Anne style in ornamentation, with more angular shapes and heavier carving of shells, leaves, scrolls. Chinese Chippendale furniture employs chiefly straight lines, bamboo turnings, and as decoration, fluting, and fretwork in a variety of lattice patterns.

Colonial Revival: building style (1880–1955) featuring a classic box design with a dominant front door elaborated with pilasters and either a pediment (Georgian-style) or a fanlight (Adam-style); double-hung windows symmetrically balanced.

corbel: an architectural member that projects from a wall to support a weight and is stepped outward and upward from the vertical surface.

Corinthian: column popular in Greek Revival style for support of porch roofs; the capitals are shaped like inverted bells and decorated with acanthus leaves.

cornice: projecting horizontal carving or molding that crowns a wall or roof.

country, folk Victorian: simple house form (1870–1910) with accents of Victorian (usually Queen Anne or Italianate) design in porch spindlework and cornice details. Also known as carpenter Gothic.

Craftsman: building style (1905–1930) with low-pitched, gabled roof and wide, unenclosed eave overhang; decorative beams or braces added under gables; usually one-story; porches supported by tapered square columns.

dentil: exterior or interior molding characterized by a series of small rectangular blocks projecting like teeth.

dependencies: buildings that are subordinate to the main dwelling; i.e., a detached garage or barn. *See* also garçonnière.

Doric: column popular in Greek Revival style for support of porch roofs; the simplest of the three styles, with a fluted column, no base, and a square capital.

Eastlake: architectural detail on Victorian houses, commonly referred to as "gingerbread." Typically has lacy spandrels and knob-like beads, in exterior and interior design, patterned after the style of Charles Eastlake, an English furniture designer. Eastlake also promoted Gothic and Jacobean Revival styles with their strong rectangular lines; quality workmanship instead of machine manufacture; and the use of varnished oak, glazed tiles, and unharmonized color.

Eclectic movement: architectural tradition (1880–1940) which emphasized relatively pure copies of Early American, Mediterranean, or Native American homes.

eyebrow dormer: a semi-circular, narrow window over which the adjoining roofing flows in a continuous wave line; found on Shingle or Richardsonian Romanesque buildings.

faux: literally, French for "false." Refers commonly to woodwork painted to look like marble or another stone.

Federal: *See* Adam.

four-poster bed: variation on a tester bed but one in which the tall corner posts, of equal height, do not support a canopy. Carving of rice sheaves was a popular design in the Southern states, and signified prosperity.

Franklin stove: metal heating stove which is set out into the room to conserve heat and better distribute it. Named after its inventor Benjamin Franklin; some designs resemble a fireplace when their front doors are open.

gambrel roof: a two-slope, barn-style roof, with a lower steeper slope and a flatter upper one.

garçonnière: found on antebellum estates; a dependency housing unmarried male guests and family members.

Georgian: building style (1700–1830) featuring a classic box design with a dominant front door elaborated with pilasters and a pediment, usually with a row of small panes of glass beneath the crown or in a transom; cornices with decorative moldings, usually dentil.

Gothic Revival: building style (1840–1880) with a steeply pitched roof, steep gables with decorated vergeboards, and one-story porch supported by flattened Gothic arches. Windows commonly have pointed-arch shape.

Greek Revival: building style (1825–1860) having a gabled or hipped roof of low pitch; cornice line of main and porch roofs emphasized by a wide band of trim; porches supported by prominent columns (usually Doric).

half-tester bed: a bed with a low footboard and a canopy projecting from the posts at the head of the bed. Pronounced "half tee'-stir."

Ionic: column popular in Greek Revival style for support of porch roofs; the caps of the column resemble the rolled ends of a scroll.

Italianate: building style (1840–1885) with two or three stories and a low-pitched roof with widely overhanging eaves supported by decorative brackets; tall, narrow windows arched or curved above with elaborate crowns. Many have a square cupola or tower.

keeping room: in a Colonial-era home, the equivalent of a modern family room; it was usually warm from proximity to kitchen, so infants and the ill were "kept" here.

kiva: stuccoed, corner beehive-shaped fireplace common in adobe homes in Southwestern U.S.

latillas: ceiling of unpeeled, rough sticks, supported by vigas (rough beams); seen in flat-roofed adobe homes

Lincrusta (or Lincrusta-Walton): an embossed, linoleum-like wallcovering made with linseed oil, developed in 1877 in England by Frederick Walton.

lintel: horizontal beam, supported at both ends, that spans an opening.

mansard roof: having two slopes on all sides with the lower slope steeper than the upper one.

Mission: building style (1890–1920) with Spanish mission-style parapet; commonly with red tile roof, overhanging, open eaves, and smooth stucco finish. In furniture, the Mission style is best represented by the work of designer Gustav Stickley. Using machine manufacture, he utilized simple, rectangular lines and favored quarter-sawn white oak for the rich texture of the graining.

Palladian window: typically a central window with an arched or semicircular head.

Pewabic (tile): glazed tiles made in the Detroit, Michigan, area, in the first half of the 1890s, whose unique manufacturing process has been lost.

pocket doors: doors that open by sliding into a recess (pocket) in the wall.

portal: (or *portale*) in Spanish-style homes, the long, narrow porch that opens onto an internal courtyard; it functions as a sheltered passageway between rooms.

post and beam: building style based on the Medieval post-and-girder method, where upper loads are supported by heavy corner posts and cross timbers. In contemporary construction, the posts and beams are often left exposed on the interior.

Prairie: building style (1900–1920) with low-pitched roof and widely overhanging eaves; two stories with one-story wings or porches; façade detailing that emphasizes horizontal lines; massive, square porch supports.

Pueblo Revival: building style (1910 to present) with flat roof, parapet above; corners and edges blunted or rounded; projecting vigas, stepped back roof lines, and irregular stucco wall surfaces. Influenced by the flat-roofed Spanish Colonial buildings and Native American pueblos; popular in Arizona and New Mexico; common in Santa Fe and Albuquerque.

Queen Anne: building style (1880–1910) with a steeply pitched roof of irregular shapes; an asymmetrical façade with one-story porch; patterned shingles, bay windows, single tower. In furniture design the Queen Anne style was prevalent from 1725 to 1750, characterized by a graceful, unadorned curve of the leg (known as cabriole) and repeated curve of the top crest and vase-form back (splat) of a chair.

quoin: wood, stone, or brick materials that form the exterior corner of a building and are distinguishable from the background surface because of texture, color, size, or material.

rice-carved bed: *See* four-poster bed.

Richardsonian Romanesque: building style (1880–1900) with massive masonry walls of rough, squared stonework and round-topped arches over windows, porch supports, or entrances; round tower with conical roof common.

Santa Fe: *see* Pueblo Revival.

Second Empire: building style (1855–1885) with mansard roof adorned with dormer windows on lower slope; molded cornices above and below lower roof, and decorative brackets beneath eaves.

Shaker: style of furniture which represents the Shaker belief in simplicity. The finely crafted pieces are functional, without ornamentation. Chairs have ladder backs, rush seats, and simple turned legs; tables and cabinets are angular, with smooth surfaces.

Sheraton: named for English furniture designer, Thomas Sheraton, of the Federal period (early 1800s); style marked by straight lines, delicate proportions, wood inlays, and spare use of carving; characteristically tapered legs.

Shingle: building style (1880–1900) with walls and roofing of continuous wood shingles; no decorative detailing at doors, windows, corners, or roof overhang. Irregular, steeply pitched roof line and extensive porches common.

shotgun: simple 19th century house form suited to narrow urban lots, featuring a single-story, front gable building one room wide. Rooms and doorways are in a direct line, front to back; theorectically, a bullet fired through the front door would travel through the house unobstructed.

spandrel: decorative trim that fits the top corners of doorways, porches, or gables; usually triangular in shape.

Spanish Colonial: building style (1600–1900) of thick masonry walls, with low pitched or flat roof, interior wooden shutters covering small window openings, and multiple doorways. Pitched roof style often has half-cylindrical tiles; flat style has massive horizontal beams embedded in walls to support heavy roof of earth or mortar. Internal courtyards or cantilevered second-story porches are common.

Stick: building style (1860–1890) with a steeply pitched, gabled roof, usually with decorative trusses at apex; shingle or board walls interrupted by patterns of boards (stickwork) raised from the surface for emphasis.

Territorial: a variation of the Spanish Colonial building style found in New Mexico, western Texas, and Arizona. The flat roof and single story are topped by a protective layer of fired brick to form a decorative crown.

tester bed: a bed with a full canopy (the tester), supported at all four corners by tall posts. Pronounced "tee'-stir."

transom: usually refers to a window placed above a doorway.

trompe l'oeil: literally, French for "to trick the eye." Commonly refers to wall paintings that create an optical illusion.

Tudor: building style (1890–1940) with steeply pitched roof, usually cross-gabled; decorative half-timbering; tall, narrow, multi-paned windows; massive chimney crowned with decorative chimney pots.

vergeboard: decorative trim extending from the roof overhang of Tudor, Gothic Revival, or Queen Anne-style houses.

vernacular: style of architecture employing the commonest forms, materials, and decorations of a period or place.

viga(s): exposed (interior) and projecting (exterior) rough-hewn wooden roof beams common in adobe homes in Southwestern U.S.

wainscoting: most commonly, narrow wood paneling found on the lower half of a room's walls.

widow's walk: a railed observation platform built above the roof of a coastal house to permit unobstructed views of the sea. Name derives from the fate of many wives who paced the platform waiting for the return of their husbands from months (or years) at sea. Also called a "captain's walk."

Windsor: style of simple chair, with spindle back, turned legs, and usually a saddle seat. Considered a "country" design, it was popular in 18th and early 19th century towns and rural areas.

For more information:

A Field Guide to American Houses (Virginia and Lee McAlester, New York: Alfred A. Knopf, 1984; $19.95, paperback) was an invaluable source in preparing this glossary, and is highly recommended. Its 525 pages are lavishly illustrated with photographs and diagrams.

Clues to American Architecture (Marilyn W. Klein and David P. Fogle, Washington, D.C.: Starrhill Press, 1985; $6.95, paperback) is a handy, affordable 64-page pocket guide to over 30 architectural styles, from the Colonial period to contemporary construction. Each is clearly described in easy-to-understand language, and illustrated with numerous detailed sketches. Also in the same style and format is *Clues to American Furniture* (Jean Taylor Federico, Washington, D.C.: Starrhill Press, 1988; $6.95), covering design styles from Pilgrim to Chippendale, Eastlake to Art Deco. If your bookstore doesn't stock these titles, contact Starrhill directly at P.O. Box 32342, Washington, D.C. 20007; 202–387–9805.

Regional itineraries

Contributing editor Suzanne Carmichael has prepared these delightful itineraries to lead you from the best-known towns and cities through beautiful countryside, over less-traveled scenic highways to delightful towns and villages, to places where sights both natural and historic outnumber the modern "attractions" which so often litter the contemporary landscape.

To get a rough idea of where each itinerary will lead you, take a look at the appropriate map at the back of this book. But to really see where you'll be heading, pull out a detailed full-size map or road atlas, and use a highlighter to chart your path. (If you're hopeless when it comes to reading maps, ask the AAA to help you plan the trip with one of their Triptiks.) Some of our routes are circular, others are meant to be followed from one end to another; some are fairly short, others cover hundreds of miles. They can be traveled in either direction, or for just a section of the suggested route. You can sample an itinerary for a weekend, a week, or even two, depending on your travel style and the time available. For information on what to see and do along the way, refer to our state and local introductions, and to a good regional guidebook. For a list of places to stay en route, see the list of towns at the end of each itinerary, then refer to the entries in the state chapters for full details.

Ocean Auto Cruise: Cruise back roads cooled by sea breezes, loll on ocean beaches, and explore both historic southern towns and barrier islands along the South's prettiest stretch of ocean. Begin in gracious Charleston, South Carolina, where pastel houses peek out from behind lacy iron gates and horse-drawn carriages clomp by on cobblestoned streets. Visit revolutionary era and 19th-century homes, stroll the walkways at Charles Towne Landing park, and peruse items for sale at City Market (especially the Gullah Blacks' sweetgrass baskets).

Head south on Route 17 to South Carolina's Low Country and resort islands, with a stop in historic Georgetown. Pause in Beaufort, where Spanish explorers arrived 100 years before the Pilgrims landed at Plymouth Rock. Absorb the town's 18th century atmosphere as you walk past palmetto trees and moss-covered oaks. Before turning south, take Route 21 to Hunting Island State Park, where you can climb to the top of a 140-foot lighthouse for superb island, ocean, and mainland views.

Continue south on Route 170 to Route 17 and the Georgia border, detouring if you wish on Route 278 to Hilton Head Island, the largest sea island between New Jersey and Florida and a popular, though crowded, resort area. Savannah welcomes you to Georgia. A town of public squares (21 of them) with the country's largest urban historic district, Savannah was founded in 1733 as the seat of our 13th colony.

Route 17 now meanders slowly south through sleepy villages, across river channels and towards the area's famous Sea Islands. Turn east from Victorian Brunswick to visit Saint Simons Island, a vacation center with lush resorts and sophisticated shops. Or continue south, then turn east on

Route 50 to Jekyll Island where you can "hyde" away on golden beaches or bicycle through stands of stately palms. Another detour, just north of the Florida border, is to take Route 40 to St. Marys where you can ferry to Cumberland Island National Seashore to glimpse wild horses, collect shells, and swim on pristine beaches.

It's time to explore northeastern Florida. To maintain your vacation mentality, leave Route 17 and skirt north of urban Jacksonville by turning east at Yulee on Route 200, to Route A1A which runs south along barrier beaches for 105 miles. Turn north first to Fernandina Beach, famous for its Victorian architecture and infamous as an early 19th-century haven for pirates and smugglers. South on Route A1A is Amelia Island, the only area in the U.S. to have been governed under eight different flags.

Follow Route A1A to St. Augustine, the end of your ocean auto cruise. A center of Spanish influence since 1513, St. Augustine is the oldest U.S. city. Be sure to visit the restored Spanish quarter, as well as Castillo de San Marcos, a rock fortress made from coquina, a local limestone of shells and coral.

Sample southern hospitality at accommodations in these towns (in order of the appearance above): Charleston, Georgetown, McClellanville, and Beaufort (South Carolina); Savannah, Saint Simons Island, Jekyll Island and St. Marys (Georgia); Amelia Island and St. Augustine (Florida). Orange Park, south of Jacksonville, is another northeastern Florida option.

Appalachian Highland Routes: North Carolina's Highland area is known for its beauty: ancient weathered and rounded mountains, gentle pastures, waterfalls and tumbling trout-filled streams, hillsides vivid with wild flowers. Equally enduring are the legacies of the Cherokee Indians and the craft traditions of the area's Appalachian residents. We suggest both a northern and a southern loop route, both starting in Asheville.

Before setting off on either journey, pause in Asheville to visit the impressive Biltmore Estate, with its gardens and winery. Start your northern journey by following I-40 and Route 70 onto the Blue Ridge Parkway, a 470-mile road tracing mountain ridges north to Virginia. Numerous overlooks and attractions dot the parkway. Look particularly for The Folk Art Center (Milepost 382; 1/2 mile north of Route 70) which offers an excellent introduction to regional crafts, and Craggy Gardens (Milepost 364.6, 17 miles northeast of Asheville), which are spectacular in spring.

Take short detours from the parkway to see the double waterfalls at Linville Falls, and Blowing Rock's unusual rock formation. Leave the parkway at Route 16 to head northwest through Glendale Springs, then turn south on Routes 221 and 194. Wind through small Appalachian hamlets such as Banner Elk, continuing south on Route 19E. Pass through Spruce Pine, then take a short detour north to Penland, home of the famous Penland School of Crafts and its impressive gallery. Return to Route 19E, continuing past Burnsville to Mars Hill. Follow Route 213, then Route 251 back to Asheville (or drop south from Mars Hill on Route 19 for a high-speed return to the city).

Begin your southern loop in Asheville by heading west on Route 19 through the picturesque Great Smoky Mountain foothills and small towns such as Clyde. Detour several miles south to Waynesville for a peek at the Museum of North Carolina Handicrafts, then return to Route 19. Continue to Cherokee, home of the eastern branch of the Cherokee tribe. Just north, on Route 441, visit Oconaluftee Indian Village, a reconstructed 1750 Cherokee town where residents create top-notch crafts (available for purchase at Qualla Arts & Crafts, next door).

From here you may want to detour south on Route 441 along the Tuckasegee River to Dillsboro, and Sylva (note the architecture of the county courthouse). Return to (or continue on) Route 19 through Bryson City, at the southern edge of the Great Smoky Mountains National Park. Just past Lauada, turn north on Route 28 to Robbinsville, on the shore of Lake Santeetlah, near excellent white-water rafting on the Naantahala River. From here follow Route 129 south, turning (south again) on Route 141 to Brasstown, home of the John C. Campbell Folk School, best known for its stable of talented woodcarvers.

Go north from Brasstown to Route 64 and head east. You'll pass through scenic countryside and, just before Highlands, near five waterfalls in the Cullasaja River Gorge. Farther along, Cashiers and Lake Toxaway are popular resort areas. Continue north passing through Brevard, known as "Land of the Waterfalls." Follow Route 280 which runs alongside the southern boundary of the Pisgah National Forest back to Asheville.

Recommended accommodations in this area can be found in (in order of appearance above) Northern Loop: Asheville, Black Mountain (just east of Asheville), Blowing Rock, Boone, Glendale Springs, Banner Elk, Spruce Pine, Burnsville, and Mars Hill; Southern Loop: Asheville, Clyde, Waynesville, Dillsboro, Bryson City, Robbinsville, Highlands, Cashiers, Lake Toxaway and Brevard.

Lower Mississippi River Route: Bustling river cities and small, languid towns, Confederate and Acadian-French historical sites, plantation mansions and sugarcane fields all vie for travelers' attention along the lower Mississippi River. Our route takes you from Jackson, Mississippi, to New Orleans through a variety of settings. Plan to spend three to five days on this route, leaving yourself plenty of time to enjoy New Orleans too.

Begin in Jackson, the state's capital, where you can see Confederate trenches in Battlefield Park, and visit Mynelle Gardens botanical park. Head west on Route 20, a superhighway that will whisk you to Vicksburg and your first glimpse of the mighty Mississippi. Known for its Civil War sites, Vicksburg also has several plantation mansions open to the public.

Turn south on Route 27 to the Natchez Trace Parkway, which stretches 500 miles from Natchez to Nashville, Tennessee. Originally a footpath used by rivermen to "trace" their way back north after taking goods down river, today the two-lane road passes green fields, forests, huge rhododendrons, and flocks of wild turkeys. Take the parkway south to Natchez, stopping to see Port Gibson's historic homes. Overnight in Natchez, and tour plantation homes, Natchez-Under-the-Hill, and the Grand Village of the Natchez Indians.

Head south on Route 61, driving past pecan orchards and oak trees dripping with Spanish moss. Make your first Louisiana overnight in St.

Francisville to see Rosedown Plantation, then take a short detour up Route 965 to the Audubon State Commemorative Area. Leave St. Francisville via Route 10 south continuing to the river's edge. Board a small car ferry here to cross the Mississippi, then follow Route 10 to Route 415 which winds behind river dikes, through sugarcane fields and rice paddies, and past signs advertising "fried pig tails."

Turn east on Route 190, following it through Baton Rouge, then picking up Route 30 south of the Old State Capitol. Turn south on Route 75 which follows the river's oxbow turns. At Carville head again to river's edge and another car ferry which will take you across the Mississippi to White Castle. From here scenic Route 1 travels along Bayou Lafourche past Napoleonville to Thibodaux in the heart of Louisiana's "sugar belt."

Take Route 24 south to Houma, a historic Cajun city laced by seven bayous and more than 50 bridges. Walk through the local historic district, embark on a boat tour of nearby bayous and swamps, or stroll by the Intercoastal Waterway which begins south of Tallahassee, Florida, and stretches to Brownsville, Texas. Before heading to New Orleans on Route 90, an optional detour (128 miles round-trip) is for those who like to "go to the end of the road." Take Route 1 south as it parallels Bayou Lafourche and ends at Grand Isle State Park on the Gulf of Mexico, near the entrance to Barataria Bay.

Overnight accommodations in this area include ones in the following towns (in order of their appearance above): Jackson, Vicksburg, Natchez (Mississippi); St. Francisville, White Castle, Napoleonville and New Orleans (Louisiana).

Criteria for entries

Unlike many guidebooks, *we do not collect a membership or listing fee of any kind from the inns and hotels we include.* What matters to us is the feedback we get from you, our readers. This means we are free to write up the negative as well as the positive attributes of each inn listed, and if any given establishment does not measure up, there is no difficulty in dropping it.

Free copy of *INNroads* newsletter

Want to stay up-to-date on our latest finds? Send a business-size, self-addressed, stamped envelope with 52 cents postage and we'll send you the latest issue, *free!* While you're at it, why not enclose a report on any inns you've recently visited? Use the forms at the back of the book or your own stationery.

Key to Abbreviations and Symbols

For complete information and explanations, please see the Introduction.

¢ Especially good value for overnight accommodation.
♦♦ Families welcome. Most (but not all) have cribs, baby-sitting, games, play equipment, and reduced rates for children.
✕ Meals served to public; reservations recommended or required.
🎾 Tennis court and swimming pool and/or lake on grounds. Golf usually on grounds or nearby.
♿ Limited or full wheelchair access; call for details.
Rates: Range from least expensive room in low season to most expensive room in peak season.
Room only: No meals included; European Plan (EP).
B&B: Bed and breakfast; includes breakfast, sometimes afternoon/evening refreshment.
MAP: Modified American Plan; includes breakfast and dinner.
Full board: Three meals daily.
Alc lunch: À la carte lunch; average price of entrée plus nonalcoholic drink, tax, tip.
Alc dinner: Average price of three-course dinner, including half bottle of house wine, tax, tip.
Prix fixe dinner: Three- to five-course set dinner, excluding wine, tax, tip unless otherwise noted.
Extras: Noted if available. Always confirm in advance. Pets are not permitted unless specified; if you are allergic, ask for details; *most innkeepers have pets.*

We Want to Hear from You!

As you know, this book is effective only with your help. We really need to know about your experiences and discoveries. If you stayed at an inn or hotel listed here, we want to know how it was. Did it live up to our description? Exceed it? Was it what you expected? Did you like it? Were you disappointed? Delighted? Have you discovered new establishments that we should add to the next edition?

Tear out one of the report forms at the back of this book (or use your own stationery if you prefer) and write today. *Even if you write only "Fully endorse existing entry" you will have been most helpful.*

Thank You!

Alabama

The Tutwiler Hotel, Birmingham

There's much to see and do in Alabama, from Huntsville's Alabama Space and Rocket Center to historic Mobile, and the gorgeous gardens at Bellingrath. To sample Gulf Coast beaches, drive south from Mobile to Dauphin Island, a scenic sliver of land where you can rent boats, swim, and watch huge ships enter Mobile Bay. In northern Alabama visit Russell Cave National Monument, an enormous limestone cave that was used as a seasonal shelter by people beginning in 6500 B.C. Birmingham, a major commercial center, is also known for the unusual "geologic walkway" carved into a mountain at Red Mountain Museum.

If you'd really like an in-depth look at Alabama's B&Bs, pick up a copy of *And to Y'all a Good Night* (Seacoast Publishing, P.O. Box 26492, Birmingham AL 35226; $8 plus $1.50 p/h) written by frequent contributor Lynn Edge. Lynn describes dozens of B&Bs, along with recipes for their breakfast favorites.

ANNISTON

Textile mills and blast furnaces were built in Anniston after the Civil War to help the region recuperate from the ravages of war. Today it's better known as the home of Fort McClellan; although the fort's Chemical Corps Training Command is off-limits to civilians, those intrigued by peculiar museums can make an appointment to visit the Chemical Corps Museum, tracing the history of chemical warfare. More appealing is Anniston's Museum of Natural History, best known for its bird collection (but the kids will prefer the Egyptian mummies). Anniston is located in northeast-ern Alabama, one hour's drive east of Birmingham via I-20, and about two hours west of Atlanta, Georgia.

The Victoria ¢ ♁ ✕   *Tel: 205–236–0503* ✠
1604 Quintard Avenue, P.O. Box 2213, 36202   *Fax: 205–236–1138* Good

Built in 1888 and listed on the National Register of Historic Places, The Victoria wears its name well, with a three-story turret, beautiful stained and etched glass windows, a conservatory, and colonnaded verandas. Restored and expanded in 1985, the inn consists of the original building, housing a restaurant and three suites, plus a recently constructed annex which wraps around a courtyard and swimming pool. Rates include a continental breakfast.

"Though bordered by busy streets at front and back, its setting on a hill surrounded by trees and well-kept flower beds insulates it from traffic noise. Our room in the annex was attractively furnished with period reproductions, including a king-size bed with a brass headboard, comple-mented by white wicker furniture—a chaise longue, glass-topped table and several chairs." *(Jeanne Smith)* "Our charming room in the new wing had a bay window, lots of white wicker, and pretty prints." *(Ruth & Derek Tilsley)* "The suites in the original building are enormous with antiques and old-fashioned beds. Best public restaurant in the area, with outstand-ing soups, acceptable wine list. Also on the property is a century-old carriage house, restored as a lovely art gallery called the Wren's Nest, emphasizing artwork by well-known local wildlife artist Larry Martin." *(Carol Flaherty)* "We were impressed with the landscaping and the way the addition complements the lovely Victorian home and site. Once on the grounds it was not apparent that we were close to anything else—much less McDonald's, Wendy's, or Radio Shack!" *(MR, also Laura Patterson)* "The service was fantastic from the moment we arrived." *(Lynn Edge)*

Area for improvement: "Breakfast was served on a lovely glassed in wraparound porch, on tables made from converted pedal sewing ma-chines; perhaps we hit an off-day, but neither the coffee nor the sweet rolls seemed fresh."

Excellent dinner.

Open All year.
Rooms 1 cottage, 3 suites in main house, 44 doubles in annex. All with private bath, telephone, TV, air-conditioning.
Facilities Restaurant, bar/lounge, swimming pool, art gallery, valet parking.
Location 60 m E of Birmingham. From I-20, take Exit 185 (Oxford/Anniston); go 4 m N on Quintard (Hwy. 21/431) to inn. Make a U-turn at 17th St. & enter from Quintard.
Credit cards Amex, CB, DC, Discover, MC, Visa.
Rates B&B, $80–145 suite, $69 double, $59 single. Extra person, $10. Children under 12 free.

BIRMINGHAM

Also recommended: In the historic Five Points South section of Birming-ham is the 63-room Art Deco-style **Pickwick Hotel** (1023 20th Street

South, 35205; 205–933–9555 or 800–255–7304). One frequent contributor liked the convenient location and free parking, the friendly staff, and her clean, comfortable room with good reading lights and well-equipped bathroom. Less appealing was the traffic noise in front rooms; she also wished more care could be given to the afternoon tea, evening wine and cheese, and continental breakfast which the rates include ($109 double, $82 corporate).

The Tutwiler Hotel 🏃 ✗ ♿

Park Place at 21st Street North, 35203

Tel: 205–322–2100
800–HERITAGE
Fax: 205–325–1183

Built in 1914, the Tutwiler was restored in elegant and luxurious style, with antique reproduction furnishings created especially for the hotel. The hotel restaurant serves classic American cuisine in an environment meant to simulate that of a private club. Heritage Club rates include use of the Club Lounge, with free breakfast and evening hors d'oeuvres.

"Room well appointed and immaculate; gracious atmosphere. The dining room is a real attraction, with marvelous food served by a fine staff. Other appealing features include the convenient valet parking, and the location across from a beautiful park and within walking distance of the excellent Birmingham art museum. Stop by the Birmingham Public Library a block away to see the interesting Ezra Winter murals." *(HJB)* "Elegant period reproduction furnishings. Friendly, helpful service. Above average restaurant." *(KM)* "One of the best restaurants in the South. Ladies can set their feet on a 'springy' stool during dinner—it's great!" *(BJ Hensley)*

Open All year.
Rooms 52 suites, 96 doubles—all with full private bath, telephone, radio, TV, desk, air-conditioning. Extra amenities on Club floor.
Facilities Lobby, restaurant, lounge with weekend evening entertainment, terrace, patio. Valet parking (fee). Guest passes to health club with Nautilus, swimming pool, tennis, racquetball.
Location Downtown.
Restrictions No smoking in some guest bedrooms.
Credit cards Amex, CB, DC, Discover, MC, Visa.
Rates B&B, Room only, $118–179 suite, $102–159 double, $82–139 single. Extra adult, $15; Free second room for children 18 and under when accompanied by parent paying hotel rate. Weekend discount. Prix fixe dinner, $27. Alc breakfast, $4–13; alc lunch, $12; alc dinner, $50.
Extras Wheelchair access; 6 rooms specially equipped for disabled. Airport/station pickup. Crib; babysitting by prior arrangement. Member, Historic Hotels of America, Heritage Hotels.

DECATUR

Although too small for a full entry with two spacious guest rooms, most readers will enjoy a visit to **The Dancy-Polk House Inn** (901 Railroad Street, N.W., Decatur 35601; 205–353–3579). Despite its location next to the railroad tracks in a modest neighborhood, readers were delighted with the inn's immaculate interior, beautifully decorated with antiques; Pam and

Ned Anderson, the warm and hospitable owners; and the delicious breakfasts of fresh-squeezed orange juice and just-baked blueberry muffins. B&B double rates are $50, and children are welcome. Situated 70 miles north of Birmingham, the inn is 20 minutes west of the Rocket and Space Museum in Huntsville.

EUFAULA

Kendall Manor ¢ ♿
534 West Broad Street, 36027

Tel: 205–687–8847

Known for its lovely antebellum homes, Eufaula has broad, tree-lined streets with handsome Victorian mansions. Kendall Manor was built in the 1860s by James Turner Kendall, and is listed on the National Register of Historic Places. Purchased by Barbara and Timothy Lubsen in 1993, this Italianate-style home has sixteen-foot ceilings, gold leaf cornices, Italian marble fireplaces, and ruby-colored glass windows. An open porch wraps around three sides of the house with 52 carved supporting columns; the two-story home is topped by a belvedere (or cupola) which bears the names, dates, and comments of the five generations of Kendalls who lived here. Guest rooms are simply furnished with antiques and Oriental rugs; most have four-poster queen or king-sized beds. A typical breakfast starts with baked apples stuffed with cranberries, raisins, and nuts, followed by poached eggs in a mushroom wine sauce atop an English muffin, ham, and Swiss cheese.

"Tim and Barbara Lubsen welcomed us with freshly baked cookies and hot chocolate; we sat and talked until bedtime. Evening turndown service with brownies left at our bedside was a thoughtful touch. The ruby glass panes were especially pretty in the morning when the sun shone through. After a wonderful breakfast of scones with jams, French toast with fresh strawberries and syrup, country bacon, juice, and coffee, we toured the belvedere and were allowed to pick a space on the walls to inscribe our names along with those that dated back to 1894." *(Kelly & Lane Atchley)*

Open All year.
Rooms 5 doubles—all with private bath and/or shower, clock, air-conditioning, ceiling fan. 2 with desk.
Facilities Dining room with fireplace, living room with fireplace, sun room with stereo, books; library with fireplace, books, TV/VCR; sitting room with books, porch. 3 acres with off-street parking, croquet, bicycles. Fishing, boating on Lake Eufaula; golf nearby.
Location SE AL, at GA border. 50 m S of Columbus, GA; 75 m N of FL border. Historic district. 2½ blocks from town. From Hwy. 431, go right onto W. Broad St. to inn on right.
Restrictions No smoking. Children over 14.
Credit cards MC, Visa (credit card surcharge).
Rates B&B, $75–95 double, $65–70 single. Extra person, $7. Golf, hunting packages. Minimum stay during April Pilgrimage. Corporate, military rates.
Extras Limited wheelchair access. Local airport pickup.

EUTAW

Kirkwood ¢ **†**
111 Kirkwood Drive, 35462

Tel: 205–372–9009

Construction of this antebellum plantation house was halted in 1860 by the Civil War. Although continuously occupied, the building was not completed until it was bought and restored by Mrs. R.A. Swayze in 1972. Now listed on the National Register of Historic Places, this American Greek Revival mansion has a roof supported by eight massive Ionic columns, two stories high. The rooftop cupola—not built until the 1970s—can be reached from the third floor billiard room. Inside are Carrara marble mantels, Waterford crystal chandeliers, and windows with the original 9-over-9 with wavy glass. Furnished primarily with original antiques, the bedrooms have four-poster beds.

"Mary Swayze lives here with her daughter and granddaughter in a separate part of the house. They rarely spend time in the main part of the house, which made me feel like I was in this big plantation home alone. The two upstairs bedrooms share a huge, nicely decorated bath, although I didn't have to share. Breakfast was delicious and plentiful and included scrambled eggs, bacon, fried tomatoes, ham, and fresh orange juice. Homemade waffles on the second morning were a special treat. During the day I took a walking/driving tour of the town to see the many fascinating antebellum homes." *(Bill Novack, also MR)*

Open All year.
Rooms 2 doubles share 1 bath. Both with radio, fan, fireplace, balcony.
Facilities Dining room, breakfast room, living room, family room with books, TV; guest laundry, screened porch. 8 acres with children's swing set, gardens, woods. Swimming pool, tennis nearby.
Location W AL, 32 m SW of Tuscaloosa, 100 m NW of Montgomery. From I-20/59, take Exit 40 (Hwy 14). Drive E 2½ m, turn left on Kirkwood Drive.
Restrictions No smoking.
Credit cards None accepted.
Rates B&B, $75 double, $38 single. Children's rate.
Extras Airport/station pickup. Pets by prior arrangement.

FAIRHOPE

Fairhope makes an ideal base for touring Mobile and the Alabama coast. It's a charming little town, with appealing shops, a lovely park and fishing pier on Mobile Bay, and several enjoyable restaurants. Within an easy drive are the sugar sands of the Gulf beaches, Fort Morgan and the ferry across the bay, and the dozens of factory outlet shops of Riviera Centre. Golf, tennis, and horseback riding are all available through the Grand Hotel (see below).

Fairhope is located on the Eastern Shore of southern Alabama, 15 miles southeast of Mobile. Take I-10 E across Mobile Bay to Route 98 south. Follow 98 south for 8 miles, then turn right at sign for Fairhope/Point Clear, and follow road (Section Street) into Fairhope.

Reader tips: "Fairhope has a delightful selection of restaurants. We heard good things about Maggie's Bistro and The Wash House, but didn't have a chance to try them. We'd highly recommend the Old Bay Steamer for huge platters of steamed shrimp, crab, crawfish, and oysters at very reasonable prices. For wonderful water views and an inexpensive meal, go to the spanking clean Yardarm, right on the fishing pier." *(SWS)*

Also recommended: Although too big for a full entry at over 300 rooms, we wanted to share the comments of well-traveled contributors about the elegant old **Grand Hotel** (Route 98, Point Clear 36564; 800–544–9933 or 800–228–9290) on the bay in nearby Point Clear, now owned by Marriott. "Grounds are beautiful, with live oaks and magnolias everywhere. Public areas are lovely, with water views, vaulted ceilings, bricks and beams visible, pegged floors." *(SHW)* "Our corner room had spectacular sunset and water views. The Boardwalk offers a mile-long walk between the water and beautiful homes; the energetic can rent a bike and take the two-mile path into town." *(Glen Lush)* Also: "Comfortable rooms, good facilities, in a typical big-hotel atmosphere." *(Rita Langel)* "Housekeeping responded to our request for additional pillows and hangers with great efficiency. Service at breakfast was delightful one morning, lackadaisical the next." *(SWS)* Also: "We stayed in one of the new, standard-hotel-style rooms added by Marriott and were disappointed; overall, it was too big, too anonymous for our tastes." *(JMS)*

Information please: Located on Mobile Bay is the **Point of View Guest House** (19493 Highway 98, P.O. Box 231, Fairhope/Point Clear 36564; 205–928–8501), an early 1900s family compound owned by B'Beth and Butch Smith. Accommodations include two 2-bedroom cottages with kitchen and living room, plus a one-bedroom suite in the main house. Guests are welcome to use the 375-foot wharf and private beach, or relax in the flower gardens.

Bay Breeze Guest House   ⅗ ¢

742 South Mobile Street, 36533

Tel: 205–928–8976
Fax: 205–990–1493

As you might expect from its name, the Bay Breeze Guest House sits right on Mobile Bay, offering lovely water views from its common rooms, a beach to explore, and decks for fishing and crabbing. Owners Bill and Becky Jones welcome guests to their stucco home, built in the 1930s, now restored, remodeled, and enlarged. Furnished with family heirlooms and period antiques dating back five generations, the decor includes wicker, stained glass, hooked and Oriental rugs. Under the same ownership is the **Church Street Inn** (205–928–5144), offering three guest rooms with turn-of-the-century ambiance just steps from Fairhope's charming shops and galleries.

"Our cottage was tastefully furnished, immaculately clean, with careful attention to detail. We felt like we were staying with good friends. The owners are always ready for a chat or to answer a question, but leave you alone if desired. Delicious self-serve breakfast." *(P.A. Van Buuren)* "Bill and Becky were helpful with sightseeing and restaurant advice. I especially liked the landscaping; the driveway is lined with shells. Home-baked muffins, poppy seed bread, juices, and more; nothing was overlooked." *(Rebecca Dugger)*

Open All year.

Rooms 2 cottages, 2 doubles—all with full private bath and/or shower, clock, TV, air-conditioning, fan. 2 with telephone, radio, desk. Cottage with kitchenette.

Facilities Dining room, sitting room with fireplace, piano; living room with books, family room with TV/VCR; glassed-in porch, family kitchen. 3 acres with camelia, azalea gardens. On beach with private pier; fishing, crabbing.

Location From U.S. Hwy. 98 exit right onto Scenic/Alt. Hwy. 98 at "Welcome to Fairhope" sign. At 3rd light (Magnolia Ave.), turn right. Go 4 blocks, turn left on S. Mobile St. at Municipal Pier. Go approx. 1 m to inn on right.

Restrictions No smoking. No children.

Credit cards Amex, MC, Visa.

Rates B&B, $85 suite, $75 double. Extra person, $10. Some weekend minimum.

Extras 1 cottage wheelchair accessible. Limited Spanish spoken.

GREENSBORO

"Blue Shadows" Guest House ¢ 🏃   *Tel: 205–624–3637*
Route 14, RR 2, Box 432, 36744

After traveling the world as a pilot for TWA, Thaddeus May and his wife Janet were inspired to offer the same type of B&B accommodation in Alabama that they had enjoyed abroad. Their 1940s home is shaded by mature trees; guest rooms in the main house are decorated with antiques, while the guest house has contemporary furnishings.

Janet notes that "we attract people who want a quiet elegant place to relax, take long walks, fish, or sit on the deck." Breakfast is continental, and afternoon tea or sherry is served. Located in the "Black Belt" (a reference to the richness of the region's prairie soil), Greensboro blossomed during the reign of "King Cotton" and the antebellum homes that dot the area are a testimony to the wealth of the early cotton growers. The Mays will gladly help with sightseeing plans to visit the historic nearby towns of Eutaw, Demopolis, Selma, and Tuscaloosa.

"Relaxing atmosphere, with fresh fruit, flowers, and lots of reading material in your room." *(Mrs. Betty Hedberg)* "Janet and Thad are friendly, interesting hosts. Sarah, their delightful dog, led us on the nature trail, but was never obtrusive or bothersome." *(Lance Bond)* "The balcony offered a view of the gardens and a pecan orchard." *(Madeline C. Ritchie)* "Thick towels, spotlessly clean." *(Miriam Mason)*

Open All year. Closed Thanksgiving week.

Rooms 1 guest house with private bath, living room, bar, kitchenette, balcony; 2 doubles in main house share 1 bath. All with radio, TV, air-conditioning, ceiling fan.

Facilities For main house guests: breakfast room, living room with piano; sun parlor, balcony. 320 acres with nature trail, gardens, pecan and fruit orchard, barn, bird sanctuary, children's play equipment, picnic area. Private lake for fishing, boating. 2 m jogging trail. Golf, tennis privileges at local club.

Location W central AL. 35 m S of Tuscaloosa, 90 m W of Birmingham, Montgomery, 3 m W of Greensboro, on Rte. 14.

Restrictions No smoking. Children welcome in guest house.

Credit cards None accepted.

Rates B&B, $65 cottage, double, $50 single. Extra person, $10.

Extras Crib, babysitting.

JEMISON

Jemison is roughly halfway between Birmingham and Montgomery, just off I-65.

Also recommended: For Southern hospitality in the heart of an old-fashioned small town, try the **Jemison Inn** (212 Highway 191, Jemison, 35085; 205–688–2055 or 800–438–3042). The three guest rooms are furnished with antiques, with fresh flowers and fruit to welcome you; rates range from $55–60, including a full breakfast. "We toured the inn and spent a delightful hour with Nancy Ruzicka; we can't wait to return for an overnight stay." *(Lynn Edge)*

Information please: About ten miles from town is the **Horse-Shoe Bunkhouse B&B** (356 County Road 164, Jemison, 35085; 205–646–4109), a working horse farm. Owner Kay Red Horse serves a breakfast of eggs to order, meat, homemade rolls, preserves, homemade Southern gravy, grits, a variety of fruits, juice and coffee. B&B double rates for the three guest rooms range from $55–65. Kay's experiences out west are reflected in the cowboy decor of one guest room, Native American in another; she'll fix you Navajo tacos for dinner if you don't want to go into town.

MOBILE

Reader tip: "Although Mobile has some museums and sights of interest, we preferred staying in Fairhope, about 15 miles away across the bay. In contrast to Mobile, we found Fairhope to be clean, safe, and friendly, and just as convenient for touring the area." *(MW)*

Malaga Inn ¢ ✗ ♿   *Tel:* 205–438–4701
359 Church Street, 36602   800–235–1586

The Malaga Inn, listed on the National Register of Historic Places, was originally two separate town houses built by two brothers-in-law in 1862. When it was converted into a hotel, over 25 years ago, a wing was added to connect the two buildings, enclosing a courtyard.

"The inn has a large reception area, with most of the guest rooms surrounding a central courtyard with a fountain. Our spacious room had two big four-poster beds, a roomy armoire, marble fireplace, ceiling fan, and hardwood floors. We had access to a balcony trimmed with wrought iron. The bath was small but clean." *(MFD)*

"With 14-foot ceilings, wide-board floors, and a New Orleans-style balcony, our room was grand yet comfortable." *(Allison & Bob Young, also Sidney Flynn)* "Although they cost slightly more, I'd recommend a room in one of the original townhouses. Their antique flavor is more pronounced; those overlooking the courtyard have motel-style furnishings. Our meal was pleasant and inexpensive; the elderly woman who served us made it feel like we were lunching at grandma's house." *(SWS)*

Open All year.
Rooms 3 suites, 37 doubles—all with full private bath, telephone, TV, desk, air-conditioning.
Facilities Restaurant, lounge, garden courtyard with fountain, swimming pool.
Location Gulf Coast. Church Street historic district. From I-10 E, take Canal St. exit. Cross Canal to Jackson. Follow Jackson to Church & go left. From I-10 W, take Gov't. St. exit from Bayway through Bankhead Tunnel. Follow Gov't. St. to Claiborne & go left. Right on Church.
Credit cards Amex, DC, Discover, MC, Visa.
Rates Room only, $125 suite, $76–79 double, $72–76 single. Extra person, $5. Alc lunch, $5–12; alc dinner, $15–25.
Extras Elevator for wheelchair access. Crib.

MONTGOMERY

State capital of Alabama, Montgomery also served as the first capital of the Confederacy; today it is equally renowned for its role in the Civil Rights movement. For evening entertainment, call 800–841–4273 for information on the Alabama Shakespeare Festival, which offers high quality repertory theater by the Bard as well as contemporary playwrights. Montgomery is located in central Alabama, 85 miles south of Birmingham, 160 miles north of Mobile.

Lattice Inn ¢   *Tel:* 205–832–9931
1414 South Hull Street, 36104   800–525–0652
                Fax: 205–264–0075

Michael Pierce welcomes guests to the Lattice Inn, built in 1906, and restored as a B&B in 1993; he notes that he "strives to be attentive without intruding on guests' privacy."

"Our favorite place to stay when we attend the Alabama Shakespeare Festival. Exquisite yet comfortable furnishings, highlighted by the host's personal collections. He is an excellent cook and our room was always stocked with homemade cookies and fresh fruit. Breakfast was served on the deck overlooking the pool." *(Marion Ruben)* "The inn has a beautiful dining room and two living areas where guests can watch TV, read or chat. The location is ideal, in a historic neighborhood just three blocks from the Governor's Mansion, charming for jogging or walking. Michael personally designed and oversaw the restoration of the house and the interior design work. His selection of colors, fabrics, wallpapers and furniture have created a comfortable and authentic environment. In the backyard, he added a large deck and swimming pool offering privacy and comfort in the shade of lovely hardwood trees. Breakfasts are a highlight, with a wonderful bowl of fresh-cut fruit (kiwi, raspberries, blackberries, and more), and an array of delicious homemade muffins. Michael frequently offers traditional Southern breakfast treats such as French toast or eggs and sausage." *(Joy Satterlee)*

"The neighborhood is quiet and unhurried, yet conveniently located for access to the interstates, downtown or suburbs. Michael is witty, urbane, erudite, and charming. Our champagne breakfast included mixed fresh fruit, muffins and other homemade baked goods, juice and coffee, two kinds of quiche—seafood and bacon." *(David Clark)* "Michael helped us find places to eat and interesting sights to see. Exceptional service, cleanliness, and quiet." *(Chris & Susan Blazer)* "The rooms have high, beamed ceilings, four-poster beds, antiques, and an elegant country feel." *(Vicki Ford)*

Open All year.
Rooms 1 cottage, 4 doubles—all with full private bath, radio, clock, desk, air-conditioning, fan. 2 with telephone (on request), fireplace, deck; 1 with TV. Cottage with living room, kitchen.
Facilities Dining room, living room with fireplace, library with TV, fireplace; porch, decks. Gazebo, swimming pool, limited off-street parking.
Location 1 m from downtown in historic garden district. Exit I-85 at Union St., & go W on Service Rd. to Hull. Go S on Hull to inn on right, between Maury & Earl.
Restrictions No smoking. Children welcome in cottage.
Credit cards Amex, MC, Visa.
Rates Room only, $50–65 cottage, $50–65 double. B&B, $55–65 cottage, double. Extra person, $5–10. 5% senior, AAA discount.
Extras Limited wheelchair access.

Red Bluff Cottage ¢

551 Clay Street, P.O. Box 1026, 36101

Tel: 205–264–0056
Fax: 205–262–1872

Anne and Mark Waldo built Red Bluff Cottage in 1987 to offer a base to those visiting the city for business or pleasure. Mark is a retired Episcopal minister, and together the Waldos have raised six children, making them old hands at extending Southern hospitality to family and friends. Situated in a neighborhood of 19th century cottages, and pre- and post-Civil War homes, the Waldos built their home in the traditional style of a raised cottage; the decor is highlighted by family antiques. The bedrooms are on the ground floor while the common rooms are on the upper level. Guests are served a breakfast of pancakes, waffles, or maybe eggs and grits in the dining room, or on the front porch overlooking the river plain; if your timing is right, fresh-picked Alabama blueberries or peaches will start off your day.

"Clean and comfortable, with a delicious hearty breakfast." *(Cynthia Blakely)* "Well furnished with antiques and historical memorabilia." *(Mary Morgan)* "Gracious, kindly, warm owners. Lovely antiques, Oriental rugs, interesting books; ample common areas in which to relax." *(Margaret Powell)*

Open All year.
Rooms 1 family suite, 3 doubles, 1 single—all with private bath and/or shower, air-conditioning, fans. Some with desk.
Facilities Dining room, family room with fireplace, music room with harpsichord, porch. Off-street parking.
Location Central AL. From I-65, take Exit 172. Take Heron St. (downtown) 1 block to Hanrick. Go left 100 ft. Parking area on right.
Restrictions No smoking. Special arrangements for children under 8.
Credit cards MC, Visa.

Rates B&B, $75 suite, $65 double, $55 single.
Extras Crib. Train station pick-up. Airport pick-up with prior arrangement.

ORANGE BEACH

Also recommended: "The most beautiful beach in the USA," is how *Marion & Ethan Ruben* describe Perdido Beach, and having seen its sugar-fine white sand and clear Gulf waters, we've placed it high on our list of favorites, too. Their favorite place to stay is the **Perdido Beach Resort** (27200 Perdido Beach Boulevard, 36561; 205–981–9811 or 800–634–8001), a 345-room Hilton beachfront hotel offering "personal attention and lovely rooms." All guest rooms have gulf views, and facilities include a heated indoor/outdoor swimming pool, four lighted tennis courts, health club, children's program, restaurants, and golf packages.

Information please: The **Original Romar House** (23500 Perdido Beach Boulevard, Orange Beach 36561; 205–981–6156 or 800–48–ROMAR), was built in 1924, and offers stained glass windows, Art Deco-type furnishings, and water views. The rates ($120 double in peak season) include breakfast, afternoon wine and cheese in the Purple Parrot Bar, off-street parking, beach access, and use of the hot tub. "Our room, #3, was somewhat small but nicely furnished with a ceiling fan, excellent queen-sized bed, unusual green lamps, and carved wooden furnishings. Eaten at tables on the deck, breakfast was the same each day: juice and coffee, canned fruit salad, biscuits, cereal, Danish, scrambled eggs, and cheese grits and ham one day, hash browns and sausage the next. Innkeepers Burke and Roxanne Chance were friendly, but rarely around, since both have other jobs." *(KW)*

PRATTVILLE

Plantation House B&B ¢   *Tel:* 205–361–0442
752 Loder Street, 36067

Prattville is named for Daniel Pratt, inventor of the cotton gin; Pratt Industries' buildings, dating from 1850, are still in use producing cotton gins to this day. Built in 1832, the Plantation House is a clapboard over brick structure, with a portico and four columns typical of the Greek Revival style. John and Bernice Hughes bought the house in 1989, after a devastating fire destroyed the rear of the building, and restored it as a B&B. The result is a happy combination of 19th century southern charm and 20th century comfort, the antique furnishings and fireplaces are enhanced by central air-conditioning and thermal sound insulation.

"A winding staircase takes you up to the guest rooms, which offer lovely views of the grounds. The Master Bedroom has a queen-size four-poster bed, hardwood floor, and a huge bathroom with a fireplace and Jacuzzi. Breakfast was served in a small breakfast area overlooking the grounds. Bernice and John are friendly and charming, willing to answer questions and be of service." *(Glenn & Delane Goggans)* "Mrs. Hughes served delicious quiche, croissants, and homemade preserves at the beautifully set dining room table." *(Jill Gilbert)* "Meticulously kept; immaculate. Breakfast was highlighted by a soufflé and apple pastry." *(Randall Merritt)*

Open All year.
Rooms 2 doubles—both with full private bath, telephone, TV, desk, air-conditioning, fan, balcony. 1 with working fireplace, whirlpool tub.
Facilities Library with fireplace, books; two lounges, sun porch. 4½ acres with swimming pool, hot tub, koi pond. Swimming, boating, fishing nearby.
Location Central AL, Autauga County. 10 m NW of Montgomery. 1 m from downtown. Exit I-65 at Main St. & drive toward town. After passing Hwy. 31, watch for Loder St. Turn right on Loder & watch for inn on right.
Restrictions No smoking in guest rooms. No children under 12.
Credit cards MC, Visa.
Rates B&B, $55–65 double, $50–60 single. 10% senior, AAA discount. Weekly rates. Family rates.

SELMA

Grace Hall   *Tel:* 205–875–5744
506 Lauderdale Street, 36701   *Fax:* 205–875–9967

After 1850, Alabama architecture is typified by a mixture of the older Greek Revival neoclassicism with "newer" Victorian trends. Listed on the National Register of Historic Places, Grace Hall exemplifies this eclecticism. Rates in this restored mansion, owned by Coy and Joey Dillon, include refreshments on arrival, a tour of the mansion, and breakfast. A recent morning feast featured fresh fruit compote, freshly squeezed orange juice, omelets filled with sautéed vegetables, bacon, homemade croissants, and banana nut bread.

"Mrs. Dillon provided a list of historic sights, made our dinner reservations, and told us the history of the house while she showed us through it. Delicious breakfast, highlighted by homemade biscuits and gravy." *(BJ Hensley)* "Well worth a detour for this well-documented restoration. Friendly, loquacious hostess." *(John Blewer)* "Immaculate housekeeping, outstanding breakfast. Wonderful wallpapers, drapes, beautiful floors." *(Nancy Bernard)* "Comfortable bed with good pillows. Delightful innkeeper; Joey's mother, plus several cats and a dog made us feel included in everything going on." *(Dianne Crawford)*

Open All year.
Rooms 1 suite, 5 doubles—all with shower bath, telephone, TV, desk, air-conditioning, ceiling fan, fireplace. 3 rooms in annex.
Facilities Dining room, double parlor, library, family room with TV, all with fireplace; porches, patio, English garden with fountain. Health club across st., $5. ½ m to jogging, tennis, river for boating.
Location Central AL. 50 m S of Montgomery. 90 min. from Birmingham. 2 blocks from center. Follow signs to Chamber of Commerce; inn is across street.
Restrictions No smoking in house. No children under 6.

Credit cards Amex, MC, Visa.
Rates B&B, $110–135 suite, $75–100 double, $65–90 single. Extra person, $15. Prix fixe lunch $17; dinner, $35.
Extras Airport/station pickup, $25. Hungarian spoken.

STERRETT

Twin Pines ♦ ♿   *Tel:* 205–672–7575
1200 Twin Pines Road, 35147

Once the weekend getaway home of the Saunders family, Twin Pines is now a resort and conference center owned by Bob Saunders and managed by Tom Scott. Although popular with corporate groups, individual and family groups are most welcome. "A wonderful, secluded place to relax. Comfortable guest rooms in recently built log lodges, each with a balcony overlooking the lake. Beautiful walking trails through the woods, with lots of peacocks, ducks, and flowering plants. Excellent food and service." *(Marion Ruben)*

Open All year.
Rooms 6 suites, 44 doubles—all with full private bath, telephone, clock, balcony, coffee maker, hairdryer. Most with clock/radio, desk, TV, refrigerator. Suites with kitchen, sitting area, fireplace. Rooms in 8 buildings.
Facilities Dining room, living room, family room, library, conference center, decks. 200 acres on 46-acre private lake for swimming, paddle boats, fishing, canoeing; hiking trails, tennis, softball, horseshoes, shuffleboard, playground, gazebo.
Location 30 min. S of Birmingham. Take Hwy 280 S. Exit on Hwy. 43 to Hwy 45, then to Twin Pines Rd. 12 m from Hwy 280.
Credit cards Amex, MC, Visa.
Rates Room only, $112 suite, $80 double, single. Extra person, $10. Full board, $135 suite, $100 double, single. Extra person, $34. 10% service. Children's rates. Senior discount. $50 Thanksgiving through Dec.
Extras Wheelchair access; some rooms specially equipped. Crib.

TALLADEGA

The Governor's House ¢ ⚡   *Tel:* 205–763–2186
Embry Cross Road, Lincoln   205–763–3336
Mailing address: 500 Meadowlake Lane, 35160

When people mention a "mobile home," they're usually don't have an 1850 Greek Revival house in mind, but that's just what the Governor's House became for the short trip from downtown Talladega to its present location on Meadowlake Farm, overlooking Logan Martin Lake. Built by Alabama Governor Lewis Parsons, Mary Sue and Ralph Gaines moved the building onto their farm in 1990, restoring it as a B&B and furnishing it with family antiques and quilts. Guests enjoy watching the farm's horses, Hereford cattle, chicken, and pet goats, or trying their luck at fishing in the lake and bass-stocked pond. A typical breakfast might include fresh fruit and juice, eggs or a cheese souffleé, garlic grits, fresh-baked biscuits and sweet rolls with homemade jellies and strawberry butter, and bacon, ham, or sausage.

"Best of all is the setting, on a knoll overlooking the lake, surrounded by rolling pastureland where cattle graze. The long front porch is furnished with white wicker and a swing—a serene place to relax." *(Cheryl Stone)* "Country ambience only two miles from the interstate. Squeaky clean; beautifully furnished. Guest refrigerator loaded with juices, cheese, breads, wine and soft drinks." *(Milly Cowles)* "Mary Sue provides an early breakfast if required, and offered excellent restaurant recommendations." *(Petra Smith)* "We were welcomed with a just-baked pecan pie, and helped with dinner reservations. Around the house are framed newspaper clippings which explain the history of the farm, antique shop, and the house itself." *(Staci Valentine)* "Mrs. Gaines is cheerful, interesting and congenial. Loved the homemade jams and jellies at breakfast." *(Clara Melton)*

Open All year.
Rooms 1 guest house, 3 doubles—1 with private shower bath, 2 with maximum of 4 sharing bath. All with radio, desk, air-conditioning, fan.
Facilities Dining room with fireplace, living room with electric fireplace, TV, books, porch with swing. 7-acre grounds with tennis court, antique shop; 157-acre farm. Lake adjacent to farm with boat ramp, fishing pier, swimming.
Location E central AL. 35 m E of Birmingham, 15 m W of Anniston, 105 m W of Atlanta, GA. From I-20, take Exit 165, and go S 2 m on Embry Cross Rd. 6 m W of Alabama International Motor Speedway and Hall of Fame.
Restrictions No smoking. No children under 12.
Credit cards None accepted.
Rates B&B, $60–70 double, $55–65 single. Family rates. Picnic baskets. Prix fixe lunch, $7; prix fixe dinner, $15.
Extras Airport/station pickups, $15.

Free copy of *INNroads* newsletter

Want to stay up-to-date on our latest finds? Send a business-size, self-addressed, stamped envelope with 52 cents postage and we'll send you the latest issue, *free!* While you're at it, why not enclose a report on any inns you've recently visited? Use the forms at the back of the book or your own stationery.

Arkansas

Williams House, Hot Springs

Rugged mountain individualism is one of the first things that comes to mind when Arkansas is mentioned. Although the Ozarks are a very old mountain chain and not terribly high, the terrain is rugged and transportation was, until quite recently, very difficult. Distinctive crafts, cuisine, and culture developed as a result, much of which has been preserved through the Ozark Folk Center, located in Mountain View (see listing). Many famous springs dot this region of northwestern Arkansas as well, particularly Hot Springs National Park, 55 miles southwest of Little Rock, and Eureka Springs, in the north.

If you want to add sparkle to your Arkansas trip, visit Crater of Diamonds State Park, southeast of Hot Springs—it's America's only public diamond-hunting field. Outdoor enthusiasts generally head to the state's rivers for white-water canoeing or a fight with a largemouth bass, while amateur spelunkers visit what experts call the greatest cave find of the 20th century, Blanchard Springs Caves near Mountain View.

Reader tip: "For Appalachian antiques and crafts, avoid the overpriced shops of Eureka Springs, and stop in Van Buren, near Fort Smith and I-40, at the Antique Warehouse and Mall; the shops in the restored downtown area are also worth a look." *(MA)*

ALTUS

Information please: A modest B&B in eastern Arkansas, just south of I-40, is **St. Mary's Mountain Guest House** (501 St. Mary's Mountain

Road, P.O. Box 100, 72821; 501–468–4141), located near a golf course, the Mulberry River for canoeing, and several wineries. "Our room in this simple contemporary home had sliding glass doors opening onto a balcony overlooking over the yard and woods beyond." *(Phyllis Wikoff)* Breakfast, which can be enjoyed on your balcony or in your room, includes homemade blueberry coffee cake and cinnamon rolls, coffee, fruit and juice. B&B double rates for the three guest rooms are $42.

BRINKLEY

Information please: The sleepy town of Brinkley was once a major transportation hub. In 1916, the town served over 30 passenger trains, and to accommodate the numerous passengers, a modern, fireproof commercial hotel was needed. In 1981, Stanley and Dorcas Prince purchased the building and began its restoration, renaming it **The Great Southern Hotel** (127 West Cedar, 72021; 501–734–4955). The first floor guest rooms are simply furnished with period antiques, wall-to-wall carpeting, and soft floral wallpapers. Rates include a full breakfast. The restaurant specializes in such Southern favorites as pecan fried chicken and fried steak with milk gravy. Desserts include praline pecan ice cream pie and Arkansas derby pie. The hotel was for sale when we went to press; reports appreciated.

EUREKA SPRINGS

Eureka Springs is the site of natural springs first discovered by the Indians, then lost for decades until rediscovered in the 1850s by a local doctor. The curative powers of the spring waters soon became renowned, and by the 1880s this hillside town boasted dozens of hotels. As the decades passed and medicine advanced, the town was forgotten and its Victorian charms thus preserved. The local Historic District Commission now stands guard to make sure that nothing is changed without its approval.

Local attractions include dozens of art galleries and mountain craft shops, the steam train ride through the Ozarks, the Passion Play, and the Pine Mountain Jamboree. Beaver Lake and the Buffalo and White rivers are nearby for swimming, boating, float trips, fishing, and canoeing.

Eureka Springs is located in northwest Arkansas, 50 miles northeast of Fayetteville, 200 miles northwest of Little Rock, and 100 miles south of Springfield, Missouri. It is best reached via Highways 62 or 23.

Reader tips: "Parking on Eureka Springs' narrow, hilly streets ranges from difficult to impossible. Once you have found a space on the street or at your inn, leave your car and get around on the convenient trolley, which stops in front of many of inns." *(GR)*

Also recommended: A 60-year-old Tudor-style B&B, the **Ellis House** (1 Wheeler Street, 72632; 501–253–8218), is decorated with local art and antiques. Some guest rooms have double whirlpool tubs, king- or queen-size beds. "Secluded location with a spectacular view overlooking the town. The grounds were full of honeysuckle, irises, peonies and lilies of the valley. When we arrived, a note invited us to help ourselves to tea, coffee, and treats. For breakfast we had fresh strawberries, cheese omelets, sausages, muffins and juice." *(Karla Riley)*

Bonnybrooke Farm Atop Misty Mountain   Tel: 501–253–6903
Route 2, Box 335A, 72632

Shaded by huge oak trees and surrounded by rock gardens, Bonnybrooke Farm Atop Misty Mountain was built in 1988, and offers secluded cottages with mountain and woodland views.

"Owner Bonny Pierson has thought of everything—wood for the fireplace, ample hot water for the Jacuzzi, plush towels, large bars of soap, hair dryer, and beautiful flowers." *(Elaine & David Miller)* "Though our cottage consisted of one mid-size room, the glass-walled solarium made it seem far more spacious. It was decorated in a floral print, with comfortable chairs, and reading material (mostly Christian). We enjoyed eating at the Café Armagost on the road into town." *(Beverly Floyd)*

"You are welcomed by the resident tour guide, Slick, a beautiful Sheltie who loves to visit with guests and take them hiking. For your arrival, Bonny leaves freshly baked bread or muffins, along with fresh fruit on your table. She has also stocked the kitchen with gourmet teas and coffees. Each cottage is decorated with beautiful antique mirrors and other pieces that Bonny has collected over the years. Soft music is playing as you enter, and audio and video tapes await your pleasure. Each cottage is different: in one, you go to sleep under the stars; in another, you can shower by moonlight. Each cottage has an album with the menus from all the local eating establishments, plus brochures from all area attractions." *(Bill & Debi Keeney)*

Open All year.
Rooms 5 cottages—all with full private bath, double Jacuzzi, TV/VCR/tape recorder with audio/video tapes; radio, clock, desk, air-conditioning, fan, books, games, fireplace; stocked kitchen with coffee maker, microwave, deck with barbecue grill.
Facilities 20 acres with hiking, gardens.
Location 4 m from downtown. Directions with confirmation.
Restrictions No smoking. "Not designed for children."
Credit cards MC, Visa for deposit only.
Rates Room only, $85–125. 2-3 night weekend/holiday minimum. (Welcome basket of fruit and breakfast bread; also coffee, tea).

Bridgeford House ¢ 🏃   Tel: 501–253–7853
263 Spring Street, 72632

An Eastlake-style Queen Anne home built in 1884, Bridgeford House has been owned by Denise and Michael McDonald since 1980.

"The parlor and guest rooms at the front of the house have Victorian furnishings. We stayed in the Greenbriar Suite, added on to the back of the house, with 'country modern' furnishings and a porch overlooking Michael's beautiful garden. Denise is a wonderful hostess, and her breakfasts kept us going until dinner." *(Mr. & Mrs. R. Thomson)* "Denise was extremely knowledgeable about events, schedules, restaurants, sights, transportation, and was pleased to help with dinner and show reservations. The house is on three levels, and all rooms have private entrances." *(Gloria Robertson)* "An easy walk to downtown shops. Our room was large and beautifully decorated in Victorian style with a clawfoot tub in the bath." *(Jeanne McDowell)* "Superb breakfasts at an antique table set with fine china, silver and crystal." *(Marcie Handrich)* "Comfortable, quiet, plenty of privacy." *(Shirley Shimota)* "Special touches: non-alcoholic drinks in wine goblets, fine tea, candies, fresh flowers." *(Cliff & Vonda Cole)* "Spacious bathroom with ample mirrors and space for a refrigerator and coffeemaker." *(Rhonda Nelson)*

Open All year.
Rooms 1 suite with kitchenette, 3 doubles—all with private bath and/or shower, radio, TV, desk, air-conditioning, refrigerator, coffee maker; 2 with fireplace.
Facilities Breakfast room, parlor, decks, porches. Off- & on-street parking, garden with fountain.
Location From Hwy 62, go ½ m N on Main St. Historic district.
Restrictions No smoking.
Credit cards MC, Visa.
Rates B&B, $95 suite, $85 double, $65–75 single. Extra adult, $20; children under 12, $15. 2-night weekend/holiday minimum. 10% discount Jan.–Mar.; also 3-day stays. Packages.
Extras Airport/station pickups.

Cliff Cottage
42 Armstrong Street, 72632

Tel: 501–253–7409
800–799–7409

Cliff Cottage is a handsome Stick-style Victorian home, painted in several shades of blue-green, accented with pale coral; it was built in 1892 and restored in 1993 by Sandra C.H. Smith. In 1994, Sandra built The Place Next Door, in a complementary Victorian style. An accomplished writer, actor, chef, sailor, and musician, Sandra will sometimes play the piano for guests. She has lived in France and sailed in the Caribbean, and her cooking reflects these influences. Guests may have breakfasts of home-baked pastries and croissants with fresh fruit delivered to their room, or can gather in the dining room for strawberry/banana French toast, eggs Benedict, or German pancakes.

"Picturesque hillside cottage. Modern luxuries included a VCR and a broad selection of movies, a large Jacuzzi, and a refrigerator stocked with tasty snacks and drinks. In the morning, a beautifully arranged plate of fresh fruit and a basket of hot pastries, wrapped in lace, arrived on our porch." *(Jan & Gary Allison)* "Our living room looked down on the shopping and restaurant district, only a quick walk away. The Victorian charm was enhanced by fresh flowers, books of poetry and fresh fruit. Our room had a hardwood floor, a king-size bed and a skylight." *(Velvet Nichols)* "Personal touches are everywhere—candles, bubble bath, fresh flowers. Sandra prepared a delicious candlelight dinner for us at our request." *(Joe & Laura Hancock)*

Open All year.
Rooms 2 suites, 2 doubles—all with full private bath, radio, clock, TV/VCR,

air-conditioning, deck. Some with double whirlpool tub, fan, desk, deck, refrigerator.

Facilities Dining room, great room with fireplace, piano, books. Occasional Sunday musicals, poetry readings. Victorian gardens. On & off-street parking.

Location Historic downtown district. Off S. Main St. Take stairway up from trolley depot.

Restrictions Children over 16.

Credit cards MC, Visa.

Rates B&B, $95–125 suite, $70–100 double. Extra person, $20. Tips appreciated. 2-night weekend minimum in season. Midweek discount; 7th night free. Prix fixe lunch, $15; dinner, $25; by advance reservation.

Extras French, Spanish spoken; some German.

Dairy Hollow House 🛏 ✕ ♿

515 Spring Street, 72632

Tel: 501–253–7444
800–562–8650

When the doors of Dairy Hollow House opened in 1981, it was one of the first bed & breakfast inns in the state. Since then, innkeepers Crescent Dragonwagon (she adopted the name after moving to Arkansas at age 18) and her husband, Ned Shank, have developed a nationwide reputation for their "Nouveau Zarks" cuisine, combining classic French with the Ozarks' best regional ingredients. The Dairy Hollow House encompasses the Farmhouse in the Hollow, a fully renovated 1880s farmhouse, housing three guest rooms, all with fireplaces, handmade quilts and period antiques; The Main House, with three suites with fireplaces; and the Restaurant at Dairy Hollow, on the garden level of the Main House. The central reception area is here also, next to the restaurant.

In addition to her innkeeping abilities, Crescent Dragonwagon is noted children's book and cookbook author (copies of her books are in the guest rooms). Breakfast specialties (delivered to your room) include fresh fruit or juice, German baked pancakes with fresh berry sauce, or perhaps featherbed eggs and chicken-apple sausages, accompanied by homemade jams and jellies, gingerbread muffins, or blueberry coffee cake. Dinner is a six-course repast; a typical menu might include smoked trout mousse; bean soup with Arkansalsa and crème fraiche; buttermilk skillet cornbread; five-lettuce salad; venison with cranberry Cumberland sauce; chocolate bread pudding with raspberry sauce and whipped cream.

"Delightful town off-season, great for walking and relaxing. The Spring Garden Suite has a lovely sun room, full of wicker furniture, a perfect spot to enjoy the amazing breakfasts. The Summer Meadows suite has a large inviting living room. Rooms in the Farmhouse are smaller, but charming and quiet." (LI) "We were welcomed with fresh flowers and hot cider. Friendly people, excellent service, outstanding meals." (Michele Coffman) "Ruffled curtains on the windows, canopy bed, and a wood-burning fireplace." (Sam Richardson) "The quiet farmhouse porch overlooking the hollow is a refreshing, peaceful haven." (Marilyn & Harry Boling)

Open Inn open all year. Restaurant closed Jan.; open weekends only Nov. 1–March 15. In season, open Thurs.–Mon.

Rooms 3 suites, 3 doubles—all with private bath and/or shower, air-conditioning, fireplace, kitchenette, coffee maker. 4 rooms with desk. 2 rooms with Jacuzzi. 1 with deck.

Facilities Restaurant, lobby. Music entertainment holidays/festivals. 3 acres with flower gardens, woods, hot tub, children's games. 15 min. to water sports.
Location 1 m from downtown.
Restrictions Restaurant noise in Main House; light sleepers should request Farmhouse rooms. Smoking restricted. BYOB.
Credit cards Amex, DC, Discover, MC, Visa.
Rates B&B, $125–185 suite, double, plus optional $2–5 daily for service. Extra person, $10. 2-3 night minimum weekends/holidays. Off-season discount for longer stays. Mystery, winter weekend packages. Prix fixe dinner, $26–36, plus service.
Extras Restaurant wheelchair accessible. Crib, babysitting.

Five Ojo Inn
5 Ojo Street, 72632

Tel: 501–253–6734

Built in 1890, this comfortable Victorian home was bought by Paula Kirby Adkins a century later. The five buildings on the property were redone as "painted ladies," and are painted in shades of mauve, with burgundy and dark green accents. After a typical 9 A.M. breakfast of eggs Benedict, sausages, potatoes O'Brien, sweet rolls, cheesecake, juice, tea or coffee, guests can relax on the front porch before taking the short trolley ride downtown.

"Despite a late arrival we were met with a big smile. A warm, cozy room and a thoughtful basket of snacks were the ideal beginning for a romantic weekend." *(Eldon Arnold)* "In the evening we unwound in the Jacuzzi and enjoyed a peaceful chat by the fire." *(Denise & Pat Bembenek)* "Our immaculate suite was stocked with snacks and beverages; ample lighting. Helpful, alert staff. Paula kindly delivered an early breakfast on our departure day." *(V.L.Hollister)* "Paula is a wonderful, energetic little woman who serves scrumptious breakfasts, and provides excellent suggestions for places to shop, sight-see, and eat. I liked to sit in the swing on our private porch in the mornings and look off to the woods, watching for deer." *(Kelli Walker)*

Open All year.
Rooms 2 cottages, 8 suites, 1 double—all with private bath and/or shower, radio, TV, air-conditioning, fan, refrigerator, coffee-maker. 5 suites with double whirlpool tub. 1 cottage with deck.
Facilities Breakfast room, living room with piano, books, games. 1½ acres with gardens, hot tub housed in gazebo, picnic area. Golf nearby. Near lakes, rivers for swimming, boating, fishing.
Location Historic District.
Restrictions No smoking. No children under 14.
Credit cards Amex, Discover, MC, Visa.
Rates B&B, $59–120 cottage or suite, $59–95 double, $55–90 single. Extra person, $20. Tipping appreciated. 2-3 night weekend/holiday minimum.

Heart of the Hills Inn &
5 Summit Street, 72632

Tel: 501–253–7468
800–253–7468

Built in 1883, Heart of the Hills was bought by Jan Jacobs Weber in 1986. She has restored its original woodwork, furnishing her B&B with period antiques and family heirlooms. Rates include a full breakfast, fresh flowers, and evening dessert. Served on the deck and porch in good weather, a typical breakfast consists of Ozark grape juice or orange juice, sliced fresh fruit, blackberry muffins, Italian sausage spinach casserole, and hazelnut coffee. Guest reports focus on Jan's warm and helpful personality, her willingness to help with reservations and information, and her excellent cooking and baking skills.

"We returned in the evening to find a homemade dessert, a turned down bed, fresh towels, and a clean coffee pot." *(Keith & Jane Stanley)* "The Hearts & Flowers Cottage has a queen-size brass bed, and every conceivable amenity, including an extra bed for a child. Jan is a native of the area, most charming and helpful." *(James Johnson)* "All of the antiques in the inn have sentimental value to Jan; she can tell you whose they were and where they came from. We loved sitting on the front porch swing, stargazing and chatting. The trolley stops right at the front door, taking you downtown in a moment."*(Cheryl LeBlanc)* "The inn is in a lovely neighborhood and we enjoyed walking around to see the other old homes." *(Janet Fisher)*

Open All year.
Rooms 1 cottage, 1 suite, 2 doubles—all with full private bath, TV, air-conditioning, fan, refrigerator, coffee maker. Suite with 2 person jacuzzi; cottage with CD player, deck, microwave.
Facilities Breakfast room, living room, porch with swing.
Location 4 blocks to downtown. From Hwy. 62 W, turn right at high school onto Kingshighway to inn on left.
Restrictions No smoking. Children welcome under 1 or over 7.
Credit cards MC, Visa.
Rates B&B, $69–109 cottage/suite, $99–109 double, $65–95 single. Extra person, $15. Weekly rates. 2 night weekend/holiday minimum.
Extras Airport pickup. Crib. Wheelchair access.

The Heartstone Inn and Cottages
Tel: 501–253–8916
35 Kingshighway (Highway 62B), 72632

Innkeepers Iris and Bill Simantel have owned The Heartstone since 1985. Guest rooms are decorated with antique and reproduction furniture and decorative Victorian touches—including plenty of hearts; most have queen- or king-sized beds.

"Iris and Bill provided candid restaurant suggestions, gave us accurate directions, and supplied us with blankets for an outside event. In the morning, guests gather for coffee on the deck overlooking the wooded hollow behind the house. Promptly at nine, Bill invites all to breakfast. Each morning we feasted on fresh fruit, sausage or bacon, fresh home-baked bread (different each morning), and a hot entrée. Most guests gravitate back to the shaded deck in the afternoon for iced tea or lemonade." *(Linda Logsdon)* "Hanging pots of Boston ferns sway lazily above the long front porch, and huge crocks spill over with salmon-colored geraniums. The Bridal Suite has an old lace wedding dress and dried bridal bouquet; a queen-size bed was covered with a red, white, and blue quilt in the double wedding-band pattern." *(Mr. & Mrs. J.D. Rolfe)* "The inn is quiet with lots of birds singing and no traffic noise; parking is reserved with excellent lighting for security." *(Carol Hawksley)*

"Breakfast was an elegant affair with the table set with crystal and fresh flowers, while two musicians played quietly on the deck." *(Harriet & Elmer Kweton)* "The inn is a beautiful pink Victorian with white trim. Our spotless room had a wonderful antique bed, dresser, and wardrobe with Victorian rose print wallpaper. We breakfasted on delicious German apple pancakes with bacon, fresh fruit, and chocolate chip muffins." *(Howard & Rebecca Harmon)* "The Victoria Cottage was built in 1882, and has lovely antique furnishings and beautiful quilts." *(Karen Hunter)* "No need for a car with the trolley stop directly in front of the inn." *(Michael Kavanaugh)* "Iris and Bill go out of their way to make sure you're having a good time. The in-house massage therapist was a wonderful treat." *(Jennifer Stansberry)*

Open Feb. 1–late Dec.
Rooms 1 2-bedroom cottage, 1 1-bedroom cottage, 2 suites, 8 doubles, all with full private bath, TV, radio, air-conditioning, ceiling fans. 1 with Jacuzzi. 4 rooms in annex.
Facilities Dining/breakfast rooms, guest lounge with piano, stereo, games, veranda, decks, gazebo; massage therapy. Off-street parking. Live music during May, Sept. festivals.
Location Historic district, 4 blocks to downtown. City bus stop near house.
Restrictions No smoking. Limited facilities for older children.
Credit cards Amex, Discover, MC, Visa.
Rates B&B, $95–115 cottage, $93–118 suite, $63–85 double. Extra person, $15. 2-3 night weekend/holiday minimum. Tipping appreciated.

Pond Mountain Lodge ¢
Route 1, Box 50, Highway 23 South, 72632

Tel: 501–253–5877
800–583–8043

Built in 1954 and transformed into an inn by Judith Jones in 1992, Pond Mountain Lodge has a beautiful setting high above the valley floor. Pond Mountain was noted as a geological mystery in the early 1900s because its two spring-fed ponds are located at the highest points of Carroll County, in apparent violation of the laws of gravity. Guests can explore the inn's extensive grounds, or enjoy the 25-mile vista from the veranda. Breakfast is served individually at guests' convenience, and typically includes fruit compote, scrambled eggs with dill, bacon, oat bran muffins and bagels, and hazelnut coffee. Rooms are furnished primarily with contemporary pieces, plus a few antiques.

"A hike to the top of the mountain revealed a dock stretching over a glorious spring-fed pond. One could fish, picnic or just take in the view." *(Erda Williams)* "We picked out a movie from Judy's extensive video library, and watched it in the privacy of our suite." *(Nancy Eaton)* "Spectacular hiking in the fall, as the leaves turn throughout the valley. In the winter, the great room is decorated for the season and a welcome fire burns in the fireplace. Hot cider and coffee is always available, as are games and books. Judy's wonderful breakfast of homemade breads and muffins, rich quiches, and blueberry or pecan pancakes is served on the veranda in warm weather, or by the fire when it's cold." *(Laurie Sanda)*

Open All year.
Rooms 4 suites, 2 doubles—all with full private bath, clock/radio, TV/ VCR, air-conditioning, refrigerator. 4 with desk, fan, whirlpool tub; 3 with balcony/deck; 1 with fireplace, 2 with kitchenette. 2 suites in duplex.

Facilities Great hall/breakfast room with fireplace, piano, VCR library; game room with books, billiards; deck, veranda. 200 acres with swimming pool, gardens, hiking trails, fishing ponds, horseback riding. 20 min. from Beaver Lake.
Location 2.2 m to downtown historic district. 2 m S on Hwy. 23 S from junction with Rte. 62 E.
Restrictions No smoking. Children over 4 preferred.
Credit cards MC, Visa.
Rates B&B, $64–125 suite, $60–80 double. Extra person $10. 5–10% midweek, AARP, extended stay, educator discounts. 2-night minimum special events. Picnic lunch, $10. Dinner with prior notice.
Extras Limited wheelchair access. Airport pickup, $25. Pets in 1 suite. Babysitting by arrangement.

Singleton House ¢

Tel: 501–253–9111
800–833–3394

11 Singleton, 72632

Barbara Gavron, who has owned the century-old Singleton House since 1984, describes her light and airy guest rooms as being "whimsically decorated with an eclectic collection of antiques, folk art, and unexpected treasures." Breakfasts differ each day; in addition to fresh fruit and juice, they might include blueberry almond pancakes, baked French toast, or an egg casserole.

"Homey, simple, clean, with an old-fashioned Victorian charm. The highlight for me is the little Victorian garden, complete with rock paths lined with wild flowers and perennials, arches with morning glories, a weeping willow over the goldfish pond, and a wonderful collection of bird houses. I love to breakfast on the balcony overlooking the bird-filled garden. From the garden there is a shaded path down the hill to shops and cafés." *(Diane Minden)* "Though small, my room was bright and comfortable; the entire house is extremely clean. Ms. Gavron is warm, witty, professional and entertaining." *(Patsy Maxwell, also E.D. Robertson)*

Open All year.
Rooms Cottage, 1 suite, 4 doubles—4 with private bath and/or shower, 1 with shared bath. All with air-conditioning; some with TV, fan, balcony, Jacuzzi. Cottage at separate location with fully equipped kitchen, Jacuzzi.
Facilities Breakfast balcony, living room with TV, nature library, guest kitchen, porch with swing. Garden with fishpond, picnic area, limited off-street parking.
Location Historic district, off Rte. 62B; Singleton is between Pine and Howell. 1 block to shops or trolley.
Restrictions No smoking.
Credit cards Amex, Discover, MC, Visa.
Rates B&B, $95 cottage, $65–75 suite, double. Discount for multi-night stay. 3-night minimum holiday/festival weekends. 2-night minimum in cottage.

HARDY

Olde Stonehouse Inn ¢

Tel: 501–856–2983
800–514–2983

511 Main Street, 72542

"Hardy, a tiny town in the northeast Arkansas region called the Ozark Gateway, offers breathtaking scenery, rich local culture, and friendly people," report Peggy and Dave Johnson, owners of the Olde Stonehouse Inn. An old railroad town, Hardy is known for its antique auctions; nearby Spring River offers good canoeing and trout fishing.

Constructed of native Arkansas stone, the inn was built in 1928 and was renovated by the Johnsons in 1992. The focal point of the living room is the rock fireplace, set with fossils, minerals, and unusual stones. A floral theme in dusty blue and soft pink colors with lace accents compliments the inn's antique and reproduction furnishings. Guest rooms have queen-size beds with firm, new mattresses—as Peggy says, "antique beds are fun, antique mattresses aren't!" Breakfast includes orange juice or musca-dine grape juice, fresh fruit, yogurt, homemade granola, muffins with strawberry butter, and baked apple pancakes or perhaps cornbread-sau-sage bake. Rates also include an evening snack of homemade brownies or cookies, with coffee or juice.

"You can stroll through town, visit the shops, walk along the river, then return to your quiet, spotless room or have a friendly chat with Peggy and Dave in the living room. Delicious food, comfortable beds." *(Jerry Clifton)* "Peggy and David were incredibly hospitable. The inn is clean, quiet, and tidy, with ample parking and a great location." *(Diane Weisenberg)*

Open All year.
Rooms 2 suites in adjacent cottage, 5 doubles—all with private bath and/or shower, air-conditioning, ceiling fan, clock. Telephone on request. Some with radio, desk, electric fireplace, refrigerator, porch. Suites with TV/VCR, mini-refrigerator, coffee maker.
Facilities Dining room, living room with fireplace, player piano; sitting room with books, games, stereo; guest kitchen; porch with rockers. Off-street parking, lawn games. Golf, tennis, fishing, swimming, canoeing, rafting.
Location NE AR. 130 m N of Little Rock. In historic "Old Hardy Town"; near shops.
Restrictions No smoking. No children. Dry county; byo wine.
Credit cards MC, Visa.
Rates B&B, $85–90 suite, $55–65 double, $50–60 single. Extra person $10. Breakfast in bed, $5 extra. 2-night weekend minimum May–Oct. 10% AAA, senior discount. Picnic lunch, $10; dinner for 2, $45. Theme packages.
Extras Bus station pickup. Limited German spoken.

HEBER SPRINGS

Water is the underlying theme of Heber Springs, located in the foothills of the Ozarks, 60 miles north of Little Rock. The eponymous springs are downtown, plus there's excellent trout fishing and canoeing on the Little Red River, and more water sports on 40,000-acre Greet Ferry Lake.

Information please: The **Anderson House Inn** (201 East Main Street, P.O. Box 630, 72543; 501–362–5266 or 800–264–5279) is owned by Larry and Sandy Anderson, who restored it in 1991. The oldest portion of the building dates to the 1880s, when the town's founder built it as a theater. The inn offers a front porch and balcony, a living room with fireplace and TV, and 16 guest rooms with private baths and ceiling fans. "Handsomely renovated, decorated with lovely local and European antiques, collected by the Andersons—many are for sale. Our rooms were comfortable, with wonderful beds. Plentiful, tasty food; helpful owners and staff." *(Gloria Robertson)*

Oak Tree Inn ¢ 👫
Vinegar Hill and Highway 110 West, 72543

Tel: 501–362–7731
800–959–3857

Owner Freddie Lou Lodge reports that although the inn's design is a New England-type Colonial, all materials used in its 1983 construction are from Arkansas. Rooms are decorated with antiques and traditional furnishings. The inn is an adults-only retreat, but Mrs. Lodge also offers family-style accommodation in her river cabins.

"Soothing colors and textures, fresh flowers, delightful chiming clock and the crackling fires in winter. Rooms are large with quality linens, imported soaps, live plants, antiques and quality reproductions. Service was impeccable but unobtrusive. Ample well-lighted parking. The grounds were well landscaped with colorful shrubs and lots of birds to watch. Superb breakfasts of eggs Benedict, Belgian waffles, and omelets." *(Larry Hughes & Lynda Gayle)* "Gracious hostess, lovely and interesting guests, and a comfortable, homelike atmosphere. Desserts and coffee are enjoyed in the evening around the fireplace." *(Mrs. David Garrett)* "Our room had a lovely bathroom, wonderful queen-size bed, beautiful Oriental rug, a ceiling fan, wood shutters, and sofa." *(Phyllis Berlin)*

Open All year.
Rooms 4 cottages with bedroom and sleeping loft—all with kitchen, fireplace, TV, laundry. 6 doubles in inn with private whirlpool baths, fan; 3 with desk, 5 with fireplace.
Facilities Common room. 1 acre with garden; swimming pool, 2 tennis courts adjacent. Swimming, boating, fishing in Greers Ferry Lake 1 block away. Tennis, hiking, trout fishing nearby. Canoe for guest use.
Location Ozarks, 60 m N of Little Rock. From Little Rock, take Rte. 67 NE to Hwy. 5, then N to Rte. 25 to Heber Springs. About 1 m W of Heber Springs on Rte. 110.
Restrictions Smoking, children permitted in cottages.
Credit cards Discover, MC, Visa. $3 service fee.
Rates Room only, $110 cottage. Inn, B&B $75–85 double; single rate on request. Extra person, $10. 2-night minimum in cottages. Weekly rates.
Extras Airport pickup.

HELENA

Edwardian Inn ¢ 👫 &
317 South Biscoe, 72342

Tel: 501–338–9155

In 1904 cotton broker William A. Short built his family their dream house at the then-extraordinary cost of over $100,000. The Shorts were not the only prosperous family in town; Helena is known for its historic houses, both antebellum and postbellum. Most of the building's original beauty, such as the fine hardware and the beveled and leaded glass in the transoms, was uncovered in the restoration, along with the handsome oak paneling and the intricate woodwork.

"We were greeted graciously by owner Cathy Cunningham and innkeeper Jerri Steed. *(E.L. Bartolotti)* "Our beautiful room had a king-sized bed with a headboard made from a church pew, an enormous bath, a glassed-in sitting area with a window seat, and access to the balcony porch. We took our delicious breakfast of homemade cinnamon rolls and carrot cake outside, and sat down in a rocking chair to eat." *(SG)* "Especially enjoyable is the sunny kitchen/dining room, complete with linen tablecloths and napkins, and fresh flowers." *(Margaret Holaway)* "The innkeepers are concerned about my comfort. The inn is well kept, clean and refreshing." *(Richard Roberts)*

Open All year.

Rooms 8 suites, 10 doubles, all with full private bath, telephone, radio, TV, individual heat/cooling unit, fan. Some with desk, fireplace, whirlpool tub.

Facilities Breakfast/sunroom. Veranda, porches. Near Mississippi Riverfront park.

Location SE AR, on Mississippi River, 70 m S of Memphis, TN.

Credit cards Amex, MC, Visa, DC.

Rates B&B, $80 suite, $60–80 double, $50–56 single. Extra person, $15. Children under 12 free in parents' room. 10% senior discount.

Extras Wheelchair access. Small pets by arrangement. Crib, babysitting.

HOT SPRINGS

A visit to Hot Springs will allow you to take your place in a long line of tradition; records indicate that the Indians used this site 10,000 years ago. The springs reached their height of popularity in the 19th century, and the area became a national park in 1921. The bath houses are still well worth a visit; the naturally hot water will soothe your aching muscles after a day of hiking or horseback riding in the surrounding Zig Zag Mountains. And the price is right—call the historic Buckstaff (501–623–2308), where steaming, soaking, and massage costs under $30 (tips extra). Several lakes—Catherine, Hamilton, and Ouachita—are nearby for all water sports. Hot Springs is located in central Arkansas, 55 miles southwest of Little Rock.

Also recommended: Though too large for a full entry with almost 500 rooms, we've had excellent reports on **The Arlington Resort Hotel & Spa** (Central Avenue and Fountain Street, P.O. Box 5652, 71902; 501–623–7771 or 800–643–1502). "The Arlington is an old-fashioned historic hotel with a large staff and excellent service at moderate prices. Fine location overlooking the national park. Large and well appointed room; buffet breakfast included in the reasonable rates." *(Duane Roller)* "This 70-year-old hotel has been updated with bright yellow flowered wall paper, and brightly painted corridors. Our room was large and clean, with a comfortable king-size bed. Breakfast was served with flowers and a smile at a reasonable price." *(Martha Banda)*

The Gables Inn ¢
318 Quapaw Avenue, 71901

Tel: 501–623–7576
800–625–7576

Built in 1905, and occupied by the same family until 1991, the Victorian Gables Inn was renovated by Shirley and Larry Robins in 1993. Along with the original pine woodwork and stained glass windows, the Robins have restored the original brass heat registers and push button switch plates, although the heating, cooling, and electrical systems are entirely new. Furnishings include queen-sized beds with handmade quilts. Breakfast consists of juice, fruit, eggs and cheese or French toast, meat, homemade muffins and breads, as well as afternoon refreshments, served in the parlor or on the porch.

"Restored with concern for both comfort and authenticity. Our immaculate room had a handsome armoire, polished hardwood floors, area rugs and a roomy shower. Friendly, hospitable owners. They supplied snacks and a canteen for our hike, and left peanut butter cookies and coffee in the TV room for us. Safe neighborhood; beautiful old-fashioned globe light fixtures illuminate the outside fully." *(Lynette Black)* "Relatively quiet street with well-lit parking in the rear. Early morning coffee in the upstairs sitting room." *(Ed & Sandy Moore)*

Area for improvement: "Bedside reading lights and tables."

Open All year.
Rooms 4 doubles—all with private bath and/or shower, radio, clock, air-conditioning, ceiling fan. Some with telephone, desk.
Facilities Dining room, living room with piano, sitting room with TV, books; guest refrigerator, porch. ½ acre with off-street parking.
Location 4 blks. to center of town. From W. Grand (Rte. 70/270) go N on Quapaw to inn on left. From Rte. 7 S, after Bathhouse Row, go right on Prospect, left on Quapaw.
Restrictions Children over 10.
Credit cards Amex, MC, Visa.
Rates $55–75 double, $45–65 single. Extra person, $10. Senior, AAA discount. 2-night weekend minimum. Bag lunches, $3.

Williams House ₵
420 Quapaw, Hot Springs National Park, 71901

Tel: 501–624–4275

Listed on the National Register of Historic Places, this imposing 1890 brownstone-and-brick Victorian has been owned since 1980 by Mary and Gary Riley. Rooms are decorated with family antiques and lots of plants. Breakfast is offered between 7:30 and 9 A.M., and might include fresh fruit, homemade bread and sweet rolls, eggs with ham, bacon, or sausage, or the daily special—ranging from eggs Benedict to pecan waffles.

"Mary and Gary Riley are attentive but unobtrusive hosts. The house is filled with antiques the Rileys have gathered; excellent food." *(Heather Fletcher)* "Despite a late arrival, Mrs. Riley directed me to an excellent restaurant nearby." *(Gary Milam)* "Our private, two-bedroom suite in the carriage house had ample sitting and reading areas. The bathroom offered a large tiled shower, a good shower head, and excellent water pressure. A full breakfast is served at the hour of your choice, a wonderful convenience for early risers." *(John Blewer)* "Delicious breakfast. Pleasant clean rooms. Delightful family." *(Mrs. Frank Herrick)* Reports appreciated.

Open All year.
Rooms 2 suites, 3 doubles—all with private bath and/or shower, radio, air-conditioning. 2 rooms in carriage house.
Facilities Dining room, living room with fireplace, baby grand piano; family room with games, TV; porches. ½ acre with patios, hammock, picnic table. Indoor heated pool at Quopow Comm. Center next door. Walking distance to Bath House Row. Several lakes nearby for fishing, swimming, boating.

Location 4 blocks to National Park headquarters. At corner of Orange and Quapaw. From Bath House Row, go S on Central Ave., right on Prospect, left on Quapaw.
Restrictions No smoking. No children under 16. Daytime traffic noise.
Credit cards Amex, MC, Visa.
Rates B&B, $85–95 suite, $70–80 double, $60–75 single. Extra person, $10. 2-night weekend minimum Mar., Apr., Oct., holidays.

JOHNSON

Inn at the Mill ¢ *Tel:* 501–443–1800
3906 Greathouse Springs Road, P.O.Box 409, 72741 800–CLARION
Fax: 501–521–8091

You want historic charm, he wants remote control TV; you want hand-stitched quilts, she has to call the office. What to do? If you're heading for the Fayetteville area, an ideal choice is the Inn at the Mill. Although it's part of the Clarion Carriage House chain, the inn is listed on the National Register of Historic Places. One of the state's oldest businesses, the mill was registered in 1835; partially burned during the Civil War, it was reconstructed in 1867. The modern renovation and addition of the adjoining hotel structure was completed in 1991, and included special art and furnishings commissioned for the inn. Continental breakfast can be enjoyed in your room, the parlor or on the deck overlooking the pond and water wheel; complimentary wine and hors d'oeuvres, and evening turndown and cookies are also included in the rates.

"The original mill building houses the lobby area highlighted by Fredrick Remington bronzes, a 1895 Frank Lloyd Wright stained glass window, antiques and contemporary quilts. A deck off the lobby overlooks the waterfall and mill pond. The rooms are spacious with hand-stitched quilts and marble bathrooms. Windows open to let in the cool Ozark air. The inn does not serve dinner but there is good dining nearby in Fayetteville and Tontitown. Personal service—not like a large chain."*(KM)*

Open All year.
Rooms 8 suites, 40 doubles—all with full private bath, telephone, TV, air-conditioning. Some with whirlpool tubs.
Facilities Restaurant, lobby, garden with lake, pond, bridge; deck with picnic area. Laundry facilities. Off-street parking. Golf nearby.
Location NW AR. 6 m N of Fayetteville. Johnson exit, Hwy. 71-62.
Credit cards All major credit cards.
Rates B&B, $130–145 suites, $67–73 double, $62–68 single. Extra person, $5.
Extras Wheelchair access. Some bathrooms equipped for the disabled. Cribs, babysitting facilities. French spoken.

LANGLEY

Country School Inn ¢ 👪 ♿ *Tel:* 501–356–3091
Highway 84 & 369, P.O. Box 6, 71952

Eddy and Charlotte Jo Ayers say that people come to their comfortable inn "to enjoy the simple things in life." Built as a schoolhouse in 1945, the

Ayers turned the classrooms into guest rooms in 1986, the former auditorium into the lounge and dining area, and the stage into the kitchen; all are decorated with antique furniture, quilts, tools, plants, and memorabilia. Nearby is the Albert Pike Recreation Area in the Ouachita Mountains, ideal for fishing and hiking. Breakfasts might consist of buttermilk biscuits, scrambled eggs and hash browns or apple puff pancakes, bacon, and sliced pears.

"The dining area has tables set with Depression glass and old china." *(Johnna McClain)* "The Ayers' three-legged dog, Jack, is everyone's friend." *(Nora & Mel Lands)* "A treat was spotting bald eagles from the inn's grounds, and fishing for rainbow trout in the river." *(Mary Tollson)* "Charlotte's breakfasts range from delicious old standards to wonderful dishes like ginger pancakes with lemon sauce."*(Medora Neale)* "The Ayers are warm and gentle people who make you feel like family." *(Connie Flanery)* "The service is great, the place is clean, and all the fixtures are in good condition." *(Diane Purifoy)*

Open Feb. through Dec.
Rooms 2 suites, 2 doubles (some sleeping 8), 1 "dorm" room, 1 single—all with private bath and/or shower, desk, air-conditioning, fan. Some with refrigerator.
Facilities Dining/living room with fireplace, piano, stereo, TV/VCR, games. Gym next door for basketball, volleyball; 3 acres with playground for badminton, horseshoes, swings, barbecue grill, picnic table. Hiking, fishing, water sports at nearby state park, lakes, rivers. Ample parking for trailered boats.
Location Pike County, bordering Ouachita National Forest. 50 m from Hot Springs. From Hot Springs, take Hwy. 70 to Salem, then follow Hwy. 84 to Langley. Inn at intersection of Hwy. 84 and Hwy. 369.
Restrictions No smoking.
Credit cards Discover, MC, Visa.
Rates B&B, $45 suite, $40 double, $35 dorm. Extra person, $8. Discount for children.
Extras Ramp for wheelchair access. Crib.

LITTLE ROCK

Little Rock is the capital of Arkansas and its largest city. Bill Clinton lived here when he was Governor of Arkansas, and the city soon adjusted to the unaccustomed glare of media attention after his election as President of the United States. The oldest section of the city is the Quapaw Quarter, which has many fine antebellum and Victorian homes; typical for a historic district, some houses are beautifully restored, others are still run down.

Reader tip: "Little Rock is like any other city: do not leave valuables visible in the car."

Also recommended: Although a bit small for a full entry with only two guest rooms, **The Carriage House** (1700 Louisiana, 72206; 501–374–7032) is enthusiastically recommended: "The spacious second floor guest rooms are simply furnished, each with a double bed with an excellent mattress and pillows. Downstairs, the comfortable sitting room has a good selection of games, books, and local restaurant menus. Fresh flowers were charming in a silver teapot, and there were plenty of beverages, fresh fruit and candies. Breakfast was served on the sunporch of the adjacent beautifully restored Eastlake Queen Anne Victorian mansion. A fresh fruit cup was followed by Grand Marnier French toast and Canadian bacon. Soft music complemented the spectacular array of flowers and plants." *(John Blewer)* "Charming patio. The breakfast table was beautifully set with a lace tablecloth and fine china."*(Joy Sugg)* The Carriage House is located in the downtown residential Quapaw District; the double rate is $89.

Information please: Located in the Governor's Mansion District and listed on the National Register of Historic Places, the **Hotze House** (1619 Louisiana Street, Little Rock, 72216; 501–376–6563), was built in 1900. Recently restored as a five guest-room B&B, the double rates range from $80–100 and include breakfast served in either the formal dining room or the sunny conservatory. Four guest rooms have fireplaces, and each has a private bath, telephone, TV, air-conditioning, and a king- or queen-size bed.

Capital Hotel ✕ ╟ ♿
111 West Markham, 72201

Tel: 501–374–7474
800–766–7666
Fax: 501–370–7091

Built in 1876 in the Italianate style, and renovated over a century later, the Capital Hotel is a fine example of cast iron architecture, and is listed in the National Register of Historic Places. The spectacular two-story lobby has a stained glass ceiling panel, a mosaic tiled floor, marble walls, faux marble columns, and a marble grand staircase leading to the mezzanine. Ashley's Restaurant offers regional specialities, fresh seafood, and continental dishes. Guest rooms are furnished with period reproductions, and some have canopy beds. "This restored Victorian hotel is handsomely decorated. Dinner at Ashley's was formal and elegant; the food was good but expensive." *(John Blewer)* "Thoroughly restored while retaining its historic character. First-rate professional staff. The spacious guest rooms have beautiful furnishings and four-poster beds." *(Robert Wolkow)* "Beautiful room; excellent service; superb dinner and lovely breakfast at Ashley's." *(BJ Hensley)* "The lobby is spectacular, service wonderful. The thick, plush terrycloth robe was a treat."*(KM)*

Open All year.
Rooms 5 suites, 118 doubles—all with full private bath, telephone, radio, TV, desk, air-conditioning.
Facilities Lobby, restaurant, bar/lounge, atrium, valet parking.
Location Central AR. Downtown, across from Convention Center.
Credit cards Amex, DC, MC, Visa.
Rates Room only, $260–360 suite, $131–163 double, $116–148 single. Extra person, $15. Children free in parents' room. Senior, AAA discount. Alc lunch, $15; alc dinner, $28–50. Weekend rates, packages ($105–200).
Extras Wheelchair access. Airport/station pickup, free. Crib, babysitting. French, Italian, Greek, Arabic spoken.

Quapaw Inn ¢
1868 South Gaines, 72206

Tel: 501–376–6873
800–732–5591
Fax: 501–376–6873–3*

The Quapaw Inn, built in 1905 for a prominent Little Rock surgeon, became a boarding house during the 1940s for young women working in the war effort, and was restored by Dottie Woodwind in 1987. "An attractive pink and white Victorian inn. The common areas are furnished with carved oak antiques. The high ceilings are trimmed with dark wood accents and the walls covered with green flowered wallpaper. The Quapaw Room has a Southwestern motif, and is furnished with two easy chairs and a comfortable king-sized bed in a branch and twig frame draped with lace netting. Upstairs are two rooms, Dr. Witt's (my favorite) with outstanding 1850s carved oak furnishings and the other with an Art Deco look. Our breakfast table by the window was covered with floral chintz that complemented the china and crystal; we had juice, fruit, hot breads, and homemade jam. There was a handy field guide to help us identify the birds that came to the feeder outside. Dottie Woodwind is a helpful and gracious hostess, who directed us to a good restaurant for dinner." *(Lynne Derry)* Comments appreciated.

Open All year.
Rooms 4 doubles—all with private bath and/or shower, radio, desk, air-conditioning, fan. 2 with TV.
Facilities Dining room, living room, porch, veranda. Guided tours.
Location Quapaw District; Governor's Mansion National Historic District. Exit Broadway South off I-630. At 18th St. turn right; at Gaines, turn left.
Restrictions No smoking.
Credit cards Amex, MC, Visa.
Rates B&B, $80 double, $70 single. Extra person, $10. $10 daily discount 3-night stays.

MOUNTAIN VIEW

It's hard to imagine how isolated Mountain View was until the beginning of the 1970s—no paved roads, no trains, no scheduled buses. Then, in 1973, the Ozark Folk Center opened, bringing with it improved transportation. Dedicated to preserving the local culture, the center offers daily demonstrations of indigenous crafts, music and dance, storytelling, and cooking. The perfect balance to a day spent absorbing cultural history is a good dose of natural history, exploring the fantastic formations in the Blanchard Springs Caverns, 15 miles northwest of town, in the Ozark National Forest.

Also recommended: Readers are pleased with the **Ozark Folk Center Lodge** (State Rte. 382, 72560; 501–269–3871), a pleasant, reasonably priced motel. "The single-level octagonally shaped buildings have a bungalow feel, many with a private view of the woods from two walls of windows. It's different from the usual motel experience, and is an easy walk to the crafts area, music show, and restaurant." *(Carol Moritz)* "Very nice place. We loved the craft area and the music shows." *(BJ Hensley)*

Information please: Built in 1886 as the Dew Drop Inn (no kidding), the **Inn at Mountain View** (W. Washington Street, P.O. Box 812, 72560; 501–269–4200 or 800–535–1301) offers ten guest rooms, each with a private bath and furnished with period decor. The reasonable rates include a breakfast of homemade biscuits with sausage gravy, Belgian waffles topped with fruit, scrambled eggs, fresh fruit and juice. The inn is located one block from Courthouse Square.

Wildflower Bed & Breakfast ¢ 🏃 ♿.   *Tel: 501–269–4383*
Courthouse Square, P.O. Box 72, 72560   800–36 B and B

When the Wildflower B&B was built in 1918 to accommodate commercial (i.e. business) travelers, it was appropriately called The Commercial Hotel. Todd and Andrea Budy, who restored the inn in 1982, report that they have renamed their inn to "reflect what the inn is today rather than what it once was." Now listed on the National Register of Historic Places, the inn has a relaxed and welcoming atmosphere, simple handmade curtains and dust ruffles, original iron beds and dressers, and immaculate baths. Rates include a buffet breakfast of juice, tea, and coffee, plus a variety of breads and muffins made at the Hearthstone Bakery which shares the hotel. Mountain View is a mecca for local musicians, many of whom congregate on the hotel's front porch. Summer weekends, especially Saturday nights, see many outdoor concerts and dancing on the courthouse lawn.

"Spotlessly clean, with the warmest of receptions. Freshly baked breakfast breads and cakes—apricot is my favorite." *(Cheryl Schaerer)* "Though simple in construction, everything is perfectly functional." *(Brode Morgan)* "The proximity to the wonderful mountain music played around the square at night beckons you to join in the fun." *(Susan & John Brant)* "In addition to breakfast, the bakery serves lunches which are both substantial and reasonably priced." *(William Cupo, also BJ Hensley)* "Neat, efficient, friendly." *(Jean Rees)* "We felt at home with Todd and Andrea, who enjoy getting to know their guests." *(Robert Waggener)*

Open April–Oct.; by reservation only, Nov., Dec., Mar. Closed Jan., Feb.
Rooms 3 suites, 5 doubles—6 with private shower bath, 2 rooms share 1 bath. Some with desk, all with air-conditioning. 1 with kitchenette.
Facilities Lobby, bakery with dining area, gift shop, wraparound porch with frequent live music. 1 shaded acre. Pool, tennis, hiking, caves, rock-climbing nearby. Short drive to White River, Sylamore Creek, Greers Ferry Lake, for fishing, swimming, float trips.
Location N central AR, Stone Cty. 100 m N of Little Rock, 150 m W of Memphis, TN. Hwys. 66, 9, 5/14 all lead to Courthouse Sq.; Inn on sq. at corner of Washington and Peabody Sts. 1 m from Folk Center.
Restrictions No smoking. "Dry county."
Credit cards Discover, MC, Visa.
Rates B&B, $65–85 suite, $41–65 double, $36–47 single. Extra person, $6.
Extras Limited wheelchair access. Crib. A little French spoken.

PINE BLUFF

Pine Bluff is the second oldest city in Arkansas, founded in 1819 as a trading post.

Margland II Bed & Breakfast   *Tel: 501–536–6000*
703 West Second Avenue, P.O. Box 7111, 71601

A complex of three restored Victorian homes on a quiet residential street, each suite at Margland has a different decor—French, Victorian, wicker, Pennsylvania Dutch, or country. Guests have a choice of continental or full breakfasts, brought to their room, served in the dining room, or on the terrace.

"Our room was beautifully decorated with antiques, and each morning the Little Rock paper was delivered with our coffee. Breakfast included fresh fruit salad, freshly squeezed orange juice, hash brown potatoes, eggs Benedict, or blueberry pancakes. At night a plate of homemade chocolate chip cookies, fresh strawberries, and mints were left in our room." *(Sidney Flynn)* "Though very expensive for the area, it was excellent in all respects. Our room was large and nicely appointed, with good reading lights." *(John Blewer)* "Innkeeper Wanda Bateman was most solicitous of my comfort." *(Frances Rainwater)* "Great restoration; consistent, attentive service." *(JB)* Reports please.

Open All year.
Rooms 17 suites, doubles—all with private bath, telephone, TV, air-conditioning, ceiling fans. 7 with whirlpool bath, 3 with loft bedrooms.
Facilities Dining room, living room, exercise room, terraces, gardens, swimming pool. Fax service.
Location C AR. 43 miles SE of Little Rock, 5 min. from Pines Mall, 10 min. from port, industrial park. 2 blocks from Martha Mitchell Expressway, Lake Pine Bluff, at corner of Beech St. & 2nd.
Credit cards None accepted.
Rates B&B, $65–100 double.

We Want to Hear from You!

As you know, this book is effective only with your help. We really need to know about your experiences and discoveries. If you stayed at an inn or hotel listed here, we want to know how it was. Did it live up to our description? Exceed it? Was it what you expected? Did you like it? Were you disappointed? Delighted? Have you discovered new establishments that we should add to the next edition?

Tear out one of the report forms at the back of this book (or use your own stationery if you prefer) and write today. *Even if you write only "Fully endorse existing entry" you will have been most helpful.*

Thank You!

Florida

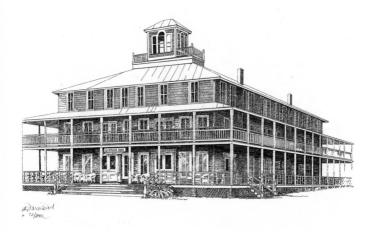

Gibson Inn, Apalachicola

There *is* a real Florida apart from giant theme parks, condo developments, and endless chains of cloned hotels and motels. It's just not that easy to find, so please be sure to share the good news whenever you discover something special. Although theme parks, beaches, and retired relatives are three popular reasons for visiting Florida, we'd like to suggest some less-well-known Florida highlights. In the southeast, visit the tranquil Japanese flower gardens at the Morikami Cultural complex west of Delray Beach, or drop by a professional polo match. On the Gulf Coast, travel back roads to find isolated coastal inlets, drop by the Salvador Dali Museum in St. Petersberg, or visit unspoiled Honeymoon and Caladesi islands that are maintained as state parks.

Although best known for its theme parks, Central Florida also boasts miles of grassy prairies, flowering fruit groves, horse farms, 1400 lakes and the world's largest sandy pine forest. In Northeast Florida don't miss the Spanish flavor of St. Augustine, the oldest city in the United States. The Florida Panhandle, in the northwest, offers miles of sugar-white sand, rolling hill country near Tallahassee, the Alaqua Vineyards (one of only four wineries in the state), and an unusual mixture of Creole, Victorian and other architecture in Pensacola's Seville Historic District.

Peak season rates in most of Florida generally extend from December 1–15 through May 1–15; off-season rates are considerably lower. Do remember that August and September are the height of the tropical storm/hurricane season, so it might be best to avoid these months when planning a trip.

Reader tips: "Distinguish yourself from the average tourist by remembering that conch is pronounced *konk*."

AMELIA ISLAND

Amelia Island's only town is Fernandina Beach, at its north end, but since the two addresses are used interchangeably, and the island name is better known, we've listed our entries here. Amelia Island is located in the northeast corner of Florida, just south of the Georgia border, and 35 miles north of Jacksonville. Area activities focus on the area's wide sandy beaches, with ample opportunities for swimming, boating, and fishing, but golf and tennis are available as well. The scent of the sea is sometimes mixed with the less appealing odor of the island's paper mills, but this doesn't seem to bother the island's many enthusiasts.

Reader tips: "The historic district of Fernandina Beach feels the way Key West did 25 years ago. Many interesting shops and good places to eat; the townspeople are exceptionally friendly." *(Joe & Sheila Schmidt)* "The Kingsley Plantation south of Amelia Island is worth visiting, as are the state parks at Little Talbot Island and Fort Clinch, where there are reenactments of military drills of the 1860s." *(April Burwell)*

Also recommended: Although far too big for a full entry with hundreds of rooms, dozens of swimming pools and tennis courts, and 45 holes of golf, we've had good reports on the **Amelia Island Plantation** (3000 First Coast Highway, P.O. Box 3000, Amelia Island 32035-1307; 904–261–6161 or 800–874–6878). Set on 1300 acres with miles of hiking trails and beautiful beaches, it's an excellent choice for families. Nothing is included with the $150–285 double rate, so be sure to ask about special packages.

For additional area entries, see Georgia, **Cumberland Island** and **St. Marys.**

Elizabeth Pointe Lodge — *Tel:* 904–277–4851
82 South Fletcher Avenue, P.O. Drawer 1210, 32034 — 800–772–3359
Fax: 904–277–6500

Constructed in an 1890s Nantucket shingle style with a maritime theme, the Elizabeth Pointe Lodge is the latest project of longtime innkeepers David and Susan Caples. Just steps from the sand dunes, the inn has a large porch with comfy rocking chairs and a cheery sunroom where a simple buffet breakfast of fresh juice and fruit, cereal, home-baked muffins and pastries, grits, and scrambled eggs is served from 7 to 9 A.M. Rates include afternoon lemonade, wine at 6 P.M., and evening desserts.

"The charming maritime theme is not overdone, and the large windows allow ample light." *(William Novak)* "Ample hot water in the large bathroom for the whirlpool tub. Friendly, helpful owners and staff." *(Rose Meyer)* "Our room had a king-size bed with a warm throw and an armoire to store the TV and our clothes. Windows, framed by simple lace panels, gave a direct view out to the dunes. Fresh flowers, Crabtree & Evelyn toiletries, and the morning newspaper at our door were all thoughtful touches." *(Rebecca Bowers)* "The roaring fire in the library fireplace was appreciated on a stormy night. An elevator takes you directly from the convenient parking area to room level." *(Marlene Jewwett)* "No detail was missed in designing this 1920s-style cottage house, from the pedestal sinks and mosaic tiles in the bathroom to the old-style wood plank floors and porch." *(Henry Bachara)* "Good provisions for the beach—baskets for shelling, towels, and an outside shower. The porch is a good place for enjoying high tide, when the water almost reaches the porch steps." *(BA)* "The light lunch menu, available until midnight, was convenient after a day's sightseeing." *(Madge Harlan)* "Our room had a queen-sized captain's bed and good reading lights. This is definitely a shore resort; if one is looking for freedom from sand, go elsewhere. Shelves are placed conveniently in the bathrooms for cosmetics. The kitchen refrigerator is always open for juice, milk, and tea; coffee is close at hand." *(Beth & Jay Childress)*

Area for improvement: "More closet space for longer stays."

Open All year.
Rooms 3 suites, 22 doubles—all with full private bath, telephone, radio, TV, air-conditioning. 7 with whirlpool tub; some with desk, refrigerator, deck. 1 suite in cottage, 4 rooms in annex.
Facilities Dining room, living room, library with fireplace, books, games; porch. Beach with swimming; beach equipment, rental bikes. Off-street parking.
Location At seaport of Fernandina. 1.5 m from Historic District.
Restrictions No smoking.
Credit cards Amex, MC, Visa.
Rates B&B, $95–150 double. Extra person, $20. Children under 6 free. Senior, AAA discount. Alc lunch, $7. Thanksgiving, Christmas packages.
Extras Wheelchair access; bathroom specially equipped for the disabled. Airport, station pickup, $22. Crib, babysitting. German, Spanish spoken.

The Fairbanks House &

227 South Seventh Street, 32034

Tel: 904–277–0500
800–261–4838
Fax: 904–277–3103

Most people think of Florida architecture in terms of high-rise hotels and pastel-colored bungalows, which makes the magnificent Italianate architecture of the Fairbanks House even more striking. Built in 1885 and listed on the National Register of Historic Places, the inn was restored by Nelson and Mary Smelker, and opened in 1994. The inn's exterior is painted in shades of gray-green with burgundy accents, and is highlighted by a Romanesque-style tower, numerous arches and pilasters; the inside offers polished hardwood floors, intricately carved moldings, and fireplace tiles with scenes from Shakespeare and Aesop's Fables. The guest rooms are appointed with antiques, Oriental rugs, and four-poster or canopy king-, queen-, or twin-size beds. Mary made all the drapes, bedspreads and pillow shams, and has done a first-rate job of balancing period charm with modern preferences for comfort and lightness. The breakfast of homemade breads, fresh fruit, and juice is served on silver, china, and crystal, and can be enjoyed in the dining room or on the patio; rates also include evening refreshments.

"The Smelkers have done a wonderful job of renovating this old rooming house into a marvelous, comfortable home. Incredible hospitality. Each morning's breakfast was a different surprise—homemade muffins, baked apples, fried bananas, all wonderfully presented and served." *(Stephen & Ellen Filreis)* "Beautiful mansion with high ceilings, spacious rooms. In the entry, layers of old paint were stripped away to reveal the beautiful wood underneath. Spacious, attractive grounds." *(Don & Karen Jones)* "The owners were never too busy to stop and chat or offer information of local interest." *(Belinda Barrow)*

Open All year.

Rooms 2 suites, 8 doubles—all with private bath and/or shower, telephone, TV, air-conditioning. Nine with fan, fireplace; some with whirlpool tub, refrigerator, balcony.

Facilities Dining room with fireplace, living room with fireplace, books; porches. 1 acre with flower gardens, patios, off-street parking, swimming pool, gazebo, lawn games. 1 m to ocean; 7 blocks to river.

Location 2 blocks from town in historic district.

Restrictions No smoking. Children over 7.

Credit cards Amex, Discover, MC, Visa.

Rates B&B, $125–150 suite, $85–130 double, $80 single. Extra person, $20. Senior, AAA discount.

Extras Wheelchair access; bathroom specially equipped for the disabled. Airport pickups.

Florida House Inn ✗ ♿   *Tel:* 904–261–3300
20 & 22 South 3rd Street, P.O. Box 688, 32034   800–258–3301
                                                         Fax: 904–277–3831

One-time Florida resident Thomas Alva Edison is said to have remarked that: "Invention is 1% inspiration, 99% perspiration." When you see the "before" and "after" pictures of the Florida House, you may decide that restoring an old inn follows a similar ratio. In 1991, Karen and Bob Warner completed a total renovation of Florida's oldest surviving (but just barely) hotel. During the 19th century, its many famous guests included General Ulysses S. Grant, plus assorted Rockefellers and Carnegies; in those days, the inn had 25 guest rooms and no indoor plumbing. Rates include a full Southern breakfast; also available is a restaurant offering "boarding house" dining—fried chicken and catfish with fresh Southern-style vegetables, served family-style at tables for ten.

"Good lighting and strong showers. An excellent breakfast is served on the back porch or in the sunny breakfast room. Sipping afternoon lemonade on the wooden rockers of the second floor porch was equally pleasant. Everything is in walking distance in this delightful town." *(Shirley Hall)* "The Warners' genuine warmth promotes an instant rapport with guests. Delightful balance of Jacuzzi tubs and central air-conditioning, with four-poster beds and claw foot bathtubs. The shade of time-twisted oaks makes the porch an inviting place to gather over evening wine." *(Michael & Jeanne Green)* "Bob Warner is helpful and friendly, both on the phone and in person." *(Jim & Sibet Grantham)* "Decorated beautifully for Christmas. Fine lunch (with lots of veggies) served family-style in the dining room." *(April & Michael Burwell)* "The annual May seafood festival is conveniently located right at the inn's front door." *(Mr. & Mrs. John Cheetham)* "Insulation added during the renovations kept our room quiet." *(Robert & Donna Jacobson)* "Crisp cotton sheets; clean, spacious bathroom; warm hospitality. We loved the kittens." *(SW & AB)*

Open All year.

Rooms 1 suite, 10 doubles—all with private bath and/or shower, telephone, radio, TV, air-conditioning, ceiling fan. Most with desk; 6 with fireplace, 2 with double Jacuzzi tub. 8 rooms in North Bldg. 3 rooms in South Bldg.

Facilities Restaurant, pub with fireplace, TV; parlor with fireplace, games. Fax, copier. Off-street parking. Tennis, golf nearby. 2 m from Atlantic Ocean for boating, fishing, swimming; 2 blocks from marina.

Location Historic District. From I-95, take A1A exit to Amelia Island, Fernandina Beach. A1A turns into 8th St. on island. Follow 8th St. to the intersection of 8th St. & Atlantic/Centre St. (BP gas on left). Turn left on Atlantic/Centre St. Go 5 blocks to S 3rd St. & turn left. Florida House Inn is ½ block from Centre on left.

Restrictions Smoking only in pub, on porches, patio.

Credit cards All major.

Rates B&B, $130 suite, $65–125 double. Extra person, $10. 2-night weekend minimum.

Extras Limited wheelchair access. Local airport/marina pickups. Limited Spanish spoken.

APALACHICOLA

Although once a major Gulf port, Apalachicola is now a sleepy town in the Florida Panhandle, with shrimp and oysters being the primary cash crops.

Reader tips: "Apalachicola is near uncrowded Gulf beaches and is still basically undiscovered, except for the seafood festival in November each year." *(April Burwell)* "Useless walking tour map; in some cases, all that was left was a vacant lot. I threw it in the trash and went browsing in antique shops instead." *(BN)*

For an additional listing in the area, see **St. George Island.**

Gibson Inn ¢ ✗

100 Market Street, 32320

Tel: 904–653–2191
904–653–8282

A large blue building surrounded by two-story white verandas and topped by a cupola, the turn-of-the-century Gibson Inn dates from the town's glory days. Restored in 1983, the inn overlooks the water and St. George Island. Rooms are furnished in period, with four-poster beds, ceiling fans, antique armoires, brass and porcelain bathroom fixtures, and claw-foot tubs. Its popular restaurant serves three meals a day, from a full range of standard breakfast favorites, to a lunch of fried oysters, to a dinner of seafood gumbo; shrimp, scallop and crab Dijon; and chocolate bourbon pecan pie.

"Most rooms have four-poster beds; ours had a TV in the armoire, two chairs, and a writing table." *(April Burwell)* "Our beautiful third-floor corner room had a luxurious bath and excellent bedding." *(Imogene Tillis)* "The friendly desk clerk offered helpful suggestions, and we enjoyed a dinner of fresh local snapper. The staff was quick to fix a slow drain in our bathtub." *(HB)* "Well prepared dinner, excellent service, charming hostess." *(Bill Novak)* "Fully endorse existing entry. The dinner was wonderful, rooms clean and fresh. Excellent renovation." *(JW, also Debbie Bergstom)*

Areas for improvement: "Uninspired strawberry pancakes." And: "With only one sofa, the lobby did not seem conducive to visiting or reading. We were sorry we didn't meet the owners."

Open All year.
Rooms 2 suites, 29 doubles—all with private bath, telephone, TV, air-conditioning, ceiling fan.
Facilities Restaurant, bar with weekend entertainment, lobby, verandas, gift/craft shop. Swimming, shelling, fishing, marina nearby.
Location FL Panhandle. Center of town, 1 block from waterfront. 75 m SW of Tallahassee, 60 m SE of Panama City, at corner of Hwy. 98 and Avenue C.
Credit cards MC, Visa.
Rates Room only, $80–115 suite, $60–80 double. Extra person, $5. Senior, group, AAA, military discounts. Package rates. Alc breakfast, $3–7; alc lunch, $7–13; alc dinner, $18–35. 2-night holiday minimum.
Extras Crib. Pets, $5 per night.

AVON PARK

Hotel Jacaranda ⊄ ✕ ♟ ♿.   *Tel:* 813–453–2211
19 East Main Street, 33825

While we love inns, there are moments when the privacy a hotel affords is just what we want. But it must be a hotel with a sense of style and history, distinctive yet affordable. Such a place is the Hotel Jacaranda, built in 1925 in the Revivalist style. Unfortunately, the hotel never recovered from the decline that started with the Great Depression, and was in a sorry state when it was acquired by South Florida Community College and the SFCC Foundation in 1988. An enthusiastic crew of college staff, students, and volunteers began an extensive renovation effort, removing endless coats of paint, restoring the brass hardware and wooden floors, and modernizing the plumbing and wiring. Lunch and dinner feature regional favorites: fried chicken, barbecued ribs, ham, roast beef, Southern-style vegetables and desserts. Daily specials are also prepared by the school's culinary arts students who train at the hotel.

"Much hard work and an injection of funds have saved the Jacaranda. Rooms have new mattresses, bedspreads, white paint, and attractive prints, with clean, functional bathrooms. The partially shaded second-floor sitting porch is a wonderful place to read and relax. The hot tub and swimming pool are clean and attractive and the desk service is friendly. There is a library in the lobby, and a fine antique store specializing in glass and china." *(Bill McGowan)*

Open All year. Restaurant closed Sat.; also mid-June–Aug. 1.
Rooms 7 suites, 53 doubles—all with private bath and/or shower, air-conditioning, TV.
Facilities Restaurant with fireplace, lobby with books, games, fireplace; conference room. Indoor swimming pool, hot tub; off-street parking. Golf, tennis, lake for fishing nearby.
Location S central FL. 10 m N of Sebring, 23 m S of Lake Wales.
Restrictions No smoking in lobby.
Credit cards MC, Visa.

Rates Room only, $45–105 suite, $40–50 double. $5 less for singles. Extra person, $5. Weekly, family rates.
Extras Wheelchair access. Crib.

BIG PINE KEY

Information please: An appealing B&B is the **Casa Grande** (Long Beach Drive, P.O. Box 378, 33043; 305–872–2878), a Spanish-style contemporary hacienda set directly on the Atlantic Ocean. Full breakfasts are served among the tropical flowers of the huge, beautifully landscaped patio.

Barnacle B&B   *Tel: 305–872–3298*
Long Beach Drive, Route 1, Box 780A, 33043

Located at Mile Marker 33, with a private oceanside beach tucked into the rocky shoreline, the Barnacle is a contemporary-style home raised on a platform above the sand. Long-time owners Stephen and Joan Cornell have enhanced the tropical atmosphere with a sunny plant-filled atrium and an inviting hot tub. Rates include a morning meal of juice, fruit, eggs, breakfast meat, and coffee served at 8:30 A.M. in the atrium.

"We first visited the Barnacle nearly ten years ago, and on our return trip we were delighted to find the innkeepers have retained their enthusiasm and the inn its charm. Recommended highly for travelers who can entertain themselves and enjoy a remote location." *(Sheila & Joe Schmidt)*

Open All year.
Rooms 4 doubles—all with private shower and/or bath, telephone, radio, clock, TV, air-conditioning, fan, refrigerator. 1 room in adjacent building.
Facilities Atrium/breakfast room, 2 guest kitchens. ³/₄ acre with hot tub, beach, bicycles, beach towels and chairs, coolers, boat ramp and dock. Off-street parking. Swimming, fishing from beach.
Location FL Keys. 33 m NE of Key West, 15 m SW of Marathon. 3 m from town. Take U.S. Rte. 1 S via Marathon to Big Pine Key. After crossing Spanish Harbor Bridge, watch for Mile Marker 33 on right. Just past sign is left-hand turnoff lane that crosses median to Long Beach Dr. Go 1 m, through private gate posts, then continue ¹/₂ m to inn on left.
Restrictions No smoking at breakfast table. No children.
Credit cards None accepted.
Rates B&B, $75–100 double. 2-night minimum.
Extras French spoken.

CAPTIVA ISLAND

For a change of pace from shell collecting and lazing on the wonderful beaches, spend time hiking, canoeing, or bicycling in the "Ding" Darling National Wildlife Preserve in Sanibel, or cross the causeway back to Fort Myers to visit the winter home of Thomas Edison. You can see his home, research labs, and 14-acre botanical gardens.

Reader tip: "The one major drawback about the entire Sanibel/Captiva area is the abominable traffic. Enough to make one wonder if it is worth the trouble."

Information please: For a taste of Old Florida, leave Captiva's traffic behind and head up the coast about 50 miles to the **Gasparilla Inn** (Gasparilla Island, Boca Grande, 33921; 813–964–2201), where little has changed in decades—jackets and ties are still required for men and boys at dinner. An ideal choice for complete R&R for the family, the low key activities include bird-watching, shell-collecting, and the usual golf, tennis, swimming, and window-shopping. Most guest rooms have been hand-somely refurbished; families may prefer to request a cabin, but rooms in the hotel itself tend to have more style.

'Tween Waters Inn 🏃 ✕ 🦮 ♿

Captiva Drive, P.O. Box 249, 33924

Tel: 813–472–5161
800–223–5865
Fax: 813–472–0249

Set on a narrow strip of land between the Gulf of Mexico and Pine Island Sound, the 'Tween Waters Inn was started as a one-cabin operation in 1926. A variety of cottages were added over the years, and the inn was bought in 1976 by Rochester Resorts, which has attempted to preserve the best features of the old while adding the facilities most travelers expect in a luxury resort. While far from perfect, "old Florida charm" generally prevails, and devoted guests return year after year.

"Our room in the main inn had a breathtaking view overlooking the Gulf of Mexico. We had a screened-in deck that allowed us to enjoy the sunsets and cool ocean breezes. Our room was simple in style but com-fortable. Best of all was its location just a few minutes walk from the gorgeous, private, and shell-covered Captiva Beach. To save money, we used our refrigerator to store breakfast and lunch fixings." *(Thomas & Linda Fontana)* "This old resort consists of many cottages and two large motel-type buildings overlooking either the Gulf of Mexico or Pine Island Sound. The cottages are quite nice, but the only ones that really have a water view face the heavily traveled road by the beach." *(SN)* "Rent a canoe at the inn to paddle through a nearby nature preserve, or take long walks down the Gulf beach." *(Pamela Mack)* "Many amenities—washer/dryer for guest use, small refrigerators in the rooms—help ease the strain of traveling with kids." *(Jane Mattoon)* "Our cottage had been freshly painted and had new furniture; there's not much they could do about the old-fashioned little bathroom. The food was delicious in the restaurant and service good." *(Keri Rutherford, also Stephen Holman)*

Areas for improvement: "Parking is barely adequate." Also: "A teen club, offering night-time activities for kids age 15–21 would be super." Also: "A place this size should take American Express."

Open All year.
Rooms 10 apartments, 83 doubles, 32 cottages—all with private bath and/or shower, telephone, TV, air-conditioning, refrigerator. Many with hair dryer, kitch-enette, screened porch, balcony, in-room safe. Some with microwave, fireplace.
Facilities Dining room, lounge with live entertainment, game room, laundry facilities. 13 acres with marina, heated swimming pool, 3 tennis courts, shuffle-board, bocce, private beach on Gulf, fishing; boat, canoe, bicycle rentals; charter, sightseeing boats.

Location SW FL. 25 m W of Ft. Myers.

Restrictions Significant traffic noise in Gulfside rooms, cottages. Minimal sound-proofing in cottages.

Credit cards Discover, MC, Visa.

Rates Room only, $130–260 apt. or cottage, $90–210 double. Extra person, $15, rollaway bed, $5. 3–night holiday and/or winter minimum. No charge for children under 12. 7–night packages, midweek specials. Weekly rates. Alc breakfast, $7–15; alc lunch, $5–12; alc dinner, $20–30.

Extras Public areas wheelchair accessible; some cottages specially equipped for disabled. Pets by prior arrangement in some cottages, $8. Crib.

CEDAR KEY

"Cedar Key is the way Florida used to be before the tourists found it—quiet, unflashy. Minimal tourist traffic, quaint, uncrowded, a great area for birds and other natural joys. The old cemetery has shell-covered graves, nesting osprey, and historic tombstones. Also good restaurants, shell mounds, wildlife refuges, and historic walking tours. There's a marina, museum, park, fishing pier. A pleasant spot to visit as a destination or as a stopover, and not far from Manatee State Park." *(Celia McCullough & Gary Kaplan)* "They say Cedar Key is a smaller and quieter version of Key West as it was some 20–30 years ago." *(Caroline Lloyd)*

Information please: We've received mixed reports on the historic **Island Hotel** (2nd & B Streets, P.O. Box 460, 32625; 904–543–5111), built of cypress faced with tabby, a mixture of lime rock and crushed oyster shells. Originally built as a general store in the 1850's, the building was turned into a hotel in 1910. Much of the structure is still original, with 11-inch walls, and oak floors sloping in every direction. Tom and Alison Sanders bought the hotel in 1992, have done much to renovate it, with a continuing list of planned improvements. The $75–85 rates for the ten guest rooms include a full breakfast served with homemade poppyseed bread, one of the chef's specialities, while seafood is the favorite at dinner. One reader enthused: "Funky, laid-back Jimmy Buffet-type atmosphere; the restaurant is a favorite with locals. Absolutely delicious food; friendly, accommodating hosts; nice bar; a delightful town to explore." *(Mrs. John T. May)* Another reader felt some work needs to be done in the area of housekeeping, maintenance, and decor.

COCOA BEACH

Inn at Cocoa Beach 🌴
4300 Ocean Beach Boulevard, 32931

Tel: 407–799–3460
800–343–5307
Fax: 407–784–8632

With a magnificent view across the water to the Kennedy Space Center, the Inn at Cocoa Beach offers ringside seats for every rocket launch, plus the opportunity to stroll out on the beach at dawn and watch the sun rise over the Atlantic. A pink stucco motel complex built in 1987, the inn has public rooms with reproduction French country furniture, cool tile floors accented with Oriental rugs, and floral fabrics in shades of rose and ivory. Guest rooms have reproduction furniture in styles ranging from Queen Anne to country pine; all have ocean views. Breakfast includes fresh fruit, coffee, and freshly baked fruit breads and muffins; at sunset, wine and cheese is served in the lobby.

"This delightful place is tucked among the tacky souvenir shops, franchise motels, and condos. Request a lower level room so you can walk right out onto the beach. Our bedroom had floral fabrics and pine beds in country French style; the living-dining room is an inviting spot for breakfast." *(MB)* "The 'L.L. Bean' of the surfing world, Ron Jon's, sits between the inn and the highway." *(NB)*

Open All year.

Rooms 4 suites, 46 doubles—all with full private bath, telephone, radio, clock, TV, air-conditioning. 43 with balcony or deck. 12 with desk, 5 with in-room whirlpool tub.

Facilities Lobby, breakfast room, deck. Conference room. 2 acres on beach, with patio, fountain, swimming pool. Off-street parking. Rental beach chairs, umbrellas.

Location E central FL. 47 m E of Orlando. At intersection of SR 520 and Rte. A1A.

Restrictions No smoking in lobby, breakfast room.

Credit cards Amex, Discover, MC, Visa.

Rates B&B, $185 suite, $109 double. Extra person, $10. Children under 5 free in parents' room. 10% senior, AAA discount. 2-night holiday, special event minimum. Honeymoon, anniversary packages.

Extras Crib. Spanish spoken.

DAYTONA BEACH

Information please: We need additional reports on the **Live Oak Inn** (444–448 South Beach Street, 32114–5004; 904–252–4667 or 800–881–4667, which stands where Mathias Day founded Daytona. Owners Sandra and Vinton Fisher restored this century-old home in 1991, and have decorated the guest rooms with Victorian antiques. Rates include a continental breakfast; the inn's well regarded restaurant is open for dinner.

For an additional area recommendation, see **Lake Helen** and **New Smyrna Beach.**

DESTIN

Once a sleepy area of the Florida Panhandle best known for the prolific off-shore fishing in the Gulf of Mexico, Destin has boomed into a major resort community. Most visitors today are attracted by the dazzlingly white sand beaches and brilliant greens and blues of the Gulf surf. Known as the "Emerald Coast," the region boasts of 24 miles of beach, more than 12 miles of which are protected from any development. Prices are moderate (relative to the east and west coasts of Florida) in season and a bargain the rest of the year.

Information please: As you might expect from its name, the **Frangista Beach Inn** (4150 Old Highway East, 32541; 904–654–5501 or 800–382–2612) overlooks the beach. Rooms have clay tile floors, tongue and groove paneling, color-washed furnishings, and Adirondack chairs; most of the 21 units have kitchens, and double rates range from $50–150.

For an additional area entry, see **Santa Rosa Beach**.

Henderson Park Inn ♦   🛦 &.   *Tel:* 904–837–4853
2700 Highway 98, 32541   800–336–4853

With uninterrupted Gulf views from its private beach, the Henderson Park Inn sits among the dunes at the boundary of Henderson Park. The inn is reminiscent of a Victorian hotel, with shingles and gables, while the adjoining "villa" is designed to look like a beach cottage, with family-style efficiency suites. Inn rooms (all with water views) have reproduction Queen Anne furnishings and designer fabrics; some have four-poster or canopy beds. The villa rooms have more of a beach-cottage look. Rates include a continental breakfast with fresh baked goods and an evening get-together in the common room. "Our large suite had a comfortable sitting space, an attractive dining area, and a large bathroom with a Jacuzzi tub and ample fluffy towels. The nightly turn-down service included either chocolates or cookies. The inn's restaurant provided an extensive and tasty buffet breakfast; service was good and the multi-course dinners were exceptional." *(Robert & Donna Jacobson)*

Open All year.
Rooms 17 suites, 20 doubles—all with private bath, telephone, TV, ceiling fan, refrigerator, balcony, coffee maker, microwave oven, safe. Most with Jacuzzi. Suites with kitchenettes in adjacent building.
Facilities Restaurant, lobby, common room, deck. Heated swimming pool, beach, barbecue and picnic area. Beach lounges, umbrellas, towels. Conference room with AV services. Deep sea fishing, snorkeling, scuba diving, golf nearby.
Location Approx. 40 m E of Pensacola.
Restrictions No vacationing students under 25.
Credit cards Amex, Discover, MC, Visa (for emergency only)
Rates B&B, $100–195 suite, $100–210 double. Weekly rates.
Extras Wheelchair access; 1 room specially equipped. Babysitting, cribs.

EVERGLADES CITY

The Ivey House ¢   *Tel:* 813–695–3299
107 Camellia Street, P.O. Box 5038, 33929   813–695–4666
                                        Summer: 203–739–0791
                                           Fax: 813–695–4155
                                   Summer fax: 203–739–4470

The Tamiami Trail (now Route 41), connecting Miami and Naples, was constructed in the 1920s. Everglades City became a boom town during this period, and what is now The Ivey House was built as a recreational center for the road workers. In 1989, it was purchased and renovated by North American Canoe Tours, for use as a B&B. Each room has twin beds, a nightstand, a luggage rack, and towel bar. Rates include breakfast of coffee, juice, and muffins, and afternoon tea. Manager Sandee Dagley and her staff are happy to share their years of experience in guiding travelers through the Everglades and will suggest reconstructed Indian encampments and archaeological sites to visit. Guests also have access to a library of books on the Everglades, reconstructed Indian encampments and archaeological sites.

"Everglades City has some pleasant places to eat, airboat rides, and the western entrance to Everglades National Park. At nearby Chokoloskee Island you can rent a powerboat or canoe and enjoy the haunting beauty of this remote area. The inn is clean and well maintained, although the rooms are small, the furnishings plain, and the washrooms located down the hall." *(Joe & Sheila Schmidt)* "After dinner, guests gather on the porch for a relaxing drink and conversation." *(Mrs. S.M. Gabb)* "Various public areas afford the opportunity to meet the other guests, while still allowing for individual privacy. The staff is extremely knowledgeable about the history, flora, and fauna of the area, and are adept at directing guest to local areas/attractions of interest." *(Nicky Simpson)*

Area for improvement: "Additional showers/toilets for groups with tight schedules."

Open Nov. 1–April 30.
Rooms 10 doubles—all with air-conditioning. All share men's/women's bathrooms with multiple showers/toilets.
Facilities Living room with TV, books, decks, screened porches. Bicycles; coin-op laundry. Airboat rides, canoe, boat rentals, fishing, all-inclusive canoe tours.
Location SW FL, 32 m S of Naples. Everglades Natl. Park. From Tamiami Trail, go S on Rte. 29. After crossing bridge, turn right at Circle K store & watch for inn on right.
Restrictions Smoking & alcohol on screened porches only. No children under 10.
Credit cards MC, Visa.
Rates B&B, $40–60 double. 2-night minimum during Seafood Festival.

FT. LAUDERDALE

Riverside Hotel
620 East Las Olas Boulevard, 33301

Tel: 305–467–0671
800–325–3280
Fax: 305–462–2148

A gracious taste of "old Florida" awaits visitors to the Riverside. Bordered by Las Olas (the waves) Boulevard, filled with fine shops and restaurants, the shaded grounds of the Riverside have changed little since the hotel was built over 50 years ago.

"Like many tourist brochures, the Riverside's reflects reality—slightly enhanced. The New River is an attractive stream; the pool is lovely, but far from Olympic, and so on. In addition to the interior courtyard, there is a sizable lawn adjacent to the pool. Guest rooms in the original building, constructed in 1936, are spacious and spotless, with beautiful oak furniture. Lovely hand-painted tiles." *(Diane Wolf)* "Ask for a room with a river view. The delightful pool area is across a small road, and is on the river."

(Sheila & Joe Schmidt) "Our suite's sitting room overlooked Las Olas Boulevard and had glass French doors opening to a small terrace above the street. The decor included a sea green jungle print fabric with a green carpet. Quality toiletries and good water pressure. Excellent meals, well served at reasonable prices." *(Susan Schwemm)*

Open All year.
Rooms 116 suites and doubles—all with private bath and/or shower, telephone, radio, TV, desk, air-conditioning, mini-refrigerator. Some with patio or deck.
Facilities 2 restaurants, lobby with fireplace, courtyard, meeting room. Gardens with heated swimming pool, private marina on river. Concierge, room service.
Location Downtown, 2 m W of Rte. A1A. 10 min from airport. From airport, take Rte. 84 E to U.S. Rte. 1 and go N, crossing river. Turn right on Las Olas Blvd. to hotel on right at SE 4th Ave.
Restrictions No smoking in some rooms. Traffic noise in some rooms.
Credit cards Amex, CB, MC, Visa.
Rates Room only, $130–180 suite, $70–145 double. Extra person, $10–15.
Extras Water taxi service.

HOLMES BEACH

Information please: A 1920s-era stucco building on Anna Maria Island, **Harrington House B&B** (5626 Gulf Drive, 34217; 813–778–5444) has seven miles of powdery white sand beginning just a few feet from its door, and breathtaking views of the sun setting over the Gulf. The seven guest rooms are decorated with floral wallpapers, reproduction furniture, ceiling fans, and lace curtains. Four additional guest rooms are located in the nearby Beach House, built in the 1940s and remodeled in the same style as the inn. You'll need to swim a few early morning laps in the pool to work up an appetite for the breakfast of stuffed French toast or perhaps eggs Benedict. B&B double rates range from $80–160.

If you are staying in the area for an extended stay, the **Sailfish Apartments** (3718 Gulf Drive, 33510; 813–778–7324) may be a good choice. "The apartment was immaculate and fully furnished. Any requests were answered with a smile. Splendid view with a white sandy beach at our patio's edge that goes for miles." *(Sylvia Woide)*

INVERNESS

Crown Hotel ¢ ✗   *Tel:* 904–344–5555
109 North Seminole Avenue, 32650

The Crown began its existence as Inverness's first store nearly a century ago. It then became a hotel and was moved to Main Street. Around 1925, it was moved again, to its present location; later, the owners enlarged it by adding a third floor to the bottom of the hotel, and a fourth to the top! By 1980, the building was on the verge of collapse. Closed for 18 months and $2,000,000 worth of restoration, it was purchased by Jill and Nigel Sumner in 1990. The inn is decorated in the Florida version of an English country inn, with brass beds and reproduction Chippendale dressers and side chairs; a sweeping free-floating staircase along with a reproduction set of the crown jewels highlight the lobby. The inn's pub serves casual American fare, along with English favorites such as fish and chips and steak and kidney pie; Churchill's restaurant offers continental specialties.

"The lit-up facade of the hotel at night was a romantic treat. Breakfast included a delightful fruit concoction, together with excellent muffins and coffee." *(FH, also BJ Hensley)* "Charming small-town hotel. We enjoy strolling the sidewalks around the hotel. The rooms, though somewhat small, are convenient, comfortable, and reasonably priced. In the dining room, good food is served well." *(HB, also Sherrill Brown)* "We enjoyed playing checkers on the game table near the elegant second-floor staircase. Excellent dinner of venison and beef filet." *(Thomas & Linda Fontana)* "British flavor. Enjoyed Churchill's restaurant. *(William MacGowan)*

Open All year.
Rooms 30 doubles, 2 singles—all with private bath and/or shower, telephone, TV, air-conditioning. Some with desk.
Facilities Restaurant with weekend entertainment, pub, parlor with fireplace. Swimming pool. Jogging trail, lakes, canoeing, golf nearby.
Location W central FL, 75 m N of Tampa, 75 m E of Orlando. Take I-75 to Hwy. 44. Go W for 16 m to town.
Credit cards Amex, MC, Visa.
Rates B&B, $100–110 double, $70–75 single. Extra person, $6. Senior, AAA discount. "Crown Jewel" package rates; includes afternoon tea, cocktails, dinner. Alc lunch, $8; alc dinner, $25.
Extras Crib.

ISLAMORADA

Information please: For a truly laidback vacation, consider **The Moorings** (123 Beach Road, 33036; 305–664–4708), a 17-acre property harboring 18 cottages, a swimming pool, a tennis court, and quantities of flowering hibiscus and bougainvillea. Cottages are self-sufficient, most with a kitchen, TV, telephone, washer and dryer. Though Islamorada is crowded and commercial, The Moorings has the feel of an isolated island, with the languid pace of the tropics, yet its two fine restaurants are a short walk away for dinner. "One of the most beautiful pieces of property in the Keys. The beach, the pool and grounds are magnificent." *(Joe Schmidt)*

Cheeca Lodge 🏃 ✕ 🎣 ⚕.   *Tel:* 305–664–4651
Mile Marker 82, Overseas Highway   800–327–2888
P.O. Box 527, 33036   *Fax:* 305–664–2893

As usual, we are putting reader opinions before any arbitrary size distinctions. Despite its size, several well-traveled readers have pointed out that Cheeca is indeed a special place. Spiffed up by a multi-million-dollar restoration, the rooms are luxurious, the food first rate, the service excellent, and the atmosphere relaxing. Although long acclaimed for its superb fishing, Cheeca is now known for its first-rate facilities for vacationing families as well.

"A splendid example of creative restoration. The rooms are well maintained and many have a fine view of the ocean. The warmth and charm of the public spaces and fine outdoor facilities make it an excellent resort." *(Joe & Sheila Schmidt)* "First class, from the front desk to housekeeping to the recreational staff. When we asked for additional towels, they arrived swiftly from a smiling housekeeper and were replenished without another request all week. Our room and the lodge overall was clean, beautiful, well-kept. The three swimming pools allowed for serious water exercise without time restrictions. The dining was top quality and the presentation appetizing and inviting. The set-up allowed both childless couples and families with young children to enjoy the resort in their own way. The par three golf course is a fun practice area for golfers who want to practice their short game; next time I'll bring my own irons. Even the gift shop is filled with wonderful, artistic finds." *(Linda Bohm, also Jane Todd)*

Open All year.
Rooms 60 suites, 143 doubles—all with full private bath, telephone, radio, TV, VCR, air-conditioning, fan, mini-bar. Most with balcony.
Facilities 2 restaurants, lounge with big screen TV. 27 acres with 3 swimming pools, 5 Jacuzzis, private beach, 6 lighted Laykold tennis courts, 9-hole par-3 golf course. Summer/holiday children's program, deep-sea fishing, on-site dive shop, parasailing, playground, boating, sailing, scuba, snorkeling, windsurfing. Water aerobics, massage.
Location Florida Keys, 75 S of Miami. Rte. 1, Mile Marker 82.
Credit cards All major credit cards accepted.
Rates Room only, $200–825 suite, $125–500 double. Extra adult, $25. Children under 16 free in parents' room. Minimum stay required holiday, special event weekends. Alc lunch $17, dinner $30. Golf, tennis, fishing packages.
Extras Wheelchair access. Round-trip airport transfers, $125 for van. Crib, baby-sitting. Spanish, German, French spoken.

JACKSONVILLE

For an additional area entry, see **Orange Park**.

House on Cherry Street ¢
1844 Cherry Street, 32205

Tel: 904–384–1999
Fax: 904–981–2998

Those who have stereotypical ideas of Floridian decor will be amazed when they see the House on Cherry Street, a Colonial-style home built in 1909, overlooking the St. John's River, and owned by Carol and Merrill Anderson since 1984. Its guest rooms are handsomely decorated in rich, deep colors, with period antiques, canopy beds, hand-woven coverlets, and Oriental rugs. The historic mood is further enhanced by the owners' collections of tall-case clocks, duck decoys, baskets, and pewter. No less inviting is the screened porch, equipped with an ample supply of old wooden rocking chairs.

"Beautifully preserved neighborhood. Our room had a four-poster bed with a 150-year-old woven coverlet, antique clock, freshly cut flowers, an ice bucket, glasses and a thirst-quenching drink. Breakfast is served at the time requested, and might consist of crepes or baked eggs, with fresh fruit, juice and homemade breads. The lovely setting of pewter or elegant china is enhanced by a fresh-cut flower centerpiece at the antique gateleg table." *(Alice Schalk)* "Carol Anderson has thought of everything that makes one comfortable; she is attentive yet never intrusive; her husband is equally charming." *(Nancy & Peter de Vos)* "The Duck Room is decorated with duck paintings, duck decoys, and duck wallpaper. It is small but comfortable with its own sitting room across the hall, looking out to the river. I breakfasted on fresh sliced pears and juice, eggs, sausage and homemade muffins." *(William Novak)* "Exceptional cherry muffins. Evening wine and hors d'oeuvres give guests the opportunity to meet the Andersons and each other, share stories and recommendations." *(Linda Hardy)*

Open All year.
Rooms 4 doubles—all with private bath or shower, telephone, radio, TV, desk, air-conditioning, fan. Some with balcony/deck.
Facilities Dining room, living room, family room, screened porch. 1 acre with lawn games. On-street parking. Fishing, dockage, tennis, golf nearby.
Location NE FL. Riverside; 10 min. from downtown; 5 min. from I-95; 25 min. from airport. 1 block from St. John's Ave. Call for directions. On bus rte.
Restrictions No smoking in guest rooms. No children under 10.
Credit cards MC, Visa.
Rates B&B, $80 double, $70 single. Extra person, $10. 2-night minimum special events.
Extras Station pickup.

KEY LARGO

Information please: Not far from John Pennekamp Underwater Park, **Largo Lodge** (101740 Overseas Highway, 33037; 305–451–0424 or 800–IN–THE–SUN) consists of six duplex concrete-block cottages, set far back from the road, each with a kitchen/dining and living room area, a separate bedroom with two double beds, and a screened porch. The long dock has many comfortable lounge chairs, and is romantically lit at night. The double rate is $75–95. "A delightful, idiosyncratic place, run by two sisters who opted out of the New York race decades ago. Something of old Florida is preserved in their approach to the lodge. The decor was established sometime in the '50s and no need to change it has ever arisen. The lodge grounds are entered through a dense, well-tended tropical garden. There is also a sandy beach and lovely places to sit and read. Nearby are restaurants, shops, and all manner of places to dive, snorkle, and visit marine parks." *(EH)*

KEY WEST

Key West is the southernmost city in the continental United States, located 161 miles south of Miami. The completion of the Overseas Highway in 1938 brought major changes to Key West. No longer a sleepy fishing village, the town is often filled with tourists and hustlers.

Its gay population is estimated at 25 percent. International travelers discovered its allures, and are providing a foreign accent to the goings-on. Key West is currently riding an upscale wave, with a gentrifying trend away from tacky tee shirt shops and dive bars to quality clothing and art stores. It's not a place people are neutral about. One of our readers wrote that "Key West is lovely—unlike any other place I've been in America. Sophisticated and funky. Even the tacky is interesting." *(Elaine Malsin)* Another reported that: "Key West is a tourist trap, overcrowded and crawling with escapees from the north, but that's what's so endearing about it. The Key West Aquarium and Audubon House are well worth visiting, but the fabled sunset festival—complete with fire-eaters, jugglers, and fortune tellers—at Mallory Dock is overrated." *(Wayne Braffman)*

If the sun and water overwhelm, some other Key West sights of interest include Ernest Hemingway's Home, Key West Lighthouse Museum, Wrecker's Museum, and Mel Fisher's exhibit of sunken treasure. Those who feel their stay will be incomplete without a taste of key lime pie (or two or three), may want to sample the offerings at the Deli Restaurant, the Buttery, Pier House, or Sloppy Joes; remember the real thing is *never* green or thickened with gelatin—it's yellow, creamy, and sweet.

A word of advice about navigating in the Keys—the Florida Keys' Overseas Highway (U.S. 1) is studded with 126 mile markers starting at the corner of Fleming and Whitehead streets in Key West and ending near Florida City. Watch for the small green signs with white writing, found on the right shoulder of the road, since they're often used as reference points when directions are given.

Budget travelers should note that hotel rates are substantially lower from June through November, with the exception of holiday weekends.

Reader tips: "On your way to or from Key West, stop at Montes at MM 25 in Summerland Key, for excellent seafood, inexpensively served in a casual setting." *(Sheila & Joe Schmidt)* "The streets of Key West are narrow and congested, making car travel a problem. Park your car and walk!" *(Howard Addis)* "Distinguish yourself from the average tourist by remembering that conch is pronounced *konk*."

Also recommended: The Mermaid & The Alligator (729 Truman Avenue, 33040; 305–294–1894) was named for two statues (a mermaid kissing an alligator) located behind the inn's octagonal-shaped Jacuzzi pool. A Queen Anne Victorian built in 1904, each of the five guest rooms has a private bath and different decor: Art Deco, Queen Anne, Southwest, and so on. Breakfasts of juice, coffee, a fresh fruit medley, cheese and smoked meat platters, boiled eggs, and a variety of breads and breakfast cakes are included in the B&B double rates of $70–$175. "Elegant old home, nicely renovated, furnished with antiques, old and new paintings—all tastefully put together. Large tropical garden with sun deck, pool, and lounge area. Helpful, friendly owners; wonderful breakfasts." *(Wolf Krusemark)*

Information please: Listed in past editions, we need reports on the well-known **Curry Mansion Inn** (511 Caroline Street, 33040; 305–294–5349 or 800–253–3466) Listed on the National Register of Historic Places, this lavishly detailed house includes original woodwork, stained and bevelled glass, and heirloom antiques. Although four guest rooms are located on the mansion's second floor, eleven are found in a new wing overlooking a deck and swimming pool. The owners hold a complimentary happy hour every night in the courtyard, and offer a breakfast buffet in the same place at 8:30 A.M.—juice, cereal, muffins, and rolls. B&B double rates range from $125—180.

The **Artist House** (534 Eaton Street, 33040; 305—296—3977 or 800—582—7882) is a Queen Anne Victorian house, complete with gingerbread trim, etched-glass windows, and a turret. Each of the five guest rooms have antique and reproduction furnishings accented with hand-painted period wallpapers. Built in the 1920s, the **Duval Gardens** (1012 Duval Street, 33040; 305—292—3379 or 800—296—3060) offers four apartments; the $75—195 rates include a full breakfast, nightly cocktail hour, and use of a private beach resort and a health club membership. The **Eden House** (1015 Fleming Street, 33040; 305—296—6868 or 800—533—KEYS) is a renovated 1924 Art Deco hotel, with porches, balconies, verandas, wicker furniture, and tropical plants. Amenities include a swimming pool, hot tub, garden cafe, off-street parking, and bike rentals; rates range from $45 for a modest room with a hall bath, to $275 for a luxury suite. Formerly a private residence, the **Gardens Hotel** (526 Angela Street, 33040; 305—294—2661 or 800—526—2664) was refurbished as a luxury hotel in 1993. The 17 guest rooms overlook a half-acre garden of fragrant flowering plants. Double B&B rates range from $200—525.

Andrew's Inn &.

Zero Whalton Lane, 33040

Tel: 305—294—7730
Fax: 305—294—0021

Andrew's Inn was built in 1920, and was opened as a B&B in 1988 by Tim Gatewood and (the late) Andrew Cleveland.

"Right behind Hemingway's Key West home is this delightful B&B with enchanting secluded gardens. Most days, breakfast is eaten in the open courtyard; one morning we had eggs Benedict, the next banana pancakes. The guest rooms are charming and private, eclectically furnished with queen- or king-sized beds." *(Geraldine Hoyt)* "Walton Cottage was furnished in vintage wicker, with bright fabrics and iron window louvers to let in the breeze but maintain privacy. The garden was a marvel of huge palms, brilliant hibiscus, cats and wrought iron furniture, positioned so that each guest could have a private corner. Tim and his staff are charming, generous, unobtrusive, and helpful." *(Pamela Roby)*

Open All year.
Rooms 1 2-bedroom cottage, 7 doubles—all with full private bath, telephone, TV, desk, air-conditioning, fan, balcony/deck, private entrance. Some with radio, fireplace, refrigerator.
Facilities Breakfast room, bar/lounge, guest kitchen/laundry, deck. Courtyard with small lap swimming pool; off-street parking.
Location Center of Old Town. At 900 block of Duval St., turn on Whalton LA. ½ block off U.S. 1.
Restrictions "Well behaved children welcome."
Credit cards Amex, MC, Visa.
Rates B&B, $178—270 cottage, $98—158 double. Extra person in cottage, $10. 10% senior, AAA discount. Minimum stay some holidays.
Extras Wheelchair access. Airport, station pickups. Pets with approval. French, Italian, Spanish spoken.

The Banyan Resort
323 Whitehead Street, 33040

Tel: 305–296–7786
800–225–0639
Fax: 305–294–1107

Located in the heart of Old Town Key West, the Banyan Resort consists of seven historic conch homes; several are listed on the National Register of Historic Places. Now converted into luxury suites (sometimes sold as time-shares), each is decorated in soothing neutral shades, with comfortable couches and lots of natural wicker. Intertwined with winding gravel paths, the grounds are lush and tropical, with many varieties of palm trees, hibiscus, and two enormous banyan trees over 200 years old. Interesting finds were uncovered during the restoration—Cosgrove House originally had a secret room and a dungeon, while Delaney House was built over two 15-feet deep vaults.

"The Banyan retains the flavor of Old Key West, with a delightful laid-back atmosphere." *(Warren Collins)* "Exceptionally beautiful garden and pool areas; excellent service." *(Michael & Dina Miller)* "Our suite had lots of windows overlooking lush gardens. Helpful staff." *(Debbie Bergstrom)*

Open All year.
Rooms 38 suites in 7 buildings—all with private bath, telephone, radio, clock, TV, air-conditioning, fan, refrigerator/kitchen, patio/balcony.
Facilities Bar/lounge, laundry, off-street parking. 1 heated pool, 1 unheated pool; gardens.
Location Center of town. Old Town Key West, at end of U.S. Rte. 1, between Eaton and Caroline Sts.
Restrictions Children over 12.
Credit cards Amex, DC, Discover, MC, Visa.
Rates Room only, $115–265 suite. Extra person, $20.
Extras Some Spanish spoken.

Duval House
815 Duval Street, 33040

Tel: 305–294–1666
Fax: 305–292–1701

Choosing just the right spot for relaxing may be the most difficult part of your stay at Duval House. Will it be poolside or under the century-old banyan tree? In the lounge, or on the balcony to watch the rest of Key West stroll by? This inn, formed by a cluster of Victorian homes, is furnished with a comfortable mix of wicker and antiques, freshened by hibiscus flowers, picked daily. The inn has been owned by Richard Kamradt since 1989, and is managed by James Brown.

"Helpful, friendly innkeepers. The inn is amazingly quiet for its location; it is easy to spend time beneath the trees quietly reading despite the traffic on Duval Street. Our small room was spotless and well-maintained. Breakfast includes cereal, muffins, bagels, coffee cake, donuts, and juice; coffee is served continuously throughout the day. The pool is located in a tropical garden surrounded by a deck, with enough chairs for all the guests. The gazebo is an equally appealing place to relax and enjoy the garden." *(Michael & Dina Miller)* "Our delightful room had a balcony overlooking the tropical courtyard where breakfast is served. The location is central, so we parked the car and walked everywhere." *(Glenn & Lynette Roehrig)* "Endorse existing entry. Wonderful staff. We'll return." *(Steve & Elise Holman)*

Open All year.
Rooms 3 suites, 26 doubles—all with private bath and/or shower, air-conditioning, ceiling fan, deck. Some with desk.
Facilities Lounge with TV, books, games; breakfast room. Swimming pool, gazebo. Golf nearby. Snorkeling, swimming nearby.
Location Historic district. 120 m S of Miami, 90 m N of Havana, Cuba. Bus. Rte. #1 to Duval St., right on Duval.
Restrictions Light sleepers could be affected by traffic noise in two rooms. No children under 14.
Credit cards Amex, DC, Discover, MC, Visa.
Rates B&B, $110–240 suite, $75–175 double. Extra person, $15. 2-night holiday minimum.

Marquesa Hotel ✕ ৬.
600 Fleming Street, 33040

Tel: 305–292–1919
800–UNWIND–1
Fax: 305–294–2121

Listed on the National Register of Historic Places, the Marquesa is a 1880s boarding house rescued from near destruction by hard work, good taste and $2,000,000. A concierge tends to your every whim, and your senses will be soothed by bedtime Godiva chocolates, fresh flowers, and Caswell Massey toiletries. The hotel restaurant, the Cafe Marquesa, offers a creative menu, with such dishes as lobster ravioli with seafood sauce; sesame rack of lamb; and Brazilian-style pork.

"Once a decayed boarding house, it was converted into an exceptional small hotel by Richard Manley and Erik deBoer. The rooms are bright, cheerful, and immaculate; most have porches overlooking the pool. Each morning the *New York Times* was delivered to our door and when we went out to dinner, the bed was turned down, the towels changed and waste baskets emptied. The staff remained unobtrusively in the background but were instantly available to offer service." *(Sheila & Joe Schmidt)* "Perfect location, on a quiet street off Duval, just a short walk to Mallory Square. Antiques abound throughout, and the marble baths are beautiful. Wonderful breakfast, served in the room or by the pool and fountain." *(Bill & Kim Barnes)* "The excellent restaurant has an imaginative menu and style that is reminiscent of the San Francisco-style of dining. An expensive, but elegant experience." *(Stephen & Ellise Holman)*

Open All year.
Rooms 15 suites, doubles—all with full private bath, telephone, TV, air-conditioning, stocked wet bar, ceiling fan. 7 with deck.
Facilities Lobby, restaurant, terraces, decks. Heated swimming pool. Off-street parking.
Location Historic district, corner of Fleming and Simonton Sts. 5 blocks from Gulf, 10 blocks from Atlantic, 1 block to center.
Credit cards Amex, DC, MC, Visa.
Rates Room only, $150–265 suite, $120–215 double. Extra person, $15. 2-night holiday minimum. Alc dinner $40; early-bird special.
Extras Wheelchair access. Babysitting.

Seascape ₵
420 Olivia Street, 33040

Tel: 305–296–7776
Fax: 305–296–7776

Built in the Bahamas around 1840, Seascape was shipped in pieces to Key West and reconstructed in 1889; Alan Melnick bought this typical conch house in 1987, and opened Seascape in 1989. The outside is painted white with royal blue shutters and awnings; inside, guest rooms are furnished in white wicker with royal blue accents and are provided with fresh flowers. Breakfast includes orange juice, fresh fruit, pastry, and coffee; a complimentary sunset wine hour is served from December through April.

"Despite its central location, the inn was peaceful and quiet." *(Scott Elliott)* "The rooms are spotless, scented with potpourri. Breakfast was served on the terrace with fresh cut flowers on the table and soft classical music playing." *(James Lampke)* "Three rooms have French doors opening onto a beautifully landscaped pool area, complete with a blooming bougainvillea and a fountain—private and relaxing." *(Debbie Alexander)* "We looked down from our balcony at the blue mosaics of the pool, matching the inn's awnings and shutters." *(Elsa Hahn)* "Our bright and airy room had a deck with a view of the Hemingway house. Extremely hospitable hosts." *(Julie Donaldson)* "Every morning, delicious muffins, fresh fruit, juice and coffee greeted us. Chilled wine was served by the Jacuzzi-equipped pool in the evening. Alan and Danny gave much needed directions, suggestions for the best restaurants, and even a list of places to avoid." *(Howard & Sharon Addis)*

Minor niggle: "Although innkeepers will take messages, outgoing calls must be made via the pay phone next to the pool."

Open All year.
Rooms 5 doubles—all with private bath, clock/radio, TV, air-conditioning, ceiling fan. 4 with deck.
Facilities Breakfast patio, lobby with piano, unscreened porch. Heated pool-spa.
Location Center of Old Town. Follow Rte. 1 to Key West. Bear right following signs 'Rte. 1 Downtown'. Rte. 1 becomes Truman Ave. Stay on Truman Ave. until Whitehead St. Go right onto Whitehead St. First right is Olivia St.
Restrictions No children under 15.
Credit cards Amex, Discover, MC, Visa.
Rates B&B, $69–109 double. Extra person, $20. Minimum stay holiday periods.

LAKE HELEN

Clauser's B&B   Tel: 904–228–0310
201 East Kicklighter Road, 32744   800–220–0310
                                          Fax: 904–228–2337

Owned by Marge and Tom Clauser, longtime Florida residents, this 1890 Victorian home has lots of porches, well supplied with rockers and wicker furnishings. Guest rooms are decorated with family heirlooms, handmade quilts and afghans; each room has a different decorating theme—English garden, Pennsylvania Dutch, Old West, and so on. Early morning coffee is set out on the porch; a country breakfast is served at 9 A.M., and might include sautéed cinnamon apples, bran muffins, cheese omelets, and ham. Rates also include afternoon fruit, beverages, and home-baked treats, plus evening sherry or port.

"Central but very quiet—thick woods with pileated woodpeckers. Large, tasty farm breakfast. Interesting repeat clientele from many backgrounds." *(Bill McGowan)*

Open All year.
Rooms 2 doubles in main house, 6 in carriage house. All with private bath and/or shower. 6 with private screened porch. 2 with Jacuzzi, 1 with fireplace.
Facilities Dining room, parlor with fireplace, living room with TV/VCR, stereo; reading room with TV, books, games; gift shop; porch with rockers, swing. 2 acres with off-street parking, gazebo/hot tub, lawn games, picnic area. 25 min. to beach, 15 min. to state park.
Location NE FL. 20 m SW of Daytona Beach; 35 m N of Orlando. From I-4, take Exit 55 & go E on Main St. Go right on High St. to Ohio St. Jog left & turn immediately onto Macy Marion St. Go left on E. Kicklighter to inn on right.
Restrictions No smoking. Children over 15.
Credit cards Amex, Discover, MC, Visa.
Rates B&B, $65–120 double, $60–120 single. Senior discount. 2-night minimum special events. Extra person, $20.
Extras Airport/station pickups.

LAKELAND

Information please: We'd like reports on **Magnolias in the Park** (255 North Kentucky Avenue, 33801; 813–686–7275), about halfway between Disney World and Tampa. Built in 1914, it's been restored with modern comforts and decorated in period. The inn has four air-conditioned guest rooms with private baths, but is best known for the delicious and reasonably priced lunches served in its restaurant. "A clean and attractive B&B. We did not stay overnight, but were delighted with their extensive menu of sandwiches and salads, made from the freshest ingredients, beautifully presented. Scrumptious homemade pies. By far the best choice for lunch when visiting the antique stores of Lakeland's historic district." *(Mimi Cohen)* B&B double rates are $95.

LAKE WALES

Reader tips: "Take time to see the Bok Tower Gardens, off Alternate Route 27 of Tower Boulevard. The tower is striking (pink Georgia marble with tile work at top), the carillon is worth hearing, and the gardens are pleasant. The coffee shop is surprisingly good and you can eat outside. Visitors are encouraged to buy food for the carp and squirrels, which kept our kids busy while we enjoyed the grounds. What a change from Disney World."*(Diane Wolf, also LG)* "The old railroad depot with its interesting memorabilia is also worth a look." *(HB)*

Chalet Suzanne 👪 ✕ ♿   *Tel:* 813–676–6011
U.S. Highway 27 and 17A North,   800–433–6011
3800 Chalet Suzanne Drive, 33853   *Fax:* 813–676–1814

Amid the orange groves and alligators of central Florida is the Chalet Suzanne, set on beautiful green lawns and bordering a lake. Over sixty years ago Bertha Hinshaw turned her home into an inn and restaurant, to support the family after her husband died. The inn soon gained a reputation for good food and lodging and was included in Duncan Hines's first *Guide to Good Eating*. During World War II the main building, including the kitchen and many dining rooms, burned down completely. No building materials were available, so the stables, rabbit hutches, and chicken coops were added to existing structures. Additional rooms have been built since then, and the delightful result is an unlikely hodgepodge of munchkin-size towers, turrets, and gables that ramble in all directions on fourteen levels.

Bertha Hinshaw made eighteen trips around the world, bringing back glass, china, tiles, and stained glass windows; the chalet's Swiss, Scandinavian, French, Oriental, Spanish, and Turkish architecture was inspired by what she saw. Guest rooms vary dramatically in size and decor, although most are spacious, with cozy seating areas and thirties-era decor; some bathrooms are dated but functional, others have been updated with whirlpool tubs, and many have stunning hand-painted tiles. Carl and Vita Hinshaw now operate the inn, with the help of their children, Tina and Eric.

"Service is attentive but unobtrusive, professional yet relaxed. The menu never changes: you start with their signature broiled grapefruit with chicken liver, followed by the peppery romaine soup, a seasonal salad, and their addictive potato rolls. The choice and originality of the main courses is limited, but they are prepared to perfection, and portions are extremely generous." *(SWS)* "The charm here is the inn's quirkiness—a quality that doesn't necessarily appeal to everyone." *(Diane Wolf)* "In-room touches included fresh flowers, a fruit basket with chocolates and hard candy, and a decanter of sherry. My small room also had a little sitting area, two bureaus, two small closets, and a double bed; the bath had a skylight and was beautifully tiled." *(Mary Morgan)* "Our room was large and comfortable, with good bedside lighting. Expensive but outstanding shad roe and lobster Newburg; excellent desserts. Swedish pancakes—as many orders as you want—were a treat—especially since you could eat anytime from 8–11 A.M." *(Robert & Ellie Freidus)*

Area for improvement: "Our bathroom window needed painting, the bathroom tiles a thorough scrubbing." And: "I loved everything about our dinner but the astounding price." Reports welcome.

Open All year. Restaurant closed Mon. only, May through Dec.
Rooms 4 suites, 26 doubles, 1 single—all with private bath and/or shower, telephone, TV, air-conditioning. Some with radio, desk, fan, balcony, courtyard or patio, Jacuzzi tub.
Facilities Restaurant, bar, lounge, living room, wine dungeon, library, patio, gift shop, antique shop. Pianist or accordionist in restaurant. 70 acres with swimming pool, private lake, badminton, croquet. Mystery weekends. Private airstrip. Self-tours of soup cannery. Tennis, golf nearby.
Location Central FL; Polk County. 1 hr. SW of Orlando, 40 min. S of Disney World, 4 m N of Lake Wales. From I-4, take Rte. 27 S to Rte. 17A. Go E on Rte. 17A to inn.
Credit cards Amex, CB, DC, Discover, JCB, MC, Visa.
Rates B&B, $125–185 suite, double, single; extra person, $12. MAP, $315 suite. Alc lunch, $28–40; prix fixe dinner, $59–73, plus 18% service. MAP packages May–Nov.; honeymoon packages.
Extras Wheelchair access. Airport/station pickups. Pets by arrangement. Crib, babysitting. German, French spoken.

LITTLE TORCH KEY

Little Palm Island ✕ ♿   *Tel:* 305–872–2524
Mile Marker 28.5, Route 4, Box 1036, 33042   800–343–8567

If you'd like to escape to a private tropical island, complete with hand-thatched bungalows, luxurious South Seas–style decor, and gourmet French cuisine—just 120 miles from Miami—read on. Occupying the whole of a five-acre island, Little Palm Island is located at the western end of the Newfound Harbor Keys, where the Newfound Harbor meets the Atlantic. This advantageous location gives it a sand and coral base, not mangrove like most other islands. Originally known as Little Munson Island and long used as a private family retreat and fishing camp, the island was a favorite vacation spot of President Truman. John Kennedy came here to watch the filming of *PT 109* in 1962, and because of his visit, the state of Florida supplied the island with water, telephone and electric service. In 1988, the island was converted into a luxury resort. The original fishing lodge is now the Great House, home to the restaurant and two suites. Most guests are accommodated in bungalows holding two suites each.

"The spacious suites are decorated with wicker furnishings, vivid prints, and Mexican tile accents. The atmosphere is quiet and relaxed, even when the inn is fully booked. The entire island is beautifully landscaped, and the pool area is lovely, with comfortable lounge chairs and big plush towels." *(Ken & Karen Gruska)* "The refrigerator and bar in each room was always kept fully stocked. While not functionally necessary, the mosquito netting over our king-sized bed was a very lovely touch." *(J. Hatcher Graham)* "Managing partner Ben Woodson and his staff work hard to make everyone feel welcome and cared for. The food is good by any standard, but its quality is even more impressive when you realize that everything has to be shipped down to the Keys, transported to the island by boat." *(Bob Blitz)* "Expensive but worth it. Our bungalow had a thatched roof, a porch for sitting, with hammocks scattered among the palms. Lovely 20-minute boat ride to the hotel." *(Jane Mattoon)* "We came for a delightful lunch, then we escorted back to the launch." *(Robert Safire)* Comments appreciated.

Open All year.
Rooms 30 suites—all with full private bath with whirlpool tub, double sinks, and outside shower; desk, air-conditioning, ceiling fan, deck with hammock, coffee maker, wet bar.
Facilities Restaurant, store. 5 acres with swimming pool, beaches, bicycling, fishing, snorkeling, sailing, kayaks, exercise facility. Dive shop, fishing; scuba certification.
Location FL Keys. 120 m S of Miami. At Mile Marker 28.5 (Little Torch Key), turn into Dolphin Marina and park at shore station (pink building on R) for Little Palm Island. 30-min. drive from shore station to Key West.
Restrictions No smoking on launch boat. No children under 12.
Credit cards Amex, MC, Visa.
Rates Room only, $330–465 suite. Extra person, $52. MAP, $75 per person extra; full board, $95 per person extra.

Extras Wheelchair access. Pickup from Key West airport, $40 per couple. French, Spanish spoken.

MAITLAND

Thurston House   *Tel:* 407–539–1991
851 Lake Avenue, 32751

Overlooking Lake Eulalia, this Queen Anne Victorian home was built in 1885, and was restored as an inn in 1992 by Carole and Joe Ballard. Architectural features include the cross gable roof and corbeled brick chimneys, while the inside is highlighted by the beautifully restored pine and cypress woodwork and floors. The rooms are spacious and airy, furnished with an attractive mix of Victorian antiques, Colonial reproductions, and traditional pieces. The Hirsch Room is done in blue and white, with sponge-painted walls in Wedgwood blue, a Sheraton-style highboy, and a queen-size lace-canopy bed, while the Cubbedge Room is painted apple green, with a beautiful hand-stitched quilt in a fan pattern. In addition to juice, tea, and coffee, a typical breakfast might include honey peaches, granola, French toast casserole with maple syrup, raisin scones, and zucchini bread, or perhaps melon and kiwi, citrus puffs, cranberry muffins, and buttermilk biscuits.

"Beautifully remodeled old house with lots of character, lovely guest rooms. Carole and Joe were friendly and accommodating. We enjoyed wine and cheese upon arrival and a delicious breakfast the next morning." *(Linda & Alan Peck)* Comments appreciated.

Open Sept. 1–July 31.
Rooms 4 doubles—all with private bath and/or shower, telephone, clock, desk, air-conditioning, ceiling fan.
Facilities Dining room, front parlor with fireplace, back parlor with TV/VCR, stereo, books; screened porches. 5 acres with off-street parking, fruit trees, herb garden; on Lake Eulalia for fishing, croquet, horseshoes.
Location Central FL. 5 m N of downtown Orlando. From I-4, exit at Lee Rd. & go N on Wymore Rd. to Kennedy Blvd. Go right to inn on left, where road jogs right & changes name to Lake Ave.
Restrictions No smoking. Children over 12.
Credit cards Amex, MC, Visa.
Rates B&B, $80–90 double. Extra person, $10. 10% AAA, senior discount. 2-night holiday minimum.
Extras Station pickup.

MARATHON

Also recommended: Travelers who prefer a resort with a full range of family activities will enjoy **Hawk's Cay** (Mile Marker 61, Duck Key 33050; 305–743–7000 or 800–432–2242) with eight tennis courts, a dolphin and sea lion training facility, kids' program, fitness center, several restaurants, and more. Like most of the Keys, Duck Key, a 60-acre island, has no beach, but a sand-bordered lagoon has been created to fill the gap. Duck Key is eight miles north of Marathon, and the resort's 180 guest rooms rent for $140–335 double; numerous packages are available.

The **Conch Key Cottages** (RR 1, Box 424, Marathon, 33050; 305–289–1377 or 800–330–1577) on Little Conch Key offers five one- and two-bedroom cottages, each with air-conditioning and full kitchens. Daily rates range from $100–185, with weekly rates available. Dockage is free to all guests, restaurants are nearby, there's quick access to the coral reefs and fishing, and pets are welcome. "Rustic but appealing." *(Sheila & Joe Schmidt)*

MIAMI

Reader tip: "Miami, once known for Jackie Gleason on Saturday night, bathing beauties on the beach and a new showplace hotel each year (in 1955, a night at the Fontainebleau Hotel cost an astronomical $55), has become a sophisticated sub-tropical city. Leading attractions are the beach and lighthouse at Bill Baggs State Park, the Seaquarium, Parrot Jungle (arrive early for breakfast and to watch the parrots placed on their roosts), tropical Fairchild Garden, Viscaya, and the world class Metro-Zoo. In the winter there is opera, in summer a film festival. Outdoor concerts and speedboat races are held at the Marine Stadium. For strolling and sidewalk cafes, try the Art Deco area of Miami Beach, Coconut Grove or Bayside. The most exotic stores can be found at Bal Harbor Shops. Sport enthusiasts will find the Dolphins, the Heat, the Marlins, Grand Prix, Lipton Tennis, and the Doral Open. Hialeah Racetrack is one of the country's most beautiful. You don't have to bet; have lunch and enjoy the scenery. The best buy is a half-hour ride around downtown on the rubber wheeled people-mover, which stops conveniently near the Bayside shops. On Saturday afternoon, park on the MacArthur Causeway and watch the parade of departing cruise ships. South Miami Beach and Coral Gables have many outstanding ethnic restaurants; check the 'Weekend' section of the Friday *Miami Herald*. For a special treat, breakfast at the beautiful Grand Bay Hotel in Coconut Grove. As in any large city, *exercise caution* as you travel; most innkeepers will happily offer guidance." *(Joe Schmidt)*

Information please: We need current feedback on several Miami area hotels. The **Miami River Inn** (118 S.W. South River Drive, 33130; 305–325–0045 or 800–HOTEL–89O) Havana was created from nine buildings, some dating back to the early 1900s, overlooking the vibrant Miami riverfront. Guest rooms are individually decorated with antiques and period pieces, and the $60–80 rates include continental breakfast and afternoon tea. "An interesting restoration in the oldest area of Miami, now known as East Little Havana. While the breakfast room is small, the adjacent pool area is lovely and perfect for enjoying your meal. The rooms and grounds are spotless, the staff pleasant, the manager helpful." *(JS)* "The experience was so novel for us, the restoration of the complex is so well carried out, and the inn is so well run, that we thoroughly enjoyed ourselves. We walked to nearby restaurants and across the river into downtown Miami. Some people might find this somewhat rundown area threatening, but we didn't; when returning from dinner, we were careful to use well-lighted, busy streets; security at the inn is excellent. A good choice for adventurous readers." *(Steve Holman)* On the southwestern edge of Miami in Coral Gables is **The Colonnade Hotel** (180 Aragon Avenue, Coral Gables 33134; 305–441–2600 or 800–843–6664), an elegantly restored 1920s Mediterranean masterpiece; its 157 luxurious guest rooms have dark mahogany furniture, softly lit with brass lamps, and all the amenities one expects of a deluxe hotel, including a fine restaurant. "Located in the heart of Coral Gables, the hotel is within easy walking distance of shops, movies, and fine restaurants." *(JS)* The **Hotel Place St. Michel** (162 Alcazar Avenue, Coral Gables 33134; 305–444–1666 or 800–848–4683) built in 1926, was a favorite of such celebrities as Hedda Hopper, Douglas Fairbanks, and Gloria Swanson. The hotel fell into decay in the 1950's, but was totally restored and refurbished in 1979. The restaurant gets fine reports, but more comments are needed on the rooms.

MIAMI BEACH

Known as South Beach or SoBe, the mile-square Art Deco district of south Miami Beach encompasses 800 buildings dating from the 1930's and 1940's. Wander along Ocean Drive between 5th and 9th Streets to see the best of them. Many have been restored as hotels, as noted below. In general, rooms in the Art Deco hotels are smaller than most modern hotel rooms are today.

Don't forget that Miami is a big city, where the twin scourges of crime and drugs can quickly sour the vacation of any traveler who isn't citywise. Consult your hotel staff about which neighborhoods are safe, and which routes to walk.

Reader tip: "Your visit will not be complete without a dinner at Joe's Stone Crab Restaurant in Miami Beach. Close to 400,000 diners annually enjoy terrific seafood from mid-October to mid-May; the restaurant closes when crab is out of season." Also: "Remember that water view rooms on Ocean Drive are *noisy*—day and night."

Also recommended: At the heart of the action is the **Cardozo Hotel** (1300 Ocean Drive, 33139; 800–782–6500), a 44-room hotel built in 1939, and newly refurbished in all-out Art Decor glory. "Owned by Gloria Esteban, it's a favorite with musicians, models, photographers, foreign tourists, a sprinkling of gays. Although street noise forced us to keep our windows closed and the air-conditioning on, this was also part of the hotel's appeal. Simply watching the passing parade was the source of endless fun. The excellent restaurant had a large outdoor cafe, a perfect spot for watching roller bladers of all sizes, ages, shapes, sexes, and passing media types. The Portuguese-speaking staff was wonderful— informal, helpful, and friendly. Breakfast included fresh juice, just-baked breads, and excellent coffee. The guest rooms were well-maintained but small." *(Steve Holman)* Doubles range from $110–135; suites to $225, including breakfast and a drink on arrival.

Information please: We'd like your comments SoBe's many other restored hotels, including the **Art Deco Hotels** (1320 Ocean Drive, 33139; 800–OUTPOST), representing **The Marlin, The Cavalier,** and **The Leslie;**; The Marlin, with its Caribbean-style decor and Jamaican restaurant is perhaps the best-known of the three. A small but classy choice is the **Park Central Hotel** (640 Ocean Drive, 33139; 305–538–1611), a six-story Art Deco classic with lavender trim and the obligatory porthole windows, offers rooms with Art Deco reproductions, and has a bar/restaurant great for people watching; in the same complex is the Imperial Hotel. Popular with Hollywood types is the **Raleigh** (1775 Collins Avenue, Miami Beach FL 33139; 305–534–6300), known for its beautiful swimming pool, white sand beach, well-equipped guest rooms, and excellent restaurant.

Lafayette Hotel ✕ &.
944 Collins Avenue, 33139

Tel: 305–673–2262
Fax: 305–534–5399

An eclectic Mediterranean-style hotel built in 1935 and listed on the National Register of Historic Places, the Lafayette was purchased by the Cattarossi family in 1991. The original red tile floors and stairs, hand-wrought iron railing and vintage elevator were restored, and all new wiring, plumbing, doors and windows were added, along with strong make-up lights in the sparkling white bathrooms. Fresh flowers, solid wood furniture, tropical plants, and water fountains extend the Mediterranean feel throughout the hotel.

"Spotless, fully carpeted rooms with modern wood furniture. The reception area was generously proportioned and tastefully decorated." *(John-Christopher Wolf)* "A comfortable, good-looking hotel, with a warmer atmosphere than the hotels in the heart of the Art Deco district." *(Juan Manuel Reyes)* "Mercifully quiet setting." *(GR)* "Graziella Cattarossi was accommodating, charming, and genuinely kind." *(Palma Rose Venezia)* "Excellent location, close to Ocean Drive and to the quieter area of Washington Avenue. Courteous and discreet staff." *(Marc Biscayart)* "Attention is personal; rooms are clean and well kept." *(Kenneth Klein)* "We loved the patio with tropical plants. Quiet, yet just steps away from the beach, fashionable shops, and restaurants. " *(Marg & Laura Mancini)*

Open All year.
Rooms 5 suites, 49 doubles—all with private bath and/or shower, TV, air-conditioning, closet safe. Some suites with VCR.
Facilities Lobby, meeting room, patio with fountain. Beach towels. Close to beach, health club (discount rate) golf, tennis nearby. Limited off-street parking.
Location Take I-95 & exit at MacArthur Cswy (I-395). Go E across bay to Miami Beach. Stay in center or right lane. In Miami Beach, continue on 5th St. to Washington Ave. (7 blocks). Go left (N) on Washington Ave. Go 5 blocks to 10th St. & go right. Go right again on Collins to hotel between 9 and 10th Sts.
Restrictions Some no-smoking rooms.
Credit cards Amex, DC, MC, Visa.
Rates B&B, $135–245 suite, $99–148 double. Corporate rates.
Extras Limited wheelchair access. Crib. French, Italian, Spanish, German spoken.

MICANOPY

Reader tips: "Micanopy (pronounced Mick-uh-NO-pea, not "my canopy") is a tiny sleepy Old Florida town about ten to fifteen minutes south of Gainesville, with many enticing antique shops." *(TS)* "Cross Creek (about 10 miles east), the restored home of Marjorie Kinnan Rawlings, is very popular. We stopped there first, to put our name on the waiting list for a tour, then had lunch—catfish, hush puppies, lime pie—at the Yearling Inn. Just outside town on Hwy 441 is the Wildflower Cafe, open for lunch and dinner. Though casual, the food is very good; our grouper and desserts were exceptional." *(HB)*

Herlong Mansion ₵   *Tel:* 904–466–3322
402 NE Cholokka Boulevard, P.O. Box 667, 32667

Although the Herlong Mansion dates back to 1845, it was completely rebuilt in 1910 in the Colonial Revival style, with a wide veranda supported by four massive Roman-style columns. It sits back from the street, surrounded by old oak and pecan trees. A 1987 restoration (requiring 162 gallons of paint stripper) has returned the mansion to its original splendor, showcasing its leaded glass windows, mahogany, oak, and maple inlaid floors, and "tiger oak" paneling. In 1990, H.C. "Sonny" Howard purchased the mansion and has done a great deal to enhance the inn's charms. Breakfast might include Herlong decadent bread—a type of bread pudding—accompanied by fresh fruit, juice, and bran-and-buttermilk muffins.

"The mansion is convenient to antique shops and a bookstore, housed in original old buildings, giving the village an early 1900s air." *(HB)* "My grandchildren loved hearing about the mansion's ghost." *(Noreen Cutler)* "Sonny is a charming, helpful host and a hopeless romantic. The antique-filled rooms are tastefully and thoughtfully decorated; the home-cooked breakfast was accompanied by Sonny's entertaining stories about the house and its history. His 150-piece collection of canes is a study in itself." *(Miriam Cohen)* "On the walls are fascinating letters and genealogical information about the Herlong family. Our room had two double brass beds with good reading lights." *(April Burwell)*

Open All year.
Rooms 4 suites, 7 doubles—all with private bath and/or shower, radio, air-conditioning. 10 with fireplace, 5 with balcony.
Facilities Parlor, dining room, living room, library, all with fireplace; conference room; veranda. 2 acres with garden and gazebo.
Location 12 m S of Gainesville, 24 m N of Ocala; take Micanopy exit off I-75 or Rte. 441 to inn in center of town.
Restrictions No smoking.
Credit cards MC, Visa.
Rates B&B, $110–135 suite, $60–105 double. Extra person, $10. Rollaway bed, $5. No charge from children under 2.
Extras Airport pickups, $25.

MOUNT DORA

Reader tips: "This delightful community is known for its antique shops and is sought after for nearby lakes, and hills for bicyclers. Special shows and programs, devoted to the arts in February, antique boats in April, and antique cars in the fall provide amusement all year." *(Joyce Wood)* "A welcome refuge from the hustle of Disney and Orlando." *(Sheila & Joe Schmidt)*

Information please: We've had mixed feedback on the **Lakeside Inn** (100 North Alexander Street, 32757; 904–383–4101 or 800–556–5016), a historic inn built in the 1880s and updated in the 1920s, when it was a fashionable resort frequented by F. Scott Fitzgerald, among others. Saved from the wrecking ball in the 1980s, renovation and refurbishing has been extensive and on-going. Now listed on the National Register of Historic Places, the hotel has a lovely, quiet setting, overlooking the swimming pool and lake beyond. Its extensive porches have plenty of old-fashioned rockers, perfect for reading or conversation. Inside, the inn is decorated with Laura Ashley fabrics and wall coverings and period reproduction furnishings; the color scheme is ivory, dusty rose, and soft blue or green. While most readers are pleased by their experience overall, several noted areas for improvement in terms of maintenance and house-keeping. The hotel has 87 guest rooms, and double rates range from $75–135.

Raintree House	*Tel:* 904–383–5065
1123 Dora Way, 32757-3734	*Fax:* 904–383–1920

Overlooking Lake Dora, the Raintree House was built in 1942, and restored as a B&B in 1992 by Dottie Smith. Breakfast is served between 8:30 and 9:30 A.M.; rates also include afternoon refreshments and snacks; early evening wine; bedtime liqueur and chocolates; and two complimentary tickets for the local theater.

"Beautifully decorated guest rooms, two overlooking the lake. Considerable grounds by Florida standards, handsomely landscaped." *(Joyce Wood)* "The immaculate bedrooms are airy and spacious, with excellent beds and both down and non-allergic pillows. We had an interesting chat with her when we returned from a day's antiquing to find cold drinks, wine and snacks set out for us on the shady porch." *(Karen Ramsay)* "Our room was decorated in Laura Ashley fabrics; the bathroom was supplied with lots of towels, terry robes, and English soap and shampoo. Early morning coffee is a thoughtful touch; juice, bottled water, and soft drinks are always available. Breakfast was served on the back porch overlooking the garden, and included a wide variety of fresh fruit, cold cereal, fresh-squeezed orange juice, Danish pastry, and muffins. We enjoyed chatting with Dottie during breakfast, comparing travel stories. Good lighting in the yard at night; covered parking." *(Eleanor MacDonald)*

Open Sept. 1–May 31.
Rooms 3 doubles—all with private shower/bath, radio, clock, air-conditioning, ceiling fan.

Facilities Dining room, living room with TV, fireplace, books; guest refrigerator, laundry, screened porch with hot tub. 1 acre with off-street parking, croquet, horseshoes. Overlooks Lake Dora; boating, fishing, golf, bicycling nearby.

Location Central FL. 25 m NW of Orlando. 1 m from town. At intersection of Old 441 and Dora Way, overlooking Lake Dora.

Restrictions Smoking only on screened porch (except during breakfast). Children over 12.

Credit cards MC, Visa.

Rates B&B, $85–110 double, $80–105 single. 10% AARP, AAA discount. 2-night minimum festival weekends. Weekly rates.

NAPLES

An elegant community of gracious homes and trendy shops and restaurants, Naples' key attraction is its seven miles of white sand beaches, ideal for sunning, swimming, and shelling. Visitors can choose from a full menu of water sports, visits to nature sanctuaries, golf, and tennis.

Inn by the Sea ₵   *Tel:* 813–649–4124
287 11th Avenue South, 33940

Built as a tourist house in 1936, the Inn by the Sea was restored as a B&B in 1989, when it was featured as a designer showcase. Decorator elements have been combined with such "old Florida" touches as heart pine and cypress woodwork, white iron and brass beds, wicker furnishings, and floral fabrics. Surrounded by tropical plantings of coconut palms, birds of paradise, and bougainvillea, the inn is listed on the National Register of Historic Places. Its pink wooden cove siding and metal roof were common during the thirties but are unusual today. Guests receive a breakfast of homemade muffins, scones, or bread, granola, fruit, and fresh-squeezed orange juice, right from the backyard tree.

"You can park your car and not get in it all weekend. Breakfast varied daily, light enough for the tropical climate yet substantial and plentiful." *(Mr. & Mrs. Robert Maser)* "The warm and friendly owner showed us all around this homey, comfortable inn." *(Elizabeth Church)* "Pleasant grounds with lovely flower beds. The cozy guest rooms were done in a country motif. The table was set prettily for breakfast and all looked clean and well cared for. Super location, close to the beach and excellent shopping. Lovely and quiet, with inviting table and chairs in the garden, protected by ample shrubbery." *(Louise Sims)*

Worth noting: "Watch carefully for address; the city limits signage and we saw their name only on the mailbox."

Open All year.

Rooms 2 suites, 3 doubles—all with private bath and/or shower, desk, air-conditioning, fan.

Facilities Living room with stereo, TV/VCR; library; dining room; sun room; patio, garden. Beach chairs, towels; bicycles. 2 blocks to beach for swimming, shelling, boating, fishing. Tennis, golf nearby.

Location Gulf coast. Olde Naples Historic District. 30 m S of Ft. Meyers, 100 m W of Miami. From I-75 or SW Regional Airport, take I-75 S to Exit 16. Bear right to Goodlette Rd. and turn left. Go 4 m to end and turn right on U.S. Rte. 41 and continue to 5th Ave. South (toward beach), then turn left on 3rd Ave. South. Continue to 11th Ave. South to inn at corner.

Restrictions No smoking. No children under 14.
Credit cards MC, Visa.
Rates B&B, $85–156 suite, $65–138 double.
Extras Local airport/station pickup.

NEW SMYRNA

Reader tip: "JB's Fish Camp, seven miles down the A1A from the 'big curve southward,' on the beach side, is outstanding. Not just another fried fish shack, this is a place where one can get bay scallops, blue crab (fresh and lots of it), plump and tasty oysters, and several kinds of fresh fish, even genuine key lime pie. They have an amusing sign: 'Parents: you are responsible for your children. One child nearly drowned. Unattended children will be used for crab bait.' Guess what? Beautifully behaved children." *(Bill MacGowan)*

Riverview Hotel ✕ ♿
103 Flagler Avenue, 32169

Tel: 904–428–5858
800–945–7416
Fax: 904–423–8927

The porches of the Riverview Hotel provide the perfect vantage point for surveying the yacht traffic on the Intracoastal Waterway. Built in 1885, this bridgetender's house was restored by Christa and Jim Kelsey in 1990, adjacent to their a contemporary restaurant and marina. The decor provides a tropical flavor with wicker furnishings, louvered wooden shutters, and brightly painted Haitian art. The restaurant, Riverview Charlie's, features a wide variety of seafood. Rates include continental breakfast delivered to your door with the morning paper (at your choice of time), and evening turndown service.

"The Kelseys rescued the building and did a great job renovating and decorating it with Victorian charm. Cordial, friendly staff." *(Jack & Bette Cochrane)* "Spotless bathrooms are classy with polished brass fixtures." *(Gregory Hilliard)* "Plants everywhere, inside and out. Good parking at hotel, but arrive early because of the popular restaurant next door." *(Joe Hansen)* "The dolphin watching is incredible. Best gift shop in town." *(Steve & Sandra Ross)* "Solicitous staff, never intrusive. Bed turned down at night with chocolates on the pillow and terry robes laid out. Breakfast was served on time, presented beautifully, hot and fresh." *(Andrea Barbera)* "Every room has an outside covered sitting porch. Big trees and flowering shrubs." *(Bill McGowan)*

Open All year.
Rooms 4 suites, 14 doubles—all with private bath and/or shower, telephone, TV, air-conditioning, fan. 9 with desk, 16 with balcony.
Facilities Restaurant, bar/lounge with spring, summer entertainment; guest kitchen, gift shop. Parking, swimming pool, docks for boats, bicycles. Golf, tennis nearby. 4 blocks to beach.
Location 15 m S of Daytona. 50 m E of Orlando. 5 minutes from downtown. Take I-95 to New Smyrna Beach exit at Rte 44. Go E and follow signs to beaches. After

crossing Intracoastal Waterway, at 1st light go left onto S. Peninsula Ave. At 1st light go left onto Flager Ave. to hotel on left.

Credit cards Amex, DC, Discover, Enroute, MC, Visa.

Rates B&B, $100–150 suite, $65–100 double. Extra person, $10. Senior, AAA discount. 5-night minimum stay special events, some holidays. Alc dinner $7, dinner $29. Overnight dockage, $.65 per foot.

Extras Wheelchair access. Airport, station pickups. Crib, babysitting. French, some Spanish spoken.

OCALA

The center of Florida's thoroughbred racing industry, many streets in Ocala's historic district are lined with gracious Victorian mansions, shaded by moss-draped oak trees. Nearby is the town of Silver Springs, famous for its crystal clear waters. Ocala is located in north central Florida, about 28 miles south of Gainesville, and about 55 miles northwest of Orlando.

Reader tip: "Although nearby Silver Springs is the area's best-known attraction, our favorite was Ocala's Appleton Museum, with wonderful objects from many parts of the world." *(Robert Freidus)*

Seven Sisters Inn &
820 S.E. Fort King Street, 32671

Tel: 904–867–1170
Fax: 904–732–7764

Imagine a century-old Queen Anne Victorian, complete with turret and verandas, surrounded by green lawns and old-fashioned flower beds. Outside of town, thoroughbred horses gallop over rolling hills bordered by white fencing. Quite a vision, you say, but in Florida? In fact, that's just what you'll find at the Seven Sisters Inn, a gracious, three-story home built in 1888, purchased in 1990 by Bonnie Morehardt and Ken Oden. Such period details as handmade quilts, antique wicker chairs, armoires, and brass and iron and four-poster beds, are highlighted by a light and sunny atmosphere. Breakfast is served at 9:00 each morning at tables for two; along with fresh fruit and juice, and home-baked muffins, a different entrée is served each day—perhaps cheese-stuffed French toast with ginger peaches, baked apple walnut oatmeal, or tomato zucchini quiche. Early morning coffee is set out in the hallway, and guests can help themselves to sodas from a refrigerator in the back.

"Our little room had a theme of white and red roses, a sitting area with magazines and books, and reading lights on both sides of the bed. The armoire was hand-painted with roses to match those in the wallpaper. The spotless bath had a claw-foot tub and a shower ring, a pedestal sink and matching wallpaper. Plenty of fluffy white towels and beautifully trimmed white sheets." *(April Burwell)* "Loretta's room has a four-poster bed and an antique armoire with hat boxes decorating the top. The front porch with its wicker chairs and tables was a delightful place to sit and read." *(Stephanie Robertson)* "Bonnie and Ken are delightful and helpful with area information. Housekeeping is impeccable, down to the ironed sheets." *(Sheila & Joe Schmidt)* "Sylvia's Room is spacious and elegant, done in green and cream, with a gorgeous king-sized bed. Blueberry French bread cobbler was a breakfast treat." *(Donna & Robert Jacobson)* "Comfortable beds, lovely fresh decor, absolutely superb breakfast." *(Elizabeth Church)* "Convenient yet secluded parking; great attention to detail; comfort a top priority." *(C.S. Lazier)*

Area for improvement: "We could not open the windows in our room."

Open All year.

Rooms 7 doubles—all with full private bath, desk, air-conditioning, fan. 1 with fireplace, 2 with TV, telephone/data port.

Facilities Breakfast room with fireplace, club room with TV, games; guest refrigerator, porch. ½ acre with lawn, garden.

Location From I-75, take Exit 69 to Rte. 40 E (Silver Springs Blvd.). Go 3 m. After passing town sq., turn right on 8th St. or Wenona St., left on SE Fort King St. to inn on right.

Restrictions Limited soundproofing/privacy in Lottie's Loft. No smoking. Children over 12.

Credit cards Amex, Discover, DC, MC, Visa.

Rates B&B, $105–135 suite, double. 2-night holiday minimum. Weekday corporate, military, senior, "frequent sleeper" rates. Mystery weekends.

Extras Wheelchair access; bathroom specially equipped.

ORANGE PARK

The Club Continental ¢ 🏃 ✕ 🎣
2143 Astor Street, P.O. Box 7059, 32073

Tel: 904–264–6070
800–877–6070
Fax: 904–264–4044

A beautiful waterfront location, a choice of either contemporary or historic accommodations, fine food, good sports facilities, reasonable prices, a welcome to both kids and pets—who says you can't have your cake and eat it too? Built in 1923 as the private winter estate of Caleb Johnson, founder of the Palmolive Soap company, the property was converted from a private residence to country club in 1964, and guest rooms were soon added. Now owned and run by the brother/sister team of Caleb and Karrie Massie, Johnson's great-grandchildren, the inn has expanded to include the River Suites, completed in 1993. Rooms are also available in the Inn at Winterbourne, an 1870 Victorian frame building on the Club's grounds, while the dining and sitting rooms are in the Spanish-style clubhouse building. Bordering the St. John's River, the complex also includes the Riverhouse Pub, an antebellum waterfront cottage, with decks overlooking the water. Guests at the inn enjoy all the club's facilities.

"Old-style Southern charm with modern convenience. Beautifully manicured grounds. Staff always willing to please. Elegant dining." *(Patricia Johnson)* "Have enjoyed both the Tower Apartment at Winterbourne and the River Suite accommodations. Wonderful setting with superb views of the wide St. John's River, and 200-year-old oak trees draped with Spanish moss. Breakfast includes cereal, fruit, Danish, juice, and coffee; wonderful dinners are served at their private dining club. The River Suites combine the comfort and convenience of the new with the charm and beauty of the old." *(Wayne Disch)* "Make reservations ahead for the Sunday brunch." *(LC)*

Open All year. Restaurant closed Sun. night, Mon.
Rooms 7 suites, 15 doubles—all with full private bath, telephone, TV, desk, air-conditioning. 8 with whirlpool tub, 18 with refrigerator, microwave, balcony. 2 with fireplace. 7 rooms in 1870 mansion; 15 in River Suites.
Facilities Restaurant, Riverhouse pub with weekend entertainment. Gardens, 3 swimming pools, 7 tennis courts (2 lighted), lawn games, marina, fishing.
Location 10 m S of Jacksonville. From I-10 or I-95, take I-295 to Hwy. 17. Go S on 17 to Kingsley Ave. & go left, then right on Astor St. to inn on left.
Restrictions Some nonsmoking rooms.
Credit cards Amex, MC, Visa.
Rates B&B, $115–120 suite, $56 double. Extra person, $10. Alc lunch, $7–10; alc dinner, $10–20.
Extras Wheelchair access; 1 bathroom specially equipped. Pets with approval. Cribs. Boat dockage with notice.

ORLANDO

Reader tip: "For a fun evening, visit Church Street, a historic railroad depot converted into an entertainment center, with a wild-west saloon and 'opera house,' a ballroom and dessert cafe, a seafood bar, and a wine cellar."

For additional area entries, see **Lake Wales, Maitland, Minneola,** and **Winter Park.**

Courtyard at Lake Lucerne ¢ 🛉 ♿
211 North Lucerne Circle East, 32801

Tel: 407–648–5188
800–444–5289
Fax: 407–246–1368

You may be surprised to find out that there is more to Orlando than theme parks and chain hotels, as you will learn at the Courtyard at Lake Lucerne. While this group of three buildings shares a common courtyard, the architecture and decor of each is totally distinct. The 1885 Norment-Parry Inn is Orlando's oldest house, and is furnished with American and English antiques, accented with floral wallcoverings and fabrics. The Wellborn, one of the finest surviving Art Deco buildings in town, has been furnished with the eclectic styles popular in the Twenties, including chairs carved in the shape of elephants, Erté posters, bronze sconces, and glass block walls. The I.W. Phillips House, a 1916 antebellum-style manor house, has wooden verandas wrapping around three sides and a Tiffany stained glass window. Guest rooms have a Belle Epoque atmosphere with ornately carved furniture, marble-topped tables, and brocade fabrics. Rates include a breakfast buffet, plus a welcoming bottle of wine.

"Owner Charles Meiner has done an outstanding job, bringing these renovated buildings together around a lush courtyard. The Wellborn suite has a black and white kitchen and bathroom. The bedroom was done in pastel pink and aqua, with a brass bed, and both Art Deco and contemporary light fixtures. Breakfast, served buffet-style in the ballroom of the Phillips House, was abundant—fresh strawberries, orange juice, fruit compote, English muffins, blueberry muffins, bagels and cream cheese, and a selection of cold cereals. Sitting on the veranda, by the gently splashing fountain, smelling the fragrances of the courtyard, it's hard to believe you are right in downtown Orlando." *(NB)* "Lovely accommodations, friendly, helpful staff; early morning breakfast before our flight was a thoughtful touch." *(CBC)* Comments welcome.

Open All year.
Rooms 2 suites with double tubs, 1 suite with Jacuzzi, steam shower in I.W. Phillips House; 11 suites with kitchens, 1 with Jacuzzi, steam shower in Wellborn; 6 doubles with private bath and/or shower in Norment-Parry. All with telephone, TV, air-conditioning
Facilities Reception hall with piano, kitchen. Verandas, garden with fountain. Parlor with fireplace in Norment-Parry Inn. Health club, tennis, golf nearby.
Location 20 min. from Walt Disney World, 20 min. from Orlando airport. From I-4 E, exit at Anderson St. and go E on Anderson to Delaney & turn right. Go 1 block & turn right on N. Lucerne Circle E., to inn on right. From I-4 W, exit at Gore St. and go E. Turn left on Delaney, go 2 blocks to N. Lucerne Circle E. to inn on right.
Restrictions No smoking in Norment-Parry Inn.
Credit cards Amex, MC, Visa.
Rates B&B, $85–150 suite, $65–85 double. Extra person, $10. AARP, AAA discount.
Extras Wheelchair access to I.W. Phillips House. Crib, babysitting.

Perri House ¢ 🏃
10417 State Road 535, 32836

Tel: 407–876–4830
800–780–4830
Fax: 407–876–0241

Designed as a B&B, Perri House was built by Angi and Nick Perretti and their family in 1990; this one-story, pale brick building is located literally at the back door to Disney World, yet the surrounding area is rural. The Perretis bring experience in the restaurant, nightclub, and catering business to their latest enterprise, and have skillfully planned their home to provide space and privacy for their guests (all rooms have queen- or king-sized beds and outside entrances). The buffet breakfast, served from 7–10 A.M., includes fresh fruit, giant muffins, pastries, toast, and cold cereal. We heard from a number of the Perretti's guests; all unanimously praised the Perretti's exceptional hospitality, and the combined comfort and attractiveness of their B&B.

"Nick Perretti built the house more or less by himself, and is constantly working to improve it." *(Sid & Ruth Geller)* "Along with their two daughters, Nick and Angie joined us for a delightful breakfast; they provided invaluable advice about the area, and helped us plan our day at Epcot. Our spacious guest room was furnished with a four-poster oak bed and dresser, contrasting with the dark traditional fabric of the bedspread and curtains. Angie designed and made most of the window treatments and accessories." *(Diane & Keith Colville)* "The sitting area has a refrigerator stocked with complimentary sodas and beer. After fighting crowds all day, we really enjoyed relaxing at the Perri House."*(Lynne Derry)*

"Minutes from Epcot, Disney, and MGM, yet totally peaceful. Each morning, I saw rabbits, Great Blue Herons, and egrets." *(Sharon Bias)* "Lots of fun to pin my home city on the Perretti's giant wall map and read the guests' names on the welcome board." *(Ann Christoffersen)* "Nick and Agni provided us with an ice chest, quilt, and beach towels for a beach trip.

They were equally accommodating to families with young children as to a retired Japanese businessman." *(Nancy Koudelka)* "You can eat at the long table in the breakfast room, or take a tray to the patio or your room. Our room had good mattresses and towels, with a quiet ceiling fan; handy soap/lotion/shampoo dispenser in the bathtub. Angi gives a thorough introduction to all aspects of the inn." *(NB)*

From the Nothing's Perfect Department: "Nightlights for the bathroom."

Open All year.

Rooms 6 doubles—all with full private bath, telephone, radio, TV, desk, air-conditioning, fan.

Facilities Living room with stereo, honor bar; breakfast room, laundry, guest refrigerator, porch, deck. 20 acres with heated swimming pool, hot tub, barbecue, gazebo, bird sanctuary. Cypress Equestrian center adjacent for riding. Golf nearby.

Location 15 m W of downtown. From I-4, take Exit 27-Lake Buena Vista/Disney Village, turn right. Go to 2nd traffic light (Texaco Station), turn left. Go 3.4 m & look for Perretti bird house on right. Approx. 5 min. to Disney World via WDW Village.

Restrictions No smoking.

Credit cards Amex, Discover, MC, Optima, Visa.

Rates B&B, $65–85 double, $50–60 single. Extra adult, $10; child, $5. 10% weekly discount. 2-3 night holiday minimum.

Extras Cribs, babysitting with advance notice. Airport/station pickups, $35–40

PALM BEACH

For additional area entries, see listings under **West Palm Beach. Information please:** Twenty miles south of Palm Beach is the **Seagate Hotel & Beach Club** (400 South Ocean Boulevard, Delray 33483; 407–276–2421 or 800–233–3581), with a 400-foot white sand beach, swimming pool, a good restaurant, and 60 comfortable, attractive suites; double rates range from $100–260. "The Seagate is located in a residential area along the 'A1A,' a 25-mph road that runs between the Intracoastal Waterway and the ocean. Our suite overlooked the hotel courtyard and swimming pool, but was well screened by lush tropical foliage. It was decorated in soft peach tones accented with flowered chintz. The fully equipped kitchen had coffee and tea supplies replenished daily; maid service was good. The full bathroom, with big wall mirrors, had a separate dressing room, plus thick towels and toiletries. The individual thermostat and ceiling fans kept the rooms fresh. The staff was friendly and helpful, but it's the quiet location and the gorgeous beach that would bring us back." *(Dick Horn)*

Plaza Inn ¢ 🏃
215 Brazilian Avenue, 33480

Tel: 407–832–8666
800–BED–AND–B
Fax: 407–835–8776

The pale pink, Art Deco-style Plaza Inn, built in 1940, is situated on a palm tree-lined, residential street, close to the beach and the shops and restaurants of famous Worth Avenue. Wicker, mahogany, pine, brass, or oak furnishings are complemented by green and burgundy draperies, linens, and wallpaper.

"Wonderfully central location, yet high hedges and ample landscaping make the pool area lush and private. The outside lighting accents flowers, trees, and the entire building beautifully. The renovation was obviously done with great care to retain original architectural details." *(John Leach)* "Bathrooms contain straw baskets of soaps and shampoos, and plenty of big towels. The dining room is snug and appealing with ruffled print curtains and flowered china. English-style breakfasts of juice, fruit, cereal, eggs, meat, and fresh muffins are served." *(Elaine Williams)* "This B&B hotel is comfortable, spotless, unpretentious, and homey. The manager was cordial, friendly and helpful, welcoming me immediately. The next morning the same gentleman was touring the sunny breakfast room, making sure we all had the directions we needed for our day's travel, enough orange juice to drink, and that our breakfasts were satisfactory." *(Natalie Foster)* Reports welcome.

Open All year.
Rooms 1 suite, 47 doubles—all with full private bath, telephone, radio, TV, air-conditioning, ceiling fans, refrigerator. Some with desk.
Facilities Lobby, breakfast room, piano bar with entertainment, heated swimming pool, hot tub. Room service. 1 block from public beach. Tennis, golf, fishing, boating nearby.
Location E FL. 60 m N of Miami, 4 blocks from Worth Ave.
Credit cards Amex, MC, Visa.
Rates B&B, $150–225 suite, $75–195 double, $60–140 single. Extra adult, $15; child under 12, $7. $1 per person daily breakfast gratuity. Weekly rates.
Extras Airport/station pickup, $10. Small pets permitted. Crib; babysitting arranged. Spanish spoken.

PENSACOLA

Pensacola has one-upped St. Augustine by having flown five flags during its history: French, Spanish, British, American, and Confederate. Today, principal sights here include the Naval Air Station and aviation museum, and the ruins of a seventeenth-century Spanish fort. Other attractions include the museums and restored houses of the historic district and the gorgeous beaches of the Gulf Islands National Seashore.

Reader tips: "Jamie's French Restaurant (904–432–5047) is located in an 1860s Victorian home, elegantly furnished with walnut sideboards, mirrors, and lace curtains. The seafood and desserts were wonderful. It's located on Zaragossa Street, in the appealing Seville District, with an interesting mix of shops and homes, and reservations are advisable." *(HB)* "Try Maguire's Restaurant for good steaks and hamburgers in an Irish family-style setting. Their gimmick is over $90,000 in one-dollar bills hanging from the ceiling! Go early as it gets crowded early." *(Debbie Bergstrom)*

New World Inn 🏃 ✕ ♿. *Tel:* 904–432–4111
600 South Palafox Street, 32501

The New World Inn reflects Pensacola's international history in its decor, utilizing reproductions of Louis XV, Chippendale, and Queen Anne in its individually decorated guest rooms. Handsome woodwork highlights the lobby area and stairs to the second floor, giving the inn an older, gracious feeling. Photographs of early Pensacola highlight one of the inn's dining rooms, while the other has beautiful windows overlooking the courtyard; the bar is English in style. Rates include a continental breakfast; the cuisine at lunch and dinner is continental, emphasizing seafood.

"Large, clean, comfortable rooms. Manager and front desk staff unfailingly helpful, considerate, and polite." *(J.R. Norcliffe)* "The inn is well located for exploring the downtown area with its recycled buildings, now full of shops, art galleries, and restaurants. Palafox Street is full of great stores for buying and browsing and interesting old architecture." *(HB, also Debbie Bergstrom)*

Open All year. Restaurant closed Sun.
Rooms 2 suites, 14 doubles—all with full private bath, telephone, radio, TV, air-conditioning, fan. Most with desk.
Facilities Restaurant, bar/lounge, lobby. Courtyard, fountain, gardens. Bicycles. Swimming, tennis, charter fishing nearby.
Location W FL panhandle, near Alabama border. Follow Rte. 29 to end; becomes Palafox St. Inn in downtown historic harbor area, adjacent to New World Convention Hall.
Credit cards Amex, CB, DC, Discover, MC, Visa.
Rates Room only, $100–125 suite, $75–80 double, $65–70 single. Extra person, $10. Weekend, weekly, corporate rates. Alc breakfast $6; lunch, $10; dinner, $45.
Extras Airport/station pickups. Wheelchair access. Crib, babysitting. French, Spanish spoken.

ST. AUGUSTINE

St. Augustine, founded in 1565, is the oldest city in North America. With a few interruptions, it was under Spanish rule until 1821; many of its restored Spanish colonial homes were built in the 1700s. The city's architecture also has a strong Victorian component, dating back to the 1880s, when Henry Flagler did much to popularize St. Augustine as a fashionable resort. St. Augustine is on the northeast Florida coast, 30 miles north of Daytona and south of Jacksonville, and 100 miles northeast of Orlando. Beautiful coastal beaches are a five-mile drive away, and opportunities for golf and tennis are ample.

Reader tip: "Parking in St. Augustine is a horror. Ask your innkeeper for specific advice and information." And: "Many inns include free passes to the Oldest House in their rates."

Also recommended: Built in 1885, the **Carriage Way B&B** (70 Cuna Street, 32084; 904–829–2467) is owned by Bill and Diane Johnson. The nine guest rooms have private baths and rent for $70–110, and the decor includes period antiques. Breakfast includes homemade breads, fresh fruit, and a hot entrée; bicycles are available for touring. "Convenient location two blocks from St. George Street; we parked in the inn's lot and never touched it until departure. The Johnsons offered warm hospitality, excellent restaurant advice." *(Karla Larson)*

For an additional area entry, see **Orange Park**, 40 miles north.

Cedar House Inn
79 Cedar Street, 32084

Tel: 904–829–0079
800–CEDAR–INN
Fax: 904–825–0916

Built in 1893, Cedar House was restored as an inn a century later by Nina and Russ Thomas. The inn has ten-foot-high ceilings and polished heart-of-pine floors, and is furnished with queen-size beds, period antiques, and reproductions. Breakfast is served at guests' convenience at individual tables, and includes juice, home-baked muffins or coffee cake, fresh fruit salad, and a hot entrée.

"Victorian B&B in the heart of St. Augustine. We were greeted with wine and chocolates, and offered a tour of the inn. Nina and Russ are very accommodating. Their lovely home is spotless and quiet. Upon returning from dinner, we found dessert waiting for us. Breakfast consisted of coffee, juice, muffins, fruit, and delicious baked French toast with pecans. A thoughtful extra was the coffee and tea supplies in our room." *(Jan Linden)* "Excellent recommendations for dining and sightseeing." *(FS)*

Open All year.
Rooms 1 suite, 4 doubles—all with full private bath, radio, clock, TV, air-conditioning, fan, balcony. 1 with whirlpool tub, 3 with fireplace.
Facilities Dining room, parlor with fireplace, player piano, Victrola, books; sitting room with TV/VCR, games, stereo. Front courtyard, off-street parking, hot tub. Walk to Intracoastal Waterway, marina.
Location Center of historic district. From I-95 S, take SR 16 (Exit 95) E to US 1 (Ponce de Leon). Turn right & go to 2nd light. Turn left on King St. & go through 2 lights. Turn right on Granada St. & go 1 block to Cedar. Turn right to inn on left. From I-95 N, take SR 207 (Exit 94) E to US 1 (Ponce de Leon). Turn right on King St. & follow directions above.
Restrictions No smoking. Children over 10.
Credit cards Discover, MC, Visa.
Rates B&B, $100–150 suite, $60–100 double. Extra person, $10. Senior, AAA, midweek discount. Prix fixe dinner, $25 per couple (advance notice).
Extras Bus station pickup.

Kenwood Inn ¢
38 Marine Street, 32084

Tel: 904–824–2116
Fax: 904–824–7712

This historic neighborhood was already old when the Kenwood was built between 1865 and 1885; just a few blocks away is the Oldest House, built in the early 1700s. This former boarding house was renovated in 1984; Mark, Kerriane, and Caitlin Constant became its owners in 1988. Rooms are decorated in a wide variety of New England styles, from Shaker to country Victorian, but all are light and airy, with soft floral fabrics.

"The owners make you feel like a welcomed family friend. The self-service breakfast includes fresh orange juice, freshly baked goods, and coffee. The common areas are comfortable, homey, and inviting." *(Ted & Laura Phelps)* "The owners invited us to look at the rooms before choosing our favorite. Delicious lemon-flavored poppy seed cake and date-nut bread." *(Barbara Charlton)* "Mark Constant was most helpful in recommending restaurants and sights." *(Glenn & Lynette Roehrig)* "Perfect for our needs: romantic, conveniently located, and reasonable." *(Edward & Kathryn Brett)*

Open All year. Restaurant closed Christmas.
Rooms 4 suites, 10 doubles—all with private bath and/or shower, clock-radio, air-conditioning, fan; some with desk, TV, fireplace, balcony.
Facilities Sunroom with TV, stereo, books, living room with fireplace, dining room with fireplace, TV/game room. Courtyard, swimming pool.
Location St. Johns County. Historic district. 3 blocks S of Bridge of Lions.
Restrictions No smoking. No children under 9. Some street noise in two rooms. On-street parking only; very limited due to narrow streets. Guests leave bags at inn, park 1 block away.
Credit cards Discover, MC, Visa.
Rates B&B, $95–125 suite, $65–95 double, $45–65 single. Extra person, $10. 2-3 night weekend, holiday minimum. 10% senior, AAA discount Sun.–Thurs.

Old City House Inn ✕ &

115 Cordova Street, 32084

Tel: 904–826–0113
Fax: 904–829–3798

We may think of recycling as a '90s concept, but when it comes to architecture, it's old hat. Built in 1873 as a stable, the Old City House Inn has been used as a boarding house, hat shop, antique store, apartments, and an office building. In 1990, Bob and Alice Compton renovated this tile-roofed, Spanish-style building as an inn. Breakfast varies daily, but might consist of frittata, seafood and Brie omelets, or ham and mushroom crepes. The dinner menu changes often, but might include a grilled pork tenderloin, maple-glazed chicken, or seafood strudel.

"Bob and Alice Compton are gracious hosts who happily advise on St. Augustine's charms. The guest rooms are eclectically furnished with a pleasing combination of antiques, reproductions, and memorabilia; ours had a comfortable queen-size bed and a lovely stained glass window crafted by Alice Compton. Bathroom amenities include big soft towels, English soap and complimentary toiletries. Wonderful, filling breakfasts with fresh orange juice. The inn is next to a public parking lot; the Comptons keep the meters fed. You can walk everywhere, so you won't need the car. In the restaurant downstairs, the atmosphere is pleasant, with low beams and tiled tables; the sesame muffins are especially tasty." *(Barbara DeVries)* "Umbrella tables and rocking chairs on the upstairs deck create a great place to relax and meet other guests. Bob and Alice serve wine and cheese here in the early evening." *(Adele & Bob Schnell)* "Spotless, well-lit room, supplied with reading material and candy. Polite, courteous staff. " *(Robert & Laura Bellospirito)*

Open All year. Restaurant closed Mon.
Rooms 5 doubles—all with private bath and/or shower, clock, TV, air-conditioning, fan, outside entrance. 4 with balcony.
Facilities Restaurant with fireplace, bar/lounge, upstairs deck, courtyard. Bicycles. Adjacent to public parking lot.
Location Historic district. From U.S. Rte. 1, go right on King St. At St. George St. go right. Parking on right next to inn. Adjacent to Flagler College, across from Lightner Museum.
Restrictions No smoking.
Credit cards Amex, DC, MC, Visa.
Rates B&B, $50–105 double. Extra person, $10. 2-3 night weekend/holiday minimum. Alc lunch, $5–10; alc dinner, $25.
Extras Restaurant wheelchair accessible. Airport, station pickup, $25–40. Spanish spoken.

St. Francis Inn ¢   *Tel: 904–824–6068*
279 St. George Street, 32084

The St. Francis Inn was built in 1791 of *coquina*, a limestone formed of broken shells and coral cemented together. The inn was used as a private residence until 1845, when it became a boardinghouse; a guide to St. Augustine published in 1869 describes it as one of the city's best.

"You really feel the inn's history—the floors creak, the balconies slope." *(Stephanie Robertson)* "You can eat breakfast in the sitting room, or pick up a tray to take to your room." *(June Harrah)* "Decorated throughout with an eclectic assortment of antiques, wicker, and Persian rugs, old and new books." *(Janet Lay)* "Our third-floor apartment had a sitting room, kitchen, and king-sized bed." *(Alison Young)* "One evening we smelled popcorn and found a big bowl awaiting us downstairs." *(Lynn Burdeshaw)* "The innkeepers explained local folklore, and made restaurant and sightseeing suggestions." *(Christine Woolard)* "Innkeepers Stanley and Regina Reynolds are wonderful people, congenial and caring." *(Virginia DeConto)*

"Conveniently located, this historic inn has lots of crooked stairways, nooks, and crannies. The lovely patio is surrounded by wrought iron and tropical plantings, with a small hidden swimming pool." *(Evelyn Zak)* "Breakfast includes fresh fruit and juice, cereal, sweet rolls, coffee and tea; coffee is always available. Though within walking distance of major sights, the inn sits on a quiet one-way street." *(Pamela Allhands)*

Minor niggles: "A mirror in our room would be helpful." And: "Our room had a minuscule bathroom."

Open All year.
Rooms 6 suites, 7 doubles, 1 2-bedroom cottage—all with private bath and/or shower, TV, air-conditioning; some with desk, fireplace, kitchenette. Separate 2-bedroom cottage with kitchen, fireplace, sleeps 4.
Facilities Living/family room with TV, piano, fireplace, books; breakfast room with fireplace; balcony. Bicycles. Patio, courtyard, swimming pool. Ocean swimming and fishing nearby. On-site parking.
Location Historic district; 3 blocks from restored town.
Restrictions No smoking in guest rooms.
Credit cards MC, Visa.
Rates B&B, $140 cottage (for 4), $65–97 suite, $52–75 double. Extra person, $10. Weekly, monthly rates available.
Extras Crib.

ST. GEORGE ISLAND

St. George Inn ¢ ✕   *Tel: 904–927–2903*
Franklin Boulevard & Pine Street, HCR Box 222, 32328–9706

It took a lot of determination for Barbara Vail to construct the St. George Inn; twice the causeway was washed away by hurricanes, and boats were needed to haul building materials. Barbara feels it was worth the effort to be able live on an island with pristine beaches, a small population, and spectacular sunsets. The inn sits right in the middle of this long, narrow barrier island, and is just 660 feet from the Gulf of Mexico in one direction and 650 feet from Apalachicola Bay in the other. The guest rooms have French doors opening to a wraparound porch and water views of the bay or gulf, and all have one or two queen-sized beds. The restaurant has a simple dinner menu, with French onion soup as an appetizer and entrées of broiled chicken, ribeye steak, and fresh local seafood.

"While the building is quite new, you feel as if you've stepped back in time. The hotel's simple Shaker-style beauty is matched by Barbara's warmth and hospitality." *(Susan Santiago)* "Immaculate rooms; welcoming lounge; meals are delicious homestyle repasts." *(Susan Baldino)* "Relax with a book on the upstairs wraparound porch. At the state park, walk over the dunes to get a good look at the intriguing vegetation on the Apalachicola Bay side. Excellent swimming." *(Bill MacGowan)* "I unwound in my room with the shades up, watching the sunset. For dinner, I had tasty stuffed grouper served by a cheerful young waitress." *(Bill Novak)*

From the Nothing's Perfect department: "I was in my room when one woman on the porch actually cupped her hands to the glass to look inside my room."

Open All year.
Rooms 8 doubles—all with full private bath, TV, air-conditioning, fan, balcony.
Facilities Dining room with fireplace, lounge with TV, piano, books; wraparound porch.
Location 75 m SW of Tallahassee, 60 m E of Panama City, 15 m SE of Apalachicola.
Restrictions Children over 12 preferred.
Credit cards Discover, MC, Visa.
Rates Room only, $60–65 double. Extra person, $10. 2-night weekend minimum June–Aug. Alc dinner, $17.
Extras Local airport pickup, $10.

ST. PETERSBURG

St. Petersburg is located on the Gulf of Mexico, just across the bay from the city of Tampa, to which it is linked by a series of bridges and causeways. A string of sandy islands (actually keys), separated from the mainland by the Intracoastal Waterway, it offers miles of sparkling beaches and an unlimited supply of condominiums, motels, shops, and restaurants. The separate communities have names like Treasure Island, Madeira Beach, and Pass-A-Grille, and local residents refer to these places just like a New Yorker does in referring to the Upper East Side or the Bronx.

Two of the entries below are in tiny Pass-A-Grille, and on the southernmost of St. Petersburg's islands. Building restrictions have limited development, so there are only a couple of buildings that rise more than two stories, and the public beach is lined with parking spaces, not condos. The town, now a National Historic District, is one of Florida's oldest settlements. Bicycling is a popular pastime, along with fishing in Boca Ciega Bay; a handful of restaurants offer a variety of seafood entrées in a casual atmosphere.

Also recommended: About 10 miles north of St. Petersburg is the

365-room **Belleview Mido Resort Hotel** (25 Belleview Boulevard, P.O. Box 2317, Clearwater 34617; 813–442–6171 or 800–237–8947), built in 1897 and said to be the largest occupied wooden structure in the world. Recently restored at a cost of millions, the hotel overlooks the intracoastal waterway, and offers a full range of activities: tennis, golf, swimming, and a health spa. "The spacious guest rooms are newly refurbished, as are the common areas. Enjoyable Sunday brunch." *(Pat Borysiewicz)*

Information please: In a quiet residential neighborhood overlooking Old Tampa Bay is the **Bayboro House B&B** (1719 Beach Drive S.E., 33701; 813–823–4955). This Queen Anne home is decorated with beautiful Victorian antiques, and the four guest rooms have private baths and color TV. The $75–85 double rates include a continental breakfast. "Great attention to detail is seen everywhere, from the collection of antique teddy bears in the entry to the dolls and carriage on the landing. Our lovely room had an unobstructed view of Old Tampa Bay. The entire inn is spotless and has a wonderful veranda facing the bay with lovely wicker chairs and lounges."

The **Five Oaks Inn** (1102 Riverside Drive, Palmetto, 34221; 813–723–1236 or 800–658–4167), is located halfway between St. Pete and Sarasota. Framed by massive oaks and magnolias, and overlooking the Manatee River, rates include a welcoming drink and a hearty Southern breakfast. The dark oak woodwork throughout the house is complemented by the period decor; guests especially enjoy relaxing on the wicker rockers of the airy sunporch. B&B rates for the three doubles—all with private bath—are $55–85; the suite costs $90–110.

The Inn on the Beach ¢ ♦ ⚹   *Tel: 813–360–8844*
1401 Gulf Way, Pass-A-Grille, St. Petersburg Beach 33706

Owner Ron Holehouse began the renovation of this 1920s house in 1989, and added ceramic tile floors, private baths, oak kitchen cabinets, and 1,000 square feet of decks. Each unit is individually decorated with brass, wicker, and antique accents. A continental breakfast is offered in the courtyard on weekends. "A cozy, pleasant place to stay; friendly staff. Our room had a king-sized brass bed and glass wall tiles; another room had a huge balcony overlooking the Gulf." *(Karen Fixler)* "Clean, quiet, relaxing, with comfortable furnishings; just across the street from the beach, with restaurants close by. Get a room on the Gulf side or one with a balcony; the buildings form a pleasant courtyard, just right for lounging in the winter sun." *(NB)*

Open All year.

Rooms 12 efficiency apartments—all with private bath, telephone, TV, desk, air-conditioning, fan, refrigerator. Some with radio, fireplace, balcony.

Facilities Center courtyard with deck, gas grill; off-street parking. Bicycles, beach chairs, fishing poles, gas grills. Tennis, beach, boat rentals nearby.

Location Pass-A-Grille. 10 m to downtown St. Petersburg, 30 m to Tampa. From I-275 S, take Exit 4 (Bay Way). Go W on Bay Way across toll bridge to Gulf Blvd. Left on Gulf to 14th Ave. (about 20 blocks). Go right at 14th Ave. to inn on right.

Credit cards None accepted.

Rates Room only, $40–150. Weekly rates. Extra person, $10.

Extras Wheelchair access. Airport pickup, $10. Crib.

Island's End Resort   *Tel:* 813–360–5023
1 Pass-A-Grille Way, St. Petersburg Beach 33706   *Fax:* 813–367–7890

Since they purchased the Island's End in 1987, Jone and Millard Gamble have created a cozy retreat from the five buildings that form the inn. Weathered cedar siding and palm-shaded decks complement expansive views of the Gulf of Mexico. The cottages have wood-panelled interiors and comfortable, contemporary furniture. Three times a week, breakfast of freshly squeezed juice, croissants, cakes and coffee are served in the gazebo; on clear nights, you can see spectacular sunsets across the Gulf.

"Plants grow abundantly around the inn. While the island's tallest building (only four floors) lies just to the north, you feel like you've been transported to your own private island." *(NB)* "Peaceful, relaxing, yet close to interesting places for sightseeing; helpful owners and staff. We have morning coffee with friends and neighbors, then walk the seven miles of beaches, and finish up by trying our luck on the fishing dock." *(Chet & Jan Schanhofer)*

Open All year.
Rooms 6 cottages—all with private bath, telephone, TV/VCR, kitchen. 1 3-bedroom house with heated swimming pool, private bath, telephone, TV, air-conditioning, heat, kitchen with microwave.
Facilities Deck, gazebo, courtyard, laundry room. Lighted fishing pier; swimming pool.
Location S tip of Pass-A-Grille. 10 m to downtown St. Petersburg, 30 m to Tampa. From I-275 S, exit on Rte. 652. Go W on Rte. 652, crossing Pinellas Bayway (toll causeway) to Gulf Blvd. and turn left. Go S on Gulf Blvd. to the end (1st Ave.) and turn right. Inn immediately on left.
Credit cards MC, Visa.
Rates Room only, $61–160 double. Extra person, $8. 4-night holiday minimum.
Extras Crib, babysitting. Lithuanian, Latvian, Russian spoken.

Mansion House ¢   *Tel:* 813–821–9391
105 Fifth Avenue Northeast, 33701   *Fax:* 813–821–9391

Alan and Suzanne Lucas exchanged the mountain mists of Wales for Florida sunshine in 1991, when they decided to open a B&B. They found a rundown turn-of-the-century home in a good location, one block from the water, close to the Sunken Gardens, Salvador Dali Museum, and Museum of Fine Arts. After ten months of renovation, the result is a soft and inviting color scheme of peach and sea foam, "giving an air of Florida with a hint of England mixed in," reports Suzanne. Guest rooms are named for Welsh castles (mercifully pronounceable ones like Raglen and Caephilly). Contemporary furnishings are offset by gleaming wood floors and the soft floral patterns of the wallpaper and comforters. Rates include an English breakfast of cereal, juice, sausage, eggs, bacon, fried tomatoes, home fries, Welsh cake, toast, preserves, coffee and tea. "Alan and Suzanne are excellent and informative hosts. Everything from service to cleanliness is first rate." *(C.J. Whyte)* Comments appreciated.

107

Open All year.
Rooms 6 doubles—all with private shower bath, clock, air-conditioning, fan. 1 room in carriage house (above garage).
Facilities Dining room, living room, sunporch with books, TV; guest refrigerator, screened porch. Off-street parking. Close to fishing pier, swimming pool, beach.
Location 5 min. walk to downtown. 1 block to water, 4 blocks N of pier. From I-275 S, take Exit 10, I-375 E to Suncoast Dome. Take Exit 2 to 4th St. N. Go straight through 4 set of lights. Turn left at 5th light; inn is on right corner at next light.
Restrictions Smoking on porch only.
Credit cards MC, Visa.
Rates B&B, $65–70 double. 10% AAA discount. Weekly rate.
Extras Crib.

SANIBEL ISLAND

Information please: Of interest is the **Song of the Sea** (863 East Gulf Drive, Sanibel Island 33957; 813–472–2220 or 800–231–1045), a 30-room European-style seaside inn, made up of a cluster of pink buildings framed by tropical foliage, right on the beach. Each unit has a kitchen, dining area, bathroom, screened porch, ceiling fan, air-conditioning, TV, VCR, and telephone; the decor includes French country furniture, Mediterranean tile floors, and down-filled comforters. The $135–300 rates include wine and flowers, free bicycles, swimming pool and hot tub, laundry facilities, and a breakfast of pastries, bagels, coffee, tea, and juice; golf and tennis privileges are offered at a nearby club. "Excellent breakfast, convenient location, free videos, friendly innkeepers." *(Robert Mandell & Deborah Brown)*

Another possibility is the **Island Inn** (3111 West Gulf Drive, P.O. Box 659, 33957; 813–472–1561 or 800–851–5088) dating back to 1895. Encompassing eight buildings, the 56 guest rooms rent for about $189 each in season—all with water views and most with screened porches—including breakfast, dinner, and service for two. Facilities include the restaurant, two tennis courts, a swimming pool, and 500 feet of beach frontage. Menus are traditional: eggs, pancakes, waffles, or French toast for breakfast; dinner entrées of broiled grouper, prime rib, or stuffed pork chops.

SANTA ROSA BEACH

Information please: The **Sunbright Manor** (606 Live Oak, DeFuniak Springs 32433; 904–892–0656) is located 25 miles north of Santa Rosa. "After touring the historic district, we enjoyed cool drinks on the front porch of this 1886 Queen Anne Victorian house. In addition to the inn's tower, a striking architectural feature is its extensive porches, with some 1,600 spindles and 33 columns. Both our room and bath were spacious. Our breakfast of cheese and egg soufflé, fresh fruit, and homemade muffins was delicious." *(HB)* The manor has three guest rooms, two with private baths, and the reasonable $75 B&B double rate includes early morning coffee, full breakfast, and evening tea.

For an additional area entry, see **Destin**.

A Highlands House ¢ ♔   *Tel:* 904–267–0110
10 Bullard Road, P.O. Box 1189, 32459

Only in Florida would an elevation 70 feet above sea level be considered a "highland," but only in western Florida would you find miles of beaches with sugar-soft white sand lapped by the bright blue-green waters of the Gulf of Mexico. Named for the area's 70-foot-high sand dunes, A Highlands House was designed and built as a B&B in 1991 by Joan and Ray Robins, in a re-creation of the antebellum raised cottage style. Guest rooms have reproduction four-poster rice beds and wingback chairs, with matching floral drapes and bedspreads; they open onto the wide front porch, where you can catch cooling breezes off the Gulf, along with glimpses of the water, about 200 feet away, via a sandy path. Breakfast is served family style at 8:30 A.M., and menus vary daily, with an especially generous meal on Sunday mornings, when you can feast on juice, fresh fruit, chocolate chunk coffee cake, scrambled eggs, home fries with peppers and onions, grilled sausage, and biscuits. On a second day, you might be served cinnamon coffee cake and batter-dipped French toast with sour cream and strawberries.

"The Gulf between Destin and Panama City is relatively underdeveloped. This handsomely designed inn has a quiet location. Comfortable, modestly-sized bedrooms and bathrooms are balanced with spacious, appealing common areas. The Robinses are friendly, casual, interesting people. Excellent location, a half-block from the beach, near the fabulous Lake Place restaurant." *(Mr. & Mrs. Robert Cargill)* "Joan went out of her way to accommodate our young child." *(Jim & Susan Previtera)*

Open All year.
Rooms 1 suite, 4 doubles—all with full private bath, clock, air-conditioning, ceiling fan, balcony, private entrance. 1 with TV, refrigerator. 1 room in carriage house.
Facilities Dining room, living room with fireplace, TV, stereo; porch. Small garden, off-street parking for five cars. 300 ft. to Santa Rosa beach. Golf nearby.
Location W FL Panhandle. 70 m E of Pensacola, approx. 15 m E of Destin. Beach Highland Area, Dune Allen Beach. 4 m from town. From I-10, take Rte. 331 S from DeFuniak Springs to Rte. 98. Go right (W) on 98, then left (S) on Rte. 83 to Rte. 30A (beach road). Go right (W) to inn.
Restrictions No smoking.
Credit cards None accepted.
Rates B&B, $80–150 suite, $55–90 double. Extra person, $10. Children under 10 free in parents' room.
Extras Crib, babysitting.

SEASIDE

Reader tip: "To avoid endless tourist tackiness, follow Route 30A right along the water and sand dunes, instead of Route 98."

For an additional area entry, see **Santa Rosa**, above.

Information please: We'd like current reports on **Seaside** (P.O. Box 4717, 32459; 904–231–1320 or 800–277–TOWN), a recently designed Victorian-style community which has won numerous architectural awards. About 150 cottages are available for sale or rent, at rates ranging from $120–550, depending on style, size, and location. Facilities include a beautiful beach, children's playground, tennis courts, croquet, shuffleboard, three swimming pools, plus several restaurants, markets and shops.

STEINHATCHEE

Steinhatchee Landing 👫 ✕ ☂   *Tel:* 904–498–3513
Highway 51 North, P.O. Box 789, 32359   *Fax:* 904–498–2346

Creeping condo-itis has overspread Florida quicker than kudzu, making sleepy Taylor County one of Florida's last real backwaters: electricity wasn't available until 1945, telephones until 1950. With the recent development of Steinhatchee Landing, visitors can explore an undeveloped part of Florida in comfort and style. In 1990, Dean and Loretta Fowler began construction of this resort on the shores of the Steinhatchee River, offering accommodation in handsomely built units in three regional styles; additional accommodations are available at the Steinhatchee River Inn, a motel a half-mile away. The restaurant specializes in seafood, with such entrées as grouper with pecans and lemon butter, swordfish in mustard cream, or Gulf shrimp to taste.

"Enjoyed getting to know the owner. A relaxing place—lovely house and wonderful restaurant with a blazing fire, delicious food, and outstanding service. Beautiful setting." *(Brian & Judy Sanders)* "More-than-pleasant stop by the river, under large live oaks. The interior decor was a nice blend of elegant and casual comfort, with a vase of just-picked roses. Quiet and unassuming. Steinhatchee (locals call it STEEN-hatchee) itself, a few miles down the road, is a working fishing town that has not been duded up, with two or three seafood restaurants. Good view of tidal marshes and islets." *(Bill MacGowan)*

Open All year. Restaurant closed Mon–Wed.
Rooms 15 1-4 bedroom cottages, 16 motel suites ($^1/_2$ m away)—all with full private bath, radio, clock, TV, desk, air-conditioning, fan, refrigerator. 15 with fan, 7 with fireplace, 15 with porch/deck. Some with telephone, VCR, stereo.
Facilities Restaurant, bar/lounge, kitchen, laundry, porches. 25 acres with nature trails, gardens, 2 pools, 2 hot tubs, tennis court, gazebo, lawn games, bicycles, canoes, boats, playground, parking. Scalloping, fishing, diving on river. 3 m from Gulf.
Restrictions Some non-smoking rooms.
Location NW FL, Taylor Cty. 70 m W of Gainesville. Take U.S. Hwy 19 to Tennille Crossing. Go W on Hwy 51 for 8 m to Landing on left.
Credit cards Amex, MC, Visa.
Rates Room only, $115–255 cottage; sleep 4–10. 2-3 night weekend/holiday minimum. Motel, $50–60. Maid service, $15 daily.
Extras Wheelchair access in restaurant only. Airport/station pickup. Pets with approval. Cribs, babysitting. Spanish spoken.

STUART

The Homeplace ¢
501 Akron Avenue, 34994

Tel: 407–220–9148

Built in 1913 by one of Stuart's first developers, owners Jim Smith and Jean Bell restored The Homeplace in 1989, decorating it with antiques and collectibles. One handsome guest room has wainscotting on the walls and ceiling, a brass bed, and a dark blue and red color scheme; another is more feminine with frills and ruffles. Breakfast includes home-baked muffins and bread with freshly picked fruit, plus "Old Florida" recipes and Victorian egg dishes.

"Beautifully restored with lots of personal touches. *(Margie & Albert Rosenbaum)* "Welcoming warmth and hospitality. Nostalgic touches included the empty milk bottles left outside the front door, the bedroom keys tied with a ribbon, and bedtime mints set on a heart-shaped doily." *(Jacqueline Jacobson)* "Comfy place with pleasant, harmonious accents. The garden area is equally inviting, and the many shrubs and flowers attract songbirds." *(Bill MacGowan)*

Open All year.
Rooms 3 doubles—all with full private bath, air-conditioning, fan. Telephone, radio, TV on request.
Facilities Dining room, parlor with piano, TV, books, self-serve bar; sun room, porch. ⅓ acre with swimming pool, hot tub, garden, lawn games, bicycles. 5 min. to tennis, beaches, boating, fishing.
Location SE central FL. 45 min. N of Palm Beach, 2 hrs. S of Orlando. 2 blocks from historic area. At corner of Akron & 5th St., 2 blocks from S.R. 76.
Restrictions Smoking discouraged. No children under 12.
Credit cards MC, Visa.
Rates B&B, $65–85 double, $60–75 single. Extra person, $15. 10% senior discount midweek. 2-night holiday minimum.
Extras Airport/station pickups, $20–25.

TALLAHASSEE

The capital of Florida, Tallahassee is also home to Florida State University and Florida A&M; other sites of interest include the Tallahassee Junior Museum, a favorite with children, and the Maclay State Gardens, stunning in early spring for their azaleas, camellias, and dogwood.

Reader tips: "Just diagonally across the street from the Governor's Inn is Andrew's Second Act which is consistently superb in quality, taste and presentation of food." *(HJB)* "For a nice meal, try Chez Pierre, 115 North Adams Street, 904–222–0936." *(Bill MacGowan)*

Governors Inn 👤 ♿
209 South Adams Street, 32301

Tel: 904–681–6855
In FL: 800–342–7717
Fax: 904–222–3105

The Governors Inn opened in 1985 in a century-old building which once housed a general store. Each guest room is named after a former Florida

111

governor and furnished with four-poster beds, black oak writing desks, and rock maple armoires.

"This inn was created by gutting a giant livery stable and an abutting two-story office building. The architect did an excellent job of meeting the challenge. A post-and-beam construction dominates an atrium-like area in the stable section, with two levels of rooms off each side. Although inviting and attractive, these rooms are small, with no outside windows. Our room was in the office building section, with twelve-foot ceilings and huge windows opening onto a side street. All the staff, from bellman to chambermaid, were warm, outgoing, and obviously dedicated." *(DB)*

"Well-kept and maintained property; excellent service. Our room had a valet for hanging clothes and comfortable chairs for reading. Rates included a breakfast of juice, melon, muffins, and croissants, and an afternoon cocktail hour. Terrycloth robes, shoeshine service, and the daily newspaper of your choice were among the other amenities. The valet parking is a great convenience in this downtown area." *(HJB)*

Open All year.
Rooms 8 suites, 29 doubles, 3 singles—all with full private bath, telephone, radio, TV, desk, air-conditioning. Some with fan, fireplace, refrigerator or whirlpool bath.
Facilities Breakfast room, patio. Valet parking.
Location W FL panhandle. Center of town. 2 blocks N of Capitol, at corner of Adams and College.
Restrictions Minimal interior soundproofing. No smoking in some guest rooms. No elevator.
Credit cards Amex, DC, Discover, MC, Visa.
Rates B&B, $149–219 suite, $119–149 double, $119 single. Extra person, $10. 2-night minimum football/special event weekends. 10% senior, AAA, corporate discount.
Extras First-floor rooms with wheelchair access. Free airport/station pickups. Crib, babysitting.

VENICE

The Banyan House ¢   *Tel: 813–484–1385*
519 South Harbor Drive, 34285   *Fax: 813–484–8032*

Built in 1926, this Mediterranean-style home, with red-tiled roof and white stucco, has been owned by Chuck and Susan McCormack since 1986. Although the living room is now decorated with formal Victorian parlor furnishings and an Oriental carpet to complement the Italian sculptured fireplace, the setting was not always so posh. Just three years after the house was built, Venice went bankrupt, and Banyan House was abandoned. For three years, tramps slept on its Italian tile floors, cooking their meals in the fireplace. Meals are served with a bit more ceremony these days; at 8:30 A.M., Susan serves breakfast of fresh fruit, juice, homebaked breads, pancakes, or crepes. "Warm, friendly, unpretentious innkeepers; comfortable, relaxing environment. Guest rooms are clean, quiet, light, and airy. Breakfasts are served in a cheerful, sunny, porch-like setting, and are an enjoyable combination of Susan's creative recipes, Chuck's humor, and the guests' friendliness." *(Jeff & Margaret Thurlow)*

"Reminiscent of a Spanish hacienda, in a desirable neighborhood, close to beaches, restaurants, and shops. The well-appointed rooms have bright, modern color schemes with big, sunny windows." *(John & Jutta O'Flaherty)*

Open All year.

Rooms 5 1-bedroom apartments in annex, 3 suites, 1 double—all with full private bath, All with radio, TV, desk, air-conditioning, fan, refrigerator. Some with telephone, desk, balcony/deck.

Facilities Living room with fireplace, piano; breakfast solarium with stereo, books; laundry facility. Brick courtyard with fountain, decks, swimming pool, hot tub, bicycles. Walking distance to beach. Golf, tennis, fishing, boating nearby.

Location SW FL coast. 40 m S of St. Petersburg, 50 m N of Ft. Myers. 5 blocks from downtown. Take I-75 to Exit 35. Turn right (W) on Venice Ave., left on Harbor Dr. Inn 5 blocks on left.

Restrictions No smoking. No children under 12.

Credit cards None accepted.

Rates B&B, $69–89 suite, $49–69 double. Weekly, monthly rates for apartments. Extra person, $15. 2-night minimum stay.

WAKULLA SPRINGS

Reader tip: On the coast, about 20 miles southwest of Wakulla, is Posey Seafood, on Highway 98 in Panacea (904–984–5799). "They have a seafood buffet that draws people from all over. It is sheer heaven to eat all the bay scallops you want, and all the shrimp you can eat, too. Not at tourist prices, either. Reservations advised. There's also a good place to eat in Spring Creek, at the end of the road; no alcohol." *(Bill MacGowan)*

Wakulla Springs resort ₵ 🏃 ✕ ♿   *Tel:* 904–224–5950
1 Springs Drive, 32305   *Fax:* 904–561–7251

Wakulla Springs Lodge was built in 1937 by Ed Ball, a real estate millionaire who had fallen in love with the natural beauty of this area and preserved the 2,900 acres which now make up Edward Ball Wakulla Springs State Park. Most of the dining room staff at this state-owned lodge are students from FSU's School of Hotel and Restaurant Management.

The lodge's exterior is Spanish Mission in style; the interior is striking for its lavish use of Tennessee marble. Other decorative motifs include the Aztec Indian designs painted on the cypress ceiling beams, the Spanish tiles, and the Moorish archways. The restaurant's specialties are navy bean soup, pan-fried chicken, and broiled shrimp. Guest rooms are furnished simply with antiques and 1930s-era furnishings. The key focus of attention here is the spring itself, producing over 600,000 gallons of water a minute. Its basin reaches a crystal-clear depth of 185 feet.

"After dinner, people sit on the benches between the lodge and the spring. As you listen to the sound of thousands of frogs, ibis fly in and settle down to pick and feed at the edge of the spring, in shallow water." *(Bill MacGowan)* "The dining room was grand and the menu varied, the food good. Waitresses were efficient, friendly, and eager to please. The

113

grounds, springs, nature walks and boat ride were beautiful." *(Mrs. John T. May)*

Areas for improvement: Spruce up the rooms, improve the heating/air-conditioning systems; more attentive housekeeping.

Open All year.
Rooms 1 suite, 26 doubles—all with full private bath, telephone, air-conditioning. Some with desk.
Facilities Lobby with TV, fireplace, piano, checkers tables; restaurant, terrace, gift shop, snack bar, conference rooms. 2,888 acres with swimming, river and glass-bottom boat tours, nature trails.
Location W FL panhandle. 15 m S of Tallahassee. Midway between Apalachicola and Perry. From Tallahassee take State Rd. 61 S, then go E on Rte. 267. From E or W, take Rte. 98.
Credit cards MC, Visa.
Rates Room only, $250 suite, $60–85 double, $52–85 single. Extra person, $6. Business, off-season packages. Children's portions. Alc breakfast, $4–7; alc lunch, $6–12; alc dinner, $25.
Extras Wheelchair access. Crib, $5; babysitting with advance notice.

WEST PALM BEACH

West Palm Beach B&B	*Tel:* 407–848–4064
419 32nd Street, 33407	800–736–4064
	Fax: 407–842–1688

A cottage-style Key West home built in 1937, owners Dennis Keimel and Ron Seitz opened the West Palm Beach B&B in 1989. The inn has a Caribbean decor with a sea-green and coral color scheme, wicker furnishings, hardwood floors, and tropical art. Continental breakfast is served each morning in the dining room or by the pool.

"The Carriage House is next to the pool in the beautifully landscaped backyard. The rooms are immaculate and tastefully decorated. Our refrigerator was stocked with fresh fruits, juice, breads, cereal and a bottle of wine. Our gracious hosts helped with suggestions and directions."*(Ed Adams)* "It was lovely to come 'home' to the casual, relaxing atmosphere of the inn, decorated with fresh flowers and plants." *(Bea Harmon)* "Good parking; safe, well-lighted setting; good showers; spring water for drinking." *(RL)* "Comfortable king-size beds, spotless rooms. Dennis and Ron operate the inn with exceptional charm and grace." *(Mr. & Mrs. Walter Wall)*

Open All year.
Rooms 1 Carriage House suite with kitchen, 2 doubles—all with private bath and/or shower, radio, TV, air-conditioning, ceiling fan, fireplace, refrigerator.
Facilities Living room with fireplace, dining room, garden room, breakfast room, deck. TV, stereo in carriage house. Swimming pool, lawn games, off-street parking, bicycles. Golf, tennis, ocean nearby.
Location SE FL. Old Northwood Historic District. From I-95 N or S, exit on 45th St. East to Dixie Hwy. Head S to 32nd St., make right 3rd house in on right.
Restrictions No smoking. Traffic noise might disturb light sleepers.
Credit cards Amex, MC, Visa.

Rates B&B, $55–85 double. No tipping. 3-night holiday minimum. Weekly rates.
Extras Airport/station pickup.

WINTER HAVEN

JD's Southern Oaks   *Tel:* 813–293–2335
3800 Country Club Road South, 33881–9292   *Fax:* 813–299–4141

Just ahead of a developer's bulldozers, Juanita and Dallas Abercrombie rescued a derelict 1925 mansion, built of cypress and heart pine, and moved it two miles to its present location. After two years of restoration, they opened JD's Southern Oaks in 1991. Each guest room has a different decor, from the Victorian furnishings of the Rose Garden room, to the rustic country look of the Carriage House rooms, while the common areas are highlighted by rich red oak floors and attractive stained glass windows. Coffee is set out at 6:30 A.M., and breakfast is served from 8–9 A.M., including fresh fruit, muffins or coffee cake, egg casserole or quiche, orange juice, coffee, tea, and cereal on request.

"The Abercrombies showed us around their lovely home, all available for guests' use, except the kitchen. The bath in my room had both a shower and a claw-footed tub. We enjoyed early morning walks through the yard, overlooking the pond. Juanita is a professional florist; she cooked us delicious breakfasts before she went to her shop. Dallas kept us all entertained with stories as he served breakfast. At night a fresh rose and chocolates were placed on our pillows." *(April Burwell)* "A long driveway lined with live oaks, bordering a pond, leads to a beautifully landscaped Southern mansion. Dallas and Juanita greeted us warmly and provided immaculate accommodations." *(Stan & Marge Nesbitt)*

Open All year.
Rooms 2 suites, 3 doubles—all with private bath, telephone, radio, clock, desk, air-conditioning, fan. 2 in carriage house with TV, refrigerator, balcony/deck; 1 with kitchen.
Facilities Dining room, living room with fireplace, library, parlor, porch. 7-acre yard with 2 gazebos, hammock, swings, vegetable garden; 30-acres with barn, fields for horses, cattle; pond. Lakes nearby for fishing, boating, swimming.
Location Central FL. 50 m W of Orlando, 50 m E of Tampa, 5 m from town. 2.2 m W of U.S. 27 to Country Club Rd.; go right 1.9 m to inn.
Restrictions No smoking. No alcohol. No children. No high-heeled shoes.
Credit cards None accepted.
Rates Room only, $100 suite, $75–115 double. Extra person, $15. B&B, $110 suite, $85–125 double. Extra person, $20. 10% discount, 3-night stays. Corporate rates.
Extras Airport, station pickup.

WINTER PARK

For additional area entries, see **Lake Wales, Minneola,** and **Orlando.**
    Also recommended: Built in 1922, **The Fortnightly Inn** (377 East

Fairbanks Avenue, 32789; 407–645–4440) was restored highlighting its original oak and heart of pine floors, original brass hardware and porcelain fixtures, and clawfoot tubs. "Immaculate, impeccably furnished, antique-filled inn; most friendly innkeeper. Drive with care entering the narrow driveway from the busy, curving road." *(Mimi Cohen)* "In a few guest rooms, bath tubs are hidden by screens with water closets tucked in small nooks." *(Joe & Sheila Schmidt)* Double rates of $75–95 include breakfast of juice, fruit and pastries served between 8 A.M. and 9 A.M., plus in-room sherry.

Park Plaza Hotel ✕ ⟨wheelchair symbol⟩

307 Park Avenue South, 32789

Tel: 407–647–1072
800–228–7220
Fax: 407–647–4081

Built in the heyday of Florida railroading and fully renovated by owners John and Sandra Spang, the Park Plaza's antique- and wicker-filled rooms look out onto a plant-filled balcony that runs the length of the second floor. Beds are turned down each night with a Godiva chocolate, and the morning brings a continental breakfast accompanied by the *Wall Street Journal.* The first floor houses the Park Plaza Gardens restaurant, serving seafood and meat dishes in a glass-enclosed patio garden. This downtown area of Winter Park attracts pedestrians who stroll among the shops, restaurants, and galleries.

"Our room had comfortable furnishings, and a plant-laden balcony overlooking a rose-filled park. Breakfast included jumbo blueberry muffins, and dinner at the hotel's restaurant was superb. After a stroll around the park, we enjoyed coffee and dessert in the piano bar, with the pianist enthusiastically taking all requests." *(Pat Falk)* "Wonderful 1920s hotel, beautifully appointed, with old-world European style." *(Miriam Cohen)* "My room was comfortably furnished with a separate sitting area and balcony. Friendly service. The restaurant is excellent although pricey." *(KM)*

Open All year.

Rooms 11 suites, 16 doubles—all with full private bath, telephone, TV, desk, air-conditioning, ceiling fan. Some with balcony.

Facilities Restaurant, bar, piano lounge, lobby with fireplace, balcony. Fishing 2 blocks away. Valet parking. Golf nearby.

Location N central FL. 5 min. N of downtown Orlando. From I-4, take Fairbanks Exit E to Park Ave. and go left.

Restrictions No children under 5. Significant early A.M. train noise in some rooms.

Credit cards Amex, CB, DC, MC, Visa.

Rates B&B, $135–185 suite, $75–110 double. 10% senior, AAA, corporate discount. Weekly rates available.

Extras Wheelchair access. Station pickups. Crib. Spanish, Italian, French spoken.

Lion's Head Inn, Savannah

There's more to Georgia than peaches and peanuts, Jimmy Carter and Scarlett O'Hara. For urban delights, visit Atlanta, one of the country's most sophisticated cities combining contemporary culture and "Old South" charm; tour graceful historic homes in Savannah; or time-travel to Macon's antebellum mansions. In northwestern Georgia, visit New Echota (outside of Calhoun), the former Cherokee capital where Sequoyah developed a written language for his people; then stop by nearby Chatsworth to see the Vann House, a mansion built by a Cherokee chief and noted for its unusually colored interior paint. In northeastern Georgia, tour the mountains, then stop by 1000-foot Tallulah Falls. Want more water? Get your fill canoeing through the Okefenokee Swamp or visiting posh St. Simons Island.

Important note: The 1996 Summer Olympics are taking place in the Atlanta area from July 19–August 4, 1996. Starting in late June, expect accommodations (as well as everything else) to be both overcrowded and overpriced; rates listed in this chapter for area accommodations will *not* be in effect within a 100-mile radius (or more) of the city. If you have tickets for the games, it will probably be well worth the trouble; if not, visit another time! For Olympic information, call 404–224–1996.

ATLANTA

Virtually leveled by General Sherman during the Civil War, Atlanta recovered fairly quickly, becoming a major rail hub by the end of the century. Today, Atlanta is a modern city whose population has exploded in the past three decades; its airport is one of the busiest in the country, and its traffic jams rival those of Los Angeles.

Also recommended: When you're in the mood for the best in a big city hotel (551 rooms), the **Ritz-Carlton Buckhead** (3434 Peachtree Road NE, 30326; 404–237–2700 or 800–241–3333) "is worth the money for an all-around luxurious yet friendly atmosphere. Wonderful rooms done in antique reproductions, and baths with all the extras, thick fluffy towels and robes, full length mirrors, nightly turn-down service. Ask for a room with the Phipps Plaza view—you can see to the horizon, or splurge on a room on the Concierge Floor. Good food and service in both restaurants too." *(SHW)*

Twenty minutes north of Atlanta are the **Stanley and Marlow Houses** (236 Church Street, Marietta 30060; 404–426–1881), two 19th century houses on the same block. The 12 guest rooms are furnished with reproductions and antiques, and the $75–85 rates include a breakfast of fruit, juice, cereal, boiled eggs, muffins, and bagels, served in the dining room at 8 A.M. "Handsome and comfortable accommodations within walking distance of the downtown square, and excellent restaurants. The trains were audible but did not bother us at all." *(Celia McCullough)*

About 30 minutes north of Atlanta is a charming century-old B&B called **Ten Fifty Canton Street** (1050 Canton Street, Roswell 30075; 404–998–1050), offering three guest rooms at B&B double rates of $70. Roswell offers magnificent antebellum homes, appealing sidewalk cafés and shops, and rafting in the Chattahoochee River. "Clean and appealing; charming, helpful innkeepers. Great bed and ample continental breakfast. Suggest shopping at American Sampler and Chandler; eat at the Public House on Roswell Square." *(Dianne Crawford)*

Information please: Listed in past editions is the **Ansley Inn** (253 15th Street N.E., 30309; 404–872–9000 or 800–446–5416), with a superb location in a quiet tree-lined neighborhood in midtown Atlanta. A Tudor mansion built in 1907, it was totally renovated in 1989. The decor includes marble floors, crystal chandeliers, Oriental rugs, brass beds, and four-poster rice-carved beds. The $80–195 rates include continental breakfast and afternoon refreshments; reports on staffing and maintenance have varied. Comments?

For affordable homestay B&Bs and unhosted apartments, a good choice is **Bed & Breakfast Atlanta** (1801 Piedmont Ave. N.E., Suite 208, 30324; 404–875–0525), a reservation service that arranges accommodations in selected homes, guest houses, inns, and condominiums in Atlanta and vicinity. For an additional area entry, see **Newnan**.

Oakwood House ¢ 🏃 ♿   *Tel:* 404–521–9320
951 Edgewood Avenue N.E., 30307   800–388–4403
                        Fax: 404–521–9320, 9 A.M.–5 P.M. only

Named for the huge oak tree in the backyard, the Oakwood was built in 1911, in Atlanta's oldest suburb, Inman Park. Longtime residents Judy and Robert Hotchkiss restored the residence in 1992, furnishing the inn in a comfortable, uncomplicated style. Breakfast includes fresh baked muffins—perhaps blueberry, chocolate chip, or bran—fresh sliced fruit, orange juice, and hot or cold cereal.

"Wonderfully high ceilings and beautifully restored original woodwork. Our spacious room had a comfortable king-size bed. Tables were set for breakfast in the living room and foyer, adorned with fresh flowers and Christmas decorations." *(Paula Hill)* "Judy and Robert were extremely gracious, informative and accommodating. Exceptionally clean and scrupulously maintained. Our room had a supportive mattress, and fluffy peach-colored bathrobes. Downstairs is an inviting library, its shelves brimming with books and magazines." *(Lyndell Anderson)*

Open All year.
Rooms 5 doubles—all with private bath and/or shower, telephone, radio, clock, air-conditioning. 1 with whirlpool tub, TV, fan, balcony.
Facilities Common area with TV, books; laundry; fax, copier; porch, decks. Off-street parking, small garden.
Location Inman Park. 2 m east of downtown Atlanta. From I-75/85 N, take Exit 94, Edgewood Ave., & turn right. Take 3rd left onto Edgewood. From I-75/85 S, take Exit 95/Butter-Houston Sts. Go straight 3 blocks, left onto Edgewood. Short walk to MARTA station.
Restrictions No smoking.
Credit cards MC, Visa.
Rates B&B, $70–110 double, $65–85 single. 1 child free in parents' room. AAA discount. 3-night minimum major conventions.
Extras Wheelchair access; 1 room specially equipped. Crib, babysitting.

Shellmont Bed & Breakfast Lodge ¢ 👫   *Tel:* 404–872–9290
821 Piedmont Avenue N.E., 30308

Built in 1891, and listed on the National Register of Historic Places, Shellmont is an excellent example of Victorian design. Stained, leaded, and beveled glass abound, as do intricately carved interior and exterior woodwork, elaborate mantels, mosaic-tiled fireplaces, documented Bradbury and Bradbury wall coverings, and accurately reproduced original stenciling. The inn is furnished throughout with Victorian antiques. Ed and Debbie McCord, owners since 1984, are not resting on their innkeeping laurels; recent improvements in various rooms of the inn include new window treatments, upgraded furnishings, and retiled showers. Every bedroom has a ceiling fan/light combination and a minimum of three lamps with three-way lights; all vanities have electric make-up mirrors. The Shellmont is located in midtown; some of the city's best restaurants, live theaters, art cinemas, museums, and shopping are within walking distance.

"This lovely Queen Anne home is painted pale green with cream trim; the carved shell woodwork above the bay window is gorgeous. The parlor sitting room has window seats in the lovely curved windows; lace curtains puddle on the floor. Breakfast is served in the dining room at either 7:30 or 8:30 A.M. weekdays (an hour later on weekends), and consists of an assorted fresh fruit plate, juice, fruit pastries, granola, fruit, cereals, coffee, and tea. At night, the lovely Tiffany window is back lit from inside the house." *(SHW)*

"Delicious homemade whole wheat croissants with butter and jam, served on a delicate blue-flowered china." *(Mary Rafferty)* "The inn is in a tree-lined section where many beautiful old homes are being restored." *(Carolanne Graham)* "The carriage house was perfect for our family, with plenty of room and a kitchen (ideal when traveling with kids)." *(Jimmy & Kimberly Fike)* "Perfect landscaping. Deb gave us lots of background about the history of the house and area." *(Gloria & Richard Hampton)* "Debbie was interested in her guests and their enjoyment of Atlanta. She intuitively knew when chitchat was welcomed or solitude preferred." *(Barbara Cordaro, also Susan Doucet)* "My room had a comfortable antique bed with a matching dresser, a modern tiled shower with tons of hot water, and plush towels. The high ceilings were painted a beautiful shade of dark green with a stenciled border. Scrumptious chocolates were put on the pillow at night; fresh fruit and an assortment of soft drinks were set on the dresser." *(Nina Piccirilli)*

Open All year.

Rooms 1 carriage house suite, 4 doubles—all with private bath and/or shower, air-conditioning, radio, ceiling fan. Suite with TV, kitchen, telephone.

Facilities 3 parlors, library, all with books, magazines, games, fireplaces; guest refrigerator/pantry; veranda. Shady garden with fish pond; bicycles. Off-street parking. 1/4 m to Piedmont Park.

Location Midtown; 1 1/4 m from city center. Exit I-75/85 N Peachtree to Piedmont; Exit I-75/85 S at North Ave. to Piedmont. MARTA stop nearby.

Restrictions Traffic noise in some rooms. Children under 12 in carriage house only. Limited off-street parking.

Credit cards Amex, MC, Visa.

Rates B&B, $87–127 suite, $79–97 double, $69–87 single. Extra person, $15. No tipping. AARP discount. Children under 6 free. 2-night minimum weekend stay.

Extras Crib in carriage house. Bicycles.

The Woodruff ¢
223 Ponce de Leon Avenue, 30308

Tel: 404–875–9449
800–473–9449
Fax: 404–875–2882

The Woodruff was built in 1906 by a prominent local doctor for his family. Purchased in the 1940s by Miss Bessie Woodruff, it was run as a legitimate massage parlor, but was also well-known as a "house of ill repute, popular with many prominent businessmen and politicians of the day." By the time Joan and Doug Jones bought the building in 1989, it was dilapidated and run down. They restored the original stairways—the balustrades carved with hearts—and open front porches, beautiful stained and beveled glass windows, decorating with period furnishings, antique double beds, and Oriental rugs. Breakfast is served in the main dining room, on the sheltered porch, or by arrangement, in your room. "Friendly, open hosts; agreeable room; central location. Hearty Southern breakfast of eggs, huge muffins, fresh fruit plate, grits and bacon." *(Cynthia Gibat)* Comments appreciated.

Open All year.

Rooms 4 suites, 8 doubles—11 with private bath and/or shower, 2 with maximum of 4 sharing bath. All with telephone, radio, clock, desk, air-conditioning, fan. Some with whirlpool tub, fireplace, refrigerator, balcony/porch. TV on request.

Facilities Dining room, living room, sitting room with TV, foyer, guest laundry, porches. Off-street parking, hot tub, gazebo.

Location Midtown. 2 m N of downtown. Exit I-75/85 onto 10th St. Go E on 10th 10 blocks. Go S (right) 10 blocks on Myrtle St. to inn at corner of Myrtle & Ponce de Leon.
Restrictions Traffic noise in some rooms. No smoking.
Credit cards Amex, Discover, MC, Visa.
Rates B&B, $125 suite, $75 double, $65 single. Extra person, $10. Senior, AAA discount.
Extras Spanish, English, German.

AUGUSTA

Founded in 1737, Augusta became Georgia's first state capital and grew prosperous from the tobacco and cotton crops. In the past century, the city's mild winters have attracted golfers, and the Masters golf tournament draws big crowds each spring. Augusta is located 150 miles east of Atlanta via I-20, at the South Carolina border.

Information please: Listed in past editions is the well-known **Partridge Inn Suites** (2110 Walton Way, 30904; 706–737–8888 or 800–476–6888), a grand old hotel overlooking downtown Augusta. Built in 1890, this historic landmark has been retrofitted as an all-suite (105 units) hotel, each complete with bedroom, living room, and kitchen. The inn's restaurant offers Southern and continental cuisine served in the dining room or outside on the veranda. Double rates are $75–95, and the $60 weekend rate includes breakfast, cocktails, and hors d'oeuvres; children under 18 stay free. Reports about the food continue to be very good, while rooms seem to be adequate; comments welcome.

Just across the river in South Carolina are two beautifully restored 19th century mansions, **Rosemary Hall & Lookaway Hall** (804 Carolina Avenue, North Augusta, SC 29841; 803–278–6222 or 800–531–5578). The $75–150 rates include early morning coffee, full breakfast, and evening hors d'oeuvres. The 23 luxurious guest rooms are furnished with antiques, reproductions, and Oriental carpets; many have sitting areas, private verandas, and whirlpool baths. Guests are welcome to relax in the inviting common areas, on the verandas, or out in the gardens. (Under the same ownership is Kehoe House; see listing under Savannah). Just 30 minutes west of Augusta via I-20 is the **1810 West Inn** (254 North Seymour Drive, NW, Thomson 30824; 706–595–3156 or 800–515–1810). Constructed of heart of pine, this Piedmont plains plantation house inn has five guest rooms, with additional accommodation available in several restored Georgia tenant houses and a tobacco barn, set among the magnolias and pecan trees which dot the property. The B&B double rates of $45–55 (higher Master's Week) include homemade biscuits and quiche, plus afternoon refreshments. Reports please.

Telfair Inn: A Victorian Village ¢ 🛄 ✗ 🦅   *Tel:* 706–724–3315
326 Greene Street (Gordon Highway), 30901   800–241–2407
                                                        Fax: 706–823–6623

A cluster of Victorian manor houses taking up most of a city block, the Telfair Inn complex includes the guest rooms, two places to eat, an elegant

French restaurant, and a casual pub. Breakfast varies daily, with such specialities as banana pancakes or puff pastry filled with eggs, spinach, and sausage. Favorite entrées at the Maison on Telfair include rack of lamb, pheasant with polenta, and salmon with raspberry vinaigrette.

"Some minor reservation confusion, but overall a nice group of accommodations, attractively decorated, with a good breakfast which can be eaten in the lovely dining room or delivered to the room. Their superb French restaurant, just down the street, delivered our dinner elegantly to our room so the children would not have to sit quietly after a long drive." *(Celia McCullough)*

Open All year.
Rooms 22 suites, 56 doubles in 17 buildings—all with full private bath, telephone, TV, air-conditioning, coffee maker. Some with whirlpool tub, bidet, gas fireplace, desk, kitchenette, wet bar, porch.
Facilities Restaurant, pub, conference center. Swimming pool, hot tub, tennis court, off-street parking.
Location Olde Town historic district. Between 3rd & 4th Sts., Greene & Telfair Sts. 2 blocks E of Gordon Hwy. (U.S. Hwy 1/78). Walking distance to Savannah River, Bus. District, Port Royal, Riverwalk.
Restrictions Some non-smoking rooms.
Credit cards Amex, CB, DC, Discover, JCB, MC, Visa.
Rates Room only, $97–140 suite, $67–90 double. Extra person, $10–20. Corporate/government rates. Alc dinner, $35. No charge for children under 12. Senior, AAA, weekly rates.
Extras Wheelchair access; some rooms specially equipped. Airport pickup. Small pets with approval, $20.

BLAIRSVILLE

Seven Creeks Housekeeping Cabins ¢ 👫   *Tel: 706–745–4753*
5109 Horseshoe Cove Road, 30512

Marvin and Bobbie Hernden have restored one old mountain cabin and have built five more over the past twenty years.

"The cabins are snug and comfortable in the winter, cool and breezy in the summer. The facilities are modern, convenient, clean, and well furnished." *(Larry & Joyce Bradfield)* "Special touches include garden-fresh flowers or vegetables awaiting you on the kitchen table. The well-spaced cabins are set in a beautiful secluded cove with a lovely little spring-fed lake, complete with ducks and fish. Good area hiking; our toddler loved playing with the dog, goats, pony, and cats." *(Linda & Tom Reeder)*

"The pond was directly across from our cabin and the surrounding mountains cast a beautiful reflection on the clear water. Ample wood provided for the fireplace." *(Lucille Cunningham & Myrna Deshazo)* "We sat on the porch and watched the moon come up over the mountains. Our 10-year-old enjoyed exploring on his own." *(Sarah Bigelow)* "Lots of privacy. A symphony of nocturnal creatures serenade you in the evening." *(Teri Kenith)* "Although secluded, convenience stores and other services were an easy drive. Excellent directions were provided by the Herndens, who were readily available to answer questions without intruding." *(Bernice Bilger)*

Open All year.
Rooms 6 1- to 3-bedroom housekeeping cabins, sleep 4 to 8. All with private bath, kitchen, TV, radio, barbecue grill, fireplace, porch.
Facilities 70 acres with hiking trails, private lake for fishing, swimming. Covered picnic area, playground, tether ball, badminton, horseshoes; pottery shop, library, fishing poles, outdoor chapel. White-water rafting, horseback riding, canoeing, golf nearby.
Location N GA. 100 m N of Atlanta, approx. 20 m S of NC border. From Blairsville, go S on Rte. 19/129, E on Rte. 180. Seven Creeks is 1 m S of 180 (Wolfstake Rd. W) on Horseshoe Cove Rd.
Credit cards None accepted.
Rates Room only, $45–55 cabin. Extra person, $5. No charge for children under 6. 2-night minimum. Weekly rates, $285 double. Extra person, $25. (Linens extra.)

BRUNSWICK

For an additional area entry, see **Darien.**

Brunswick Manor
825 Egmont Street, 31520

Tel: 912–265–6889

Whether you'd like a taste of history en route to the Golden Isles or a delightful stopover when traveling south on I-95, a fine choice is Brunswick Manor, in the port city of Brunswick. Built in 1886, this B&B was restored in 1988 by transplanted New Englanders Claudia and Harry Tzucanow. They have decorated their inn handsomely with Victorian antiques and period reproductions, complementing the original carved oak staircase, high ceilings, and Victorian fireplace mantels with bevelled glass mirrors. The stained-glass 'eyebrow' windows on the first floor offer views of the gardens and moss-draped oaks. One elegant guest room is striking in deep blue and wine colors, accented with crisp white linens, lace curtains, and a lace-topped queen-size canopy bed. A typical breakfast consists of fresh fruit, eggs Benedict, juice, coffee and tea, served on fine crystal; also included is afternoon tea at 4 P.M., bathrobes, wake-up and turn-down service, and the daily newspaper. "Antique clocks and furnishings abound in this charming Victorian manor. Fantastic breakfasts, good conversations with the host. We became friends with the two cats and dog that live at the inn." *(Paul Munroe)* Comments welcome.

Open All year.
Rooms 3 suites, 5 doubles—all with private bath and/or shower, air-conditioning. 4 doubles in 1890 House. 2 with kitchenette.
Facilities Dining room, parlor, library, veranda with swing. Gardens, patio, greenhouse, fish pond, lawn games. Bicycling; boat charters. Tennis nearby.
Location Historic Old Town Brunswick, across from Halifas Sq. Halfway between Savannah & Jacksonville; gateway to Golden Isles. Near I-95 access. Take I-95 to Exit 7. Follow ramp S to Rte. 341. Go approx. 6½ m, turning left on Prince St. Once on Prince St., do *not* turn right to follow Rte. 341 to Jekyll Island. Stay on Prince St. 4 major blocks to Egmont St; house is on corner of Prince & Egmont.
Restrictions No smoking. Children under 12 in 1890 House.
Credit cards MC, Visa.
Rates B&B, $85 suite, $55–80 double.
Extras Free airport pickup.

BUFORD

The Allen Mansion ♿   *Tel:* 404–945–1080
395 East Main Street, 30518

Civil War veteran and tannery tycoon Bona Allen built this Italianate mansion in 1912. Restored in 1984 and opened as a B&B in 1993 by Janet Ditmore, it's furnished with period antiques; rates include a full breakfast and afternoon refreshments. "A great find. Huge, comfy, immaculate rooms; enormous bathrooms—mine had a Jacuzzi and shower stall; friendly atmosphere. Three generations live on the property." *(Ann Christoffersen)*

Open All year.
Rooms 1 suite, 2 doubles—all with private bath, air-conditioning. Some with TV, Jacuzzi, porch. 1 with kitchenette.
Facilities 2 dining rooms, great room, gallery, library; each with fireplace. 7 acres with gardens, swimming pool; bicycles. Lake Lanier nearby for water sports.
Location N GA. 35 m NE of Atlanta. Take I-85 N to I-985 N. Go W on Hwy 20, N on Hwy 13 (Buford Hwy.). Turn left on Hill St, right on Main St. to inn on right.
Restrictions Train noise in some rooms. No smoking.
Credit cards MC, Visa.
Rates B&B, $75–125 suite, $65–95 double. Extra person, $10.
Extras Limited wheelchair access. Spanish spoken. Crib.

CHICKAMAUGA

Information please: Just south of Chattanooga, Lookout Mountain, and Chickamauga Military Park is the **Gordon-Lee Mansion** (217 Cove Road, Chicamauga 30707; 706–375–4728 or 800–487–4728), a National Historic Site. Built in 1847, this classic Southern Greek Revival plantation home is beautifully furnished with 18th and 19th century antiques. During the battle of Chickamauga, the house was used as a Union Hospital, with the library used for surgery. Four guest rooms, an apartment, and a cabin are available, at double rates of $65–90, including a full breakfast and afternoon tea or wine. Comments welcome.

CLARKESVILLE

Also recommended: In Clarkesville's historic district, and listed on the National Register of Historic places is the **Burns-Sutton House** (124 South Washington Street, P.O. Box 992, 30523; 706–754–5565). Built in 1901, owners John and Jo Ann Smith have restored the wraparound porches, stained glass windows, and ornate woodwork. Rooms are furnished in period antiques, and the $55–75 rates include a full breakfast; the Smiths have opened a reasonably priced restaurant as well. "Stopped for a delicious lunch during a Christmas holiday tour." *(Trina Wellin)* "Comfortable room, welcoming owners, lovely Victorian home." *(Miriam Brigham)*

Charm House Inn ✕
Tel: 706–754–9347
Washington Street, Highway 441, P.O. Box 392, 30523

Listed on the National Register of Historic Places, the Charm House is a 1907 Greek Revival house, its massive porch supported by four Corinthian columns. Rates include a full Southern breakfast, plus afternoon tea, soft drinks, and cookies. The dinner menu ranges from rack of lamb to veal piccata to Southern fried chicken. Rooms are eclectically furnished with antiques, lots of lace, and white wicker.

"Mary and Fred Newman invite you to sit and chat in the parlor. The dining room may be the best in town. Clarksville rolls up the sidewalks early, so plan to stay and listen to their beautiful music." *(Jacqueline & Alan Granath)* "Mary and Fred are the ultimate innkeepers. When we arrived, we relaxed with a glass of wine on the porch, while Mary cooked us a delicious dinner. The beds were fabulous." *(Dianne Crawford)*

Open All year.
Rooms 5 doubles—all with private bath and/or shower, desk, air-conditioning, fan, fireplace. 1 with whirlpool tub.
Facilities Dining room, breakfast room, common area with TV/VCR, books, games; living room, porch, veranda. 1 ¾ acres with lawns, yard swing. Tennis, golf, rafting, horseback riding, fishing nearby.
Location NE GA. Equidistant from Atlanta & Greenville SC. Walking distance to center.
Restrictions "Discreet smoking allowed." No children under 10.
Credit cards MC, Visa.
Rates B&B, $75–90 double, $60–75 single. Extra person, $10. No tipping for B&B. Alc dinner, $22 plus 17% service.
Extras Limited wheelchair access.

Glen-Ella Springs Inn ✕ ♿
Tel: 706–754–7295
Route 3, Box 3304, 30523 Bear Gap Road   *Outside GA:* 800–552–3479

In the early 1900s, Atlanta tourists came to "take the waters" at the Glen-Ella Springs Inn. When Barrie and Bobby Aycock purchased the inn in 1986, it had essentially been unaltered since its construction, so the Aycocks' restoration started with the addition of indoor plumbing and electricity. Well off the highway on a quiet gravelled road, the inn is surrounded by pine forests and meadows of wildflowers. The gardens supply the herbs and vegetables for summertime dining. Breakfasts include fresh fruit compote, homemade granola, cereal, and home-baked breads, and battered French toast with orange sauce or perhaps blueberry granola pancakes—plus coffee, tea, and juice. The dinner menu might include bacon-wrapped scallops, salad with lemon dill dressing, and trout pecan or honey-roasted lamb.

"A restorative place, with its wraparound porches and white rocking chairs. The lobby has a huge floor-to-ceiling fireplace and a variety of chintz-covered sofas, chairs, and loveseats." *(Nancy & John Schultz)* "Our suite was furnished with antiques, handmade quilts and rugs. The walls, floors, and ceiling were all of pine, the bathroom modern. We relaxed on the rocking chairs on the balcony, and on the deck surrounding the beautiful swimming pool." *(Anna Culligan)* "Barrie and Bobby have their guests' peace and comfort always in mind. The seafood, beef, and veal are all first quality, and the Key lime pie is the best." *(Mary Mallard, and others)* "The breakfast buffet had hot food that stayed hot, edible eggs, and grits without lumps." *(Kay Sassi)* "Our rustic room had plenty of reading material and a checker board." *(Beth Webster)* "Wonderful picnics in charming woven baskets." *(Rebecca Bowers)* "Beautiful and restful. Outstanding food and service at dinner." *(Marion Ruben)*

Open All year. Restaurant open by reservation. Jan.–June; Tues.–Sun., June–Dec.
Rooms 2 suites with fireplace, Jacuzzi; 14 doubles—all with full private bath, telephone, radio, air-conditioning. Some with balcony. VCR avail. TV in lobby.
Facilities Restaurant, gift shop, living room with fireplace, TV/VCR, games, books; terrace. 17 acres with swimming pool, gardens, nature trails, mineral spring. Close to Lake Rabun. Tennis, golf nearby.
Location NE GA. 85 m NE of Atlanta. From Atlanta, take I-85 N to I-985, Exit 45. Becomes GA 365, then US 441 N of Cornelia. Follow US 441N for 15 m. Go left on G. Hardeman Rd. at Turnerville, then right on Historic Old 441 for 1/4 m. Left on The Orchard Rd. Follow signs 2 1/2 m to the inn.
Restrictions Thin walls make noises audible; restaurant noise in some rooms. Slow service possible in restaurant Saturday nights in season. "Well-behaved children welcome." BYOB.
Credit cards Amex, MC, Visa.
Rates B&B, $150 suite, $90–100 double. Extra person, $10. 2–3 night weekend minimum stay Oct., holiday weekends. Alc lunch $8–10, alc dinner $30. Mystery weekends.
Extras Wheelchair access. Babysitting by arrangement.

COLUMBUS

Also recommended: Although not appropriate for a full write-up, frequent contributor *Celia McCullough* was delighted with her stay at the **Columbus Hilton** (800 Front Avenue, 31901; 706–324–1800 or 800–HILTONS), built around a restored 19th century grist mill, and located at the edge of the historic district. "Delicious breakfast in one of the Hilton's attractive dining areas in the lobby, bordered by the old brick walls of the grist mill. Outstanding dinners nearby at Bludau's at the 1839 Goetchius House. Many beautifully restored antebellum houses in the area; would make excellent B&Bs." *(Celia McCullough)* Double rates for the 177 rooms run from $66–125.

COMMERCE

The Pittman House ¢   *Tel: 706–335–3823*
81 Homer Road, 30529

The Pittman House is an 1890s four-square Colonial house, owned by Tom and Dot Tomberlin since 1988. The guest rooms are spacious and inviting, with period antiques, ruffled tie-back curtains, handmade quilts, and Oriental rugs. Breakfast varies daily; in addition to juice and fresh fruit, you might enjoy a sausage cheese casserole, a potato omelet, and blueberry muffins; the next day, apple cinnamon nut pancakes with honey butter syrup, bacon, and an egg casserole might make up the menu.

"A plate of homemade cookies might await in your room, or warm brownies might be just out of the oven down in the kitchen. If you're looking for conversation, you will find a friendly gathering of guests and a Tomberlin or two; a cozy spot is always available for privacy and quiet." *(Sunny McMillan)* "Tom and Dot were gracious hosts, eager to satisfy any need or request. Our comfortable, immaculate room had lovely linens and plenty of blankets and pillows. The breakfast is bountiful and delicious, with Tom hovering in the background to make certain everything is perfect." *(Alyson Meeks)* "The owners offer a friendly welcome with delicious baked goods and an invitation to sip on a cold drink." *(Jan Howell)* Reports needed.

Open All year.
Rooms 4 doubles—2 with maximum of 4 sharing bath. All with air-conditioning, ceiling fan. Telephone, radio, TV, desk available.
Facilities Family room with TV/VCR, books; living room with books; enclosed sunporch; wrap-around porch. Tennis, golf nearby. Swimming, boating, fishing nearby.
Location NE GA. 65 m NE of Atlanta. 70 m SW of Greenville, SC. 2 blocks from town center. Take Exit 53 on I-85 to US 441 South. Go 3 1/2 m to Pittman House on right.
Restrictions No smoking. "Well-behaved children welcome." Traffic noise in some rooms.
Credit cards MC, Visa.
Rates B&B, $50 double, $45 single. Extra person, $10. Corporate rates. Advance notice required for late arrivals.
Extras Crib.

CUMBERLAND ISLAND

Reader tip: "Fifteen miles of unused beach, great stands of oak, rolling dunes, and a wealth of history about the days of the Carnegies (the museum is in their old ice house). Wild horses, some believed to be descendants of the stock left by the original Spanish settlers, roam the island. Just one shortcoming—during warm weather, ticks are everywhere, so come prepared." *(Joe Schmidt)*

For additional area entries, see listings under **St. Marys**.

Greyfield Inn ♦♦
8 North Second Street, P.O. Box 900, 32035
Tel: 904–261–6408

The natural beauty of most of Georgia's barrier islands has been overwhelmed by massive hotel and condominium projects, with tennis courts and golf courses. A welcome exception is Cumberland Island, the southernmost and largest at 17 1/2 miles long. Thomas Carnegie (brother to steel magnate Andrew) bought land on Cumberland Island in 1881, and built an imposing mansion, Dungeness. Eventually a total of five mansions were constructed, but most now lie in ruins. An imposing four-story white mansion built in 1901 for a daughter of Thomas Carnegie, the Greyfield opened as an inn in the 1960s. In 1972, much of the island was designated as a National Seashore.

Rates include three meals daily, round-trip ferry transportation, an outing with the inn's naturalist, and use of its bicycles. Breakfast consists of fresh-squeezed orange juice and fruit; homemade muffins; bacon or sausage; and eggs, pancakes, or the chef's fancy. Picnic lunches are packed and are available after breakfast. Dinner is served in the candlelit dining room with fresh flowers and a view of the sunset. The nightly entrée includes fresh seafood, Cornish game hen, lamb or beef tenderloin, home-made breads, fresh vegetables, and home-baked desserts. Hors d'oeuvres are served in the honor system bar before dinner.

"The Carnegie family once owned the entire island as a plantation for Sea Island cotton, and Carnegie descendants still own the Greyfield. Only 300 persons at a time are allowed access to the island, to cause minimum disturbance to the wild horses, deer, wild turkeys, armadillos, alligators, birds, and other wildlife that roam the island. The house is furnished with old family photos, portraits, original furniture, well-worn Oriental rugs, books, with a huge bathtub in the shared bath. Service is personal, friendly, excellent, elegant." *(Celia McCullough & Gary Kaplan)* "The comfortable downstairs suite has a private bath and is simply furnished in period pieces. Delicious meals, with a satisfying box lunch to take bicycling or hiking." *(William Novack)* "We walked for two hours and saw only one human but lots of wildlife. Gorgeous private beach." *(Lillie Galvin)* "A most intriguing experience was a Jeep ride with a local naturalist, seeing much of Cumberland Island that most day-hikers never get to see, and learning first-hand about the animals and plants indigenous to the island." *(Marsha & Bob McOsker)* "Early in the morning, wild turkeys forage under the giant oaks, while deer browse in the misty meadows." *(Bill MacGowan)*

And a word to the wise: "Plumbing is antique so be prepared." Also: "When the wind blows from the mainland, the occasional smell of a distant paper factory is unpleasant."

Open Sept. 1 thru July 31.
Rooms 1 2-bedroom cottage, 2 suites, 6 doubles, 1 single—2 with private bath, rest share 1 bath (tub—no shower). All with ceiling fans. Some with desk. Backyard shower house.
Facilities Dining room with fireplace, living room with fireplace, books; bar, library, balcony, porch with rockers, swings, fans. 1,300 acres for shelling, fishing, clam digging, birding, swimming, fossil-hunting. 50 m of hiking trails, beachcombing, Jeep tours. Bicycles.
Location SE GA, at FL border. 40 m N of Jacksonville, FL. Private ferry from Fernandina Beach, FL (1½ hrs.), Nat'l Park Service ferry from St. Marys, GA (45 min.). Private airstrip.
Restrictions Smoking in bar only. Advance notice for dietary restrictions required. Emergency radio-phone only; no regular telephone communication. No stores on island; bring along all essentials, including bug repellent, hiking shoes (winter), rubber boots or old sneakers (summer), rain gear. Children over 5. Jackets/dresses suggested at dinner.
Credit cards MC, Visa.

Rates Full board, $215–315 suite, $190–290 double, $175–275 single. Children's rates. 17% service. 2-3 night minimum weekends/holidays. Reservations for spring/fall weekends recommended at least 6 months ahead.
Extras Ferry pickups.

DAHLONEGA

Nestled in the foothills of the Blue Ridge Mountains, Dahlonega was the site of the first gold rush in the United States. The old saying "There's gold in them thar hills" refers not to California but to Dahlonega! The name of the town is the Cherokee word for precious yellow metal. Area activities include hiking, rafting, canoeing, fishing, and panning for gold. Dahlonega is located in the North Georgia mountains, 65 miles north of Atlanta; from Atlanta, take Route 19/400 from I-285.

Reader tip: "Visiting westerners will need to adjust their concept of what constitutes a 'mountain' when traveling in North Georgia. These are low hills, pretty when the leaves are on the trees, less so in the winter months."

Also recommended: Nearby is the village of Helen, a once-dying lumber town born-again as an ersatz Bavarian village (only in America!). Nevertheless, everyone seems to enjoy it. Thriving among the Alpine facades is the **Dutch Cottage** (P.O. Box 757, Ridge Road, Helen 30545; 706–878–3135), a 35-year-old house, decorated with antiques, and within walking distance of Alpine Village. B&B rates for the three guest rooms is $55–65; a chalet rents for $75. "A beautiful room, cool and clean. Nice hosts and a great breakfast." *(Susan Doucet)*

Mountain Top Lodge at Dahlonega ¢
Route 7, Box 150, 30533

Tel: 706–864–5257
800–526–9754

A gambrel-roofed barn-style inn built in 1985 by innkeeper David Middleton, the Mountain Top has guest rooms decorated with pine furniture, mountain crafts, antiques, and flea market treasures.

"Our room, #5, had a small sitting nook complete with nicely upholstered love seat, duck motifs on the wall, oak furniture, and good reading lamps. Also: classy magazines, books, antiques here and there, duck prints, nicely appointed (though small) private bath, chairs with crocheted doilies on the back, little plate with a piece of freshly baked pound cake and homemade fudge wrapped and tied with a blue ribbon. For breakfast we had excellent ham, sausage, hot fruit compote, cheese, eggs, juice, biscuits. Everyone sat around family-style at several tables and the food just kept coming and coming." *(SC)*

"David is an accomplished artist and has done a beautiful mural in the dining room; several of his other paintings grace the walls at the lodge. His friendly dogs will greet you on arrival and will keep you company during your visit." *(Sue Murphy)* "Mexican frittata and cheese biscuits for breakfast, fresh-baked chocolate chip cookies in the afternoon; and a plate of banana bread in our room. We took lots of wonderful walks." *(Gene & Helen Curtis)* "The innkeepers did not hover, but were close enough if needed. Not a speck of dust to be seen." *(Doris & Allen Watson)* "A spring or fall visit is especially lovely, when you can wander the woods admiring the dogwoods or foliage." *(Gina Killgore)* "Inviting areas for bridge, reading and conversation. Appealing deck and hot tub." *(E.S. Becker)* "Loved our luxury suite in the Hillside Lodge with double Jacuzzi and fireplace." *(Jim Clayton)* Comments welcome.

Open All year.

Rooms 2 suites, 11 doubles—all with private bath and/or shower, air-conditioning, fan. 2 with double Jacuzzi tub, gas fireplace, refrigerator, deck. 2 with balcony. Radio on request. 4 rooms in separate lodge.

Facilities Dining room, common room with stereo, piano, wood-burning stove, books; TV room, guest pantry, game room, deck, covered porch. 40 acres with hot tub, trails, picnic areas, gazebo, swing. Rafting, trout fishing, hiking, horseback riding nearby.

Location 60 m N of Atlanta. 5 m from town. From Dahlonega square, go 3 1/2 m on GA 52 W. Turn right on Siloam Rd. Go 1/2 m and turn right on Old Ellijay Rd. Follow to end and turn left into entrance.

Restrictions No children under 12.

Credit cards Amex, MC, Visa.

Rates B&B, $85 suite, $65–125 double, $55–115 single. Extra person, $10. 15% discount for 5-day stays.

Extras Wheelchair access; 1 small step to porch.

DARIEN

Open Gates ¢

Vernon Square, P.O.Box 1526, 31305

Tel: 912–437–6985

You can zoom down I-95 to Florida, refueling both body and car at identical gas, food, and sleep stations, or you can slow down here for an authentic slice of Americana. Founded in 1736, Darien soon became a thriving timber port. Burned twice during the Civil War, its Vernon Square historic district is where Open Gates was built in 1876. Restored as a B&B in 1987 by Carolyn Hodges, Open Gates is shaded by massive live oaks, hung with Spanish moss; inside, its high-ceiling rooms are simply decorated in cheerful colors with family antiques and collectibles. The Timber Baron's room has an antique sleigh bed, while the Quilt Room takes its name from the hand-stitched star-patterned quilts that adorn the queen-size bed and the walls. Breakfast, served at a mutually agreeable time, might include fresh fruit compote, pancakes served with assorted syrups, honey and apple butter, herbed shirred eggs with sausage and cheese, Belgian waffles with whipped cream, or baked apples and oatmeal.

A short drive away are the deserted rice islands and marshes of McIntosh County. Owner Carolyn Hodges provides personal tours to her guests' specifications, including boat tours of the Altamaha River Delta and a guided tour of Butler's Island from a botanical as well as historical perspective.

"Carolyn and Philip Hodges are knowledgeable about area history." *(Joe Schmidt)* "Well-appointed house on a quiet, picturesque square in this old fishing village. Best of all is Ms. Hodges, a former school teacher, avid environmentalist and self-taught historian, who makes you feel welcome immediately. Sitting down to breakfast with her is a feast of local history and politics." *(Judith Bates)* "Clean, comfortable house; delicious, creative breakfast." *(Keith Westphal)*

Open All year.
Rooms 4 doubles—2 with private bath and/or shower, 2 with maximum of 4 people sharing bath. All with clock, air conditioning; some with fan, desk. 1 room over garage with separate entrance.
Facilities Dining room, living room with fireplace, piano, TV, books; family room, porch. ½ acre with swimming pool, gardens, croquet. Game refuges, birding, river, barrier island boat trips.
Location SE GA, halfway between Savannah & Jacksonville, FL. Historic district. Take Exit 10 off I-95. Go 1.9 m SE on Hwy. 251.
Restrictions No smoking.
Credit cards None accepted.
Rates B&B, $48–55 double. Extra adult, $15; child over 10, $10. 2-night weekend minimum. 10% discount for 4-day stay.
Extras Airport pick-up. Pets possible; inquire.

DILLARD

Dillard House ¢ 🏃 ✕ 🐾
Old Dillard Highway, P.O. Box 10, 30537

Tel: 706–746–5348
In South: 800–541–0671
Fax: 706–746–3344

Overlooking a fertile valley and surrounded by the Blue Ridge Mountains, Dillard House is a year-round family resort run by generations of Dillards since 1794.

"A wonderful place for a family vacation, especially if you are interested in horseback riding. Horses and trails are available for all levels of difficulty. The Little River Ride goes up the middle of the Little Tennessee River, makes a loop through lush, green forest, and winds back down the river. Our motel-style room was clean and nicely furnished, with a view of the horses at pasture, with the mountains in the background. There are no restaurant menus at Dillard House; trays are laden with such Southern foods as fried chicken, breaded fried steak, smoked ham, corn on the cob, squash, and green beans. Stockton House in nearby Clayton offers an excellent alternative with such entrées as broiled mountain trout, chicken tempura, and shrimp scampi." *(Pat Borysiewicz)* "Wonderful country cooking. For a set price at breakfast, lunch, and dinner, they bring out bowls and bowls of delicious Southern-style food." *(Karla Riley)*

Open All year.
Rooms 4 cottages, 3 2-bedroom suites, 50 doubles—all with private bath and/or shower, telephone, TV, air-conditioning. Some with kitchenette, whirlpool tub.
Facilities Restaurant, meeting rooms, gift shop, theater. Swimming pool, 2 tennis courts, playground, petting zoo, horseback riding. Whitewater rafting, boating, fishing, golf, downhill skiing nearby.
Location NE GA, Rabun Cty. 2 hrs. NE of Atlanta. 2 m S of NC border. ¼ m E of Hwy. 441.
Credit cards Amex, DC, Discover, MC, Visa.

Rates Room only, $80–150 cottage, $75–125 suite, $55–70 double; $95 during foliage. Extra person, $5–10. Senior discount. Children free under 10. Prix fixe dinner, $12. Beds/cribs $5/night.
Extras Pets allowed, $5 daily. Petting zoo, free.

GAINESVILLE

The Dunlap House &.   *Tel:* 404–536–0200
635 Green Street, 30501   In GA: 800–462–6992

The Dunlap House was built in 1910 and was restored in 1985 as a luxury B&B inn; Ann and Ben Ventress took over as innkeepers in 1992. Guest rooms are handsomely decorated with quality reproductions, including floral chintzes and custom-made rice and four-poster queen and king-size beds, plus designer linens, oversize towels, and terry robes. Rates include the morning paper and a breakfast of fresh fruit, cereal, yogurt, muffins, and fresh-squeezed orange juice.

"A charming, elegantly appointed Southern mansion. Large, comfortable, sunny rooms; brass fixtures; beautiful fabrics and wallpapers. Ben and Ann accommodate requests with warmth, charm, and humor, in a comfortable, homey environment." *(Susan Snowe)* "The large porch is a wonderful place to relax; parking is ample and convenient." *(Blanche & Alan Williams)* "Delicious breakfasts; comfortable, well-furnished room; meticulous housekeeping. We ate well at Rudolph's, across the street. Green Street is lined with wonderful Greek revival houses; the one next door is particularly noteworthy." *(Nancy Bernard)*

Open All year.
Rooms 9 doubles—all with full private bath, telephone, TV, air-conditioning. Some with deck, fireplace.
Facilities Breakfast room, dining room with fireplace, porch. Off-street parking. Tennis, golf nearby. Lake Lanier for all water sports.
Location N GA. 60 m N of Atlanta. From I-985, take Exit 6. Go N 2 m on Rte. 129 (Butler Pkwy); changes name to Green St. at curve to right. Inn on left at corner of Ridgewood.
Restrictions No smoking.
Credit cards Amex, MC, Visa.
Rates B&B, $85–125 double, $65–115 single. Extra person, $15. 10% senior, AAA discount. Weekly, corporate rates. Packages. Special rate, 2-night minimum during Olympics.
Extras Wheelchair access; room specially equipped.

HAMILTON

Wedgwood ¢   *Tel:* 706–628–5659
132 College Street, P.O. Box 115, 31811

If you're looking for an appealing B&B near Callaway Gardens, the Wedgwood is an excellent choice. A classic Greek Revival home built in 1850, it was restored by Janice Neuffer in 1988, and takes its name from the Wedgwood blue color used in decorating, as well as the lovely pieces of this English jasper ware on display. Hand-planed wall planks up to 22′ wide indicate the age of this house, and are complemented by the period antique furnishings interspersed throughout. Rates include afternoon refreshments and an 8:30 A.M. breakfast of country ham or sausage, grits, biscuits, jellies, orange juice, or perhaps oven-baked pancakes topped with fresh fruit.

"Janice Neuffer is intelligent, informative, entertaining, hospitable. Delicious home-baked bread and creative pancakes for breakfast. Immaculate housekeeping. Outstanding continental restaurant just a block away." *(Joyce Johnson, also Susan Doucet)* "Easily accessible from the main road, in a quiet, peaceful small town. Surrounded by beautiful flower gardens. The guest rooms have quilts hand-sewn by Janice." *(Tracy & Joe Campbell)* "Clean and neat with a nice side screened porch." *(BJ Hensley)*

Open All year.
Rooms 3 doubles—all with private bath and/or shower, radio, clock, air-conditioning, fan, balcony.
Facilities Dining room, living room with piano, den with TV/VCR, stereo, books, videotapes; screened porch. Off-street covered parking, gardens, gazebo. Swimming, golf, hiking, bicycling, sailing, horseback riding nearby.
Location E GA. 22 m N of Columbus, 5 m S of Callaway Gardens, 20 m SW of Warm Springs. In historic district, on Hwy. 27, at corner of Mobley.
Restrictions No smoking. Traffic noise in front rooms.
Credit cards None accepted.
Rates B&B, $65–80 double, $55–75 single. Extra person, $10. No charge for pre-schoolers. 2-night minimum some holiday weekends.

JEKYLL ISLAND

Jekyll Island Club 👫 ✕ 🛫
371 Riverview Drive, 31527

Tel: 912–635–2600
800–333–3333
Fax: 912–635–2818

One hundred years ago, the Rockefellers, Morgans, Goodyears, Astors, Pulitzers, and other American millionaires set up a club to relax and get away from the pressures of excessive wealth. Called the Jekyll Island Club, it accepted only society's "crème de la crème," and served as a winter Newport. The club's era ended in the thirties with the Great Depression and it closed at the outset of World War II. After the war, Jekyll Island was purchased by the state of Georgia and opened for public use; most of the island is a state park, and only a third of it can be developed. The club faces the Intracoastal Waterway, while modern construction is primarily on the Atlantic beachfront side of this narrow island.

In 1986, an investment group leased the club (listed on the National Register of Historic Places) from the state of Georgia and spent $17 million restoring and refurbishing it; it's now run by Radisson Hotels. Ornate woodwork and gold leaf have been returned to their original splendor, while the baths have been modernized. Rooms are furnished with custom-made Queen Anne reproductions.

"A lively resort, wonderful for bicycling, with over twenty miles of trails. Relax in wicker chairs on verandas overlooking the river." *(Marjorie Cohen)* "Don't miss the historic tours of the hotel and nearby buildings, or the trolley tour of the historic district. Mansions once owned by the Rockefellers and Pulitzers have been restored and are now open to the public." *(Pat Borysiewicz)*

"Friendly, helpful staff. There are about 10 buildings, other than the hotel, that were part of the original complex; we visited six of the houses, and an indoor tennis club, which would be worth the visit alone. We bought tasty sandwiches at the deli, and ate them outside in the sun; had wickedly good martinis in the tearoom/bar—a beautiful semi-circular room; had a fine dinner in the pillared dining room, and a full breakfast in our room overlooking the lawns. Our enormous two-room suite had a large bathroom and a huge Jacuzzi. Regrettably, the hotel furnishings are inappropriate to the period; if ever a resort cried out for late Victorian furniture, this is it." *(Robert Freidus)*

Open All year.

Rooms 17 suites, 117 doubles—all with full private bath, telephone, TV/VCR, radio, desk, air-conditioning. Most suites with porch, fireplace, Jacuzzi. 24 rooms in San Souci Cottage.

Facilities Dining room, room service, delicatessen, snack bar (seasonal) parlors, lounges, verandas. 7 acres with beach club with all water sports, deep-sea fishing, croquet, horseshoes, volleyball, badminton, children's program, swimming pool, marina, 8 outdoor tennis courts (5 lighted), 1 indoor court, 63 holes of golf, gift shops, valet parking. Bicycle paths; short walk to ocean.

Location SE GA, Golden Isles. 75 m S of Savannah, 65 m N of Jacksonville, FL. 12 m from I-95. Club is part of 240-acre national historic district, in central part of island, on inland side.

Restrictions Non-smoking rooms available.

Credit cards Amex, CB, DC, Discover, MC, Visa.

Rates Room only, $109–180 suite; $79–130 double; $69–89 single. Extra person, $20. Meal plan, per person, per night, includes tax/gratuity: MAP, $44; full board, $59. Reduced rates for children. Sports, family, romance, murder mystery, other packages. Senior discount. Alc lunch, $12; alc dinner, $40. Trolley tour, $6.

Extras Rooms equipped for handicapped; elevator. Airport/station pickups. Shuttle service on island. Crib, babysitting, play equipment, games. Spanish, French, Italian spoken.

MACON

A trading center since its founding, Macon remains a manufacturing center to this day. Much of the downtown business area and the College Hill residential neighborhood has been designated as an historic district. The city is located in central Georgia, 82 miles southeast of Atlanta.

1842 Inn ⚑ &.
353 College Street, 31201

Tel: 912–741–1842
800–336–1842
Fax: 912–741–1842

The 1842 Inn consists of an imposing antebellum Greek Revival mansion, restored in 1984, and an adjacent Victorian cottage. The luxurious rooms are furnished handsomely with Oriental rugs, antiques, and quality reproductions; Phil Jenkins is the general manager. Rates include a light breakfast, brought to your room with the morning paper; shoeshine; afternoon coffee or iced tea; pre-dinner hors d'oeuvres; and evening turndown service.

"This beautiful Southern mansion sits on a street of beautiful houses, in a city of beautiful streets. Double-floor columns extend across the front, with splendidly proportioned rooms inside." *(Robert Freidus)* "Within walking distance of many fine antebellum homes and the fabulous Hay House home museum." *(Celia McCullough & Gary Kaplan)* "Our attractive room was off the veranda, complete with fresh flowers." *(Lee Todd)*

"Helpful, friendly check-in, convenient off-street parking. Our room, 'Nancy Hanks,' had matching wallpaper, bedspreads, and bath towels. Good lighting made reading in bed a pleasure. After dinner, we were invited to take tea by the fireplace, lit especially for us. Ample desk and storage space." *(April Burwell)* "Our room had lovely rose-colored walls and coordinating sheets." *(EP)* "Breakfast was served either on the veranda or in our room, at a time specified by us, and consisted of juices, fresh fruit, and French toast one day, bran muffins the next. The Green Jacket, opposite the old railroad terminal, was good for light salads at lunch; Leo's, an easy drive downtown, provided an excellent dinner."*(HJB)* "Our lovely, large airy room was in the Victorian annex; the excellent bathroom had a small TV in it." *(Nancy Bernard)* "First-rate service even though the inn was full. In the living room was a well-stocked bar with cheeses and snacks."*(Jo-Ann Johnsen)* "As charming as ever on a return trip. We enjoyed dinner at a new international restaurant called Ali's." *(CM)*

Other points: "When booking, ask if a group will be in residence." And: "Our room lacked adequate closet space for an extended stay."

Open All year.
Rooms 22 doubles—all with full private bath, telephone, radio, TV, desk, air-conditioning. 9 rooms in annex. Some with whirlpool tubs, gas fireplaces.
Facilities 2 parlors with piano; occasional pianist. 1 acre with garden. Off-street parking. Lake, beaches nearby.
Location 1 m from center. Exit 52 off I-75; go left on Forsyth St.; left on College to inn.
Restrictions Light sleepers should request a second floor room away from lobby, or in adjacent cottage.
Credit cards Amex, MC, Visa.
Rates B&B $89–119 double, $79–109 single. Extra person, $10. Reduced rate for children. 10% AARP discount.
Extras Wheelchair access. Crib.

NEWNAN

Information please: Lovers of Victoriana will be fascinated by **The Parrott-Camp-Soucy Home** (155 Greenville Street, 30263; 404–502–0676), an exceptionally striking house, built in the 1840s but rebuilt in 1885 as a Second Empire Victorian with the addition of elaborate moldings, woodwork, and French mansard roof. The interior is decorated with period antiques, hand-carved woodwork in oak, mahogany, cherry and maple, period wallpapers and stained glass windows. Guest comfort is not forgotten amid the period opulence; the four guest rooms have queen-sized beds, private baths and fireplaces, and are supplied with slippers and bathrobes. Outside are four acres with gardens, a heated swimming pool, and hot tub in a gazebo. The B&B double rates of $95–125 include early morning coffee, breakfast, and afternoon refreshments. A typical breakfast menu might be fresh-squeezed juice, fruit with yogurt and granola, quiche with asparagus and country ham, home-baked pastries and muffins. Newnan is halfway between the Atlanta airport and Callaway Gardens. Your opinions requested.

PERRY

Information please: Eleven miles northwest of Perry is **The Evans-Cantrell House** (300 College Street, Fort Valley, 31030; 912–825–0611), a 15-room Italian Renaissance Revival mansion, built in 1916. Located in the Everett Square Historical District, the inn was renovated in 1985 by Cyriline and Norman Cantrell. A hearty Southern breakfast is included in the double rates of $50–65.

New Perry Hotel and Motel ¢ 🚶 ✕ ♿   *Tel:* 912–987–1000
800 Main Street, P.O.Box 44, 31069   800–877–3779

There's been a hotel on this site since 1850, when the first stagecoach route came through town. In 1924, the Old Perry was razed to make room for the New Perry Hotel. The hotel has been owned for over 50 years by Yates and Harold Green, who added a motel behind the hotel. The hotel restaurant is well known for good Southern cooking at reasonable prices; at lunchtime, a modest amount buys you baked ham with corn relish, Southern fried chicken, or fried catfish, plus soup, two vegetables, hot rolls and corn sticks, while prices at dinner are only slightly higher. Desserts include your choice of apple pan pie, lemon chess pie, or pecan pie—topped with whipped cream. The hotel's location makes it a good meal-time stop if you're en route between Georgia and Florida.

"My room in the hotel was comfortable for one, with a double bed, desk, and easy chair; the bathroom was small, with only a shower. What was particularly nice was the dining room, with excellent local cuisine. Breakfast included ham, grits, biscuits and eggs. The place was bustling with mostly elderly patrons."*(Duane Roller)* "The fresh peach pan pie was absolutely divine." *(HJB)* "We stopped for lunch recently on our way home from Atlanta—the food is wonderful. The old hotel is charming and well maintained. The gardens are gorgeous." *(Sue Baker)*

Open All year.
Rooms 7 suites, 47 doubles—all with private bath and/or shower, telephone, TV, air-conditioning. 39 rooms in hotel; 17 rooms in motel.

Facilities Lobby, restaurant. Swimming pool, flower gardens, off-street parking.
Location 115 m S of Atlanta. 5 blocks S of intersection of Exit 43, I-75, & U.S. 341. At corner of Main & Bell Sts.
Restrictions No alcohol served.
Credit cards Amex, MC, Visa.
Rates Room only, $53 suite, $31–45 double. Extra person in room, $3. Alc breakfast, $3–6; alc lunch $4–7; alc dinner, $11–20.
Extras Wheelchair access. Airport/station pickups.

PINE MOUNTAIN

Also recommended: Enthusiastically recommended is **Callaway Gardens** (Pine Mountain 31822-2000; 706–663–2281 or 800–282–8181), a major resort complex too large (800 units, 5 restaurants) for a full writeup: "Located about 70 miles south of Atlanta, this resort has a golf course and lake with a full complement of water sports." *(SHW)* "Lovely location with woods and a variety of indoor and outdoor gardens. Opportunities for walking, bicycling, seeing wildlife. We had a sumptuous breakfast in the Plantation Room overlooking the garden, with interior floral displays. The butterfly house alone makes the trip worthwhile." *(Celia McCullough, also Lynn Fullman)* "Large, comfortable guest room in conference center lodge; nice soaps and towels in rooms. Good, inexpensive dinner in the Country Store restaurant." *(KLH)* "Nicely furnished cottage in the woods. The screened porch was ideal for playing cards or reading." *(Pat Borysiewicz)*

Reader tip: "Highly recommend the intimate Bon Cuisine restaurant for superb food, interesting decor." *(B. J. Hensley)*

Information please: We need current reports on the **Mountain Top Inn** (P.O. Box 147, 31822; 706–663–4719 or 800–533–6376); its 1500-foot elevation promises temperatures at least 10 degrees cooler than the valley. Accommodations are available in lodge buildings and cabins, and rates range from $45–150. Activities include fishing, boating, swimming, plus hiking on Pine Mountain Trail.

For additional area entries, see **Hamilton**, 5 miles south of Callaway Gardens, **Warm Springs,** about 15 miles northeast, and **Newnan**, about 30 minutes drive north.

PLAINS

Also recommended: Jimmy Carter fans will do well to book a room at **The Plains B&B** (P.O. Box 217, 31780; 912–824–7252), combining turn-of-the-century atmosphere with the convenience of private baths and central air-conditioning. "Located in the center of town, Mrs. Jackson's home is well maintained with clean, comfortable rooms. The house displays memorabilia of the former President, and a plaque identifies the room where his expectant mother stayed just prior to his birth. Good Southern breakfast." *(Hans Wriadt)* B&B double rates are $55.

RABUN GAP

Moon Valley Resort ✗
Patterson Gap Road, Rt. 1, Box 680, 30568

Tel: 706–746–2466

Reached by a circuitous route through the Blue Ridge Mountains, Moon Valley is located in a quiet lakeside cove, and has been owned by the Moon family since 1979. Accommodations are offered in a Scottish-style "castle," in cedar cabins with fireplaces, and in a contemporary chalet with loft bedrooms and skylights. Dinner is served in the gazebo by the lake or in the restaurant, with its fireplace and old store counter that serves as a bar. A second dining room has a high stone hearth and wooden walls decorated with old farm and kitchen tools. A recent dinner included cream of spinach soup, fresh mountain trout, rack of lamb or veal marsala.

"Meals are attractively prepared and tasty. The Moons have a great secret recipe for crackers to munch with the unusual salad, generally consisting of mixed greens, sliced fruit, avocado and/or sprouts. We almost always order the Chateaubriand (when we make our reservations) because we cannot see how anything else could be better. Desserts are large and superb." *(Barbara Show)* Comments appreciated.

Open All year.
Rooms 2 suites in "castle"; 3 doubles in chalet/townhouse; 4 cabins. All with private bath and/or shower, radio, clock, fan. Most with TV, fireplace, refrigerator, deck. 2 with air-conditioning, whirlpool tub.
Facilities Restaurant with fireplace, porch, gazebo. 130 acres with hiking trails, stocked fishing lake. 5 m to skiing, hiking.
Location NE GA. 70 m N of Gainesville, 3½ m W of Dillard, off Betty's Creek Rd. for 3½ m. Follow gravel-covered dirt road, marked by sign for ½ m.
Restrictions No children under 12.
Credit cards Amex, MC, Visa.
Rates $159 suite, $79 double. Extra person $10. 2-night weekend minimum. Alc dinner $21–28.

ST. MARYS

St. Marys is located at the southernmost corner of Georgia, just north of Fernandina Beach on Amelia Island, Florida, and is the starting point for the ferry to the Cumberland Island National Seashore. For an additional area entry, see **Cumberland Island.**

Information please: The **Historic Spencer House Inn** (Osborne at Bryant Street, 31558; 912–882–1872) was built in 1872 and restored in 1990. Three verandas overlook the quiet street below. The 14 guest rooms are decorated with antiques and reproductions, and have private baths, air-conditioning, telephones, and TV; B&B double rates range from $55–100. "Excellent accommodations; the rooms are bright and the furnishings well done. Innkeepers are pleasant and helpful; fine hospitality and service." *(Joe Schmidt)*

Listed in past editions is the 1870 **Goodbread House** (209 Osborne

Street, 31558; 912–882–7490), within walking distance of the Cumberland Island ferry. Carefully restored, it offers wide pine floors and antique decor. The rates include afternoon wine and cheese, a continental breakfast, and the morning paper. Double rates for the four guest rooms with private baths range from $50–60.

ST. SIMONS ISLAND

Little St. Simons Island ♦♦
P.O. Box 1078, 31522

Tel: 912–638–7472
Fax: 912–634–1811

To get to Little St. Simons, you leave your car at the locked parking lot on St. Simons Island and take a 20-minute boat ride. Since only 24 people can be accommodated on this 10,000-acre private island, you'll find as much solitude as you desire. With the variety of habitats on the island, and its location in the path of a number of migratory patterns, the opportunities for bird-watching are outstanding. Resident naturalists are available to answer questions, and readers report that their presence really adds to the experience. Debbie McIntyre is the long-time manager.

Rates include three meals a day, evening hors d'oeuvres, wine with dinner, snacks and hot and cold beverages on request, picnic lunches, use of all facilities and equipment, and access to all experts. The food is home-cooked, including Southern specialties, such as shrimp mull, smoked ham, cornbread, and pecan pie. Guest rooms are located in several cottages, with the main lodge dating back to 1917; the Honeymoon Cottage was built in 1920 and refurbished in 1986, while the remaining two were constructed in the 1980s.

"Great for bird-watchers (the number and variety of birds are incredible), animal-watchers (for the armadillos, alligators, deer, an occasional snake), swimmers (six miles of beach), horseback riders, surf-fishers, boaters, loafers, honeymooners, and anyone who doesn't want an 18-hole golf course and disco at their resort." *(Robert Saxon)* "Swimming in a pool fed with artesian well water was heavenly." *(EB)* "Our room had a king-sized bed, two easy chairs and a table, plenty of closet and drawer space, and a heart-stopping view of the marshes and woods beyond." *(Paula Marcus)* "Debbie and her staff give the place its friendly atmosphere and Kevin is a naturalist who makes every trip and outing a delightful experience." *(Gary & Monica Gray)* "The cottages have four bedrooms with a comfortable central living room." *(Edith Potter)* Worth noting: "Mosquitoes plentiful during our spring visit; bring repellent."

Open Feb. 1–mid-Nov.
Rooms 2 bedrooms in main lodge. 2 cabins with 2 bedrooms, 2 cabins with 4 bedrooms—all with private bath and/or shower, fan, screened porches, living rooms, coffee maker.
Facilities Dining room, living rooms with library/bar, fireplace; family room. Swimming pool. Slide shows, games, crafts, stargazing. 8 acres for lodge complex; barrier island is 10,000 undeveloped acres, with 6 m of ocean beach. Swimming, surf-casting, shelling, boating, bird-watching, hiking, horseback riding, canoeing.
Location SE GA, Glynn County. 70 m S of Savannah, 70 m N of Jacksonville, FL. Northernmost of the Golden Isles. Nearest mainland town, Brunswick, GA.

Restrictions No smoking in dining room, guest rooms. No children under 5. Children must have good table manners.
Credit cards MC, Visa.
Rates Full board, $300–400 double, $200–300 single. Extra person, $100.
Extras Airport/station pickups; varying fee. No charge for boat transportation from St. Simons to Little St. Simons.

SAVANNAH

Savannah was founded in the eighteenth century by the English general James Oglethorpe and has been a major port ever since. Today, elegant yachts have replaced the pirate ships and China clippers of the early days, but a surprising number of Savannah's original buildings have survived. In fact, Savannah now claims to have the largest urban National Landmark District in the U.S., with over 1,000 restored homes in an area 2½ miles square. Some are now museums; many more are inns and restaurants. In fact, it seems to us that Savannah has more B&Bs these days than you can shake a croissant at!

Savannah is located 255 miles southeast of Atlanta, 136 miles north of Jacksonville, Florida, and 106 miles south of Charleston, South Carolina. It's an 18-mile drive to the Atlantic Ocean beaches of Tybee Island. Start your exploration of the town at the Visitors Center on West Broad Street. There's an audiovisual program to introduce you to the city, lots of brochures, and a well-informed staff to answer questions.

Worth noting: Walking at night in some parts of Savannah is inadvisable; ask your innkeeper for advice. Parking in Savannah's historic district can also be a problem. Some inns have a limited number of on-site spaces, while others do not. If you're traveling by car, be sure to get details. The front doors of most historic inns in Savannah are reached by a flight of steps; guest rooms at the ground level look out onto a sidewalk at the front of the house and the garden to the back, and usually have exposed brick walls and more rustic furnishings than upstairs guest rooms; these "garden-level" rooms are often dark and sometimes lack privacy.

Reader tips: If you don't mind waiting on line, head for Mrs. Wilkes Boarding House (107 West Jones Street) where enormous Southern-style breakfasts are served at penny-pinching prices. There's no menu, but your table will be covered with a dozen dishes; one reader thought lunch was worth the wait, while another reported that "we waited 70 minutes on line and then were rushed out in 20 minutes." *Kip Goldman & Marty Wall* recommend the Chutzpah Panache, "a delightful European cafe and clothing boutique, a great stop for a light lunch or dinner, or just coffee and dessert." "Savannah is made for walking; if you like *real* bookstores, stop by Shaver's, on a beautiful square in the historic district; it's just across from the ugly DeSoto Hilton. Browse in the shops and galleries of the City Market, and pick up a light lunch at one of the cafés. Well worth a splurge was dinner at Elizabeth on 37th, in a handsome mansion; standout appetizers included a three-mushroom dish, and another with eggplant and goat cheese; favorite entrées were grouper with pecans and shrimp and okra; desserts were just OK. Not a neighborhood for strolling, though." *(SWS)*

Also recommended: River tugboats are docked just outside of the **Olde Harbour Inn**, (508 East Factor's Walk, 31401; 912–234–4100) a three-story warehouse building along the cobblestone streets of Factor's Walk. Originally planned as condominiums, the inn's one and two-bedroom suites have living rooms and fully equipped kitchens. Included in the $95–155 double rates are a light breakfast of cereal, muffins, biscuits, juice, and coffee; evening wine and cheese; a bedtime bowl of ice cream; and turn-down service. "Our suite had stone walls and massive wooden support ceiling beams, and a great view of this working harbor. There were always more big, thirsty towels than we needed. Security was good, with keys required for the outside door and our suite." *(Imogene Tillis)*

Ballastone Inn & Townhouse	*Tel:* 912–236–1484
14 East Oglethorpe Avenue, 31401	800–822–4553
	Fax: 912–236–4626

Originally known as the old Anderson House, the Ballastone Inn dates back to 1838. When the inn was restored, the original owners renamed it the Ballastone in recognition of the ballast stones of which much of the city had been built. In the early nineteenth century, English sailing ships dumped their ballast stones at nearby Yamacraw Bluff, to make room for the bales of cotton to be taken to England.

Rates at the Ballastone include a welcoming glass of sherry and bowl of fruit, continental breakfast with fresh flowers and a morning paper, brandy and chocolates at bedtime, overnight shoeshines, and terry robes in the bath. Rooms are individually decorated in a variety of styles, with antiques, queen- and king-size beds, and modern baths. Authentic Savannah colors are used throughout, coordinated with Scalamandre fabrics. Late-afternoon tea and cocktails are served in the garden, bar, or in the antique-filled parlor. The inn was purchased by Richard Carlson in 1988.

"This small hotel is surprisingly warm in feeling, due in large part to the friendly staff. Meal suggestions were wonderful, and menus were available to help in the decision." *(Caroline & Jim Lloyd)* "Each floor has five or six rooms, with spacious halls and sitting areas. The doors of unoccupied rooms are left open for guests to sneak a peek; all we saw were spacious and beautifully decorated, with canopy or Charleston rice beds. Breakfast of fresh orange juice, strawberries and pineapple, and muffins, was delivered to our room on a silver tray at the appointed hour with the Sunday paper." *(Linda Bamber)* "Our bed had an excellent mattress and reading lamps on each side of the canopied bed. We enjoyed the small garden off the parlor—a lovely place to sit with a glass of sherry." *(Amy Peritksy)*

"We had willing assistance with our considerable luggage. The elevator took us to our spacious fourth-floor room, with two comfortable queen-sized beds. The air conditioning was efficient and relatively quiet; the bathroom had plenty of towels, a hairdryer, and toiletries provided the first night." *(Alex Williams)* "My spacious third floor room, Gazebo, had dark green walls with an English-style cabbage rose print border, repeated on the bedspreads and accent pillows on the couch. Exceptionally good lighting. Sherry, fruit, tea, coffee, and cookies are always available in the living room." *(SWS, also Elaine Bounds)*

Open All year.
Rooms 7 suites, 15 doubles—all with private bath and/or shower, telephone, radio, TV/VCR, air-conditioning. Some with whirlpool bath or fireplace. 4 suites in Ballastone Townhouse, 4 blocks from inn.
Facilities Parlor with fireplace, videotape library, gift shop, florist, bar/lounge, patio. Small garden. Off- and on-street parking.
Location Historic district. 6 blocks from riverfront. Adjacent to Juliette Low House.
Restrictions No children under 12. Traffic noise in some rooms.
Credit cards Amex, MC, Visa.
Rates B&B, $175–200 suite, $95–155 double. Extra person, $10. Corporate rate Sun.–Thurs.
Extras Limited accessibility for disabled, elevator. Small pets allowed.

East Bay Inn 🛏 ✕ ♿
225 East Bay Street, 31401

Tel: 912–238–1225
800–500–1225
Fax: 912–232–2709

Built in 1853 as a cotton warehouse, the East Bay Inn was created in 1982, and has been owned by J. Roger Hammond since 1991; Jean Ryerson is the manager. Typical of the period, this sturdy brick building has a first-floor facade made of cast iron, as are the interior columns visible in the parlor and some guest rooms. Amenities include evening wine in the parlor, nightly turndown service with Savannah pralines, in-room coffee and the morning newspaper. Skyler's restaurant offers such specialties as crab cakes with remoulade sauce, shrimp with Jack Daniels cream sauce, and garlic chicken with eggplant.

"Friendly, helpful staff; gracious living room/lobby area; spacious, comfortable rooms. My room had been recently redone in a handsome deep red and blue-green color scheme, and had high ceilings, a brick wall, an armoire for the TV and storage, and two reproduction four-poster rice double beds. Breakfast is served in the sunny, appealing bar, and included juice, melon, yogurt, cereal, English and sweet muffins, pastry, with a choice of regular coffee, decaf, or tea. The privacy of a hotel with the friendliness of an inn." *(SWS)* "A fine meal in their downstairs restaurant." *(BJ Hensley)*

Open All year. Restaurant closed 1st week Jan., 1st week July.
Rooms 28 doubles—all with full private bath, telephone, radio, clock, TV, air-conditioning, coffee maker. 3 with desk, 2 with patio.
Facilities Restaurant, bar/breakfast room, parlor. Limited off-street parking.
Location Historic District, across from Emmet Park, near Savannah River. From I-95 take I-16 East until it ends at Montgomery St. Go straight on Montgomery. Turn right on Bay St. to hotel on right after 3rd traffic light.
Restrictions Traffic noise in some rooms. No smoking in public areas; some nonsmoking guest rooms.
Credit cards Amex, CB, DC, Discover, MC, Visa.
Rates B&B, $89–129 double. Extra person, $10. Off-season specials. No charge for children under 12. 10% senior, AAA discount. Alc dinner, $25.
Extras Wheelchair accessible; 1 room specially equipped. Cribs, babysitting. Pets under 30 lbs.; $25 fee.

The Foley House ♦♦
14 West Hull Street, 31401

Tel: 912–232–6622
800–647–3708
Fax: 912–231–1218

Foley House was built in 1896 and restored in 1982. Among the more interesting finds of the renovation was a skeleton lying behind a wall—a knife still stuck in its breast bone! Although no ghost sightings have been reported, any returning spirit would undoubtedly be impressed with the lovely decor and service here. Rooms are beautifully furnished with four-poster Charleston rice beds, antiques, and Oriental rugs, and have modern baths. Breakfast includes croissants, bagels and Danish pastry with fresh fruit, juices, coffee or tea, served with the morning paper in the room or in the courtyard. The rates also include afternoon tea; evening sherry, port, wine and soft drinks; and shoeshine and turndown services.

"Excellent service, comfortable bed, large room with attractive decor." *(Dawn Allison)* "High quality, extremely comfortable." *(William MacGowan)* "If you don't mind a climb, rooms on the upper floors are slightly less expensive than the lower ones but are just as nice, with a better view over the city." *(SWS)*

Open All year.
Rooms 20 doubles—all with full private bath, telephone, radio, TV, desk, air-conditioning, gas fireplace. Some with Jacuzzi, VCR, balcony, refrigerator. 4 rooms in carriage house.
Facilities Parlor with fireplace, videotape library. 2 courtyards with gardens, fountain, hot tub. Valet parking (fee); on-street parking.
Location Center of historic district. On Chippewa Sq., between Whitaker and Bull Sts.
Restrictions No off-street parking; staff will feed meters on weekdays (weekends free). Smoking limited to certain rooms.
Credit cards Amex, MC, Visa.
Rates B&B, $85–190 double. Extra person, $10. 10% AAA, senior discount. Children under 12 free. Extra person, $10. Dec.–Feb. (exc. hol.), 3rd night free.
Extras Crib.

The Gastonian ♿
220 East Gaston Street, 31401

Tel: 912–232–2869
800–322–6603
Fax: 912–232–0710

From California modern to Savannah historical was quite a change in location and life-style for Hugh and Roberta Lineberger. But they were sure enough of their innkeeping plans to invest $2 million in the 1986 restoration of two connecting Savannah mansions, built in 1868 in the Regency Italianate style. The interiors are highlighted with fine woods and heart pine floors, decorative moldings and brass, and wallpapers in the original Scalamandre Savannah pattern. Depending on the room, the luxurious decor ranges from French, Italianate, English, Victorian, or Colonial, but both common areas and guest rooms are stunning with authentic antiques, Persian rugs, and rice poster or Charleston canopied beds.

"Located in a quiet residential area near Forsyth Park, the inn is within walking distance of Savannah's attractions. Hugh and Roberta are the most gracious of hosts, always helpful and concerned about their guests, friendly and pleasant." *(Susan Rasmussen)* "Breakfasts were friendly occasions for getting acquainted with the innkeepers and other travelers. Our room was high up in the connecting house, next door, with a four-poster bed and a separate sitting room." *(Lee Todd)* "The Julia Scarbrough room was exceptionally lovely." *(Nina Elliott)* "Wine and fruit awaits when you check in, and peach liqueur and a praline is placed in your room every night. The Caswell-Massey toiletries are a nice extra, as are the terrycloth robes. The Linebergers are knowledgeable about Savannah, and made terrific restaurant recommendations. Breakfast is served family style in either the kitchen or the lush dining room, depending on the number of guests; the food is good, especially the bacon quiche." *(Rachel Gorlin, also SWS)*

Area for improvement: "My room needed a second bedside light and table; its mattress was softer than I'm accustomed to."

Open All year.
Rooms 3 suites, 10 doubles—all with private bath and/or shower, telephone, radio, TV, air-conditioning, fireplace. 6 with whirlpool tub. Some with desk, fan.
Facilities Kitchen/breakfast room, parlor, dining room. Courtyard with hot tub. Limited off-street parking.
Location Historic district.
Restrictions No smoking. No children under 12. Minimal interior sound-proofing.
Credit cards Amex, MC, Visa.
Rates B&B, $195–250 suite, $115–185 double. Extra person, $25. Corporate rates.
Extras Wheelchair access; some rooms equipped for the disabled; elevator.

The Kehoe House ♿
123 Habersham Street, 31401

Tel: 912–232–1020
800–820–1020
Fax: 912–231–0208

An imposing mansion built in 1892, The Kehoe House was restored as an inn in 1993, and is owned by Consul Court Property Management; Peggy Holmes is the manager. Rates include a full breakfast and evening hors d'oeuvres served at 6 P.M. The inn's common areas include an enormous double parlor, furnished with handsome antiques and highlighted by a beautiful Chinese screen. The beautiful guest rooms are furnished with equal care, luxurious yet not fussy, restfully done in soft colors.

"Our suite, overlooking Columbia Square, was beautifully coordinated—from the love seat and armchairs to the handsome queen-size sleigh bed, from the draperies to the wallpaper. Hors d'oeuvres were delicious: open-faced finger sandwiches and little pastries of salmon mousse. Breakfast was equally appetizing. We were seated in the parlor at two small tray tables covered with white linen place mats, and served chilled orange juice, muffins and croissants, a composed fruit plate napped with a light custard, and Belgian waffles. The elevator is convenient to the parking area, which is just across the street from the inn." *(Jeanne Smith)*

Open All year.
Rooms 2 suites, 13 doubles—all with private bath and/or shower, telephone with data port, radio, clock, TV, desk, air-conditioning, fan. 10 with balcony. 2 suites in adjoining building.

Facilities Double parlor, music room with piano, conference room, fitness room. Off-street parking.
Location Historic district, Columbia Square. Take I-16 to end, go right on Oglethrope Ave. Go left of Habersham St. to first square, Columbia.
Restrictions No smoking. Children over 12.
Credit cards Amex, CB, DC, Discover, MC, Visa.
Rates B&B, $195–225 suite, $100–175 double. 15% senior, AAA discount.
Extras Wheelchair access; 1 room specially equipped.

Lion's Head Inn 🛏 ♿

120 East Gaston Street, 31401

Tel: 912–232–4580
800–355–LION
Fax: 912–232–7422

Named for the lion's head that appears on the foundation of this 1883 mansion as well as the brass knocker on the front door, the Lion's Head Inn was restored as an inn in 1992 by Christy and John Dell'Orco. The double parlor and dining room are furnished in the formal Empire style of the early 1800s while the guest rooms have four-poster beds and richly colored walls. Breakfast is served from 8:30–10 A.M., and includes fresh fruit salad; homemade blueberry, banana nut, or bran muffins; zucchini or cranberry bread; croissants, cinnamon rolls, or bagels; granola and cereal; and juice, tea, and hazelnut coffee.

"Easy walking distance to anywhere in historic Savannah. Michigan transplants Christy and John have painstakingly restored the house with beautiful antiques. Christy, a licensed guide, can take guests on walking tours of the historic district and John is always available to answer questions. Breakfast is served in the formal dining room, plus afternoon tea, with wine and cheese, crackers and munchies. At night, a peach-shaped white chocolate is placed on your pillow, along with a glass of sherry by the bed." *(Kip Goldman & Marty Wall)* "Rooms beautifully decorated, immaculately clean. The owners go out of their way to be accommodating, giving directions, offering ideas for dining and entertainment, suggesting places to visit and explore, and offering many thoughtful extra touches." *(Larry Koehn)*

Open All year.
Rooms 2 suites, 4 doubles—all with private bath and/or shower, telephone, radio, clock, TV, desk, air-conditioning. some with fan, fireplace, refrigerator, VCR.
Facilities Dining room, living room, library with books, stereo, videotapes; all with fireplace. Veranda with swing, garden courtyard with fountain, pond. Limited off-street parking.
Location Historic district, on E. Gaston between Drayton & Abercorn; ½ block from Forsyth Park. Follow I-16 to end at Montgomery St. Go right at first light. At Liberty St. go right and continue 3 lights to East Gaston. Go right to inn on right.
Restrictions No smoking. No windows in 2 ground level rooms.
Credit cards Discover, MC, Visa.
Rates B&B, $95–135 (for 4), $110 (for 2) suite; $65–110 double. Extra person, $10. Corporate rate, $70, Sun.–Thurs. Discount for 4-night stay. Off-season rate. Tips welcome. 10% senior discount. Infants free. 2-night minimum holiday weekends.
Extras Limited wheelchair access. Airport/station pickups. Crib, babysitting.

River Street Inn ₵ ♁ ✕ ♿
115 East River Street, 31401

Tel: 912–234–6400
800–253–4229
Fax: 912–234–1478

Situated between historic Factor's Walk and River Street, this appealing hotel overlooks the working river port of Savannah and is within walking distance of all historic areas. Originally built in 1817 as a storage warehouse for raw cotton, the building was enlarged in 1853 by the addition of the top three floors. Access to each level was necessary to get the cotton bales in and out of the building, so a series of alleys and walks were created on the bluff, and bridges were built to provide street access to each level. The alleys, known as "Factor's Walk" after the factors who graded the cotton, are one of its unusual design features. Rooms are furnished with four poster and canopy beds, Oriental rugs and polished brass bath fixtures. Some guest rooms have French balconies and floor-length windows, providing river views. Rates include the morning paper, a full breakfast buffet, and a wine and cheese reception Monday through Saturday. Before retiring, guests can stop in at Mates, the cafe just below the inn on River Street. "The location is ideal for night life." *(Naomi Moschitta)* "Lovely people, excellent cuisine, attractive rooms. Took the elevator down to the River level and had a super dinner at the Shrimp Factory." *(BJ Hensley)*

Open All year.
Rooms 44 suites, doubles—all with private bath and/or shower, telephone, TV, air-conditioning, desk. Some with balcony.
Facilities Restaurant, billiard room, lounge, atrium lobby with sitting areas. Health club privileges; fax/copier services.
Location From I-95, take I-16 E to end at Montgomery St. Go straight on Montgomery to Bay St. Turn right on Bay. Inn is on left after 3rd light, between River & Bay Sts.
Restrictions Some non-smoking rooms.
Credit cards Amex, CB, Discover, Enroute, MC, Visa.
Rates B&B, $79–139 double, $69–129 single. Extra person, $10. No charge for children under 18. Corporate rates. Alc lunch, alc dinner $6–12. AAA, off-season rates.
Extras Small pets with approval. Wheelchair access.

SENOIA

Senoia is located in central Georgia, about 37 miles south of Atlanta. Senoia is 9 miles south of Fayetteville, between Griffin & Newnan, at the intersection of routes 85 and 16, just a half-hour drive to the Atlanta airport.

Information please: Under new ownership is **The Culpepper House** (35 Broad Street, P.O. Box 462, 30276; 404–599–8182) purchased by Maggie Armstrong and Barbara Storm in 1994. This Queen Anne Victorian style home has gingerbread trim and stained glass windows, and is located in Senoia's historic district. The double rates of $75 include a full breakfast.

The Veranda ♦ ♿
252 Seavy Street, Box 177, 30276

Tel: 404–599–3905
Fax: 404–599–3806

A white clapboard building with Doric columns, The Veranda was built in 1907 and is listed on the National Register of Historic Places. Bobby and Jan Boal purchased the house in 1985, and after extensive restoration opened its doors as an inn. Many rooms feature the original tin-covered ceilings and stained-glass windows. Antiques and memorabilia, including Oriental rugs, a player piano, and a bookcase owned by President McKinley, add to the old-fashioned atmosphere. Guest rooms are spacious with high ceilings, armoires, rocking chairs, and handmade quilts. After the beds are turned down at night, guests often discover a small "pillow treat," such as a homemade fruitcake or a miniature kaleidoscope. The gift shop downstairs offers an extensive collection of kaleidoscopes and unique games. Breakfast includes a variety of juices and hot beverages, fresh fruit with strawberry sorbet or stewed dried fruit, granola, and such entrées as cheese soufflé with basil and sweet pepper, quiche with chicken and broccoli, or cheddar mushroom omelets with asparagus and seasoned grits. Dinners are no less tempting—a recent meal included corn chowder with corn sticks, salad with edible flowers, smoked trout with watercress and whole wheat sourdough bread, veal with pasta and carrot soufflé, and angel cake with raspberries and whipped cream.

"Jan and Bobby are hospitable, attentive innkeepers. The many sitting areas come equipped with unusual books and magazines; the many games provide opportunities for conversation between guests." *(Alice Young)* "Our room had a four poster bed; the immaculate modern bathroom was stocked with toiletries. After a wonderful dinner, the tempting desserts included a cobbler, cheesecake, or fruit tarts. Delicious breakfast of apple crepes with whipped cream, homemade muffins, jam, jelly, and grits." *(Binnie Anne Davidow)* "My initial phone conversation with Bobby Boal was a clue to the outstanding hospitality we would experience. We stayed in the Bird Watcher room—a soft yellow upstairs room with windows on two sides. After a wonderful night's sleep, crickets and the crowing of roosters awakened us to a royal breakfast." *(Marion Ruben)*

Open All year. No dinner Sun.
Rooms 9 doubles with full private bath, air-conditioning. 4 with radio, desk. 1 with fan. 1 with whirlpool tub.
Facilities Dining room, parlor with player piano and pipe organ; veranda, gift shop.
Location In historic district. ½ block from town center.
Restrictions No smoking. Alcohol only in guest rooms. Well-supervised children.
Credit cards Amex, Discover, MC, Visa.
Rates B&B, $85–105 double, $65 single. Extra person, $20. Prix fixe dinner, $29 (by reservation).
Extras Wheelchair access. Playpen. Babysitting by arrangement.

TATE

Also recommended: An hour north of Atlanta is the **Tate House** (P.O. Box 33, 30177; 404–735–3122 or, inside GA, 800–342–7515) built in 1926 by Colonel Sam Tate, president of the Georgia Marble Company, and designed to exhibit the treasures of his quarry. The Etowah marble exterior of the house is complemented by formal gardens, marble walks, fountains and statues. Restored and opened in 1985 by Ann Laird, guests can also enjoy the tennis courts, swimming pool, and horseback riding. The mansion has four luxurious suites, while the nine log cabins have stone fireplaces, hot tubs, and sleeping lofts. Double rates, including tax, are $83 weekdays with a continental breakfast, $132 weekends with a full breakfast. "Tate is known as the marble capitol of the U.S. We had a tour of the entire mansion and extensive grounds." *(BJ Hensley)*

Information please: About 1 mile from Tate is **The Woodbridge Inn** (411 Chambers Street, Jasper, 30143; 706–692–6293). We've had excellent reports on the restaurant, housed in an 1850s farmhouse. Motel-like accommodations were available in an adjacent contemporary building, damaged by fire in 1994, now being rebuilt.

THOMASVILLE

Thomasville is centrally located in south Georgia, 28 miles north of Tallahassee, Florida. Once the train lines were repaired after the Civil War, wealthy Northerners traveled here to hunt quail, breathe the pine-scented highland air, and escape the harsh winters; many built lavish "cottages" and "shooting plantations" for the winter season. The mild winter climate hasn't changed over the last century; now travelers detour off I-10 or I-75 to enjoy Thomasville's leisurely pleasures—visits to historic homes and plantations, two challenging golf courses, tennis, and sporting clays. During the Rose Festival, held the fourth week of April, reservations are essential.

Reader tip: "Thomasville has small museums and many beautiful old homes. The Rose Test Gardens are a must for any rose lover. The citizens of Thomasville have great civic pride, and roses are everywhere. The people are friendly and helpful." *(HJB)* "We enjoyed a nice meal at Melissa's, housed in the former laundry for the 19th century tourist hotels. We toured the historic district and nearby Pebble Hill Plantation." *(Celia McCullough)*

Also recommended: Listed on the National Register of Historic Places and overlooking Paradise Park, **Our Cottage on the Park** (801 South Hansell Street, 31792; 912–227–0404), is a Queen Anne Victorian home built in 1893 and opened as a B&B by Connie Clineman in 1992. B&B double rates for the two guest suites are $60 double, and guests are delighted with its comfortable atmosphere and welcoming proprietor. "Connie takes pride in her cottage and town, making guests feel right at home. Chocolates are left by your bed at turndown, and the excellent breakfasts include French toast with heart-shaped poached eggs or crepes with peaches and strawberries, served on Royal Doulton china." *(Robert Mast)* Connie notes that children of all ages are most welcome.

1884 Paxton House ¢   *Tel:* 912–226–5197
445 Remington Avenue, 31792   800–278–0138

One of the first seasonal residences in Thomasville, the Paxton House was built in 1884, and restored as an inn in 1992 by owner Susie Sherrod. This

Victorian Gothic home has twelve (decorative) fireplaces, a circular stair-case, and twelve-foot ceilings. The rooms are decorated with Susie's collections of china, antiques, and quilts. Breakfast is served at guests' convenience, and includes fresh fruit, juice, home-baked breads, and per-haps stuffed orange French toast and bacon or fruit crepes with ham. Rates also include in-room fresh flowers, bedside chocolates, turndown service, and refreshments in the butler's pantry.

"The owner is a real character; the house is quite amazing; our room was very comfortable. Breakfast was delicious and bountiful." *(Elizabeth Church)* "Susie Sherrod and her mother run this B&B as an impressive, comfortable, and authentically furnished home. During her military career, Susie collected ceramics and other objects from around the world and displays them throughout the house. She is knowledgeable about the history of the house and the town." *(Celia McCullough)*

Areas for improvement: "An updated bathroom; a reading light for my side of the bed."

Open All year.
Rooms 4 suites, 2 doubles—all with full private bath, telephone, radio, clock, TV, air-conditioning, ceiling fan. Some with desk, VCR. 2 doubles in Garden Cottage.
Facilities Living room, guest pantry, porches. 1.6 acres with off-street parking, garden. Historic district walking tours.
Location Historic district near center. One block from U.S. 84; 2 blocks from U.S. 319. At corner of Hansell & Remington.
Restrictions No smoking. Children over 10.
Credit cards MC, Visa.
Rates B&B, $75–120 suite, $65–75 double. Midweek corporate rate, $60–70. Midweek, off-season rates. Extra person, $20. 2-night minimum high season or 10% single-night surcharge.
Extras Crib, babysitting. German spoken.

Evans House B&B ¢
725 South Hansell Street, 31792

Tel: 912–226–1343
800–344–4717
Fax: 912–226–0653

Built in 1898, the Evans House is located in an area of late Victorian houses built across from 27-acre Paradise Park, in what was then suburban Thomasville. Its transitional style bridges the asymmetry of the Victorian era and the formality of the emerging Neo-classical style. Lee Puskar, who has owned Evans House since 1989, has furnished it with a mixture of turn-of-the century and contemporary pieces. Breakfasts vary daily, but might include fresh squeezed orange juice, melon with strawberries, sau-sage, eggs to order, grits, buttermilk biscuits, and blueberry bran muffins one day; and sparkling cranberry juice, grapefruit garnished with grapes, apricot French toast (from home-baked bread), sugar-cured ham, and homemade strawberry jelly roll the next.

"Friendly owners put me quickly at ease, and I felt I'd known them all my life. With their security system I felt extremely safe." *(Rita Gable)* "Genuine warmth and welcome; exceptionally comfortable beds. Lee Pus-kar respected my lactose intolerance while preparing delicious French toast." *(EMJ)* "Our room, with twin beds, two comfortable chairs, and good lighting was clean and quiet. The bathroom was vintage but ade-quate and well supplied with towels. Superb breakfast with fresh peach crepes and excellent coffee."(ELC) "After settling in, Lee brought me a plate of homemade brownies and iced tea, and provided helpful information about the area's historic homes." (Bill Novak)

Open All year.
Rooms 1 suite, 3 doubles—all with private bath and/or shower, radio, desk, air-conditioning, fan.
Facilities Dining room, living room with TV, entrance hall & library with fireplaces, guest kitchen with refrigerator and refreshments. Off-street parking, bicycles. Paradise Park across street.
Location Park Front Historic District. $1/4$ m from downtown.
Restrictions No smoking.
Credit cards None accepted.
Rates B&B, $95 suite, $50–75 double, $50–65 single. Weekly, commercial rates.
Extras Airport/station pickups. Pets by prior arrangement.

The Grand Victoria Inn ¢   Tel: 912–226–7460
817 South Hansell, 31792

Built in 1893, Anne Dodge restored this eclectic Victorian mansion as an inn in 1991.

"Anne is an exceptionally warm person. The Sheridan Room has antique walnut furniture and a four-poster king-size bed, with soft down pillows and a floral comforter with a deep burgundy background; there's an adjoining screened sleeping porch with a hammock. The Jenny Lind room has a queen-size wicker bed, oak antiques, and a small sitting area with a fluffy floral couch. Breakfast treats include fresh fruit crepes and egg casseroles. We loved sitting on the front porch rockers, overlooking the wooded park, sipping iced tea and chatting with Anne." (Shannon Mikell) "The Hoosier Room is decorated in crisp blue and white with an original Hoosier cabinet, a double pencil post canopy bed, down comforter, and luxurious towels. Our favorite breakfast is pecan-stuffed French toast with raspberry syrup, and accompanied by fresh-squeezed orange juice. Anne is flexible about the timing, trying to accommodate all her guests. Tea, coffee, hot chocolate and soda are always available, and fresh baked goods are often offered." (Tom & Carol Kehoe) "Special touches include mints on your pillow, afternoon tea and scones." (Melissa White) "Friendly and attentive service, ample parking, elegant decor." (Cynthia Hinrichs Acree) "Wonderful from the delicious breakfast to the evening snack of chocolate cake and cookies." (Bob & Anne Huffman) "Relaxing reading areas—books and magazines everywhere and even a meditation garden outside." (Caroline San Juan)

Open All year.
Rooms 4 doubles—all with private bath and/or shower, radio, clock, fan, air-conditioning. 2 with gas fireplace, 1 with balcony, screened sleeping porch, whirlpool tub.
Facilities Dining room with piano; living room, family room with TV/VCR, stereo; library; veranda with swing. 1 acre with gardens, patio with fountain, off-street parking. Paradise Park across street.
Location Walking distance to town. From U.S. Rte. 19, go E on U.S. Rte. 319 or Smith Ave. to Hansell St. & turn left to inn on left. On Hansell between Old Monticello Rd. & Smith Ave.

Restrictions No smoking. Alcohol discouraged. Well-behaved children welcome.
Credit cards None accepted.
Rates B&B, $55–80 double, $50–75 single. Extra adult, $10; child under 3, $5. 2-night minimum Rose Week.
Extras Crib, babysitting. Picnic baskets.

Susina Plantation 𝕋

Tel: 912–377–9644

Meridian Road, Route 3, Box 1010, 31792

"Susina is a Greek Revival residence built in 1841 and listed on the National Register of Historic Places. The high-ceilinged rooms are furnished with carefully chosen antique four-poster beds, chests, and hand-crocheted bedspreads. The parlor is large and comfortable with scrapbooks full of historic details. The dining room focuses on a majestic table which seats over 12, but there are smaller tables for those who prefer more private dining." *(Judith Wilkins)*

"Susina is surrounded by lawns and woodlands. The grounds are wonderful for admiring the live oaks draped with Spanish moss, magnolias, and flowering bushes. Long-time Swedish owner Anne-Marie Walker provides quality cuisine, fluffy towels, firm comfortable beds, and plenty of plantation atmosphere." *(HB)* "Anyone who is looking for perfect plumbing, manicured lawns, or impeccable housekeeping, should look elsewhere. The beauty of Susina is its air of slightly decayed luxury." *(John Freebairn)* "Dinner was divine—with a perfectly spiced shrimp and eggplant Creole dish—and the table was formally set with beautiful silver. Breakfast was first class, including the freshly squeezed orange juice." *(Jo-Ann Johnson)*

Open All year.
Rooms 8 doubles—all with private bath and/or shower, desk, air-conditioning, porch.
Facilities Dining room, living room, screened verandas. 115 acres with 2 m jogging trail, fishing pond, swimming pool, tennis court. Golf, hunting nearby.
Location SE GA, just N of FL border. 12 m S of Thomasville, 22 m N of Tallahassee. Watch carefully for Susina signs off Rte. 319 to Meridan Road (S.R. 155).
Credit cards None accepted.
Rates MAP, $175 double, $125 single. Prix fixe dinner with wine, $35.

WARM SPRINGS

Information please: Best known as the home of Roosevelt's Little White House, Warm Springs now attracts visitors for its historic significance as well as its numerous craft shops. In 1988, Lee and Gerrie Thompson restored the 85-year-old **Hotel Warm Springs** (17 Broad Street, P.O. Box 351, 31830; 706–655–2114). The town's only hotel in Roosevelt's day, members of the press, secret service, and assorted dignitaries stayed here when Roosevelt was at the Little White House. Two honeymoon suites with king-size beds and heart-shaped Jacuzzi tubs were recently added; breakfast in bed, chocolates, flowers and champagne are included in the honeymoon rate. B&B rates for the three suites are $80–160; $58–73 for the 11 doubles. "We liked the hotel's simplicity and character, and admire the tremendous amount of personal effort the Thompsons have put into the restoration." *(Steve & Elise Holman)*

Key to Abbreviations and Symbols

For complete information and explanations, please see the Introduction.

¢ Especially good value for overnight accommodation.

🛏 Families welcome. Most (but not all) have cribs, baby-sitting, games, play equipment, and reduced rates for children.

✕ Meals served to public; reservations recommended or required.

🎾 Tennis court and swimming pool and/or lake on grounds. Golf usually on grounds or nearby.

♿ Limited or full wheelchair access; call for details.

Rates: Range from least expensive room in low season to most expensive room in peak season.

Room only: No meals included; European Plan (EP).

B&B: Bed and breakfast; includes breakfast, sometimes afternoon/evening refreshment.

MAP: Modified American Plan; includes breakfast and dinner.

Full board: Three meals daily.

Alc lunch: À la carte lunch; average price of entrée plus nonalcoholic drink, tax, tip.

Alc dinner: Average price of three-course dinner, including half bottle of house wine, tax, tip.

Prix fixe dinner: Three- to five-course set dinner, excluding wine, tax, tip unless otherwise noted.

Extras: Noted if available. Always confirm in advance. Pets are not permitted unless specified; if you are allergic, ask for details; *most innkeepers have pets.*

Kentucky

Inn at the Park, Louisville

Kentucky's history is a rich and complex one—Daniel Boone explored and hunted here, Abraham Lincoln was born here, and Stephen Foster and Harriet Beecher Stowe wrote about Kentucky. In the development of the U.S., Kentucky has served as a bridge state: Linking the north and south, it was a slave state but fought for the Union in the Civil War; from Virginia to Missouri, settlers passed through on their way west.

And there is far more to present-day Kentucky than Churchill Downs, the Derby, and horses. A key common denominator is the dominant limestone strata responsible for the state's bourbon (the water), bluegrass (the color), and dramatic scenery (cliffs, canyons, and caves). At Cumberland Falls State Park visitors can walk out on flat limestone slabs to watch a 125-foot-wide, 68-foot-high swathe of water plunge dramatically to the boulders below. During a full moon, the resulting pervasive mist forms a rare "moonbow" visible only here and at Victoria Falls in Zimbabwe, Africa. If you're not claustrophobic, explore some of the 300 miles of charted limestone passages in Mammoth Cave, including some areas used for human habitation over 4,000 years ago.

Other spots to explore: Shaker Village at Pleasant Hill, with its architecturally distinctive buildings where superb design emphasizes stately simplicity; nearby Harrodsburg's Old Fort Harrod—site of the first permanent English settlement west of the Alleghenies; Hodgenville, where visitors can see Abe Lincoln's birthplace and an enormous sinkhole; and the many TVA lakes scattered throughout the state, which offer limitless recreational opportunities.

Reader tip: If you're traveling on I-64 between Louisville and Frankfort or Lexington, stop in Shelbyville for lunch at the **Science Hill Inn**, a beautifully restored historic complex including some attractive shops, a gallery of English antique furniture and silver, and a restaurant specializing in Kentucky rainbow trout, corn bread, and lemon chess pie (502–633–2825).

Worth noting: Expect higher rates and minimum stays in Louisville and surrounding areas during the Kentucky Derby.

BARDSTOWN

Bardstown is one of Kentucky's oldest towns, with many historic buildings, and it is a center for the growing of tobacco and the distilling of bourbon. Sights of interest include the local historical museum, the Getz Museum of Whiskey History—from colonial days to Prohibition—and My Old Kentucky Home State Park. This park is home to Federal Hill, a mansion that probably inspired Stephen Foster to write "My Old Kentucky Home." From June to early September the "Stephen Foster Story," a musical pageant featuring the composer's melodies, is sung in the park's amphitheater. Bourbon aficionados will want to take the tours of the nearby Jim Beam and Maker's Mark distilleries. Here also is a Trappist abbey that sells a very distinctive (and strong) cheese.

Bardstown is in central Kentucky's Bourbon County, 35 miles south of Louisville.

Information please: The well-known **Old Talbott Tavern** (107 West Stephen Foster Avenue, 40004; 502–348–3494 or 800–4TAVERN) is one of Kentucky's most historic inns. Among the tavern's famous visitors were King Louis Philippe of France, Abraham Lincoln, Jesse James, Daniel Boone, Stephen Foster, and James Audubon. Meals include both typical American cuisine—steak, shrimp, chicken—and old Kentucky favorites—rabbit, quail, fried chicken with cream gravy, and catfish with hush puppies. Although worth visiting both for its historical significance and for its downhome cooking, reader opinions indicate that an overnight stay may not be the best choice.

We'd like to hear more about two B&Bs owned by Kenny Mandell: **Glenmar Plantation** (2444 Valley Hill Road, Springfield, 40069; 606–284–7791 or 800–828–3330) is about ten minutes from Bardstown off the Blue Grass Parkway. This 200-acre Colonial estate and working farm includes two log barns with hand-hewn timbers measuring up to 60 feet in length and a manor house built around 1785. The menagerie of animals will delight children—especially the llamas and the peacocks. Breakfast at the plantation might include sausage gravy with homemade biscuits, eggs, grits, and fried apples. Rates range from $85–125. **Amber LeAnn B&B** (209 East Stephen Foster Avenue, Bardstown, 40004; 502–349–0014), named for Mr. Mandell's granddaughter, is surrounded by an acre of land and houses five guest rooms, each with king-sized bed, private bath and a fireplace. Rates include a full breakfast and evening dessert. Comments?

Jailer's Inn ¢   *Tel:* 502–348–5551
111 West Stephen Foster Avenue, 40004

After two centuries as a jail, Fran and Challen McCoy bought the old jail and jailer's residence at public auction in 1987, and have converted it into an unusual B&B. Five guest rooms have been decorated with antiques and Oriental rugs; the sixth, the former women's cell, is done in prison black and white, with framed reproductions of cell-wall graffiti hung on the walls. Public tours are given from 10 A.M. to 5 P.M.; guests check-in from 5 to 7 P.M.

"We could take a late shower without disturbing the other guests; the stone walls are so thick, no sound gets through. The delicious breakfast included orange juice, cereals, sausage bread, and croissants served at a gleaming mahogany table." *(Rita Langel)* "The smallish sitting area has an Oriental theme, with a large couch; the breakfast table was set with beautiful china, and included wonderful blueberry peach muffins. Our room, #3—The Library—had green walls, a wallpaper ceiling border, red accent curtains, pretty pictures, a king-sized bed with a brass headboard, two brocade sitting chairs, and a modern bath." *(Lynne Derry)*

"Breakfast was served in the flower-filled fortress courtyard." *(Gail Greco)* "The Library and Colonial rooms were beautifully decorated, roomy and comfortable. The private garden in back was wonderful for relaxing." *(MW)* "The innkeeper thoughtfully prepared a special dish to meet my dietary needs, and everyone was courteous, pleasant, and helpful with dining and sightseeing suggestions. I enjoyed their collection of jail memorabilia." *(Patricia Davis, also John & Marie Lawley)*

Open March 1–Dec. 31.
Rooms 6 doubles, 1 cottage—all with private bath, desk, air-conditioning, fan. 1 with double Jacuzzi.
Facilities Breakfast room, TV/VCR room, courtyard garden, gazebo, picnic area. Off-street parking. Swimming pool, golf nearby.
Location 35 m S of Louisville. 65 m SW of Lexington. Center of town. Adjacent to Court Square.
Restrictions No smoking in guest rooms. House tours held 10–5 P.M.
Credit cards Amex, Discover, MC, Visa.
Rates B&B, $55–85 double, $65 single. Extra person, $10.
Extras Limited wheelchair access. Pets by arrangement. Crib, babysitting.

1790 House ¢   *Tel:* 502–348–7072
110 East Broadway, 40004   800–229–1790

The 1790 House is furnished with period antiques and reproductions; each guest room has a queen-size four-poster or canopy bed. Owners Linda and Ken Anderson have preserved the oversized fireplace and exposed wood beams in the living room, where they encourage guests to curl up with a good book. Breakfast is usually served at 8:30 (9:00 A.M. on Sunday), and includes fresh-squeezed orange juice, a fruit course, and home-baked bread or muffins, followed by such entrées as baked pancakes, featherbed eggs, or five-cheese pie.

"The Colonial colors and beautiful furniture make for an authentic 1790 restoration." *(BJ Hensley)* "Linda and Ken were gracious and hospitable hosts. Our room on the second floor had a four-poster lace-canopy bed with a crocheted cream-colored bedspread and lots of candles; the bath had fluffy towels and almond-scented soaps. The first-floor bedroom has high ceilings and a lovely blue and white color scheme. The wonderful kitchen has exposed beam ceilings and the original brick floor. Magnificent herb and perennial gardens. Delicious breakfast of cheese-stuffed French toast." *(Laurie Projansky)*

Open All year.
Rooms 3 doubles—all with private bath and/or shower, air-conditioning. 2 with gas log fireplace.
Facilities Living room with fireplace, dining room, kitchen with fireplace, den, patio, gardens.
Location Downtown historic district. 2 blocks N of Court Sq., between 2nd & 3rd Sts.
Restrictions Smoking in den only. Children over 12.
Credit cards Amex, Discover, MC, Visa.
Rates B&B, $70–85 double.

BELLEVUE

Weller Haus B&B ¢   *Tel: 606–431–6829*
319 Poplar Street, 41073

While a convenient location, good food, and comfortable accommodations are essential to any B&B, it's the innkeepers themselves that set some places above the rest, and so it is with the Weller Haus. After their children had grown, Mary and Vernon Weller renovated their Victorian Gothic home as a B&B in 1990; in 1992, they purchased the house next door and restored it as well. Inveterate collectors and antiquers, they've decorated each room with a different decor, from Victorian, to French cottage, to Art Deco. Breakfast is served on antique linens, glass, and porcelain, and includes fresh fruit and home-baked muffins and breads; cinnamon bread is a speciality.

"Though the neighborhood is modest, the restoration is extraordinary. A small wrought iron fence surrounds both the original family home and the second building next door. All the rooms are lovely but the Jacuzzi suite was my favorite. The breakfast, afternoon treats and well-stocked guest refrigerator are incredible." *(Penny Poirier)* "The Wellers anticipate your every need. If they learn that you have a preference—for muffins without nuts, for example—they remember when you return." *(Susan Kirby)*

Open All year.
Rooms 3 suites, 2 doubles—all with private bath, radio, desk, air-conditioning, fan. 2 with private entrance; 1 with TV, porch, double Jacuzzi.
Facilities Great room with TV/VCR, radio, stereo, books, fireplace; guest kitchen. Garden, on-street parking.
Location Historic Taylor Daughters' District. Just E of Covington; 5 min. from downtown Cincinnati. From Cincinnati, cross river on I-471 (Daniel Carter Beard Bridge). Take Exit 5 (Newport & Bellevue) & bear right to Dave Cowens Dr. (KY. 8). Changes name to Fairfield Ave. in Bellevue. Go right on Washington, right on Poplar to inn on right.
Credit cards MC, Visa.
Rates B&B, $85–110 suite, $68–70 double. Corporate, off-season rates.

BEREA

Boone Tavern Hotel ¢ 🛏 ✕ 🎿 ♿︎

Berea College
Main & Prospect Streets, CPO 2345, 40404

Tel: 606–986–9358
800–366–9358

Berea College was founded in 1855 to provide quality education for financially needy but academically gifted Appalachian students. Students pay no tuition, but all are required to work at least 10 hours a week in one of the 120 work programs. Berea is known for having preserved the skills of mountain craftsmen; students operate six different craft shops where furniture, games, weaving, toys, ceramics, brooms, and wrought iron are crafted by traditional methods. Walking tours are provided by students every day but Sunday.

Boone Tavern Hotel was founded in 1909 as a guest house for the college. Although it's been expanded and modernized many times since then, it's still 80% student-operated. Many of the students are majoring in hotel management, and most of the guest-room furniture has been made by students.

"The young staff are generally proficient, courteous, and plain fun." *(Jim Lyle)* "Our room was huge with a magnificent king-size bed. Meals were inexpensive, and the service everywhere was great. Excellent shopping in immediate area." *(Carol & Nick Mumford)* "Beautiful hand-made furniture; everything in our recently refurbished room was immaculate. Our room was right on the main street but there was no late-night noise; it might be a problem if you wanted to sleep late. We had a choice of a 6 or 7:15 P.M. dinner seating (doors close at 7:30 so be on time). Be sure to take the one-hour campus tour—a pleasant walk with fascinating information. The hotel is in the middle of campus, but Berea has no movie theaters and no real entertainment, so bring a good book." *(Ben & Peg Bedini)* "Consistently a delightful experience; excellent dining room." *(Duane Roller)* "Love the Kentucky fried apples for breakfast." *(HB)*

Open All year.
Rooms 57 doubles—all with private bath and/or shower, telephone, radio, TV, desk, air-conditioning.
Facilities Restaurant, gift shop, lounge with TV, parlor, bridge rooms. 140-acre college campus, with tennis courts, running track, heated swimming pool, golf, hiking trails.
Location Central KY; foothills of the Cumberland Mts. In center of town 50 m S of Lexington, 2 hrs. N of Knoxville, TN. Just off I-75.
Restrictions No alcohol. No smoking in restaurant. Dress code at dinner.
Credit cards Amex, DC, Discover, MC, Visa.
Rates Room only, $66–87 double, $57–76 single. Extra person, $7. Rollaway bed, crib, $10. No tipping. Alc breakfast, $3.50–7.50; alc lunch, $5–12; alc dinner, $10–18.
Extras Wheelchair access; some rooms specially equipped. Pets by arrangement. Crib. French, German, Spanish spoken.

COVINGTON

Covington is located in north central Kentucky, on the Ohio River, two miles south of Cincinnati, Ohio, and 90 miles north of Lexington. Of particular interest is the River Center, a mixed-use development project, and home to Covington Landing, a floating entertainment complex with a theater, replica steamboat, and a turn-of-the-century riverfront atmosphere.

For an additional area entry, see **Bellevue**.

Amos Shinkle Townhouse 👫
215 Garrard Street, 41011

Tel: 606–431–2118
800–972–7012

Former Covington mayor Bernie Moorman and his partner, Don Nash, bought this 1850s brick town house in 1983 and began its renovation, uncovering some of the original wall murals in the process. Many of the original plaster ceiling medallions and cornices were preserved, and several of the public rooms retain their Rococo Revival chandeliers. Much of the decorating was completed by a group of Cincinnati-area design firms when the house was showcased as a local fund-raiser. In 1987, the carriage house was restored, providing additional rooms with simple early American decor; the original horse stalls have been redesigned as sleeping quarters for children. "The main house has unusual 16-foot ceilings both upstairs and down." *(Suzanne Johnson)* "Our carriage house room was sparkling clean, with candies, delightful handmade shades for the tiny windows, and fluffy towels. Breakfast, served from 7:00–9:30 A.M., was elegantly presented on Noritake china." *(Zita Knific)* "Breakfast started with warm homemade coffee cake and fruit salad, and proceeded through eggs or French toast to order. Wonderful neighborhood; we took a lovely evening stroll along the 'Riverwalk,' a beautiful park which runs along the two rivers of Cincinnati, with interesting statues and loads of atmosphere." *(Wendy Garen)* "Even though the street is fairly busy, my front room was quiet. The bathroom had walls in a faux marble pattern, a crystal chandelier, and theatrical lighting around the mirrors. Equal to it was the bedroom: sponge-painted wallpaper in shades of lavender and violet, accented with a burgundy pinstripe, a massive carved walnut bedroom suite, a fainting couch and two Victorian chairs, an Oriental rug, an oval Empire table, and two alabaster vases on the painted mantel. The Carriage House rooms are not as lavish, with wall-to-wall carpeting and a mix of antiques and upholstered pieces. Best of all are the friendly and considerate owners, Bernie and Don, who make the inn so special." *(SHW)*

Open All year.
Rooms 7 doubles, all with full private bath, radio, TV, air conditioning. 3 in main house, 4 in carriage house. 1 with whirlpool tub; 2 with desk; 4 with telephone.
Facilities Dining room, parlor with grand piano, pump organ; porches. Garden patio.
Location 1½ blocks from river, in Riverside Historic District; across the Roebling Suspension Bridge from Riverfront Stadium. From I-75/71, take Exit 192, 5th St/Covington exit. Follow 5th St. to end. Go left & follow Garrard St. N 2½ blocks to house on W side of St.

Credit cards Amex, DC, Discover, MC, Visa.
Rates B&B, $69–120 double, $59–110 single. Extra adult, $15. No charge for children under 13. No tipping. Senior discount.
Extras Airport/station pickups, $5. French, German spoken. Ticket service for greater Cincinnati area.

Sandford House ¢ ♀ *Tel: 606–291–9133*
1026 Russell Street, 41011

Sandford House was built in 1820 as a private home by Thomas Sandford, northern Kentucky's first U.S. Congressman. Although the original design was Federal, the building was remodeled in the Victorian Second Empire style (with a mansard roof) after a fire in the 1880s. Owned by Linda and Dan Carter since 1988, it was totally remodeled as a B&B in 1990. Breakfast includes fresh fruit and juice, with French toast, waffles, or an egg casserole.

"Our cozy room's pastel walls accented the high corniced ceilings and plush carpeting. The counter for the bathroom sink was originally part of an altar, recycled from one of the house's earlier uses. Breakfast was served on fine china in the beautiful dining room." *(Zita Knific)* "We stayed in a lower level room, redone in modern decor, which looked out on the pretty backyard." *(Jeffrey Rosenberg)* "Dan took the time to walk us around the neighborhood to show us the different styles of historic homes. Breakfast in the garden gazebo was wonderful. Location convenient to the waterfront, restaurants, and shops." *(Gina & Bob Weitzel)* "Good reading lamps over the beds and an abundant supply of large, comfortable pillows." *(Shelley Goldbloom)* "The beautifully manicured garden added to our enjoyment." *(Joan Wilson)* "The sodas in our refrigerator were a homey, welcoming touch. Sandy, their golden retriever, and Amber, their cat, roamed the house making instant friends of all. Terrific breakfast entrées—sausage, mushroom and artichoke casserole, ham soufflé. Parking was convenient and equipped with motion sensor lighting for security." *(Tammy Lea Thomason)* "The suite is quiet and private, with handsome contemporary furnishings and a lovely garden view." *(Sandy Chapman)*

Minor niggle: "I would have liked a full-length mirror in the room."

Open All year.
Rooms 2 apartments, 1 suite, 1 double—all with full private bath, radio, TV, air-conditioning. 1 room with waterbed. Suite with whirlpool tub, patio, refrigerator. Apartment with desk, refrigerator, washer/dryer; 2-bedroom carriage house with living room, dining room, kitchen.
Facilities Dining room, living room with fireplace, family room with TV/VCR. Laundry facilities. 1 acre with gardens, hot tub, patio, gazebo.
Location Old Seminary Square Historic District. 10 min. from downtown Cincinnati, 5 min. from Covington Landing, 2 blocks from Basilica. Exit I-75 at 12th St. & go E. Turn left on Russell St. to inn between 11th St. & Robbins.
Restrictions Train noise might disturb light sleepers. Smoking in living room only.
Credit cards MC, Visa.
Rates B&B $85–95 suite, $55 double, $50–90 single. Extra person, $10. No charge for children under 12.
Extras Airport/station pickups.

CUMBERLAND FALLS STATE RESORT PARK

Dupont Lodge ¢ ♔ ✕ 🎣   *Tel:* 606–528–4121
7351 Highway 90, Corbin 40701-8814   800–325–0063
                                                  Fax: 606–528–0704

Plan to combine a visit to Cumberland Falls with one to the Big South Fork National Recreation area to the south, including a ride on the scenic railway to the Blue Heron mine. Known as the "Niagara of the South," Cumberland Falls forms a 120-foot wide curtain of water that drops 60 feet into the gorge below. On clear nights during a full moon, the mist of the falls creates the only moon bow in the Western Hemisphere. "The lodge is an interesting, well-maintained old facility, with comfortable, if uninspired rooms. The dining room has a great view of the Cumberland River." *(Joe and Sheila Schmidt)* Reports needed.

Open All year. Closed Dec. 22–28. Coffee shop open April–Oct.
Rooms 52 doubles, 26 1-2 bedroom cabins—all with private bath, telephone, radio, TV, air-conditioning; some with wet bar, refrigerator. Cabins also with kitchen, heat.
Facilities Restaurant, coffee shop, gift shop, meeting rooms. Hiking, fishing, shuffleboard, horseshoes, nature center & trails, picnic tables, playground, recreation program, swimming pool, tennis court, white water rafting.
Location S central KY. From I-75, take Exit 25 in Corbin. Follow Hwy 25 W to Hwy 90.
Credit cards Amex, CB, DC, MC, Visa.
Rates Room only, $42–60 double, $32–50 single, $55–120 cabin.
Extras Wheelchair access.

GEORGETOWN

Also recommended: The **Log Cabin B&B** (350 North Broadway; 502–863–3514) is a chinked log cabin built in 1809. Clay and Janis McKnight moved and reassembled this cabin, equipping it with two bedrooms, a living room with fieldstone fireplace, a bathroom, telephone, TV, and a kitchen/dining area, and furnishing it with primitive antiques and quilts. "Set in the innkeepers' backyard, but completely private. You have your own fenced yard, back and front porch, and attentive innkeepers who supply an expanded continental breakfast. We felt perfectly safe and at home. Great for people who don't feel like socializing at breakfast." *(C.J. DeSantis)* Rates for this B&B are about $75 per couple, including a continental breakfast; pets and children welcome.

Blackridge Hall B&B   *Tel:* 502–863–2069
4055 Paris Pike, Georgetown 40324   800–768–9308

A 10,000-square-foot southern Georgian-style mansion overlooking the rolling bluegrass landscape, Blackridge Hall B&B was built by Jim Black in 1990, who opened it as a B&B in 1993. Jim notes that they try to pamper guests in an elegant setting, while maintaining a family atmosphere; rooms are furnished in 18th and 19th century reproductions. The candlelight breakfast is served on china, crystal, and silver; entrées might include bacon quiche, baked French toast, eggs Benedict, sausage-egg casserole, or waffles accompanied by a fresh fruit plate and just-baked muffins or bread.

"Wonderful breakfasts, exquisite accommodations in My Old Kentucky Home suite. Personalized attention lavished on us by innkeepers." *(Rhonda Edwards & Bill Wise)* "An incredibly lavish, elegant home, starting with the winding tree-lined drive leading up to the four 20-foot columns that frame the double front doors, opening to the marble foyer and double curved staircase. The bathroom in my suite was bigger than my bedroom at home, and had beautiful hand-crafted wooden cabinets. Enormous silk flower arrangements are everywhere, and soft music is piped into each room. Jim prepared and served an excellent breakfast." *(Nancy Debevoise)*

Open All year.

Rooms 2 suites, 3 doubles—all with private bath and/or shower, telephone, radio, clock, TV, air-conditioning, fan. Some with whirlpool tub, desk, fireplace, balcony.

Facilities Living room, dining room, family room with TV/VCR, sun room, guest refrigerator, veranda. 5 acres. Swimming, tennis, golf, horseback riding nearby.

Location 10 m N of Lexington, 3 m W of town. From I-75 N, take Exit 125 to Rte. 460 E; from I-75 S, take Exit 126 to Rte. 460 E. Go 2½ m to inn on right.

Restrictions No smoking. "Children not encouraged."

Credit cards Amex, Discover, MC, Visa.

Rates B&B, 149–159 suite, $89–109 double. 2-night minimum special events, holidays.

Extras Airport/station pickups.

Jordan Farm B&B ¢   *Tel:* 502–868–9002 (daytime)
4091 Newtown Pike, 40324   502–863–1944 (evening)

Built in 1993 by owners Becky and Harold Jordan, Jordan Farm is a working Bluegrass horse farm. Each of the three suites has a separate entrance as well as a deck overlooking the farm. "Suites are lavishly decorated with floral carpets in a dark rose, and splashy prints. A full breakfast is served in each individual suite." *(Susan Schwemm)* "It was a unique experience walking around the farm in the early morning, watching the horses. The countryside is lovely; the accommodations most comfortable." *(Pam Phillips, also Joyce Ward)*

Open All year.

Rooms 3 suites; 2 in carriage house, 1 in main house. All with full private Jacuzzi bath, telephone, radio, clock, TV, air-conditioning, refrigerator, deck.

Facilities 100-acre horse farm, fishing lake, swimming pool.

Location 12 m N of Lexington. 4 m to center of town. 5 minutes from Ky. Horse Park.

Restrictions No smoking.

Credit cards None accepted.

Rates B&B, $75 suite. Extra person, $5. 2-night minimum.

GHENT

Ghent House *Tel:* 502–347–5807
411 Main Street, U.S. Rte. 42, 41045

A restored 1833 Federal-style house, the Ghent House overlooks the Ohio River and is simply furnished with antiques and collectibles from the nearby Amish community. Although steamboats no longer ply the river, guests still enjoy watching the river traffic from the second-floor porches and from the lovely gardens, which Diane and Wayne Young planted when they restored Ghent House as a B&B in 1990. The rose garden has over 45 varieties, while the English garden has winding brick paths. A typical breakfast menu might include homemade bread or muffins, French toast with orange butter, and fresh fruit; guests are welcomed with Diane's cookies or other home-baked treats.

"Lovely decor with a mixture of antiques, handmade items, and family pieces. Everything is clean, well arranged, and gives the appearance of openness and light. Breakfast is delicious, homemade and plentiful. Personal touches include early morning coffee, and evening soft drinks and snacks. The Youngs enjoy what they do and it shows; they always try to anticipate guests needs and make them feel at home." *(Marjorie Mueller, and others)*

Open All year.
Rooms 3 suites—all with private bath and/or shower, air-conditioning, refrigerator. 2 with telephone, desk, porch; 1 with fireplace, TV, double whirlpool tub.
Facilities Dining room, breakfast room, living room with fireplace, TV; porch. Flower gardens with gazebo. 400 ft. from Ohio River for fishing, boating. Skiing, golf nearby.
Location N KY. 1 hour SE of Cincinnati; halfway between Cincinnati & Louisville. From I-75, take Carrollton exit. Take Rte. 227 N to US 42 (1½ m). Take US 42 W 7 m to Ghent; inn is 1st brick bldg. on left.
Restrictions No smoking.
Credit cards Amex, MC, Visa.
Rates B&B, $90 suite, $60 double, $55 single. Extra adult, $25. Children $15.
Extras Train pick-up, $10. Crib, babysitting.

GLASGOW

Four Seasons Country Inn ¢ ♿ *Tel:* 502–678–1000
4107 Scottsville Road (Hwy 31-E), 42141

Travelers who enjoy country inn ambience but are reluctant to sacrifice motel comfort will appreciate the Victorian-style Four Seasons, built in 1989. Rooms have queen-sized four poster beds and oversized wingback chairs, and most have a hide-away trundle bed to accommodate an extra guest. Breakfast includes pastries, yogurt, fruit juices, milk, tea, and coffee. Numerous antique shops, Mammoth Cave National Park, the Barren River Lake State Park, and the Horse Cave theater, are among the nearby attractions.

"Large, well-equipped rooms; 35-channel TV, comfortable chairs and beds, nice bathrooms. Good sound-proofing; a party of fisherman left at 5 A.M. and we didn't hear a thing. The owners are pleasant and helpful about local attractions and restaurants, and the common area is inviting." *(Duane Roller)* "Comfortable four-poster bed. Excellent dinner at the only restaurant in town; the food was fresh, the quantities ample." *(Deanna Yen)*

Open All year.
Rooms 17 doubles—all with full private bath, telephone, radio, TV, air-conditioning, desk. Some with refrigerator, balcony/deck.
Facilities Parlor/lobby with fireplace; veranda, sundeck. 3 acres with swimming pool. Parking lot with basketball, 30 spaces for boat hookups. Golf, horseback riding, biking, boating nearby
Location S central KY. Heading S on I-65, take Exit 53 at Cave City. Turn left & follow Hwy 90 E 10 m to Glasgow. Turn right at 2nd light onto Hwy. 31-E & go S about 5 m to inn on right. From I-65 N, take Exit 43. Take Cumberland Parkway 11 m to 1st Glasgow exit. Turn right on Hwy 31-E & go 2 m S to inn on right. Approx. 2 1/2 m S of town.
Restrictions Traffic noise in front rooms. Some non-smoking guest rooms.
Credit cards Amex, CB, DC, Discover, MC, Visa.
Rates B&B, $50–60 double. Extra person, $5. 10% senior, AAA discount. Tipping welcome.
Extras Wheelchair access; 1 room specially equipped. Crib.

HARRODSBURG

The Harrodsburg area is home to two of Kentucky's finest inns. If your time in the state is limited, this town, oldest in the state, is probably the one to visit. Sights of interest include Old Fort Harrod State Park, with its historic buildings and amphitheater, featuring dramatizations of the stories of Daniel Boone and Abraham Lincoln; Morgan Row; and Shakertown at Pleasant Hill (see page 164).

Harrodsburg is located in central Kentucky's Bluegrass Region, 32 miles southwest of Lexington.

Reader tip: "Mercer County is dry, so come prepared. If you'd like to enjoy a glass of wine with dinner, phone the restaurant in advance to see if it's OK."

Beaumont Inn 🛏 ✕   *Tel:* 606–734–3381
638 Beaumont Drive, 40330   800–352–3992

Listed on the National Register of Historic Places, the Beaumont dates back to 1845. Long used as a girls' school and college, it was purchased by Annie Bell Goddard and her husband in 1917 and converted into an inn. Ownership and management passed to her daughter, Mrs. Pauline Dedman; four generations later, Chuck and Helen Dedman continue the family tradition. The inn's rooms are spread out over a number of buildings, including the original main building of the school, a brick building with Greek Revival–style Doric columns, as well as other buildings and cottages of varying sizes. Restaurant specialties include the inn's own Kentucky-cured ham, fried chicken, corn pudding, and orange-lemon cake.

"Situated well off the main highway on a peaceful knoll. The sitting room is gracious—large mirrors, lace curtains, floral wallpapers, and velvet-covered furniture." *(MFD)* "A majestic-looking building, with lots of lovely trees on the grounds. The bedroom of our suite was comfortably furnished with two antique spindle beds, an antique bureau, bedside table and several comfortable chairs. The balcony was heavenly, with old-fashioned gliders. Our living room had good reading lamps, a hide-a-bed sofa, several comfortable lounging chairs, and a great secretary desk. The set dinner included a great cauliflower soup, a cucumber and tomato salad, ham, mock oyster casserole, lima beans, delicious homemade biscuits, ice cream, and coffee. Breakfast is an enormous array of hot and cold cereal, pancakes, eggs, grits, hot breads, fruit, and more. The Beaumont is a very busy place. Young families might be best off staying in the buildings away from the main inn; the elegant dining experience is best for older children." *(Joyce Whittington)* "Our room in the main building was large, decorated in authentic heavy Victorian furnishings, with floral wallpaper and cabbage rose carpets; bathrooms are basic, but clean and functional." *(SHW)*

"Immaculate housekeeping, excellent service, warm hospitality, wonderful food, lovely gift shop. Early morning coffee is set out in the sunroom." *(Betty Lou Hickey)* "Special requests are always treated with respect and attention. Wonderful long-time employees. True Southern fare in the dining room, well prepared, hot and fresh, with seconds offered. Upkeep and maintenance of the inn is excellent, both on the surface and beneath." *(Lynne Brown)* "Parking is ample and easily accessible." *(Carmen McNeill)*

Minor niggle: "An extra shelf or cabinet in the bathroom."

Open Early March–mid-Dec.
Rooms 1 cottage, 33 doubles—all with private bath and/or shower, telephone, TV, air-conditioning. Some with refrigerator. Rooms in total of 4 buildings—main building, Bell Cottage, Goddard Hall, Greystone House.
Facilities Restaurant, parlors, lounge, library, conference room. 30 acres with 2 tennis courts, swimming pool, gift shop. Fishing, boating, golf nearby.
Location Central KY, Bluegrass Region. 32 m SW of Lexington.
Restrictions No smoking in dining room.
Credit cards Amex, Discover, MC, Visa.
Rates Room only, $77–90 double, $55–75 single. Extra child, $15; adult, $20. Full breakfast, $6; alc lunch, $6–10; alc dinner, $14–18. 15% discount, 5-night stays. Mid-week & off-season packages. 10% AARP discount on 3-night stays.
Extras Airport/station pickups. Crib.

Shaker Village of Pleasant Hill ¢ 🛗 ✕ ♿   *Tel:* 606–734–5411
3500 Lexington Road, 40330   *Fax:* 606–734–5411

Shaker Village preserves 33 original 19th-century buildings, accurately restored and adapted. Visitors take self-guided tours of the buildings where interpreters and craftsmen explain the Shaker approach to life and religion. Shaker music programs are also offered on many weekends. Shakertown at Pleasant Hill is a nonprofit educational corporation, listed on the National Register of Historic Places; it is the only historic village offering overnight accommodation in original buildings. *John Blewer* speaks for most readers when he notes that "Shaker Hill is a wonderful experience that shouldn't be missed, excellent for families and history buffs. Visit for a meal or a tour, even if you can't stay overnight."

"Rolling Kentucky bluegrass, with peaceful vistas in all directions. Tasty down-home cooking with fried fish, fried chicken, and steaks. Family-style vegetables—perhaps green beans with bacon and corn pudding. Furnishings are authentically plain—reproduction Shaker furniture, rag rugs, white walls, dark woodwork. The rooms are clean, the bathrooms basic. To reach the idyllic Tanyard Brick Shop cottage, you wind through cow pastures down to a small farm pond, surrounded by weeping willows." *(SHW)* "A serene mood settles over the village in the evening after all the day visitors have gone home." *(Mrs. Perry Noe)* "The trundle beds enable a family to share one large room, each with a comfortable bed. Meals are served in the Trustees' House, with spectacular twin spiral staircases." *(Ann Delugach)*

"Our two-room suite in the East Family Wash House was large and private. The furnishings were good Shaker reproductions, plus serviceable couches and chairs in subdued colors." *(Joyce Ward)* "We enjoyed our stay in the Old Ministry's workshop, with a fireplace and comfortable bed. At night we saw a spectacular sunset over the rolling fence-lined hills of Kentucky. Meals were excellent and abundant." *(Deanna Yen)*

"My room had a comfy bed with soft pillows and linens and a handsome Shaker spread. The staff was friendly and helpful, and all took seriously the Shaker admonition that there is no dirt in heaven. Superb country breakfast buffet—scrambled eggs, bacon, sausage, assorted fruits, juices, grits, gravy, cereal, bite-sized biscuits, and pumpkin muffins." *(Carol Moritz)* "The West Lot Conference Center is ideal for family reunions. Also delightful is the 1½ mile lane that wanders from the village through woods and past fields being plowed." *(SHW)*

Minor niggles: "The neighbors had their TV on really loud." Also: "The adults were charmed, but our kids were bored after a couple hours in the 90° heat with no swimming pool."

Open All year. Closed Christmas Eve and Day.
Rooms 1 cottage, 2 conference centers, 78 doubles with full private bath, telephone, TV, desk, air-conditioning. Accommodations in 15 restored buildings.
Facilities Sitting rooms, restaurant. 2,700 acres. Riverboat rides on Kentucky River. Craft shops, demonstrations.
Location Central KY, Bluegrass Region. 80 m SE of Louisville, 25 m SW of Lexington, 7 m NE of Harrodsburg, on US Rte. 68. Use caution on winding, hilly road after dark.
Restrictions No alcoholic beverages in dining room (dry county). Traffic noise in North Lot dwelling.
Credit cards MC, Visa.
Rates Room only, $150 cottage, $58–100 double, $48–90 single. No charge for children under 17 in parents' room. Extra adults, $8. Country buffet breakfast, $7.50; alc lunch, $6.50–9.50; alc dinner, $13.25–17.75. Children's menu. No tipping. Seasonal overnight packages for special events.
Extras Crib. Dining room, public restrooms wheelchair accessible.

LEXINGTON

A city wealthy from the tobacco industry, Lexington is home to the University of Kentucky, Transylvania University, and many beautiful antebellum and Victorian buildings, a number of which are now open to the public as museums. But the real attraction here is thoroughbred horses. Head for the Kentucky Horse Park, for 1,000 acres of bluegrass, where you can learn everything you ever wanted to know (and more) about equines, then sign up for a tour of the area's best horse farms.

Lexington is located in central Kentucky, 101 miles south of Cincinnati, Ohio, and 78 miles east of Louisville.

Information please: Listed in past editions, we need current feedback on the **Gratz Park Inn** (120 West Second Street, 40507; 606–231–1777 or 800–227–4362), located downtown in the historic Gratz Park area. This 44-room luxury hotel is housed in a 1916 Georgian Revival–style building, with a lovely lobby, and pleasant guest rooms with English antique reproduction furniture, king- or queen-size pencil post or rice four-poster beds, wall-to-wall plush carpeting, floral print comforters, and armoires that conceal TVs. The reasonable rates include a buffet breakfast, morning paper, limo service to the airport and downtown restaurants, and turndown service with cookies and flowers.

Just 15 minutes west of Lexington in historic Versailles are two B&Bs of interest. The **Rose Hill Inn** (233 Rose Hill, Versailles 40383; 606–873–5957) is an early 1800s home, a block from downtown. The four guest rooms have private baths, and a hot breakfast is delivered to your room; double rates range from $70–90 and also include access to a guest pantry stocked with fresh fruit and home-baked treats. Listed in previous editions is the **Sills Inn** (270 Montgomery Avenue, Versailles 40383; 606–873–4478 or 800–526–9801). Built in 1911, this three-story Victorian-style home offers five guest rooms with private baths, and is decorated with antiques. Rates range from $60–100, and include a full breakfast. Reports welcome.

For additional area entries, see listings under **Georgetown,** about 10 miles north of Lexington.

LOUISVILLE

Louisville is known best for the Kentucky Derby (the most famous two minutes in sports), and as the state's cultural center year-round, with great jazz clubs, superb live theater, and several truly gracious residential areas where homes date from the 1870s. Louisville is located in the north central part of the state, on the Ohio River, across from Indiana.

Also recommended: Visitors to Louisville are fortunate to have their choice of two lovely, well-maintained, historic luxury hotels, The Brown, and The Seelbach, each with approximately 300 guest rooms. Although regular double rates at both are in the $150–175 range, both offer enticing weekend packages, and promotional rates to AAA members.

Comments on **The Brown** (4th & Broadway, 40202; 502–583–1234 or 800–866–ROOM): "Our large corner room, complete with sitting area, overlooked Theater Square. Downtown Louisville is undergoing a renewal, and the hotel is clearly a focal point. Service is warm and friendly. The formal restaurant has an intimate atmosphere and graciously serves imaginative cuisine. We were also pleased with the continental breakfast buffet." *(Jean Rees)* And on **The Seelbach** (500 4th Avenue, 40202; 502–585–3200 or 800–333–3399): "Perfect downtown/convention center location. Lots of places to eat, close to the pedestrian mall. Hotel is absolutely lovely, very old-worldish and German. We had a huge and charming corner room. Room service and food exquisite and extremely reasonable, large servings. When we return, we'll request a room without a connecting door, because we could hear our neighbors talking." *(JMW)*

Inn at the Park ¢ 👫
1332 South Fourth Street, 40208

Tel: 502–637–6930
800–700–PARK

In 1886, Russell Houston, president of the L & N Railroad, built a 10,000-square-foot mansion in the massive Richardsonian Romanesque style, with blocks of roughly squared stonework, rounded arches, stone balconies, and more. The interior is equally lavish, with a striking mahogany staircase, rich hardwood floors, 14-foot ceilings, marble fireplaces, and crown moldings. Opened as an inn in 1993 by Theresa and Bob Carskie, the rooms are furnished in period with antiques and reproductions. Breakfast is served at guests' convenience, and includes fresh baked muffins, croissants, and breads, fresh fruit and juice, coffee and tea, and a choice of such entrées as banana-walnut pancakes with maple syrup and bacon, made-to-order omelets with grilled ham and whole wheat toast, or vanilla yogurt with granola and honey.

"Elaborate architectural details—numerous quoins, lintels, sills, and columns. Theresa managed two successful inns in Boulder, Colorado, and her experience shows: needed extras are offered—from lotion and shampoo, to a hair dryer. Common areas are ample and attractive; the living and dining rooms have magnificent fireplaces, and there's a well stocked guest pantry with soft drinks, beer, and wine. From the original master suite, I had a view of the park, and felt like a princess in the high four-poster bed. Both the bedroom and bath have working fireplaces; the bath has the original marble walls. The inn is adjacent to Central Park, the setting for summer Shakespeare and the October craft fair. You can take a picnic to the park, and relax on a blanket under the towering trees." *(Lynn Grisard Fullman)*

Open All year.
Rooms 1 suite, 5 doubles—4 with private bath and/or shower, 2 with maximum of 4 sharing bath. All with telephone, radio, clock, TV, air-conditioning. Some with ceiling fan, fireplace, desk.
Facilities Dining room, living room, library (each with fireplace); family room with TV/VCR; guest refrigerator, porch; fax, copy service. Off-street parking. Park adjacent for tennis, playground.
Location Historic district, 5–10 min. of downtown, U. of Louisville, Churchill Downs. From I-65, take Exit 135 A & go W (right) on W. St. Catherine St. 4 blocks. Turn S (left) on 4th St. & go 3 blocks to inn at corner of Park & 4th.

Restrictions Smoking restricted to certain rooms.
Credit cards Amex, MC, Visa.
Rates B&B, $95 suite, $60–79 double. Extra person, $10.
Extras Free airport/station/downtown shuttle service. Crib, babysitting. Spanish spoken.

Old Louisville Inn ¢ 👥
1359 South Third Street, 40208

Tel: 502–635–1574
Fax: 502–637–5892

Most people spend 20 years in the corporate world before finding an avocation in innkeeping; Marianne Lesher found her calling a lot sooner. After graduating from college, she set out to explore the U.S. Coming back home to Louisville in 1990, she became the managing partner of Louisville's first bed and breakfast inn, built in 1901 in the Second Empire Beaux Arts style.

"Iron gates lead to a marble alcove just outside the heavy front doors. Inside is a massive entry hall that leads to the wide carpeted staircase. The huge original globe chandeliers are still in place in the hall and the living room. Both rooms also have modern ceiling mythological murals, featuring voluptuous nudes. The dining room has an elaborately carved built-in sideboard; guests sit at individual tables. Room #3 has a four poster queen-sized bed and large bow windows fronting the street. The moss green walls have cornice paper trim, and the enormous original bathroom has marble walls, a deep soaker tub, and a pedestal sink with an Ionic column base." *(SHW)*

"Excellent location in a residential area close to downtown, on a beautiful tree-lined street with stunning architecture. Restaurants, the theater, and Shakespeare in the Park are all within walking distance. Homey touches for each room include fresh flowers, potpourri, and a 'rent-a-cat' program." *(Arthur Edwards)* "The Honeymoon Suite has a king-size four-poster rice bed with a crocheted canopy, glass cases filled with antique wedding memorabilia, a Victorian chaise longue, and a table for two. Each room is charming, although some of the furnishings are modest." *(Thea Reis)* "Breakfast, served from 8–10 A.M., included granola, yogurt, melon, great popovers and fruit-filled muffins, plus freshly squeezed juice and unlimited coffee and tea." *(Minnie Miller)* "Marianne is an exceptionally caring and helpful innkeeper." *(Margaret Haterton)*

Open All year.
Rooms 3 suites, 8 doubles—7 with private bath or shower, 3 with a maximum of 6 sharing bath. All with radio, desk, air-conditioning. Honeymoon suite with double whirlpool bath.
Facilities Dining room, living room with stereo, game room with TV/VCR, videotape library, books; laundry, porch. Courtyard, picnic area, off-street parking. Tennis, golf nearby.
Location Old Louisville. Downtown on 3rd between Ormsby & Magnolia.
Restrictions No smoking in breakfast room, kitchen. Light traffic noise in front rooms.
Credit cards MC, Visa.
Rates B&B, $100–195 suite, $60–90 double, $55–75 single. Extra person, $10. Children 12 & under, free. Romance packages.
Extras Crib, babysitting.

MAMMOTH CAVE

Mammoth Cave Hotel ¢ &.
Mammoth Cave National Park, 42259–0027

Tel: 502–758–2225
Fax: 502–758–2301

You've seen the bumper stickers for years, so you might as well accept the inevitable and plan a visit to one of "the seven wonders of the New World." In addition to the cave itself, with some 300 miles of cavern corridors, the park offers 80 miles of rugged woodland and 30 miles of river to explore. Bring a sweater even on the hottest day; the cave stays at a steady 54° year-round. The contemporary brick hotel overlooks a scenic ravine, near the cave entrance, and connects to the National Park Visitor Center by a bridge. Additional accommodations are located at the Sunset Point Motor Lodge and in a variety of cottages. Least expensive are the Woodland Cottages, set in the forest a short distance from the hotel.

"Although the accommodations are ordinary, the scenic location within the park, surrounded by greenery and many hiking and walking trails, makes this place special. The dining room, while unpretentious, serves simple yet excellent Southern food. The place can be rather noisy and crowded during peak season, because of its proximity to the cave entrance. Delightful off season." *(Duane Roller)*

Open All year. Closed Christmas.
Rooms 68 doubles—all with full private bath, television, radio, air-conditioning. 38 cottages—all with private bath. Some with balcony/patio.
Facilities Restaurant, coffee shop, lobby, laundromat, visitors center, gift shop, nature program, cave tours, boat trips, hiking, tennis court.
Location S central KY. 11 m W of junction of I-65 & Hwy. 70.
Credit cards Amex, CB, DC, MC, Visa.
Rates Room only, $57–80 double, $51–73 single, $40–48 cottage. Extra person, $6.
Extras Wheelchair access.

MIDDLESBOROUGH

The RidgeRunner ¢
208 Arthur Heights, 40965

Tel: 606–248–4299

Susan Richards opened The RidgeRunner, the first B&B in Bell County, in 1989. A 20-room Victorian built in the 1890s, the house has a massive, 57-foot brick porch across its front, ornate wood paneling, and stained glass windows. The name is derived from the way the house "rides" the ridge overlooking the town, with views of the Cumberland Mountains. A short drive to the southeast is the Cumberland Gap National Historical Park, commemorating the famous Appalachian pass through which Daniel Boone and most of the early pioneers passed on their way west.

"We grow our own raspberries, blackberries, strawberries, and raise our own meat, milk, and eggs," notes Susan. Breakfast favorites are pancakes with blueberry sauce, baked eggs with ham and cheese, scrambled eggs with sausage gravy and biscuits, or yogurt with fruit, bran muffins and juice.

"Furnished throughout with antiques and memorabilia. Special touches include chocolates on the pillow with turndown service, toiletries in the bathroom, fresh flowers in the room, and fresh mint garnishing the lemonade served on the porch." *(Ann Schell)* "We had a delicious breakfast with innkeepers Susan Richards and Irma Gall, and talked about the area and their nearby farm. For dinner, we were directed to Ye Olde Tea and Coffee Shoppe, nearby in Cumberland Gap, Tennessee for a superb meal." *(Glenn Roehrig)* "Susan is a good conversationalist, sensitive to the needs and wishes of her guests." *(Lawrence Durr)*

Area for improvement: "A firmer bed."

Open All year.

Rooms 5 doubles—2 with private bath and/or shower, 3 with a maximum of 6 people sharing bath. All with radio, desk, fan.

Facilities Dining room, living room with piano, books; library, porch. Picnic area, off-street parking. Golf nearby. Cumberland Gap National Park, Pine Mountain State Park, Cudjo Caverns nearby.

Location SE KY, near TN, VA border. 50 m N of Knoxville, TN. 2 m from center. Take Rte. 25 E to Cumberland Ave. & go right on 20th St. for 2 blocks. Turn left on Edgewood Rd and bear right up hill to Arthur Heights & go right to "T" intersection. Go left to 2nd house on left.

Restrictions No smoking. No children under 16.

Credit cards None accepted.

Rates B&B, $55 double, $50 single. Extra person, $15.

RUSSELLVILLE

Also recommended: In southern Kentucky, about 25 miles west of Bowling Green, is the **Washington House** (283 West 9th Street, Highway 79 South, 42276; 502–726–7608 or 502–706–3093), built in 1824 by a cousin of George Washington. Rates for the three guest rooms, each with private bath, range from $65–70, including a full breakfast. "Owner Roy Gill is an antiques dealer of repute; it showed in the wonderful Victorian furnishings found throughout this meticulously maintained house. He willingly shared information about the area's history and sights." *(Rex Howland)*

Free copy of *INNroads* newsletter

Want to stay up-to-date on our latest finds? Send a business-size, self-addressed, stamped envelope with 52 cents postage and we'll send you the latest issue, *free!* While you're at it, why not enclose a report on any inns you've recently visited? Use the forms at the back of the book or your own stationery.

Louisiana

Bois des Chênes, Lafayette

Everybody goes to New Orleans sooner or later, and although it's a big city, you can get a good taste of its delicious food, distinctive architecture, and famous jazz in just a few days' visit. Beyond New Orleans, the state offers a potpourri of cultures and landscapes. North of the city, across Lake Pontchartrain Causeway, horse farms and dense pine forests provide a peaceful contrast to New Orleans' famous excesses. To the south, scenic Route 90 leads to Houma, the heart of Cajun country. Rent a boat here to explore and fish in Louisiana's legendary bayous, swamps and marshes. Continue west on Route 90, then detour to Avery Island, the home of McIlhenny Tabasco sauce. Up the road, visit the restored antebellum plantation homes in New Iberia.

Note: You'll frequently hear the words *Cajun* and *Creole* used in Louisiana. The former refers to the French settlers of Acadia (present-day Nova Scotia), who were expelled from Canada by the British in the 1750s and settled in Louisiana, which was then French territory. (The word *Cajun* is derived from the word *Acadian*.) The word Creole, on the other hand, describes the descendants of the early French and Spanish settlers of this region. Although time has produced some overlapping, their heritage and traditions are quite different.

DARROW

Tezcuco Plantation ¢ 👫 ✗
3138 Highway 44, 70725

Tel: 504–562–3929
Fax: 504–562–3923

Tezcuco Plantation, an antebellum raised cottage, was built in 1855 in the Greek Revival style and is listed on the National Register of Historic

171

Places. Its name is taken from the Aztec word for "resting place," and the grounds, shaded with majestic live oaks, accented with formal gardens and brick paths, ensure that the name remains accurate. The main house was restored for tours in 1982, with the original slave cottages rebuilt for B&B guests. Debra Purifoy is the long-time manager; Keith Harland has owned Tezcuco since 1991. Rates include a tour of the antique-filled main house (between 9 A.M. and 4:30 P.M.), a welcome glass of wine, and breakfast brought to your cottage or served in the restaurant between 8–10:30 A.M. The cottage breakfast includes scrambled eggs, grits, homemade biscuits, sausage, and juice; in the restaurant there's also a choice of waffles, pancakes, or French toast. At lunch, the restaurant serves such Cajun favorites as fried catfish, blackened pork, crawfish etouffée, and chicken and sausage jambalaya.

"Breakfast was brought promptly to our front door. Our rooms were clean and attractively decorated, many with handsome antiques. We especially liked the General Suite in the main house, plus the cottages La Petite Maison, Pigeonaire, La Cabane, Tennessee, and L'Autre. The cottages provide a quiet, romantic atmosphere; we relaxed on our porch rocker with an iced tea." (Joan O'Brien) "Enjoyed having books to read, appealing knickknacks, and rockers on the porch. Interesting tour of the main house." (Annette Rolfes)

Open All year. Closed Thanksgiving, Christmas, New Year. Restaurant open for breakfast and lunch.
Rooms 1 2-bedroom suite, 15 1–3 bedroom units in 9 cottages—all with full private bath, radio, clock, TV, air-conditioning, porch. Some with desk, fan, fireplace, refrigerator, stove.
Facilities Restaurant, manor house, chapel, museum, doll house, blacksmith shop. guest laundry. 24 acres gardens, off-street parking, gazebo, lawn games.
Location S LA. 60 m W of New Orleans, 30 E of Baton Rouge. From I-10, take Exit 179 & go 5½ m S on LA 44 to Burnside. Inn is 1 m N of Sunshine Bridge on LA 44.
Restrictions No smoking in suite.
Credit cards Amex, Discover, MC, Visa.
Rates B&B, $150 cottage, $55–110 double. Extra adult, $20; extra child 4–18, $12.50. Prix fixe lunch, $6; alc dinner, $12–25.
Extras Crib.

EUNICE

In the heart of Cajun country, about 70 miles west of Baton Rouge and about 30 miles northwest of Lafayette is the town of Eunice, home of the 1920s-era Liberty Center and its delightful Saturday night radio show, "Rendez-Vous des Cajuns," and of the Prairie Acadian Cultural Center (a U.S. National Park Service project) next door.

Reader tip: "Try Nick's on Second Street for fried catfish, crab and alligator, seafood gumbo, grilled shrimp, and crawfish etoufée." (MA)

Also recommended: Frequent contributor *Duane Roller* wrote to comment on **Potier's Prairie Cajun Inn & Gifts** (110 West Park, 70535; 318–457–0440): "Originally the first hospital in Eunice, all accommodations are suites. Ours consisted of a large living room with handmade Cajun wood furniture and a TV, bathroom, bedroom, and a kitchen stocked with a selection of coffees and teas. In the evening, we were given a basket with eggs and breads, milk and juice; in the morning, we prepared breakfast at our leisure. A pleasant place to stay in an area where little is available, though we'd recommend avoiding the oppressive summer heat and humidity." *(Duane Roller)* The reasonable $60 double rates include breakfast and use of the hot tub.

Information please: Another possibility is the **Seale Guesthouse** (Highway 13, P.O.Box 568, 70535; 318–457–3753), a turn-of-the century home two miles south of Eunice. The eight guest rooms have private or shared baths, plus telephones and color TV. A continental breakfast is included in the $65 B&B double rate, with rates in the $150–200 range for the luxurious honeymoon cottages. The charming decor includes antiques and appealing collectibles.

JACKSON

Information please: About 5 miles south of Jackson is **Asphodel Village** (4626 Highway 68, 70748; 504–654–6868), a complex consisting of the main house, a full-service restaurant, a gift shop, and a collection of buildings providing overnight accommodation for B&B guests. Double rates for the 16 guest rooms ranges from $55–80. The main house dates back to 1820 and is built in the Greek Revival style; it is open for tours weekdays from 10 A.M. to 4 P.M. "The cottages undergo constant maintenance and are kept immaculate; our favorite is the Woods Cottage. The renovated gift shop, and the creek and path into the woods give it an 'inn-like' feeling. Helpful owners and staff, adequate food." *(Joan & Robert O'Brien)* In town is **Milbank** (102 Bank Street, P.O. Box 1000, 70748; 504–634–5901), a classic antebellum home furnished with museum-quality antiques, including Mallard tester and hand-carved oak beds, huge old armoires, and more. There is no resident innkeeper, so single travelers may not feel comfortable. B&B double rates are $75.

LAFAYETTE

Located in south central Louisiana, Lafayette is the capital of Cajun country; many Acadians settled here after being driven out of Nova Scotia by the British in 1755. Of particular interest is Vermillionville, a recreation of the original 18th-century Cajun and Creole village; the Live Oak Gardens, especially beautiful when both azaleas and tulips are in bloom; the Acadian village, a folk museum celebrating 19th-century Acadian life; nearby plantations, and a variety of celebrations and festivals year-round. Lafayette is 131 miles west of New Orleans.

Reader tip: "Don't miss dinner and dancing at Rondol's. Wonderful Cajun food, terrific dance floor, and friendly people who didn't seem to mind two Yankees trying the Cajun dances. Vermillionville was a disap-

pointment during our July visit; no craftspeople or interpreters in sight."
(DS)

Also recommended: Seven miles north of Lafayette is **La Maison de Compagne** (925 Kidder Road, Carencro, 70520; 318–896–6529), offering four guest rooms with private baths, plus a swimming pool, at B&B double rates of $85–90. "Decorated with magnificent Victorian antiques. Careful attention to detail. Fred and Joeann McLemore made us feel like old family friends. Each morning, we were greeted with fresh coffee, juice, tea and fresh muffins, which we enjoyed outdoors on rocking chairs on the balcony. At 9 A.M., breakfast was served in the dining room. Fresh baked breads, elegant seafood dishes, superb egg dishes, and wonderful fruit frappes kept us fueled all day. The meals were served on beautiful china and crystal." *(Michael Ledger)* "Excellent restaurant and sightseeing suggestions. At departure, we were given a jar of their own honey." *(Martha Banda)* **Information please: Ti Frère's** (1905 Verot School Road, Highway 339, 70508; 318–984–9347) is a brick and cedar house built in 1880 by Ti Frère (Little Brother) Comeaux, and was bought by Pat and Maugie Pastor in 1994. The three double rooms each rent for $85, including a full breakfast.

Bois des Chênes 👥 ♿

338 North Sterling Street, 70501

Tel: 318–233–7816
Fax: 318–232–5400

Listed on the National Register of Historic Places, this Acadian-style plantation home has been restored to its original 1820 configuration, and is furnished with Louisiana French period antiques, highlighted by Coerte and Marjorie Voorhies' collections of pottery, antique weapons, and textiles. Part of the Charles Mouton Plantation, the B&B is housed in an 1890 carriage house at the rear of the plantation house. It is decorated with antique furnishings and the immaculate bathrooms have brass fixtures. Each guest room has a different decor: Country Acadian, Louisiana Empire, and Victorian. Rates include breakfast, a welcome bottle of wine, and a house tour. Coerte's expeditions into the Atchafalaya Swamp have been featured on cable TV's Discovery channel; he's happy to plan an excursion for guests.

"A quiet and peaceful place, where we were treated with care and concern. We stayed in the Louisiana Suite, with a high, firm bed. We loved the two family dogs." *(Deborah Ross & Russ Hogan)* "Mrs. Voorhies is a wonderful cook." *(Gail Hari)* "Comfortable, spotless room with good bedside lighting. Tons of towels for those multi-shower summer days. Hosts knowledgeable about restaurants and local points of interest. Coerte's small and private swamp tour was memorable; we saw lots of birds and local color." *(DS)* "Best of all was the Voorhies' kindness. They provided our toddler with a splendid antique brass child's bed, complete with teddy bear. Delicious breakfast of coffee, freshly squeezed orange juice, bacon, fresh fruit, boudin (sausage), and pain perdu (French toast). Afterwards, we got a history and tour of the plantation house, and a slide show of the before pictures." *(Barbara Mast James)* "Delicious breakfasts are served at a long common table." *(James Burr)*

Open All year. Closed Christmas Eve & Day.
Rooms 1 suite. 3 doubles—all with private bath, radio, TV, air-conditioning, fan, refrigerator.
Facilities Breakfast room, solarium, porch. 2 acres with patio, aviary. Atchafalaya Swamp expeditions.
Location Historic district. From I-10 take exit 103A S to Evangeline Thruway. Go 3 lights to Mudd Ave. Turn left and go 3 blocks to intersection with N Sterling. Inn is on SE corner. Continue on Mudd past inn and enter circular driveway on right at "35 MPH" sign.
Restrictions No smoking.
Credit cards Amex, MC, Visa.
Rates B&B, $105 suite, $85 double, $75–95 single. Extra person, $20. Children under 5 free in parents' room. Crib, $10. 10% senior, AAA discount.
Extras Wheelchair access. Airport/station pickups. Pets by prior arrangement. Crib, babysitting. French spoken.

Tante Da's   *Tel:* 318–264–1191
2631 S.E. Evangeline Thruway, 70508   800–853–REST

A one-story Queen Anne Revival cottage built in 1902, Tante Da's was purchased in 1989 by Douglas and Tanya Greenwald, who opened it as an inn in 1993 after extensive restoration work. Named for Miss Alida Martin (known as Tante Da), who lived here for 80 years, this B&B features 12-foot ceilings and hand-hewn cypress casings and doors.

"We stayed in Miss Alida's Room where Doug and Tanya's attention to detail was evident in the collection of Oriental fans and chopsticks. The furnishings included an 1860 walnut queen-sized bed with matching armoire and marble-topped dresser, with a sea-green and mauve color scheme. Warm, friendly hosts, yet not overbearing." *(Jack Oehme)* "Delicious breakfast of eggs Benedict, fresh fruit, homemade nut bread and muffins. " *(Jane & Mike Middleton)* "Spacious, bright, airy, and sunny. Wonderful aromas emerge from the kitchen where Doug is constantly putting his remarkable culinary skills to good use. His tarte Milan was as delicious to eat as it was to behold, and was served with fresh fruit and homemade banana pineapple bread. The house is immaculate, and everything smelled clean and fresh; the wood floors shone. My room had a double bed with a cozy comforter that matched the drapes and valances, vases of fresh-cut flowers, a rocking chair, and a huge antique claw-foot tub in the bathroom. The convivial cocktail hour was a special treat, when Doug and Tanya offered wine and snacks to guests in their parlor." *(Claire Falkner)*

Open All year.
Rooms 4 doubles—all with full private bath, radio, clock, air-conditioning, ceiling fan, refrigerator. TV, telephone on request.
Facilities Dining room, living room, guest refrigerator, guest laundry, porch. 1 acre with garden, off-street parking. Golf, swamp tours nearby.
Location 5 m from town.
Restrictions No smoking. Children over 12. Train tracks nearby.
Credit cards Amex, Discover, MC, Visa.
Rates B&B, $75–150 double. Extra person, $20. Weekly, corporate rates. 2-night minimum festival weekends.
Extras Airport/station pickups. French spoken.

LAFITTE

Victoria Inn ¢   *Tel:* 504–689–4757
Highway 45, Box 545 B, 70067   *Fax:* 504–689–3399

A visit to Louisiana is more than a trip to New Orleans and a bus tour
to a famous plantation. You don't have to go far to experience Cajun life
in a Cajun community, where a majority of the people still make their
living from fishing and trapping, and weekends are filled with Cajun music
and dance at a local "Fais Do Do." That's the appeal of the Victoria Inn
in Lafitte, whose inhabitants are descendants of the pirate Jean Lafitte. This
West-Indies style cottage was built in 1884 and was restored as a B&B
in 1993 by Roy and Dale Ross. Guest rooms are named after flowers from
the garden, and are decorated with antiques. Guests are welcomed with
refreshments on arrival and are offered such breakfast choices as pecan
waffles and bacon, or a crabmeat omelet; early morning coffee is ready at
6 A.M.

"The Rosses care about their guests, yet respect their privacy. Perfect
setting for strolling, with a barn full of horses and other animals, and a
dock where you can sit and listen to the lapping water. The immaculate
Magnolia Suite was furnished with antiques, the quiet broken only by the
many area birds." *(Mary Oliveira)* Comments welcome.

Area for improvement: "A reading light on my side of the bed."

Open All year.
Rooms 2 suites, 3 doubles—3 with private bath and/or shower, 2 with maximum
of 4 people sharing bath. All with clock, TV, air-conditioning, fan. Some with
porch.
Facilities Dining room, books, veranda. 6 acres with off-street parking, gardens,
lakefront, covered dock, pier for swimming, boating, water skiing, fishing, bird-
watching. Swamp tours, fishing charters, Jean Lafitte National Historic Park nearby.
Location S LA. 30 m S of New Orleans. 5 m to town. On Bayou Barataria. From
Westbank Expressway, take Barataria Blvd. (LA 45) S to LA 3134 & bear left. Road
reconnects with LA 45 at blinking light. Continue S on 45 to bridge across bayou.
Continue S 7¼ m till road crosses Goose Bayou, then watch for road for B&B on
left.
Restrictions No smoking.
Credit cards Amex, MC, Visa.
Rates B&B, $125 suite, $75 double, $50 single. Extra person, $15. No charge for
children under 6.
Extras Train station pick-ups, $15 round-trip. Spanish spoken. Pets sometimes
permitted.

LECOMPTE

Also recommended: Another appealing choice located 16 miles southeast of Alexandria is **Loyd Hall Plantation** (292 Loyd Bridge Road,
Cheneyville 71325; 318–776–5641), a 640-acre working plantation dating back to 1820. Tours of the mansion are offered, while B&B accommo-

dation is found in several restored outbuildings. "Beulah Davis conducts the tours and is a most fascinating person. Ask her to tell you about the ghosts, and what happened to the other 'L' in Loyd. Our suite in the converted kitchen building was clean and well done with antiques. It had a fully stocked kitchen with wine, an apple cobbler, and brownies, plus all the makings for breakfast the next morning—eggs, grits, coffee, juice, milk, sausage, and sweet potato muffins. Clarence the donkey and Lady the horse were a delight to watch. We picked cotton as a memento when we took a bicycle ride, and browsed in the gift/antique shop." *(Joan O'Brien)*

Hardy House ¢ ✕ ♿   *Tel: 318–776–5178*
1414 Weems, P.O. Box 1192, 71347   *Fax: 318–776–5103*

Many towns are named for famous historic figures, but very few are named for a famous racehorse, as is Lecompte; whole plantations were bet on the outcome of his New Orleans race in 1854. Staying at the Hardy House is hardly such a risky proposition. Built in 1888, and restored as an inn in 1991 by Ann Johnson, the house has an unusual architectural design, enhancing guest privacy. Breakfast is served from 7–11 A.M. in Lea's Lunchroom, specializing in Southern country food, and located four blocks away; lunch and dinner are offered from 11–7 P.M.

"Ann Hardy is the daughter of the famous old gentleman who started Lea's Lunchroom; his famous pies earned him a spot in the restaurant hall of fame. She did a beautiful job of restoring this 1888 cottage, with a honeymoon suite at the front of the house and other guest rooms behind the country kitchen. When we returned to our room late, she had left a pecan pie and brownies in the kitchen for a bed-time snack. Guest rooms are furnished with antique beds and wash basins as well as clawfoot tubs. The work of local artists highlights the decor." *(Joan O'Brien)* Reports welcome.

Open Jan.–Oct.
Rooms 2 suites, 2 doubles—all with full private bath, air-conditioning. Some with radio, clock, TV, desk. fan, fireplace, double soaking tub.
Facilities Restaurant, porch with rockers. Garden with gazebo. Bicycles.
Location Central LA. 12 m S of Alexandria on I-49. Approx. halfway between New Orleans & Shreveport.
Restrictions No smoking.
Credit cards MC, Visa.
Rates B&B, $95–110 suite, double. 10% senior discount.
Extras Wheelchair access. Crib.

MONROE

Information please: In northeast Louisiana's cotton country, where B&Bs are sparse, is **Boscobel Cottage** (185 Cordell Lane, Monroe 71202; 318–325–1550 or 800–CLIF–KAY), a 1820 Greek Revival cottage with two guest rooms furnished with antiques and queen-sized beds, private baths, TVs, and air-conditioning. The B&B double rates of $65–95 include a full Southern breakfast and refreshments upon arrival. Facing the Ouachita River, Boscobel is located 14 miles south of Monroe. Comments?

NAPOLEONVILLE

Information please: Certainly a visit to Lousiana isn't complete without spending a night on a plantation, but an equally authentic experience is a night in a trapper's swamp cabin. About 15 miles south of Napoleonville is James and Betty Provost's **Wildlife Gardens** (5306 North Bayou Black Drive, U.S. Rte. 90, Gibson 70356; 504–575–3676) located in a natural cypress swamp, with three simply furnished (but air-conditioned) cabins built right over the water. The $60 double rate includes a full breakfast; the swamp tour is a small extra fee, and children are most welcome. The Provost's mini-zoo includes bobcats, nutria, owls, deer, loggerhead turtles, and of course, alligators.

Madewood Plantation House ➠   *Tel:* 504–369–7151
4250 Highway 308, 70390   *Fax:* 504–369–9848

A 21-room Greek Revival mansion, Madewood was designed in 1846 and is a National Historic Landmark. The white-painted mansion has six imposing Doric columns and was built from bricks produced in the plantation's kiln and from cypress grown on its lands. Madewood was purchased in 1964 by Mr. and Mrs. Harold Marshall and is now owned by their son Keith and his wife Millie. Keith and Millie work in New Orleans during the week, spending many weekends at Madewood; Dave D'Aunoy and Janet Ledet are the managers. Rooms are furnished with an extensive collection of period antiques, including canopy or half-tester beds, marble fireplace mantels, hand-carved woodwork, and fanned windows. Millie notes that "Madewood is not sophisticated or luxurious, but is a large country mansion. Our food is country cooking, not gourmet; some northerners don't realize that smothered green beans are supposed to be cooked to death." Guest rooms are located in the mansion, a 1820s Greek Revival cottage, and a three-room cabin with more casual country furnishings. Rates include wine and cheese, family-style dinner, coffee and brandy in the parlor, and full breakfast in the dining room.

"A picture book plantation house. We slept in an antique four-poster bed, and woke up to find steaming coffee outside our room the next morning." *(Alan H. Smith)* "Ambiance, service, careful attention to detail." *(Diane Greeneich)* "A highlight was being free to roam the house and to look at old photos." *(SD)* "Delicious breakfast buffet of grits, eggs, biscuits, spicy sausage, bacon, and New Orleans coffee." *(Terri Dunham)* "Spacious, beautiful bedroom; delicious dinner; interesting guests." *(Nancy Sinclair)*

Worth noting: Because rooms are kept open for tours during the day, a 5 P.M. check-in and a 10 A.M. check-out is sometimes requested for rooms in the main house. Also: While readers are consistently pleased with their stay at Madewood, weekends when the Marshalls are in residence appear to be a highlight.

Open All year. Closed Thanksgiving, Christmas, New Year.

Rooms 1 cottage, 2 suites, 6 doubles with private bath and/or shower, air-conditioning. 3 rooms in annex; 1 2-bedroom cottage. Some with desk, radio, fireplace, refrigerator, balcony.

Facilities Double parlors, dining room, library, music room, verandas. 20 acres with patio, live oaks, bayou. Swamp tours nearby.

Location SE LA. Sugarcane country. 75 m W of New Orleans, 45 m S of Baton Rouge. On Bayou Laforche, facing LA Hwy. 308. 4 m from town.

Restrictions No smoking. "Front rooms 100 yds. from highway."

Credit cards Amex, MC, Visa.

Rates MAP, $165 double. Extra person, $10–50. Reduced rate for children.

Extras Playpen.

NATCHITOCHES

About 60 miles south of Shreveport on Cane River Lake, Natchitoches is the oldest permanent settlement in the Louisiana Purchase territory; it may also have one of the area's most mispronounced names—the correct one is somewhere between NAK-a-tosh and NAK-a-tish. A more recent claim to fame is that it was the setting for the movie, *Steel Magnolias*.

Reader tip: "Lazyone's Diner is famous for meat pies and Irish stew; while there, visit Just Friends on Front Street for some chocolate chip pie." *(Terri Dunham)*

Also recommended: Dating back to 1820, the **Cloutier Townhouse** (Front Street, 71457; 318–352–5242) is located in Natchitoches's historic district. "Decorated with Louisiana Empire antiques throughout. Knowledgeable innkeepers." *(Sarah Brown)* "The master bedroom has a private Jacuzzi bathroom. A Southern breakfast was left on a silver tray outside of our bedroom door, and we ate on the back balcony overlooking the courtyard; Julia Roberts slept here when *Steel Magnolias* was being filmed. Conna Cloutier, the owner, lives in the home and was flexible and helpful, allowing us a late check-out and suggesting restaurants." *(Joan O'Brien)*

Information please: Also located in the historic district, the **Fleur-de-Lis Inn** (336 Second Street, Natchitoches 71457; 318–352–6621 or 800–489–6621) offers five guest rooms with private baths, antique furnishings, and queen- or king-size beds at double rates of $65 (except December), including a full breakfast. This turn-of-the century Victorian home offers beautiful woodwork and a wraparound porch with rockers and a swing. This B&B was purchased by Tom and Harriette Palmer in 1994.

NEW ORLEANS

Cognoscenti inform us that the city under discussion here is called *Nu-Awluns*, never *New Orleens*.

The French Quarter is roughly rectangular in shape, bordered by Canal Street to the west, Rampart Street to the north, Esplanade to the east, and the river to the south. Canal Street forms a border between the French Quarter and the financial district; the big chain hotels—the Sheraton,

Marriott, Westin, etc., are all in the area around Canal. Bourbon and Royal Streets run east/west, and are very noisy; the quietest section of the quarter is the beautiful residential area to the east, just north of the French Market.

Rates are highest during Mardi Gras, Sugar Bowl, Super Bowl, Jazz Festival, and other peak festival times (not listed here); be prepared to pay the top rate *in advance.* Bargain summer rates are generally available from June through September, so ask for details when phoning. Parking can be a problem; if traveling by car, be sure to ask for specifics when reserving your room. A few hotels provide on-site parking; most have arrangements with nearby garages.

Many hotel rooms in the French Quarter tend to be small, with a bed and not much in the way of easy chairs or usable desk space. Although most inns have attractive balconies and courtyards, few offer parlors or dining rooms for guests to gather inside. If you'll be visiting when it's either too hot or too chilly to enjoy being outdoors for long, make an effort to book a room in one of the establishments that does provide interior common space.

People come to New Orleans for many reasons, but peace and quiet are not usually among them. It is a noisy city, and light sleepers should stay away from rooms in the commercial sector of the French quarter. Visitors should also be alert to the problem of street crime, a real problem at night in parts of the French Quarter and in the Garden District. Ask your innkeeper for advice.

Reader tips: "Be sure to allow plenty of time for just hanging out in front of the Cathedral in Jackson Square, where music is always playing and there's always something going on. After you've made the obligatory visits to the French Market for souvenirs and the Café du Monde for *beignets* (benyay) and *café au lait* (lay), be sure to visit the nearby Jean Lafitte Visitor Center where you can sign up for terrific free walking tours of the French Quarter and Garden District. We thought Arnaud's restaurant was good but over-rated, but had a fabulous lunch at the Commander's Palace in the Garden District after our walking tour." *(RSS)* "Café Maspero, on Decatur, across from the Jackson Brewery has fabulous mufalettas, and their pastrami sandwiches are equally renowned. Abita Beer, a local brew, is great in all its varieties. For breakfast, Croissant d'Or on Rue Ursuline, has wonderful pastries and coffee, served in a traditional coffee house atmosphere." *(Steve Holman)*

Also recommended: In the too-big-but-still-wonderful category is the **Windsor Court Hotel** (300 Gravier Street, 70130; 504–523–6000 or 800–262–2662) with 325 suites and doubles. As the city's first and only 5-diamond hotel, *Alex & Beryl Williams* describe it as "a civilized haven of peace and quiet. We had a beautifully furnished junior suite with a small balcony. The restaurant is most attractive and the food is excellent." Another good choice is the 226-room **Le Pavillon Hotel** (833 Poydras Street, 70140; 504–581–3111 or 800–535–9095), in the heart of the central business district, within a 10-minute walk of the French Quarter (not recommended at night). This elegantly appointed hotel has lovely rooms and good service, original artwork and antiques, marble floors, and a rooftop pool with a spectacular view. Suites range from $275–800;

doubles from $99–250; rates include a bedtime snack of milk or cocoa with peanut butter and jelly sandwiches.

Thirty minutes from the French Quarter is **Seven Oaks** (2600 Gay Lynn Drive, Kenner 70065; 504–888–8649), a new home built in the style of an antebellum cottage. The two guest rooms rent for $95–115, including a plantation breakfast. The handsome decor combines antiques, collectibles, and contemporary furnishings, and the surrounding gardens invite guests for a relaxing stroll. "Immaculately clean, superb decor, accommodating hostess. Interesting Mardi Gras collection. Safe neighborhood, ideal for the woman traveler." *(Joan O'Brien)*

For an additional area entry, see listing for the **Salmen-Fritchie House** in **Slidell,** just 30 minutes north of New Orleans.

Information please; French Quarter: We'd like more feedback on two of New Orleans best-known inns, the **Hotel Maison de Ville** (727 Rue Toulouse, 70130; 504–561–5858 or 800–634–1600) and the **Soniat House** (1133 Chartres Street, 70116; 504–522–0570 or 800–544–8808). The Maison de Ville consists of eight buildings, including the Audubon Cottages, about a block and a half away. Its acclaimed restaurant features Provençal and Mediterranean dishes. Rates, ranging from $100–240 include a continental breakfast, afternoon cocktails and an overnight shoe shine service. The Soniat House is probably New Orleans' best-known B&B inn, and offers lovely rooms, a peaceful setting, and a charming courtyard. B&B double rates range from $135–185; continental breakfast is $6 per person; all phone calls, $.85 each. "Loved the firm beds with top-quality linens, great water pressure, and friendly staff, but I thought it was overpriced and don't plan to return." *(DC)*

A good choice for bargain hunters is the **French Quarter Maisonnettes** (1130 Chartres Street, 70116; 504–524–9918). Built in 1825, it has maintained much of its original architecture, including the flagstone carriage drive and inner courtyard. Although the furnishings can charitably be described as utilitarian, the $55–70 double rates are a terrific bargain for the prime location.

At the northern edge of the quarter, three blocks from Bourbon Street, is **P.J. Holbrooke's Olde Victorian Inn** (914 North Rampart Street, 70116; 504–522–2446 or 800–725–2446), built in 1860. The six guest rooms (all with private bath) have period decor. The $115–165 double rates include a five-course breakfast served in your room or in the courtyard, welcoming wine and cheese, afternoon refreshments in the Gathering Room, and airport pickups and returns. If you'd like your own little apartment at the eastern edge of the quarter, try **The Lanaux House** (Esplanade Avenue at Chartres, 70152; 504–488–4640 or 800–729–4640), built in 1879, and opened as a B&B in 1989. Three suites are available, each with a private entrance, sitting room, queen-size bed, bathroom, and kitchenette. A self-serve breakfast is included in the $76–276 rates.

An affordable hotel in the French Quarter is the **Chateau Hotel** (1001 Chartres Street, 70116; 504–524–9636) with 46 individually furnished guest rooms surrounding a courtyard with swimming pool and patio. The $70–100 rates include the morning paper, continental breakfast, and valet parking. The **Hotel Provincial** (1024 Chartres Street, 70116; 504–581–

4995 or 800–535–7922) is a family-owned 100 room hotel occupying several 19th-century buildings. The hotel has five landscaped interior courtyards and patios, one with a swimming pool. The high-ceilinged guest rooms are decorated with Creole antiques, French furnishings, floral fabrics, and modern appointments. Kids will enjoy a swim in the hotel's small swimming pool, and all will appreciate its convenient but quiet location. Double rates range from $105–165. Comments welcome.

Information please; Uptown/Garden District: Small and elegant, with a Garden District location, is the **Pontchartrain Hotel** (2031 St. Charles Avenue, 70140; 504–524–0581 or 800–777–6193). Guest room decor varies from library paneling and English antiques, to chintz and wall-to-wall carpeting. Rates for the 100 guest rooms ranges from $120–600.

The Uptown **Beau Séjour** (1930 Napoleon Avenue, 70115; 504–897–3746) has five guest rooms, each with private bath and air-conditioning. B&B double rates range from $80–125. Guest rooms are simply furnished with some Victorian antiques and handmade quilts. "Convenient and peaceful in a neighborhood with huge trees and handsome Victorian homes. Owners Kim and Gilles Gagnon are helpful, warm, informative innkeepers." (Janice O'Neill) Self-described as a "little Bohemian around the edges," the **St. Charles Guest House** (1748 Prytania Street, 70130; 504–523–6556) is located in the lower Garden District and has 36 guest rooms in four century-old buildings. Continental breakfast is served in the poolside breakfast room, with double rates ranging from $48–65; backpacker rooms go for $30. Reports appreciated.

The Chimes Cottages 🛏 ¢   Tel: 504–899–2621
1146 Constantinople Street, 70115

The Chimes Cottages encircle the brick courtyard belonging to the 1876 Uptown home of innkeepers Jill and Charles Abbyad. In 1985, the Abbyads bought and restored three Victorian cottages, with gingerbread detailing and stained and leaded glass windows. Breakfast is served family-style in the dining room, and includes freshly squeezed orange juice, fresh fruit, muffins, rolls, and coffee.

"The brick courtyard is filled with flowers and plants, a delightful place to relax with a glass of wine. Charles and Jill were friendly, gracious and professional. Breakfast is served in the dining room with the other guests (or by request, in your cottage), hosted by Jill and/or Charles. They introduced the guests and encouraged the exchange of information and suggestions. Their insights made our plans easier, faster, better; they made objective suggestions for dining, tours and activities without imposing." (Ri Regina) "Unbeatable restaurant advice. Fresh gardenias from their bushes were placed by the bedside." (Beth de Anda, also Steve Soule) "Our room was furnished with a comfortable four-poster bed; the arched, bevelled windows offered a view of the shady courtyard. Softly tinkling chimes lulled us to sleep." (Katherine Madden) "The French windows in my cottage opened onto the brick courtyard, where I reclined in a hammock with a good book. The honor system refrigerator was stocked with soda, beer, and wine." (Ann Christoffersen) "Good location within walking distance of Tipitina's and the St. Charles streetcar. Wonderful bread pudding." *(Karl Bremer)*

Open All year.
Rooms 1 suite, 3 cottages—all with private bath and/or shower, telephone, radio, TV, desk, air-conditioning, ceiling fan, refrigerator, coffee-maker. 2 with fireplace.
Facilities Dining room, laundry facility, courtyard, limited off-street parking.
Location Garden district. 2 m from French Quarter; 3 blocks to St. Charles Streetcar. Take I-10 E to Business District which changes to Hwy. 90. Exit at St. Charles Ave. (last exit before Greater New Orleans bridge). Constantinople St. is located between Louisiana & Napoleon on river side of St. Charles.
Restrictions No smoking.
Credit cards None accepted.
Rates B&B, $65–125 suite, $50–90 double, $50–75 single. Extra person, $10. 2-3 night weekend minimum Oct.–May.
Extras Pets with approval. Playpen. French, Arabic spoken.

Dauphine Orleans Hotel ♛

415 Dauphine Street, 70112

Tel: 504–586–1800
800–521–7111
Fax: 504–586–1409

The Dauphine Orleans offers the hospitable atmosphere of a small French Quarter hotel. Amenities include a welcome cocktail with hors d'oeuvres, continental breakfast, morning newspaper, turndown service, afternoon tea, and downtown transportation. Guest rooms were refurbished in 1994; most appealing are the courtyard suites, dating back to the early 1800s.

"Pleasant rooms decorated with period reproductions and generic hotel furnishings. Request one on the courtyard, or overlooking the swimming pool for a little more elbow room; upstairs rooms are quiet. In the sunny kitchen is a buffet breakfast of juice, cereals, fresh fruit, toast, English muffins, and sweet rolls. The staff was friendly and helpful." *(Stephanie Reeves)* "The hotel escapes the noise and crowds of Bourbon Street, yet one can easily go everywhere in the Quarter." *(Frank Conlon)* Reports please.

Open All year.
Rooms 9 suites, 100 doubles—all with private bath, telephone, radio, TV, desk, air-conditioning, safe, mini-bar. Some with balcony, whirlpool tubs. 18 courtyard rooms.
Facilities Breakfast room, library, bar/lounge, exercise room. Valet parking, swimming pool, hot tub.
Location French Quarter between Conti & St. Louis Sts.
Restrictions Some non-smoking guest rooms. Street noise in front rooms.
Credit cards Most major cards.
Rates B&B, $165–350 suite, $135–175 double. Extra person, $15. Children under 12 free. Senior, AAA discount.
Extras Transportation (8 A.M.-8 P.M.) in French Quarter, business district. Pets by arrangement. Crib, babysitting. French, Italian, Spanish spoken.

Hotel Villa Convento ¢

616 Ursulines Street, 70116

Tel: 504–522–1793
Fax: 504–524–1902

Since Larry and Lela Campo bought the Villa Convento in 1982, they have been continuously improving and upgrading this 1848 building, a

183

single-family dwelling until the 1940s. Although the rooms are rather small and the furnishings modest, most readers feel that this is well balanced by the reasonable rates, convenient location, and helpful owners.

"The rooms facing Ursulines have traditional wrought iron balconies, while the others overlook the courtyard. A breakfast of croissants and coffee is served in the covered courtyard; they come fresh and hot from the Croissant D'Or bakery across the street. The tapestry-padded elevator is convenient because the stairs are narrow." *(Christine Pflug)* "The Campo family and their staff know the city well, and are helpful with questions about restaurants, local sights, and directions. My favorite rooms are the front balcony rooms; furnished with table and chairs, they are perfect for sipping your coffee on a sunny morning." *(Jon Legris)* "Quiet street, plenty of hot water in the bathroom, and good light for reading. I felt secure, with the front door locked at all times and a staff member at the desk twenty-four hours a day." *(Peggy DeCoursey)* "Legend has it that this hotel was the original *House of the Rising Sun*" *(Caryl Burtner)* "Our spotless room, #207, had been recently redecorated; it was small but adequate. Great coffee, croissants, and conversation at breakfast—I think all the other guests were British." *(DS)*

Areas for improvement: "Hopefully, the breakfast courtyard is scheduled for a facelift." Also: "Our tub didn't drain well; the sink stopper was hard to work."

Open All year.
Rooms 2 suites, 22 doubles—all with full private bath, telephone, TV, air-conditioning. 20 with fan, 18 with radio. Some with balcony.
Facilities Courtyard. Fax. Parking garage 2 blocks away, $8 per night.
Location French Quarter, between Chartres & Royal.
Restrictions Light sleepers should request rooms away from street. No children under 10.
Credit cards All major cards.
Rates B&B, $95 suite, $59–95 double. Extra person, $10. 2-night weekend, holiday minimum.
Extras Spanish spoken.

The House on Bayou Road

2275 Bayou Road, 70119

Tel: 504–945–0992
504–949–7711
Fax: 504–945–0993

For country atmosphere just a half-mile from the French Quarter, consider the House on Bayou Road, a West Indies-style plantation home built in 1798 for a Spanish Colonial diplomat. Owned by Cynthia Reeves since 1976, it was opened as a B&B in 1992, and is managed by Karon Baudouin. Guests are welcome to explore the antique-filled double parlors, and enjoy a full breakfast in the dining room furnished with Louisiana primitive pieces. Guest rooms are decorated with antiques, collectibles, and queen- and king-size four poster and canopy beds. Rates include breakfast, afternoon sherry, and evening turndown service with wrapped pralines. "Enjoyed the big Southern plantation breakfast, the elegant yet homey atmosphere, and the lovely grounds." *(Mary Ann Howard)* "Cynthia Reeves made our stay memorable." *(CP)* Reports welcome.

Open All year.

Rooms 2 suites, 6 doubles—6 with private bath and/or shower, 2 with maximum of 4 people sharing bath. All with telephone, radio, clock, desk, air-conditioning, fan. 4 with fireplace, 2 with porch, 1 with kitchen. 4 rooms in main house, 3 in cottage, 1 in carriage house.

Facilities Dining room with fireplace, living room, guest kitchen/laundry, sun porch, screened porches, deck with hot tub. 2 acres with brick courtyard with fountain & fish pond, off-street secured parking.

Location Esplanade Ridge Historic District. ½ m from French Quarter. Just off of Esplanade Ave.

Restrictions No smoking. Children over 10. Cats in residence.

Credit cards MC, Visa.

Rates B&B, $180–290 suite, $95–180 double. Extra person $20. 2-night minimum, except during special events.

Extras Limited wheelchair access. Airport/station pick-up. French, Spanish spoken.

Lafitte Guest House	*Tel: 504–581–2678*
1003 Bourbon Street, 70116	800–331–7971
	Fax: 504–581–2678

Long owned by Dr. Robert Guyton, the Lafitte Guest House is now managed by William B. Stuart, a retired college professor. Built in 1849, its rooms are furnished with 18th and 19th century antiques. Breakfast is served from 8–11 A.M.; in the evening, wine and hors d'oeuvres are usually served by Dr. Guyton.

"My initial telephone call was answered by a knowledgeable employee providing careful descriptions; confirmation followed promptly." *(Ernest Harmon)* "Rooms are spacious and beautifully furnished with antiques; the parlor is especially pleasant." *(Craig Brummer)* "Fourteen-foot ceilings, fireplaces with mantles, crystal chandeliers, armoires, and four-poster beds." *(David Cooley)* "The concierges are helpful in guiding guests to good restaurants, tours, clubs, and shops. Inviting private courtyard with flowers and stone floor." *(Miriam Cooper)* "Breakfast includes fresh mixed fruit, choice of bakery-fresh croissant or Danish, juice, and beverage. Spotless housekeeping. Convenient location, yet removed from crowds and noise." *(Elaine Rogers)* "The cocktail hour, with wine and plentiful hors d'oeuvres, was a pleasant way to meet and chat with the other guests." *(Helene Nelkin)* "Great advice on which streets are safe to walk at night." *(Martha Ruddell)* "They remember you from previous stays and keep track of your individual preferences." *(Peter Dibble)* "The staff greets you in the hallways with smiles and good mornings. Antique botanicals and fashion prints, canopy beds, flower borders, marble-topped dressers, and flower arrangements all contribute to the atmosphere." *(Mary Webb)*

Open All year.

Rooms 2 suites, 12 doubles—all with private bath and/or shower, telephone, radio, desk, air-conditioning, TV. Many with balcony, fireplace, refrigerator.

Facilities Parlor with fireplace, courtyard, off-street parking (fee).

Location Residential section of French quarter, at corner of Bourbon & St. Philip.

Credit cards Amex, Discover, MC, Visa.

Restrictions Traffic noise in some rooms.

Rates B&B, $265 suite, $85–165 double. Extra person, $22; children under 5 free.
Extras Crib ($10), babysitting.

Le Richelieu in the French Quarter 👫 ✗ ♿ *Tel:* 504–529–2492
1234 Chartres Street, 70116

800–535–9653

Fax: 504–524–8179

Several restored 19th-century buildings make up Le Richelieu. Long-time owner Frank Rochefort and manager Joanne Kirkpatrick make sure their staff "do their best for guests," which is probably why the hotel has such a high rate of both occupancy and returning guests. Another plus is its "self-service" parking lot, avoiding the inevitable inconvenience of valet parking.

"Our spacious room overlooked the courtyard and swimming pool. It had ample room for a king-sized bed, armoire for both the TV and drawers for clothing, easy chairs, and a workable desk. The furnishings are quality reproductions, with coordinating drapes, coverlets, and dust ruffles. The bed was firm and comfortable, the sheets soft. The bathroom was basic, with ample storage space and towels. We had a good breakfast of omelets and biscuits in the small dining area between the bar and the swimming pool. We loved the quiet location, just a block or two from the French Market." *(SWS)*

"We were delighted with our two-bedroom suite with enormous walk-in closet, ironing board, and linen closet." *(Susan Roach)* "Efficient, thorough housekeeping staff." *(JS)* "Being able to drive right into their parking lot is a big plus at night." *(Mary & Sidney Flynn)* "On return visits, we've noticed that the hotel goes from strength to strength. A few upgrade touches, constant maintenance, and pleasant staff." *(Steve Holman)*

Open All year.
Rooms 17 suites, 70 doubles—all with full private bath, telephone, radio, TV, desk, air-conditioning, ceiling fan, refrigerator, hair dryer. Some with balcony.
Facilities Lobby, café, bar/lounge. Courtyard, swimming pool, free private self-park-and-lock lot. Room service.
Location French Quarter. On Chartres St. in between Gov. Nicholls and Barracks Sts.
Credit cards Amex, DC, Discover, En Route, Eurocard, JCB, MC, Visa.
Rates Room only, $150–450 suite, $95–120 double, $85–110 single. Extra person, $15. Packages available. Alc breakfast, $5–6; alc lunch or supper, $7–10.
Extras Limited wheelchair access. Crib, babysitting. French, Spanish spoken.

Maison Dupuy Hotel ✗ *Tel:* 504–586–8000
1001 Toulouse Street, 70112

800–535–9177

In LA: 800–854–4581

Fax: 504–566–7450

Seven French Quarter town houses were restored to create the Dupuy House, owned by The Delta Queen Steamboat Company. Some rooms overlook the street, while others have French doors opening onto balconies overlooking the lushly planted courtyard and the swimming pool. The furnishings are reproduction French Provincial, and many rooms are decorated in soft pink or aqua tones. The hotel restaurant, Le Bon Creole, serves three meals a day; lunch-time favorites are the Po-Boy sandwiches and the soup and salad bar.

"On the northern edge of the French Quarter, this was the last hotel built in the Quarter before zoning kept new construction out. The swimming pool is located in a beautiful interior courtyard and is a delightful place to sip a strawberry daiquiri after a day of sightseeing." *(Tatiana Maxwell)* "Comfortable, quiet rooms, a few short blocks away from the bustle of the French Quarter." *(KM)* "Fresh and lovely; ask for a room with a balcony if you like getting fresh air." *(LR)*

Open All year.
Rooms 198 suites and doubles—all with full private bath, telephone, radio, TV, air-conditioning. 10 with refrigerator. Some with wet bar, balcony.
Facilities Bar, restaurant, heated swimming pool, exercise room, courtyard with fountain, pay valet parking.
Location N central edge of French Quarter. Between Burgundy and N. Rampart Sts., near Louis Armstrong Park.
Credit cards Amex, CB, Discover, MC, Visa.
Rates Room only, $225–800 suite, $130–200 double, $120–190 single. Extra person, $25.

Prytania Park Hotel 🛏 ♿
1525 Prytania Street, 70130

Tel: 504–524–0427
800–862–1984
Fax: 504–522–2977

The Prytania Park Hotel consists of a renovated Victorian mansion, dating back to 1850, plus several modern buildings constructed in 1984; Edward Halpern has been the manager since 1990. The high-ceilinged mansion rooms have hand-carved English pine furniture, wood floors, and exposed brick walls. Particularly convenient for those traveling with children are the rooms in the contemporary section with two queen beds, plus sleeping lofts. Breakfast is served from 7:30–9 A.M. in the lobby, courtyard, or guest rooms, and includes coffee, tea, juice, cereal, and croissants.

"Our room in the 1850 building was quiet and peaceful, beautifully furnished with lovely antiques. We had a great lunch across the street in the bistro of the Halpern's family-run furniture store—excellent dessert and coffee. Free parking is a real plus." *(Joyce Whittington)*

Open All year.
Rooms 6 suites, 56 doubles—all with private bath and/or shower, telephone, clock, TV, air-conditioning, fan. Some with radio, desk, balcony, refrigerator, microwave, sleeping loft. 6 with balcony.
Facilities Lobby, commissary, courtyard.
Location Uptown; Lower Garden District. ½ block from St. Charles Ave. streetcar. 15 blocks to French Quarter. From I-10 take U.S. 90 to Greater New Orleans Bridge. Exit at St. Charles Ave. Go 2 blocks to Thalia St. & turn left. Go 1 block to Prytania & turn right. Continue for 2 blocks. Entrance and parking area around corner on Terpsichore St.
Restrictions No smoking in lobby.
Credit cards Amex, DB, DC, JCB, MC, Visa.
Rates B&B, $99–220 suite, $109–250 double, $99–225 single. Extra person, $10. Children under 12 free. 10% senior, AAA discount. Minimum stay special events. Winter, summer rates.
Extras Limited wheelchair access. Crib, $10. Spanish spoken.

NEW ROADS

New Roads is a French Creole community dating from 1749, located across the Mississippi from St. Francisville; you can cross by ferry between the "English" and "French" sides. The town is located on the False River, a horseshoe lake created when the Mississippi River changed course.

Reader tip: "Had lunch at the Magnolia Cafe—an eclectic menu, with gumbos, nachos and tacos. Terrific muffeletta sandwich." *(Ri Regina)*

Information please: An 1820 Creole plantation house, **Mon Rêve** (9825 False River Road, 70760; 504–638–7848 or 800–324–2738) has a front gallery overlooking the False River. Constructed of cypress, old brick and bousillage (mud and moss), this B&B offers guests access to a pier across from the house. "Outstanding hospitality; loved their pet dog, Moe." *(RB)* Rates for this B&B start at $55.

The **Garden Gate Manor** (204 Poydras Street, 70760; 504–638–3890 or 800–487–3890) is a 1911 restored Victorian manor house. Guest rooms are named for Louisiana flowers, and feature period antiques and goosefeather comforters. "Flowers, candles, original art and Victorian touches create an inviting atmosphere. Our room was beautifully decorated in floral prints and lush English fabrics; the bath had a double heart-shaped soaking tub. Breakfast consisted of freshly squeezed orange juice, grapefruit, and wonderful French toast and sausage." *(Ri Regina)* B&B double rates for the seven guest rooms are $60–115.

SAINT FRANCISVILLE

Settled by the English, St. Francisville is in the heart of Plantation Country, an area much favored by Audubon when he worked in this area during the 1820s, living at Oakley Plantation. "St. Francisville is a truly lovely little town, with quiet streets set off the main highway. Listed on the National Register of Historic Places, the handsome restored historic buildings, lovely gardens, and antique shops make Royal Street well worth exploring. Make it your base to visit the area plantations (less commercial than those closer to New Orleans, two hours away); particular favorites are Rosedown (the showiest), Greenwood, Oakley, and Catalpa, the homiest." *(SWS)*

St. Francisville is set on the Mississippi River, 25 miles north of Baton Rouge and 60 miles south of Natchez, MS, via Highway 61.

Reader tip: "Stop at the Ramada Inn—St. Francis (junction of Rtes. 61 and 10; 504–635–3821), to see the Audubon Gallery, which has an original print of each of Audubon's fabulous drawings." *(SC)*

Information please: The Myrtles (Highway 61, P.O. Box 1100, 70775; 504–635–6277) dates back to 1796, and was enlarged in 1834 to create a showplace for lavish parties and balls. Louisiana specialities are served at lunch and dinner in the plantation restaurant. Guest rooms are located in the main house and a motel wing; B&B double rates of $75–130 include a full breakfast and a house tour.

Barrow House ¢   *Tel:* 504–635–4791
524 Royal Street, P.O. Box 1461, 70775

Built in the saltbox style in 1809 with a Greek Revival wing added in the 1850s, Barrow House is listed on the National Register of Historic Places and is furnished in 1860s antiques. In 1992, the Dittloffs acquired the equally historic Printer's Cottage across the street, dating from the late 1700s; its gazebo has a view of the Mississippi. Other cottage highlights include the 21 original 1840s Audubon bird prints in the sun room, and the ever-growing collection of teddy bears.

"We relaxed with a glass of wine on the screened porch to the sound of the splashing fountain, and chatted with the Dittloffs and the other guests. Our elegant dinner included shrimp salad with two dressings, and delectable rack of lamb with a Creole mustard glaze. Desserts included a dense chocolate cream, praline parfait, or strawberry crepe. Take a long walk before breakfast the next morning if you're planning to feast on Shirley's full breakfast—poached eggs with beans and rice or grits, accompanied by well-spiced Cajun *andouille* sausage." *(SWS)*

"Everything is provided, from sherry on an antique table, snacks in the refrigerator, and toiletries in the bathroom. The inn is located on a lovely, safe, quiet street of beautiful historic homes." *(Jerome Klinkowitz)* "Cleaned to perfection, the Printer's Cottage is immersed in history. You can see where a Union cannonball entered and exited the roof." *(Cindy & Bob Cameron)* "Shirley, our hospitable and loquacious hostess, provided extensive information about restaurants and other sites, and served us a delicious warm ricotta cake for breakfast." *(Christine Grillo)* "We spent a wonderful morning seeing the sights—from the historic bank with its stained-glass windows to the fascinating graveyard of the Grace Episcopal Church." *(Beverly Simmons)* "We enjoyed sleeping on the 1860 Mallard bed with its Spanish moss mattress." *(Norman & Catherine Ronneberg)*

Open All year. Closed Dec. 22–25.
Rooms 3 suites, 5 doubles—all with private bath and/or shower, TV, air-conditioning. 4 with desk, 2 with kitchen. 2 suites, 2 doubles at Printer's Cottage.
Facilities Dining room, living room, screened porch, sunroom. 1 acre with gazebo, camellia collection. Golf nearby.
Location In town, behind the courthouse.
Restrictions "Well-behaved children welcome." Porch conversation can be heard in downstairs guest room.
Credit cards MC, Visa.
Rates B&B, $100–115 suite, $75–90 double, $65 single. Extra person, $15. Full breakfast, $5 extra. Prix fixe dinner, $20–25; 24 hrs. advance notice.
Extras Port-a-crib.

Green Springs Plantation ¢ 🏃   *Tel:* 504–635–4232
7463 Tunica Trace (Highway 66), 70775   800–457–4978
                                                      Fax: 504–635–3355

Built in 1991 by Madeline and Ivan Nevill, Green Springs Plantation was constructed in the Feliciana cottage style reminiscent of the early 1800s, on land that has been in Madeline's family for nearly 200 years.

Named for a natural spring in the glen near the house, rooms overlook oak, dogwood, and magnolia trees, a creek-bottom field of Bayou Sara and a 2,000-year-old Indian mound. Inside, the inn is comfortably decorated with handsome antiques and reproduction furnishings. The family-style breakfast includes coffee, fresh fruit, sausage, eggs, grits, and hot breads; spinach Madeline is a house speciality. "Beautifully furnished, neither stiff or formal. Delicious eggs Benedict." *(Rebecca Gibson)* "Serene country atmosphere. The generous breakfast was served in the charming dining room overlooking a meadow." *(Jackie Freeman)* Comments welcome.

Open All year.
Rooms 3 doubles—all with private bath and/or shower, radio, clock, air-conditioning, fan. Some with TV, desk.
Facilities Dining room, family room with TV, porch with swing. 150 acres with hiking trails; Tunica Hill nature area. Bicycling, tennis, golf nearby.
Location On Hwy. 66, 1 m off US 61.
Restrictions No smoking.
Credit cards MC, Visa.
Rates B&B, $75–90 double, $60–75 single. Extra person, $35. Family rate for 2 rooms, $125–150. Reduced rates for children.
Extras Crib.

ST. MARTINVILLE

Settled by Acadians in the mid-1700s, St. Martinville prospered with the arrival of aristocrats fleeing the French revolution. Immortalized in Longfellow's poem, "Evangeline," the town is where the parted Acadian lovers are said to have met; the centuries-old oak that marks the spot is allegedly the most photographed tree in America. Worth a visit are the Acadian House Museum in the Longfellow Evangeline State Commemorative Area, the St. Martin de Tours Catholic Church, and several other restored buildings and museums; nearby is Avery Island, home of Tabasco.

Reader tip: "This area has lots to offer—historic homes in New Iberia, Cajun food and music (Mulate's in Breaux Bridge is fun), swamp and bayou tours. Sidewalks in St. Martinsville are rolled up around 9:00 P.M. in summer; in July, a lot of Louisiana was on vacation, which meant closed restaurants." *(Christine Grillo)*

Information please: About 20 miles southeast of Lafayette and 10 miles southeast of St. Martinville is New Iberia, home of the famous Shadows-on-the-Teche plantation. Just across the street is **Le Rosier** (314 East Main Street, P.O. Box 11707; 318–367–5306), an elegant restaurant, and just behind it, a romantic B&B. The four guest rooms in this reproduction Acadian raised cottage are furnished with antiques and reproductions, private bath, telephone and TV; the $100 double rate includes a full breakfast. Dinner might include such creative delights as crawfish spring rolls with ginger; duck breast with wild rice and sweet potato hay; and pecan tart with Bourbon whipped cream. Reports appreciated.

The Old Castillo Hotel ¢ ✗
La Place d'Evangeline
220 Evangeline Boulevard, P.O. Box 172, 70582

Tel: 318–394–4010
800–621–3017

"An excellent inn, set on the Bayou Teche, right at the Evangeline Oak. Built in the early 1800s as a hotel, the Castillo served as a Catholic girls' school until it was bought by Gerald and Peggy Hulin in 1987. Guest rooms overlook either the bayou and Evangeline Oak, or St. Martinsville's historic square. Room #1 is spacious and lovely, with antique furnishings. The casual restaurant serves excellent Cajun food and the staff is friendly and helpful." *(R.H. Mitchell)* "Delicious food at both lunch and dinner." *(Sidney & Mary Flynn)* "Thoroughly nice proprietor and staff. Homemade beignets at breakfast are a highlight." *(E.J. Sullivan)* "Stayed in a huge room with six windows looking out on the bayou and the Evangeline Oak. Gorgeous wood floors; very clean. Very pretty town." *(Carey Sutton)* "Charming atmosphere; excellent service. Good traditional breakfasts. On display are pictures from every graduating class at Mercy High School." *(Christine Grillo)* "Can't be beat for authenticity and a wonderful feeling of history." *(NJS)*

Rates include a full breakfast; favorites on the English/French dinner menu include such appetizers as fried alligator, popcorn shrimp, and seafood gumbo, with such seasonal entrées as crawfish étouffée, catfish, and broiled frogs' legs.

Open All year. Restaurant closed Thanksgiving, Jan. 1, Dec. 25.
Rooms 2 suites, 5 doubles—all with private bath and/or shower, air-conditioning. 2 with desk, balcony.
Facilities Restaurant, bar/lounge, laundry facilities. Gazebo, picnic area.
Location S LA, 10 m S of Lafayette; 60 m W of Baton Rouge. From I-10, take Exit 109 S on Rte. 31. Go 15 m to St. Martinville, turn left on Evangeline Blvd. to inn on right.
Restrictions Traffic noise possible in front rooms.
Credit cards Amex, MC, Visa.
Rates B&B, $75 suite, 45–60 double. $15 dinner ticket for overnight guests. Alc breakfast (outside guests), $3–5.
Extras French spoken.

SHREVEPORT

Set in northwest Louisiana, near the Texas border, Shreveport owes its development to its location on the Old Texas Trail. In fact, the city is a mixture of both states, with many streets named after early Texas heroes. Sights of interest include the Louisiana Downs racetrack and the Louisiana Hayride in neighboring Bossier City, the famous paintings and sculptures of Russell and Remington at the Norton Art Gallery, and the American Rose Society Gardens, a stunning sight from April through November, plus numerous other gardens and historic places of interest.

Information please: We need current reports on **Twenty Four Thirty Nine Fairfield** (2439 Fairfield Avenue, 71104; 318–424–2424), a 1905

191

Victorian house. Guest rooms are richly furnished with vintage antiques and wallcoverings, down pillows and comforters, and Amish quilts. B&B double rates for the four guest rooms range from $85–125, and include a full buffet breakfast.

Fairfield Place
2221 Fairfield Avenue, 71104

Tel: 318–222–0048
Fax: 318–226–0631

After extensive renovation and restoration work, Janie Lipscomb opened Fairfield Place in 1983, furnishing it with antiques, fine china and crystal, as well as books and paintings by Louisiana writers and artists.

"Convenient to good, downtown restaurants, the LSU Medical Center, and Louisiana Downs. Breakfast was delicious, with Cajun coffee, fresh fruit and juice, an unusual egg, spinach, and bacon casserole, marmalade muffins, fresh-baked French pastries, and strawberry butter. Janie is a perfect hostess and makes every guest feel right at home." *(Chris Mott)* "Rooms are stocked with cold drinks and fruit, and are handsomely decorated." *(MS)* "Our room upstairs in the back was smallish, but impeccably appointed and spotless, with a wonderful European featherbed." *(John Blewer)* "Gracious, well maintained, tree-lined residential area. The downstairs suite is particularly lovely with golden stars upon the ceiling. Thoughtful amenities are the thick robes, private phone line, and good collection of books and magazines." *(L. Stovall)* "The sumptuous breakfast is served in the wide center hall." *(Sarah Brown)*

Open All year.
Rooms 6 doubles with private bath and/or shower, telephone, radio, TV, desk, central air-conditioning, fan, refrigerator, hair dryer.
Facilities Parlor, balcony, porch, courtyard, garden. Boating, fishing, horse racing nearby.
Location NW LA, 319 m from New Orleans. Highland Historical Restoration district, 2 m from downtown. From I-20 W, exit at Fairfield, go left 8 blocks. From I-20 E, exit at Line Ave. S, go right on Jordan, left at Fairfield 6 blocks to inn.
Restrictions No smoking. No children under 12.
Credit cards Amex, Visa.
Rates B&B, $89–135 double. Extra person, $10.

SLIDELL

Salmen-Fritchie House ¢
127 Cleveland Avenue, 70458

Tel: 504–643–1405
800–235–4168
Fax: 504–643–2251

Listed on the National Register of Historic Places, the Salmen-Fritchie House has been owned by the same family for over 100 years, and was restored as a B&B in 1991, by Homer and Sharon Fritchie. Breakfast is served from 7:30–9:30 A.M., and a typcial menu includes fresh fruit and juice, double blueberry muffins, pecan waffles, and bacon.

"Homer and Sharon greeted us warmly, and showed us to our beautiful room. This uncluttered B&B is a fine example of good taste, with period furnishings, lovely woods, beautiful fabrics, exquisite antiques, pleasing colors, excellent lighting, and just a few feminine touches. The mattress and pillows were comfortable, and there was little traffic noise. The bathroom was well supplied with soft towels, well-lit mirrors, and convenient electrical outlets. Sharon made reservations for us at a fine Italian restaurant with exceptional calamari. We returned to find our bed turned down, the lights dimmed." *(Maryanna & Braxton Dixon)* "Charming, interesting tour of the home; everything the Fritchies do is first class. Our bedroom was clean and comfortable; the bath had modern-day comfort with a touch of 1890s charm. Delicious breakfast of apple and cinnamon muffins, Creole omelets, fresh strawberries, juice, and coffee, served in a glassed-in breakfast room overlooking the lovely grounds, complete with a 350-year-old oak, huge pecan trees, and numerous azalea and camelia bushes." *(Rodney Zeringue)*

Open Sept. through July.

Rooms 2 suites, 3 doubles—all with full private bath, air-conditioning. Most with TV, desk, telephone, clock, fireplace. 2 with fan.

Facilities Breakfast room, dining room, main hall with piano, TV; library; porch. 4½ acres with lawn games. Tennis, golf, water sports nearby.

Location 25 m N of New Orleans. From I-59, take Exit 263. Go W on Old Spanish Trail to Hwy. 11 & go right. Bear right onto Front St. & go right on Cleveland to house on right. From I-12, exit at Hwy 11 (Front St.) & go S 2 m to Cleveland Ave. on left.

Restrictions No smoking. Children 10 and over. Train noise possible.

Credit cards Amex, MC, Visa.

Rates B&B. $190 suite (for 4), $75 double, $70–90 single. Extra person, $20. 10% senior, AAA discount. 3-night minimum Mardi Gras, Jazz Fest; $95 double.

Extras Station pick-ups.

WHITE CASTLE

Information please: One of Louisiana's best-known plantations, **Nottoway Plantation** (Mississippi River Road, P.O. Box 160, 70788; 504–545–2730) is a 50,000 square-foot Italianate and Greek Revival mansion, supported by 22 massive cypress columns, saved from Civil War destruction by a Union gunboat officer. Randolph Hall, the plantation's restaurant, serves Cajun cuisine at lunch and dinner. The $125–175 double rates include a welcoming glass of sherry, plantation tour, wake-up coffee and juice, plus a full plantation breakfast. While the atmosphere is fairly commercial, readers have been relatively pleased with the mansion tour and meals, less so with the rooms and breakfasts. Reports welcome.

Mississippi

Linden, Natchez

Andrew Jackson was one of Mississippi's first heroes. After he defeated the Creek Indian nation and won the Battle of New Orleans, the state's capital was named for him. The Civil War played a major role in Mississippi's history; in addition to the famous siege of Vicksburg, innumerable battles took place across the state, leaving tremendous destruction in their wake.

Today history buffs visit Natchez and Vicksburg in search of antebellum ambience, while beach lovers head south to the Gulf Coast, for the sparkling waters and off-shore gambling. Plan to spend some time (spring and fall are best) exploring the Natchez Trace Parkway, a 400-mile parkway administered by the National Parks Service. Extending from Natchez nearly to Nashville, Tennessee, it follows the historic trail (or trace) that was one of the region's most frequented roads at the beginning of the 1800s.

For additional accommodations in historic private homes and inns, call **Lincoln, Ltd. B&B** (P.O. Box 3479, 2303 23rd Avenue, Meridian 39303; 601–482–5483), a reservation service operated by Barbara Lincoln Hall since 1983. If you're planning to spend some time exploring along the Gulf, pick up a copy of *Ramblin' and Gamblin' on the Mississippi Coast*, a delightful and informative guide written by long-time contributors Lynn Edge and Lynn Fullman ($10 including postage and handling; Seacoast Publishing, 110 Twelfth Street North, Birmingham, AL 35203, 205–250–8016).

Important note: If you're booking a room in an antebellum mansion that can also be visited by the public, remember that rooms on a tour will

194

rarely be available for occupancy before 5 P.M., and must typically be vacated by 9 A.M. Rooms in adjacent buildings may not be quite as fancy, but have more liberal check-out policies. In addition, public rooms on the tour are usually kept locked.

CORINTH

Rich in history, Corinth was the site of an intense Civil War battle in 1862, and has a national cemetery with over 6,000 graves. Twenty miles north, in Tennessee, is Shiloh National Military Park, where one of the bloodiest battles of the war was fought. It's about the same distance to Pickwick Landing State Park, for water sports and golf. Corinth is located in northeastern Mississippi, 90 miles east of Memphis, 2 miles south of the Tennesee border, 24 miles east of the Alabama border, near the intersection of Highwways 72 and 45.

Generals' Quarters ¢

924 Fillmore Street, P.O. Box 1505, 38834

Tel: 601–286–3325
Fax: 601–287–4445

The General's Quarters is a Victorian home owned by J.L. and Rosemary Aldridge. The guest rooms are simply furnished, some with antique half-tester beds. Rates include a hearty Southern breakfast. "The real highlight of this B&B is its owner. Upon our arrival in 'downtown' Corinth, we called for directions to the inn. J.L. answered our call and said, 'Wait just a minute. I'll hop in my pickup truck and come lead you in.' When I asked J.L. if he knew where I might purchase an authentic Civil War sword, he immediately got on the phone to his friends, and tracked down a fine sword at a super price." *(Elliott Kagen)* "J.L. and Rosemary make this inn special." *(Maryanna Dixon)*

Open All year.
Rooms 4 doubles—all with private bath, telephone, TV.
Facilities Dining room, parlor with fireplace, upstairs sitting area, porch.
Location Take Business Hwy. 45 N into Corinth; becomes Fillmore St. Inn is at corner of Fillmore & Linden.
Credit cards Amex, MC, Visa.
Rates B&B, $75 double.

Robbins Nest B&B

1523 Shiloh Road, 38834

Tel: 601–286–3109

Built in 1869, Robbin's Nest is a Southern Colonial-style home surrounded by oak and dogwood trees, boxwoods and azaleas, restored as a B&B in 1992 by Anne and Tony Whyte. Breakfast includes cereal, fruit, juice, eggs, bacon or sausage, grits, and home-baked breads, served on the back porch in season, where guests can relax in the antique wicker furniture beneath the cooling breezes of the paddle fans. "Comfortable house, beautiful yard; superb breakfast, extraordinarily hospitable innkeepers." *(David Adamson)*

Open All year.
Rooms 3 doubles—all with full private bath, telephone, clock, TV, desk, air-conditioning, fan. 1 with whirlpool tub.
Facilities Dining room, living room with fireplace, piano; family room with TV/VCR, stereo, books; veranda with ceiling fans. 2 acres with lawn games, off-street parking.
Location 2 m from center. From Hwy. 72, go N on Hwy 45 (By-pass) 1.8 m. Take Wenasoga Rd. exit & go E to Shiloh Rd. on left. Go 1.5 m to inn on left.
Restrictions No smoking. Children over 12.
Credit cards Discover, MC, Visa.
Rates B&B, $75–95 double, $60 single.
Extras Airport/station pickups.

JACKSON

Jackson is the capital of Mississippi and its largest city, with a population of 400,000.

Also recommended: Just ½ block from governor's mansion, is **The Edison Walthall Hotel** (225 East Capitol Street, Jackson 39201; 601–948–6161 or 800–932–6161), built in 1928 and restored in 1991. Its 208 doubles rent for $75–80, and children under 18 stay free; facilities include a restaurant, outdoor swimming pool, fitness center, and secured parking. "My room was conventional but comfortable, with a handsome downtown view. Excellent breakfast, friendly staff." *(Kevin Sellers)*

Information please: About 40 miles southeast of Jackson is **Pineview** (Old Post Office Road, Route 1, Box 28A, Magee 39111; 601–849–6270 or 601–948–3429), a spacious two-story French Provincial house set back on ten acres of pine trees. This elegantly decorated B&B has three guest rooms with private baths, telephone, and TVs; the B&B double rates are $80–125.

Fairview &.   *Tel:* 601–948–3429
734 Fairview Street, 39202   *Fax:* 601–948–1203

Built in 1908 and opened as a B&B in 1993 by Carol and William Simmons, this replica of Mount Vernon is listed on the National Register of Historic Places. Business travelers will find the inn's location especially convenient. Breakfast is cooked to order and is served at guests' convenience. "We stayed in the honeymoon suite located on the top floor of the renovated carriage house—all done in white ivory and beige. Elegant and comfortable. Carol is a well-known caterer and William is rooted deeply in Mississippi history. They are charming hosts." *(MR)*

Open All year.
Rooms 3 suites, 2 doubles—all with private bath and/or shower, telephone, clock, desk, air-conditioning, TV. 2 with fan; 1 with fireplace, whirlpool tub. 1 suite in carriage house.
Facilities Dining room, living room; library, foyer with fireplaces, garden room with piano; porch; deck with hot tub. 2 acres with off-street parking.
Location Old Jackson; near state Capitol Building, medical complexes. From I-55 S, take Exit 98A. Go W on Woodrow Wilson Dr. & turn S (left) on N. State St.

Go E (left) at Medical Plaza bldg. on Fairview to inn on left. From I-55 N, take Exit 96C & go W on Fortification St. to N. State & turn right. Turn right on Fairview as above.

Restrictions No smoking. Children over 12.
Credit cards Amex, MC, Visa.
Rates B&B, $150 suite, $80 double.
Extras Wheelchair access; 1 room specially equipped. French spoken.

Millsaps Buie House &
628 North State Street, 39202

Tel: 601–352–0221
Fax: 601–352–0221

Back in the 1880s, Jackson's social elite built mansions along State Street and gathered in each other's homes for dinner parties, tea dances, and croquet. The Millsaps Buie House dates from this period and is listed on the National Register of Historic Places. Its renovation as a bed & breakfast inn began in 1985; the house survived a near disastrous fire and opened fully restored and decorated with beautiful period antiques late in 1987. Rates include a breakfast of fresh fruit and juice, cereal, cheese grits, homebaked pastries, sausages, and muffins.

"Beautiful decor, gracious southern hospitality, spotless housekeeping. Rooms on the first and second floors are furnished with period antiques; those on the third floor have a more contemporary decor." *(Jean Rawitt)* "Our first-floor room was beautifully appointed with a king-size bed, good lighting, and excellent shower." *(John Blewer)* "We requested help with our bags, which was promptly provided. The serene back porch overlooks the garden area. The buffet-style breakfast offers a wide variety of choices. Plates are taken to smaller tables set up in an adjacent room. Tasty pralines were placed on our pillows at night." *(HJB)* "Beautifully furnished and professionally managed with all the amenities a business traveler needs. Wine was served in the parlor in the late afternoon." *(KM)*

Open All year.
Rooms 1 suite, 10 doubles—all with private bath, telephone/computer dataport, radio, TV, air-conditioning. Some with desk.
Facilities Breakfast room, dining room, parlor with grand piano. 1 ½ acres, patio, off-street parking.
Location Central MS. 5 blocks from Capitol. From I-55 N, exit at High St. & go W. Turn right at 4th light onto N. State St. House is 4th on the right.
Restrictions No smoking. No children under 12.
Credit cards Amex, DC, Discover, MC, Visa.
Rates B&B, $90–165 double. Extra person, $15.
Extras Wheelchair access.

NATCHEZ

Natchez was founded in 1716. Since then the flags of six nations have flown over the city—France, England, Spain, the sovereign state of Mississippi, the Confederacy, and the U.S. Natchez's greatest wealth and prosperity came in the early 1800s with the introduction of cotton and the coming of the steamboat. Extraordinary mansions were built during this period, which ended with the Civil War. Unlike Vicksburg to the north, Natchez was not of military importance, so although little property was destroyed during the war, further development ceased. As a result, over 500 antebellum mansions survive.

About a dozen mansions, including some of the most important, such as the palatial Stanton Hall, are open to visitors year-round. Most, however, are open only during festivals, called Pilgrimages, which are held for two weeks from early to mid-October and for a month in the spring, from early March to early April. If you plan to visit during one of the Pilgrimages, make your reservations six weeks to three months in advance. Alternative bed & breakfast lodging, as well as tickets for the house tours, can be arranged by calling Pilgrimage Tours at 800–647–6742.

Natchez is in southwest Mississippi, on the Mississippi River, 114 miles southwest of Jackson. Try to travel here via the Natchez Trace, once an Indian footpath, now a two-lane parkway run by the National Park Service between Natchez and Nashville, passing centuries of American history en route. Call the Natchez Trace Parkway Visitors Center for more information (601–842–1572).

Reader tips: "Natchez may not have Vicksburg's Civil War history, but it is small and manageable. The people are friendly and there are lots of antique shops to explore. The Pilgrimage attracts crowds, but it is well-established and organized, with two evening entertainments: *Southern Exposure*, a comedy play, and the *Confederate Pageant*. Some inns and hotels raise their rates slightly during Pilgrimage." *(SHW)* "While in Natchez, be sure to explore Natchez-Under-the-Hill, an area wedged in beneath the Mississippi River bluffs that was once home to gamblers, riverboat hustlers and other ne'er-do-wells." *(SC)* "The Cock of the Walk restaurant (Under the Hill) offered good local cuisine, reasonably priced; some tables have a river view." *(David Adamson)*

Worth noting: In many plantation homes, the common areas are kept locked, except during tours, because of the value of the antique furnishings. Guests are welcome to relax on the galleries and grounds, but rarely have "free run" of the house itself. Typically, plantation homes are found in neighborhoods where many poor people now live; expect historic Southern neighborhoods to have shacks and mansions next door to each other.

Information please: Listed in past editions, we need current reports on **The Briars Inn** (31 Irving Lane, P.O. Box 1245, 39120; 601–446–9654 or 800–634–1818) set on a hill overlooking the Mississippi River. This plantation-style mansion was built in the early 1800s and was the site of Jefferson Davis' marriage to Varina Howell in 1845; it was restored in 1975. Most of the 13 guest rooms are elegantly decorated, and the $130–145 B&B double rates include a full breakfast.

Dunleith
84 Homochitto, 39120

Tel: 601–446–8500
800–433–2445
Fax: 601–446–6094

Listed on the National Register of Historic Places, Dunleith was built in 1856 and was restored in 1976 by its current owner, William F. Heins III.

"An exquisite Greek Revival mansion, with well-manicured grounds. Long-time manager Nancy Gibbs cares about her guests and their comfort and provides wine and lemonade upon arrival. Our room had a comfortable queen-size tester bed and welcome basket of apple juice, homemade cake, dried fruit, and assorted candies. Delicious breakfast of scrambled eggs, sausage, fruit, cheese grits, biscuits, and coffee, served from 8–9 A.M."*(WA)*

"Although on a noisy street, Dunleith occupies substantial acreage, with huge trees and a great garden. Guests get a tour of the main house, including the stunning formal dining room, but are not permitted on the main floor of the house at any other time. Guest rooms in the courtyard wing are similar, with four-poster beds, a sink in the bedroom that fits into an old marble washstand, and small modern baths. Breakfast is served in a separate converted poultry house, attractive in a rustic country style, and is the same every day."*(SHW)* "Comfortable accommodations in the slave quarters; fabulous breakfast." *(P.A. Van Buuren)* "Decorated with 18th and 19th century French and English antiques. The four rooms in the main house are most impressive, while those in the courtyard are charming." *(Craig Brummer)*

Open All year except Thanksgiving, Christmas, New Year's.
Rooms 11 doubles—all with full private bath, telephone, TV, air-conditioning, balcony/deck. Most with telephone, fireplace. 3 bedrooms in main house; 8 in courtyard wing connected to back of house.
Facilities Breakfast room, gallery, gift shop. 40 acres with flower garden.
Location Homochitto connects Rtes. 61/84 and Pine/Orleans Sts.
Restrictions No children. No smoking in breakfast area.
Credit cards Amex, Discover, MC, Visa.
Rates B&B, $85–130. Extra person $15. No tipping.

The Guest House Historic Hotel
201 North Pearl Street, 39120

Tel: 601–442–1054
800–442–1054

The Guest House is an 1840s brick town house built in the Greek Revival style, restored as a small hotel by Louis and Gina Jones. Contemporary comforts and modern conveniences have been added, and guests can relax in either the downstairs parlor or the library upstairs. The guest rooms are furnished with antiques and reproductions reminiscent of Natchez history. Rates include a continental breakfast in the Garden Room, complimentary wine upon arrival, and nightly turn-down service (with a chocolate on your pillow). "The very comfortable bed in our room was so high that a little stool is provided to help you climb in. Most everything in Natchez is within walking distance." *(Donna Bocks)* "Rooms are comfortable and roomy. Friendly staff."*(KM)*

Open All year.
Rooms 18 doubles—all with private bath, telephone, radio, TV, mini-bar, coffee-maker.
Facilities Parlor, library, solarium, porches; fax machine. Courtyard.
Location Historic district. At corner of Franklin & Pearl Sts.
Credit cards Amex, Diners Club, MC, Visa.
Rates B&B, $94 double. Extra person, $15.

Linden ¢
1 Linden Place, 39120

Tel: 601–445–5472
Fax: 601–445–5472

Dating back to 1792, most of the present house was constructed between 1818 and 1849, when Linden was bought by ancestors of the current owners. Nearly all furnishings are original to the house, and Linden is especially noted for its outstanding collection of Federal furniture, including many Hepplewhite, Sheraton, and Chippendale pieces.

"At Linden, you are really 'at home' with Jeanette Feltus, in the home that her family has occupied for six generations. Now a widow, Jeanette lives here and is constantly on hand with her staff, seeing to her guests' every need. The setting is lovely, surrounded by gardens, well off the main roads with no traffic noise, yet is convenient to downtown. The hearty breakfast was served on the porch at 8:30 A.M. *sharp*, and with grits, sausages, scrambled eggs, and curried peaches one day, then ham, steamed eggs, and apricots the next, with lots of homemade biscuits, orange juice, and coffee. The light and airy guest rooms open to the porch on one side and lawns on the other. Rooms in the garçonnière are a bit smaller, but all are handsome with four-poster beds. The brief tour is interesting and fun, highlighting such features as an enormous lyre-shaped cypress punkah fan above the dining room table, originally pulled by slaves to cool the guests during dinner." *(SHW)* "It was pleasant gathering on the gallery for good conversation with the other guests. Mrs. Feltus is a lovely hostess, and Lily prepares an outstanding Southern breakfast." *(BJ Hensley)* "Breakfast served in the banquet room one morning, and in the back gallery by the courtyard the next. Attentive and pleasant service." *(GH)*

We understand that Mrs. Feltus has placed Linden on the market "because [her] children do not wish to return to Natchez;" inquire further when calling for reservations.

Open All year.
Rooms 7 doubles with private bath.
Facilities Dining room, parlor with piano, porch, galleries. 7 acres with courtyard, gardens.
Location Take U.S. Rte. 61/84 to Melrose Ave.
Restrictions No children under 10.
Credit Cards None accepted.
Rates B&B, $90 double, $80 single.

Monmouth Plantation ✕ &.   *Tel:* 601–442–5852
36 Melrose Avenue at the John A. Quitman   800–828–4531
  Parkway, 39120   *Fax:* 601–446–7762
P.O. Box 1736, 39121

Monmouth, a Greek Revival mansion listed on the National Register of Historic Places, was built in 1818 and was purchased in 1826 by John Quitman, who later became governor of Mississippi and a U.S. congressman. Monmouth stayed in the Quitman family until 1905; its restoration began in 1978, when it was purchased by Ron Riches. Period antiques, including many of the plantation's original furnishings, fill the rooms. Five-course candlelit dinners are served in the elegant dining room by tuxedo-clad waiters.

"The cocktail hour begins every day at 5 P.M., with complimentary hors d'oeuvres and an honor bar. The plantation breakfast is served on the ground floor of a brick wing of the mansion, followed by a tour of the mansion. The guest rooms in the main house are huge, with elaborate fabrics and furnishings. The whole place defines antebellum excess—it's the most luxurious setting in Natchez." *(SHW)* "Our third-floor suite was lovely and cozy; thick terrycloth robes were provided. The tasty breakfast consisted of grits, biscuits, jam, sausage, eggs, stewed apricots, and poppy seed bread. The grounds offer a relaxing setting, with garden gazebos and benches pleasant for playing cards, or reading a book." *(Darrel & Renate Kurtz)* "We had fun being the only Americans at breakfast, surrounded by a French tour group." *(BH)*

"After touring all day, it's a treat to sit at one of these formal dinner tables, lights dimmed, and imagine for a moment that you actually live in another time—and in such opulence. The rooms built on the site of the former slave quarters and carriage house are private and elegantly furnished, including a welcome basket of wine, spring water, and pecans. They don't have the historic feel of the in-house rooms, but it's not a bad trade-off." *(Lynn Fullman, also M. Marsted)*

And another opinion: "Somewhat lacking in warmth; the atmosphere is rather businesslike." Reports appreciated.

Open All year. Dinner served Tues.–Sat.
Rooms 7 suites, 12 doubles—all with private bath and/or shower, telephone, radio, TV, desk, air-conditioning. Most with fireplace. 6 rooms in mansion, 4 in original kitchen building, 4 in former slave quarters, 4 rooms in annex.
Facilities Parlors, study, courtyard patio, gift shop. 26 acres, gardens, gazebo, fish pond.
Location 1 m from downtown. At corner of Quitman Pkwy. and Melrose.
Restrictions No smoking in main house. Children over 15.
Credit cards Amex, Discover, MC, Visa.
Rates B&B, $140–175 suite, $95–140 double. Extra person, $35. Prix fixe dinner, $35.
Extras Limited wheelchair access.

Weymouth Hall ¢
Tel: 601–445–2304
One Cemetery Road, P.O. Box 1091, 39120

"This Greek Revival mansion, built in 1855, is set high on a bluff above the Mississippi River with a fine view. When it was bought by Gene Weber and Durrell Armstrong in 1975, the house had deteriorated to a shell and was on the verge of sliding down the hill into the river. An engineer was hired to assist in reconstructing the bluff and the building was saved. The inn is a total restoration; the ground floor was originally made of concrete finished to look like marble; before rebuilding, it had crumbled back to dirt. Gene Weber has a scrapbook of photos and articles chronicling the restoration. He lives on the third floor and is always available to guests.

"Rooms are furnished with the owners' collection of elaborate Victoriana from the 1840s to 1860s. They have tester, four-poster or canopied beds, and two rooms have river views. The utilitarian modern baths have fiberglass tubs and linoleum floors, with full-size bars of quality soaps." *(SHW)* "Across the street is an interesting old cemetery where many Confederate soldiers are buried." *(Victor Thorne)* "Wonderful sunset views of the Mississippi. Nancy, who runs the inn with her brother, could not have been more kind and accessible to her guests. She welcomed us with a glass of wine when we checked in. Her tour was interesting and detailed, and our room was comfortable and charming. Guests and hosts sit together for a filling breakfast of fruit, scrambled eggs, ham, sausage, grits, hash browns, blueberry muffins, biscuits, juice, and coffee, all presented with smiling, attentive service." *(NJS)* "Extra towels were stored right in the room for our use. The bed was comfortable and blankets were plentiful." *(Happy Copley)* "Clean, comfortable, and quiet. The innkeeper takes personal responsibility to see that guests enjoy the inn and Natchez." *(Glenn Roehrig)*

Area for improvement: "Brighter lighting in our room."

Open All year.
Rooms 5 doubles—all with full private bath, radio, air-conditioning. 4 with desk, 1 with private gallery.
Facilities Enclosed gallery with river view. 13 acres, gardens.
Location ½ m from town. From post office, go N on Broadway or Canal to Linton Ave. to Old Cemetery Rd. Inn on left, overlooking river.
Restrictions No smoking. Children over 14. No check-ins after 6:00 P.M. Parlors open *only* on tour.
Credit cards MC, Visa.
Rates B&B, $85 double. Individual house tours, $4.

TUPELO

Tupelo's first B&B, **The Mockingbird Inn** (305 North Gloster, Tupelo, 38801; 601–841–0286), was built in 1925 and opened in 1994 by Jim and Sandy Gilmer. Each of the seven guest rooms reflects a different location from around the world—from Athens to Africa, Sanibel to Mackinac Island. Named for the state bird, the double rates of $75–965 include a hearty breakfast and evening refreshments.

PASS CHRISTIAN

Once known as the "American Rivieria," then less favorably as the "Redneck Riviera," Mississippi's Gulf Coast is once again enjoying increased prosperity, fueled by legalized gambling at numerous dockside casinos. Those who want more from a vacation than a turn at the blackjack tables will enjoy beautiful historic homes, appealing antique shops, countless seafood restaurants, beautiful sugar-white sand beaches with warm, shallow waters, and such historic sites as Beauvoir in Biloxi, the restored home of Jefferson Davis, and a museum of the Confederacy; nature lovers can take ferries out to the barrier islands of the Gulf Islands National Seashore. Numerous golf courses, hunting, fishing and water sports are also available.

Described below are several appealing B&Bs in the Gulf Coast towns of Bay St. Louis, Biloxi, Pass Christian, and Waveland, all within a 25-mile stretch along Highway 90. Reports from "y'all" are needed if they are to become full entries.

Information please: A turn-of-the-century planter's home, **Bay Town Inn**(208 North Beach Boulevard, Bay St. Louis 39520; 601–466–5870 or 800–467–8466) is listed on the National Register of Historic Places. Owned by Judy Lipscomb, the inn features seven guest rooms, each with a private bath. B&B double rates are $75–85, and you can watch the sun come up over the Bay as you sip your morning coffee or relax in the swing under the magnolia tree.

A National Historic Landmark built circa 1841, **The Father Ryan House** (1196 Beach Boulevard, Biloxi 39530; 601–435–1189 or 800–295–1189) is one of the oldest remaining structures on the Gulf Coast and was once the home of Father Abraham Ryan, poet laureate of the Confederacy. The inn's suites are furnished with antiques; each has a queen-size bed, a view of the Gulf, an adjoining sitting room and private bath. Located on a sandy beach, the inn's 60-foot porch overlooks the Mississippi Sound. The $90–125 double rates include a continental breakfast.

Located in the antebellum seaside community of Pass Christian directly across from the beach and yacht club, the **Harbour Oaks Inn** (126 West Scenic Drive, Pass Christian 39571; 601–452–9399 or 800–452–9399) is a three-story building with covered porches on the first and second floors. French doors open onto the porches facing the Gulf; centuries-old live oak trees, draped with Spanish moss, provide shade. Owners Diane and Tony Brugger have furnished their B&B, built as a hotel in 1840 and listed on the National Register of Historic Places, with family antiques. Guests can relax on the wicker furniture on the verandas with morning coffee or complimentary wine at sunset, or enjoy the card and billiards table in the den. Breakfast is served in the elegant dining room, and includes such menus as strawberry crepes and stuffed pears, or broiled grapefruit and scrambled eggs with chives and avocado. Double rates for the five air-conditioned guest rooms with private baths range from $78–98.

An intriguing possibility is the **Gulfside United Methodist Assembly** (950 South Beach Boulevard, Waveland 39576; 601–467–4909), an interracial retreat center since 1923. Although it caters primarily to groups, accommodations are also offered to individuals in separate cottages and in the air-conditioned Longmore Inn. The reasonable rates include meals and use of the recreational facilities. "A quiet getaway spot, popular with writers, artists, and musicians, according to director Marian Martin, a really neat lady. She told us that one well-known Mississippi writer calls every time he has a deadline coming up, reserves a room, and stays until his work is done, but she wouldn't tell us who it was!" *(Lynn Edge)*

VICKSBURG

When folks talk about "The War" in Vicksburg, it's the Civil War they're referring to, not any of more recent vintage. Because of the town's controlling position, high on the Mississippi River bluffs, Union forces felt Vicksburg's surrender was essential to victory. Repulsed in repeated attempts both from land and water, the town surrendered to General U.S.

Grant only after a 47-day siege of continuous mortar and cannon bombardment.

Must-see sights in Vicksburg include the National Military Park and Cemetery and the nearby Cairo Museum, with numerous exhibits and audiovisual programs that bring the history of the battle and the period to life. Amazingly enough, many of Vicksburg's antebellum mansions survived the siege and can be visited today. Check with the Vicksburg Tourist Commission for Pilgrimage dates: 800–221–3536. For a lighter taste of history, stop at the Biedenharn Candy Company Museum to see where Coca-Cola was first bottled in 1894.

Vicksburg is located in southwest Mississippi, 44 miles east of Jackson, via I-20.

Reader tips: "The **Delta Point** restaurant is recommended for its magnificent views of the Mississippi; food good on one visit, disappointing on a return trip." *(HB)* "Good food at Delta Point; wonderful roast beef. Prices reasonable for a first-class restaurant." *(David Adamson)* "The **Top of the River** restaurant is not fancy but has excellent food, reasonably priced. A popular local favorite." *(Bob Pomeroy)*

"Although Vicksburg is well worth visiting, much of the downtown is depressingly poverty-stricken, and many handsome mansions [including a number of our entries] are set amongst dilapidated shacks. While security is not a problem and all are very happy to see tourists, plan on using your car get around, and don't plan on any extended strolls." *(SHW)* "Riverboat gambling has come to Vicksburg; we hope it helps the economy, since it doesn't do much for the quality of the historic experience." *(MW)*

Belle of the Bends ¢

508 Klein Street, 39180

Tel: 601–634–0737
800–844–2308

High on a bluff overlooking the river is the brick Italianate-style home of Wally and Jo Pratt. This 1876 vintage mansion is furnished with period antiques and steamboat memorabilia, and is named for the finest steamboat ever owned by Jo's grandfather, Captain Tom Morrissey. Fully restored in 1991, guests receive a tour of the house (also open to the public daily from 10 A.M. to 5 P.M.), a history of the Morrissey Line, and breakfast.

"The first floor rooms are done in peach and mauve, and are spacious and comfortable. The upstairs rooms are also done in light colors, an appealing contrast to the dark decor of many other mansions. Jo and Wally joined us for a breakfast of juice, ham with pineapple, cheese grits, and eggs in ramekin with cream, cheese, and bacon slivers. Biscuits and two kinds of homemade muffins were served along with plenty of hot coffee." *(Judy & Marty Schwartz)* "Top quality materials and workmanship in the restoration, providing an appropriate setting for a generous selection of Victorian antiques. Top quality linens and soaps. The Pratts provided me with a warm and enthusiastic welcome."*(Stephen Holman)* "Coming from a family of building professionals, I was unusually impressed with the quality of the Pratts' craftswork." *(Deborah Pettry)* "Comfortable sitting areas, both inside and on the veranda. Fresh flowers and lovely furnishings created an inviting atmosphere."*(Dorothy Gourley)* "Beautiful architecture and furnishings. Solicitous owner who breakfasts with guests; the meal is first class, as is everything about this B&B. Rooms are large and spacious; ours had a river view." *(David Adamson, also Keith & Sally Hall)*

Open All year.
Rooms 4 doubles—all with private full bath, telephone, radio, TV, air-conditioning, balcony access. 1 with whirlpool tub.
Facilities Dining room, living room with piano, books. 1 acre with garden. Mississippi, Yazoo River for water activities.
Location 1/2 m from center of town, 1 1/2 blocks W of Washington St., in Klein's Landing historic district.
Restrictions No smoking. "Prefer mature children."
Credit cards MC, Visa.
Rates B&B, $85–95 double. Extra person, $20.

Cedar Grove Estate ✕ 朮
2300 Washington Street, 39180

Tel: 601–636–1000
800–862–1300

One of Vicksburg's finest antebellum mansions, Cedar Grove was built in 1840 and is listed on the National Register of Historic Places. It's been owned by Ted and Estelle Mackey since 1983. Despite the Union cannonball still lodged in the parlor wall, it survived the Civil War with most of the antiques and architecture intact. Guest rooms are available in the mansion and in the poolside guest cottage; the carriage house has eight suites. Rates include a welcoming drink, a full Southern breakfast, and a tour of the mansion. Dinners are served in the Garden Room restaurant; grilled chicken, catfish, and filet mignon are among the entrées.

"Many furnishings original to the house. Most rooms in the main house have four-poster beds, including a huge one in the master bedroom. The carriage house rooms have beautiful brocade fabrics, with private patios in the rear. The suites have a mixture of antique and contemporary furnishings." *(SHW)* "We were greeted with a complimentary drink. The third floor terrace provided a stunning view of the Mississippi River, gardens, and croquet lawn." *(Lynn Fullman)* "My room had superb antiques, immaculate linens, and a river view. Elegant, ample breakfast." *(Polly Noe)* "We sat with a glass of wine, looking out over the beautiful grounds, listening to the pianist play the theme from *Gone with the Wind.* The staff was welcoming, our tour guide was enthusiastic and full of anecdotes, and the house lovely." *(NJS, also Jeanne Ferris)* "Beautifully furnished room with wonderful four poster bed and good housekeeping. Pleasant help. Beautiful gardens." *(Nancy Bernard)*

Open All year.
Rooms 11 suites, 13 doubles—all with private bath and/or shower, telephone, TV. Rooms in main house, carriage house, pool house.
Facilities Dining room, sun parlor, roof terrace, piano bar, gift shop. 4 acres with gazebo, fountains, gardens, heated swimming pool, hot tub, tennis court, croquet.
Location 1/2 m from town center. Take Exit 1A off I-20. Go N 2 m, then W on Klein.
Restrictions Smoking restricted. No children under 5.
Credit cards Amex, Discover, MC, Visa.

Rates B&B, $85–160 suite, double; $75–150 single. Extra person, $20. Alc dinner, $20–25; children's menu, $7.

The Corners ¢ 🛉 ♿   *Tel:* 601–636–7421
601 Klein Street, 39180   800–444–7421

Resident owners Cliff and Bettye Whitney will greet you on arrival at the Corners with a complimentary beverage, and you may want enjoy it in a lazy rocking chair on the wide gallery as you watch the sun set. Built in 1873, The Corners is listed on the National Register of Historic Places and was built in a style combining Greek Revival and Victorian features. The floors are original heart-of-pine boards 20 feet long and the support walls are three bricks thick. Rooms are furnished with period antiques, while baths are modern. The servants' dependency houses two guest rooms, with the original brick walls left exposed, fireplaces, whirlpool baths, and a gallery overlooking the back gardens.

"We stayed in the Master Suite, with two 12-foot windows facing the Mississippi River, and ample room for a massive half-tester bed, an armoire, straight and overstuffed chairs, a tea table, and a dresser. The bath was supplied with thick towels, and imported toiletries." *(SHW)* "Upon arrival, we were served coffee and tea in the parlor while listening to soft-playing music. Returning to the inn after dinner, Mr. Whitney lit the parlor fireplace, and we read through their many interesting books on the area and its history. The Old Court House Museum was fascinating and set the stage for our stay in Vicksburg." *(Darel & Renata Kurtz)* "We stayed in the Garden Room—spacious with a comfortable bed and a roomy, well appointed bathroom. The large parlor is congenial for meeting other guests. Breakfasts were delicious, plentiful, and different each morning." *(Happy Copley)*

"We stayed in the cottage across the street, which was comfortable although not as luxurious as the mansion rooms. For breakfast, all the guests gathered to feast on pecan banana pancakes, bacon and eggs, and homemade biscuits. Seconds were offered and eagerly accepted." *(Judy & Marty Schwartz)* "We especially enjoyed Bettye's humorous tour of the house, and Cliff's tour of his beautiful garden." *(Lynda Freeland)* Comments appreciated.

Open All year.
Rooms 1 2-bedroom cottage, 1 suite, 7 doubles—all with private bath and/or shower, TV, air-conditioning. Some with telephone, desk, fan, fireplace. 1 with radio, refrigerator. 2 rooms in former servant quarters with whirlpool tub, fireplace.
Facilities Dining room; parlor with 2 fireplaces, piano, library; country kitchen, veranda. 1½ acres, parterre gardens, croquet. Boating, golf nearby.
Location 1 m from center. From I-20, take exit 1A. Go N on Washington St., left on Klein St. to inn at corner of Klein and Oak Sts.
Restrictions Smoking in designated areas only. Train noise might disturb light sleepers; some noise in Gentlemen's Parlor due to location.
Credit cards Amex, MC, Visa.
Rates B&B, $140–150 2-bedroom suite, $85–105 double, $75–95 single. Extra adult, $20; child under age 6, $10–15; infant, free. House tours, $5.
Extras Limited wheelchair access. Pets permitted by prior arrangement.

Duff Green Mansion ♟ ♿
1114 First East Street, P.O. Box 75, 39180

Tel: 601–636–6968
800–992–0037
Fax: 601–634–1061

Duff Green, a prosperous Vicksburg merchant, built this 12,000-square-foot Paladian mansion in 1856 as a wedding gift for his bride, Mary Lake Green; her parents had provided the land as a wedding gift. Once the scene of many parties, the mansion was converted into a hospital during the Civil War (Union soldiers on the third floor, Confederates on the second). Mary Green gave birth to a son during the siege of Vicksburg, while taking shelter in a nearby cave, and named him Siege Green. The restoration of the mansion combines antiques and period reproductions with exceptionally luxurious appointments; rates include a tour and breakfast. Guests can request early morning coffee to be brought to their rooms, and can choose to eat breakfast in the dining room, on the patio, or in their rooms, and can opt for a full plantation breakfast (eggs, grits, biscuits, and bacon or sausage); pancakes and sausage, French toast and bacon, or cereal with fruit and muffins.

"Owners Harry and Alicia Sharp moved to Vicksburg from Florida in 1986 and transformed Duff Green into a showpiece, adding a swimming pool and landscaped courtyard." *(Janet Howe)* "Has more the feel of an elegant luxury hotel than a cozy homestay. It is not a museum, and the whole house is open to guests. The pine floors are original, as are the 15½-foot ceilings and 12-foot windows. The house's relatively high elevation protects it from the noise and less attractive elements of the street below. Although the grounds are limited, they are well designed and private, with brick terraces everywhere. Likable owner Harry Sharp lives elsewhere in Vicksburg, but acts as the daytime innkeeper; John Brewer is the night manager. Guest rooms are individually furnished and good sized; the Duff Green suite is massive, covering one-half the third floor." *(SHW, also Carey Sutton)* "Friendly service, beautiful rooms. We were invited to dance in the ballroom if we liked." *(NJS)* "Stayed in the Dixie room, the least expensive, yet beautifully decorated and restful. Wonderful breakfast in the lovely dining room." *(Bob Pomeroy)* "Our room had a Victorian bed and a gas fireplace; a rollaway was provided for our child; loved having breakfast options—time, place, and menu." *(Deborah Brockman)*

Little quibbles: Receptions are often held in the ballroom on the main floor; when making reservations, check to be sure one won't conflict with your visit.

Open All year.
Rooms 2 suites, 5 doubles—all with full private bath, telephone, TV, air-conditioning. 6 with gas fireplace, 5 with desk, 1 with kitchenette.
Facilities Dining room, parlor, library, porches; bar service. 1 acre with swimming pool, brick patio with fountain.
Location Historic District. From Hwy. 61, go E on 1st East St. to inn between Adams & Locust. From I-55, take National Park exit to Clay St. Go W on Clay until intersection with Cherry St; go right. Drive 5 blocks then go right on 1st East St. Drive 3 blocks to inn on right.
Restrictions Smoking discouraged.
Credit cards Amex, MC, Visa.

Rates B&B, $125–160 suite, $65–110 double. Extra adult, $15; children age 6-12, $10; under 6, free. Special winter rates.

Extras Wheelchair access in ground-floor rooms. Cribs. Spanish spoken.

We Want to Hear from You!

As you know, this book is effective only with your help. We really need to know about your experiences and discoveries. If you stayed at an inn or hotel listed here, we want to know how it was. Did it live up to our description? Exceed it? Was it what you expected? Did you like it? Were you disappointed? Delighted? Have you discovered new establishments that we should add to the next edition?

Tear out one of the report forms at the back of this book (or use your own stationery if you prefer) and write today. *Even if you write only "Fully endorse existing entry" you will have been most helpful.*

Thank You!

North Carolina

Carolina B&B, Asheville

Few states offer as much to the traveler as North Carolina—beautiful barrier island beaches and historic towns in the east, breathtaking mountain scenery in the west. Mt. Mitchell, at 6,684 feet the highest point east of the Mississippi, lies in the High Country, in the northwestern part of the state. The center of the state, called the Piedmont, is rich in industry, agriculture, and has some of the state's most beautiful golf courses.

The Blue Ridge mountains in the west are home to artisans who create fine Appalachian crafts while traditional "jugtown" potteries line the roads near Seagrove, south of Greensboro. For an introduction to the region's original residents, visit Cherokee in the southwestern corner of the state. Here you can wander through Oconaluftee Village, a reconstructed 1750 Cherokee town, or purchase top-notch tribal arts at the Qualla gallery.

In North Carolina, liquor is sold only through state-owned "A.B.C." stores, although beer and wine are sold in grocery stores in most counties. Some inns provide setups if you bring your own beverage; others prefer that drinks not be consumed in public. Some counties are completely dry, so call ahead or come prepared. State law prohibits pets in commercial accommodations.

ASHEVILLE

Asheville is in western North Carolina, at the juncture of interstates 26 and 40, 106 miles southeast of Knoxville, Tennessee; it's just an hour's drive to the Great Smoky Mountains National Park. Surrounded by more than a million acres of national forest, Asheville is known for its cool mountain summers. Golf, rafting, horseback riding, and hiking are all available nearby. It's also the home of the Biltmore House and Gardens, the Vance Birthplace, the Thomas Wolfe Memorial, and many craft shops and galleries. The Biltmore House is probably its best-known attraction; George W. Vanderbilt (of the railroad/steamship Vanderbilts) was so enamored of the area that he bought 125,000 acres and built this 255-room castle, completed in 1895. Several inns sell reduced-rate tickets to the castle.

Also recommended: A century-old home on lovely park-like grounds in the Montford Historic District, **The Lion & The Rose** (276 Montford Avenue, 28801; 704–255–ROSE) offers five guest rooms each with private bath. Double rates of $85–110 include a full breakfast and afternoon English tea and refreshments. High embossed ceilings, golden oak woodwork, and leaded and stained glass windows are enhanced by lovely furnishings and decor. "Personal service, lovely decor, comfortable bed and exceptional bath. Different breakfast every day; it tasted even better than it looked. Owner Jeanne Donaldson was knowledgeable about the area and provided excellent recommendations." (MR)

For mountain cottage charm just 1½ miles from downtown, consider the **Dogwood Cottage Inn** (40 Canterbury Road North, 28801; 704–258–9725), built in 1900. You can relax in front of the living room fireplace, watch TV in the den, or take a dip in the swimming pool. Best of all is the back porch, supported by entire tree trunks and decorated with white wicker and chintz. Guest rooms are spacious and uncluttered with antique and reproduction furnishings. The $90–100 double rates include a full breakfast, evening wine and beverages, and in-room fruit and sherry. "Beautiful, quiet mountainside location. Our room had a queen-size bed with a firm mattress, extra pillows, and good reading lights. Well-equipped bathroom. Friendly hosts, attuned to guests' needs." (Jane Chandra)

Information please: Eight miles north of Asheville is the **Dry Ridge Inn** (26 Brown Street, Weaverville, 28787; 704–658–3899 or 800–839–3899) Built as a parsonage in 1849, it served as a hospital during the Civil War. In 1992, the inn was purchased by Paul and Mary Lou Gibson, who have worked hard to improve the inn, adding air-conditioning and queen-sized beds to assure guest comfort, and building an art gallery to display Mary Lou's works. B&B double rates for the seven guest rooms range from $65–80.

Abbington Green B&B Inn	*Tel:* 704–251–2454
46 & 48 Cumberland Circle, 28801	800–251–2454
	Fax: 704–251–2872

An English theme pervades Abbington Green, from its guest rooms—all named for London gardens or parks—to its English books, paintings, and furnishings. In 1993, Valerie Larrea restored this Colonial Revival home, built in 1908, as a B&B. Floral themes are evident throughout, creating a light and airy atmosphere. Guest rooms have four-poster, canopy, or draped queen-size beds, with good bedside lighting, terry robes, and beautiful Oriental rugs. Breakfast is served at guests' convenience at individual tables, and consists of homemade cakes, a hot or cold fruit course, and such entreés as cheese crêpes with lemon sauce, or quiche Florentine. Tea and other beverages are always available.

"Breakfast was exquisitely presented on family heirloom china. Valerie Larrea didn't miss a beat preparing a low-fat breakfast." *(Valerie Rubin)* "Spotless; all utilities in good working condition." *(Michele Hyduke)* "Valerie was never intrusive, yet was always ready to help. She made dinner reservations for us, and her recommendations for both restaurants and activities were great." *(Roberta Schoenfeld)* "A beautifully restored house in a lovely, quiet area." *(Roy Farmer)* "Spacious grounds and ample parking. Public rooms are comfortable and welcoming." *(J.G. Tyror)* "Tantalizing smells of baked bread and sizzling bacon; delicious cold cherry soup and hot coffee." *(John Schoeni)*

Open All year.
Rooms 1 suite, 5 doubles—all with private bath and/or shower, clock, desk. 3 with gas fireplace, 2 with fan.
Facilities Dining room with fireplace, living room with fireplace, piano, family room/parlor with TV, VCR, fireplace, books, games; porch with swing. Off-street parking, bicycles.
Location Less than 1 m from downtown, historic district. From I-40, take I-240 to Exit 4C. On Montford Ave., go N to traffic light. Go right onto W Chestnut St. At flashing light go left onto Cumberland Ave. Go 2 blocks to Cumberland Circle. Bear right to inn on left.
Restrictions No smoking. Children over 10 preferred.
Credit cards Amex, MC, Visa.
Rates B&B, $110–130 suite; $95–130 double. Extra person, $25. 2-night minimum most weekends.

Acorn Cottage ¢ 👫 *Tel: 704–253–0609*
25 Saint Dunsten's Circle, 28803

A stone cottage built in 1925, Acorn Cottage was opened in 1993 by Connie Stahl. Her breakfasts include fresh fruit and juice, such entreés as blueberry-sour cream pancakes or garden quiche, and perhaps raspberry-cream cheese coffee cake or pear-yogurt bread; afternoon tea is also served.

"Clean, comfortable, nicely furnished, and beautifully decorated with a rich color palette. Connie is an attractive, dedicated, and effective hostess. Her knowledge of the area enhanced our visit." *(William Taylor)* "Delightful wooded setting, yet convenient to the Biltmore Estate. The lovely guest rooms have queen-size beds, but our favorite is the 'Tree' room, complete with hand-painted nature scene murals, tucked under the eaves. Ample common areas with warm ambiance. Whether it was a strata or French toast, the delicious breakfasts were always freshly cooked and beautifully presented. Marvelous muffins! " *(Elabeth Fisher)*

Minor niggle: "A reading light on *my* side of the bed."

Open All year.
Rooms 4 doubles—all with full private bath or shower, radio, clock, TV, air-conditioning. 2 with fan.
Facilities Dining room, living room with fireplace, TV, stereo, family room, porch. 1 acre with gardens, parking, swing set, gazebo. 30 m to hiking, cross country, downhill skiing.
Location 1 m from downtown. From I-40, take Exit 50 to Hwy. 25N. Follow

Biltmore Ave. Go left onto St. Dunstan's Rd. Where St. Dunstan's Rd. and St. Dunstan's Circle intersect, take driveway between "Acorns."
Restrictions No smoking.
Credit cards MC, Visa.
Rates B&B, $75–90 double, $70–85 single. Extra person, $15. 2-night minimum weekends, Mar.–Dec.
Extras Crib.

Albemarle Inn
86 Edgemont Road, 28801

Tel: 704–255–0027
800–621–7435

The Albemarle Inn is a Greek Revival mansion built in 1909 and listed on the National Register of Historic Places. Owned by Kathy and Dick Hemes since 1992, it features high ceilings, oak paneling, and a hand-crafted oak stairway with a circular landing and balcony. Composer Béla Bartók wrote his Third Piano Concerto here. Breakfast is served from 8–9:30 A.M. at individual tables; a sample menu might consist of juice, grapefruit-strawberry ambrosia, leek and artichoke strata, dill bread, and ham.

"Beautiful, spacious common areas. Kathy and Dick create a friendly atmosphere where guests are encouraged to meet one another." *(Robert & Judy Loest)* "Guest are introduced to one another at the 5:30 P.M. wine and cheese gathering, and the innkeepers help with dinner recommendations and reservations. Bedrooms and bathrooms were cleaned quickly and thoroughly each morning." *(Jean Brown)* "Our third-floor room was large, airy and clean, with handsome Victorian furnishings. After breakfast we took a walk and admired the beautiful houses in this historic neighborhood." *(Mr. & Mrs. Zack Logan)* "The cheerful Garden Room is done in white wicker and chintz. Many of the beautiful antiques and Oriental blue and white china." *(Judith G. Russell)* "Juliet's Chamber has a queen-size four-poster rice bed, Battenburg lace, a white and blue color scheme, and a balcony with table and chairs overlooking the front lawn and Norway spruces. Especially enjoyed breakfast on the sun porch; marvelous stuffed French toast and fruit salad. Best of all are hosts Dick and Kathy. Delightful swimming pool, too." *(Don & Elizabeth Harting)*

Open All year.
Rooms 1 suite, 10 doubles—all with full private bath, telephone, radio, clock, TV. Most with air-conditioning, 7 with fan, 2 with balcony.
Facilities Dining room with fireplace, stereo; living room with fireplace, stereo, books; dining sunporch, veranda. 7/10 acre with off-street parking, swimming pool.
Location 5 min. from downtown. From W on I-40 or S on I-26: take I-240 to Charlotte St.; turn left & go 9/10 m to Edgemont Rd. Turn right & go 2/10 m to inn. From E on I-40: take I-240 to Charlotte St. & go right. Follow as above.
Restrictions No smoking. Children over 13.
Credit cards Discover, MC, Visa.
Rates B&B, $135 suite, $80–135 double. Extra person, $25. 2-night minimum weekends, Apr.–Dec.

Applewood Manor
62 Cumberland Circle, 28801

Tel: 704–254–2244

Applewood Manor is owned by Susan Poole and Maryanne Young, who bought the inn in 1991. "A lovely turn-of-the-century Colonial Revival set at the top of a wooded hill, the Applewood makes you feel as if you are in the country. The front door opens onto a large foyer with a large parlor and living room to the left and dining room to the right; all are divided by pocket doors and are furnished with handsome period antiques and Oriental carpets." *(Susan McMullen)* "We enjoyed relaxing on the porch rockers and swing. The spotless rooms have cheerful wallpaper or stenciling, with charming decorator touches. We loved Susan's cinnamon cream syrup and English muffin bread." *(Polly Murphy)* "Susan and Maryanne had great suggestions for making the most of our Asheville visit. They were friendly but respected our privacy. Lovely house in a quiet old neighborhood. Delicious pineapple muffins." *(Steve Thomas)* "We were welcomed with lemonade and cream cheese brownies—fresh from the oven. We had sherry on our treetop balcony that evening and enjoyed an exquisite breakfast the next morning." *(Katherine Drew)* "This is obviously a labor of love, and it shows in the attention to detail and the friendly atmosphere throughout. Wonderful homemade pumpkin bread, omelets, and waffles." *(Chip Birdsall & Anne Randall)*

Area for improvement: "A reading light on my side of the bed."

Open All year.
Rooms 1 cottage, 4 doubles—all with private bath and/or shower, radio, air-conditioning, fan. 3 with fireplace, balcony.
Facilities Dining room with fireplace, parlor with fireplace, library, porches. Occasional live traditional music. 2 acres with flower gardens, swings, croquet, volleyball, badminton, bikes. Fitness club privileges. Tennis nearby.
Location 1 m from downtown. From Rte. 240 W take Exit 4C/Civic Center/Haywood St. Go right on Haywood, then turn right on Montford Ave. Turn right again onto W Chestnut; go to blinker at Cumberland Ave. Turn left, then bear right onto Cumberland Circle to inn.
Restrictions No smoking. No children under 12.
Credit cards Discover, MC, Visa.
Rates B&B, $85–115 double, $80–110 single. Extra person, $20. 10% senior discount in Sept. 2-night weekend minimum.

Beaufort House   *Tel:* 704–254–8334
61 North Liberty Street, 28801   *Fax:* 704–251–2082

A rambling Queen Anne mansion, built in 1894 and painted a soft coral color with terra cotta accents and white gingerbread trim, the Beaufort House was restored by Robert and Jacqueline Glasgow in 1993. Rooms are furnished with antiques, with a king-size canopy bed in one room, and a queen-size rice bed in another. Guests gather around the dining room table for breakfasts of freshly squeezed orange juice, home-baked muffins, breads, or biscuits, fresh fruit from the garden in season, plus waffles, omelets, pancakes, or French toast.

"An 1890s ambiance with 1990s amenities. Friendly, hospitable but unobtrusive owners." *(D. Bottom)* "Listed on the National Register of Historic Places and decorated with authentic antiques. The front porch is a delightful place to relax after a delicious breakfast. Great little dog named Beaufort. Convenient location on a lovely tree-lined street." *(Michele Baptiste)* "We awoke to the aroma of fresh ground coffee and baking muffins." *(Sandra Simonetti)* "Our room was impeccably appointed with comfortable chairs, an armoire, and a luxurious contemporary bathroom. A lovingly tended vegetable and flower garden provides delights for the senses and the palate. We picked blueberries for our breakfast pancakes. Special dietary needs are accommodated with skill and grace." *(Erica Rand)*

Open All year.
Rooms 1 suite, 5 doubles—all with private bath and/or shower, telephone, clock, TV/VCR, air-conditioning. 4 with double whirlpool tub, fireplace, 1 with desk. 1 room in carriage house with kitchen, deck.
Facilities Dining room, living room, den with videotape library; each with fireplace. Wraparound porch with swings, rockers, gazebo. 2 acres with off-street parking, lawn games, gardens, hiking. Watersports, tennis nearby.
Location Walking distance to historic district. From Hwy. 240, take exit 5A on Merrimon Ave. (#25). Go right at 2nd light onto Chestnut St. Go left onto Liberty St.
Restrictions No smoking. Children over 11 in mansion, any age in carriage house.
Credit cards MC, Visa.
Rates B&B, $150–240 suite, $75–135 double. Extra person, $25. 10% senior, AAA discount off-season. 2-night minimum holidays & peak season weekends.
Extras Airport/station pickup.

Cairn Brae ¢   *Tel:* 704–252–9219
217 Patton Mountain Road, 28804

Meaning "rocky hillside" in Scottish, Cairn Brae is tucked in the Blue Ridge Mountains above Asheville. Millie and Ed Adams's three-story contemporary home has a secluded setting, with great views and walking trails, yet is close to downtown. Guest rooms are individually decorated, some with lively floral wallpapers and wicker accents, and others with mellow pine walls and furniture.

"Our suite afforded a panoramic view through tall windows; it was furnished with a comfortable king-size bed and a separate dressing room." *(Barb & Al Easton)* "Coffee by the fireplace every morning was a special treat, as was the sherry and chocolate by our bed at night." *(Martha Ann Mobley)* "Exquisite linens, immaculately clean. Friendly, gracious innkeepers knew the area and helped us plan our tours." *(Norman Talner)* "The nature trail and stone patio, with its afternoon tea table, swing, and hammock, offer views of distant ridges and the fresh scents of rhododendron and laurel." *(Richard & Cindy Lacy)* "Soft music was piped into the room to let us know that breakfast would soon be served on their best china, crystal, and silverware." *(Joyce Fowler)* "Beautiful rock garden with a fish pond to enjoy." *(Cindy Voegeli)* "We were welcomed with wine and iced tea. The breakfast table was set with different china each morning, and included such creative delights as waffles with walnut butter and French toast with orange maple syrup." *(Homer & Joanne Middleton)*

Open April through Nov.
Rooms 1 suite, 3 doubles—all with private bath and/or shower, radio, air-conditioning, fan.
Facilities Dining room, living room with fireplace, TV, games, phone; deck. 3 acres with walking trails. Swimming, tennis, golf nearby. Close to river for hiking, fishing, boating, canoeing, whitewater rafting.

Location 12 min. from downtown Asheville. Exit I-240 at Charlotte St. (turn left onto Charlotte St.) Go 2 lights to College St. turn left. At the next light, turn left onto Town Mountain Rd. Turn left onto Patton Mountain Rd.
Restrictions No smoking. Children over 12.
Credit cards MC, Visa.
Rates B&B, $85–100 suite, $85 double, $70 single. Extra person, $15. 2-day minimum October, holiday weekends.
Extras Airport/station pickup, $20.

Carolina B&B ¢   *Tel: 704–254–3608*
177 Cumberland Avenue, 28801

Built around the turn of the century by Richard Sharp Smith, supervising architect for the Biltmore Estate, the Carolina B&B has a stucco exterior, graced by front and rear porches and two pairs of chimneys. Restored in 1989 by Sam and Karin Fain, the warm pine floors shine again in spacious, high-ceilinged rooms. The guest rooms, with large windows and ruffled organdy curtains, have walnut or brass beds; some have antique dressing tables. Some recent breakfast menus included pumpkin-ginger bread, spiced apple rings, and cinnamon French toast; or pineapple-kiwi-banana compote, spinach and cheese casserole, and blueberry muffins.

"An older neighborhood where many homes are being restored. The Blue Room, at the front of the house, is shaded by a huge maple tree, and is accented with antique hats and period clothing. Sam is sensitive and intelligent, willing to discuss any subject you choose." *(Nancy Cerreta)* "The Fains are friendly hosts—talkative when you need suggestions about places to see, but respectful of your privacy." *(Howard Pousner)* "Rooms are clean, comfortable and decorated without pretension. We fell asleep watching the light from the fire dancing on the ceiling and walls." *(Rick & Carol Littlehales)* "We're still making cinnamon coffee at home the way Karin makes it at the B&B. A cup of coffee or glass of wine was always available, to enjoy in front of the parlor fireplace or in our room." *(Jeff & Michelle Gardner)* "Great bed. Karin helped us choose a cozy little restaurant for a special dinner. Tasty chocolate chip cookies were left out for a bedtime snack. Delicious breakfast of apple waffles with maple syrup, grapefruit and homemade muffins." *(Deanna & Mike Yen)* "The beautifully wooded grounds (flowering dogwoods, rhododendrons, and azaleas) set the mood for a walk to the botanical gardens not far away." *(BAB)*

Open All year.
Rooms 5 doubles, 1 cottage—all with private bath and/or shower, air-conditioning, fan, fireplace.
Facilities Parlor with stereo, books, games, dining room, porches, deck. Off-street parking, garden.
Location Montford Historic District. ½ m from center of town. From I-240, take Montford Avenue exit. Turn right onto Montford Avenue then turn right at Chestnut Street. Go one block, turn left onto Cumberland and go 1½ blocks to inn, located on right.
Restrictions No smoking. Children under 12 not permitted.
Credit cards MC, Visa.
Rates B&B, $115 cottage, $80–90 double, $65–75 single. Extra person, $20.

The Colby House
230 Pearson Drive, 28801

Tel: 704–253–5644
800–982–2118
Fax: 704–259–9479

Colby House is a Dutch Tudor home built in 1924, fully renovated in 1992 by Everett and Ann Colby. Furnished with antiques and reproductions, the inn uses Williamsbury, English, and Oriental decorative motifs.

"Beautifully renovated, tastefully furnished, and immaculate. Coffee, tea, soft drinks, and home-baked goodies are always available in the butler's pantry. Wine, cheese and crackers are served at 6 P.M. every evening. For breakfast, we had juice, fruit, cereal, muffins, and pancakes on the first day, and French toast on the second. Our room had a comfortable queen-size bed, and we were pleased that no plumbing sounds could be heard from the other rooms. The gardens are Everett's special interest and it shows." *(Janet Payne)* Comments appreciated.

Open Open mid-March–Christmas.
Rooms 4 doubles—all with private bath and/or shower, telephone, clock, desk, air-conditioning. 2 with fan, 1 with fireplace, balcony.
Facilities Dining room, living room with fireplace, den with fireplace, TV/VCR, books, games; guest refrigerator. 1/3 acre with off-street parking, garden.
Location 1 min. to historic district. From I-240 , take Exit 4C & go N on Montford Ave. Go left onto Watauga. Go left onto Pearson Dr. to inn on right.
Restrictions No smoking. Children over 12.
Credit cards MC, Visa.
Rates B&B, $80–110 double. 2-night weekend minimum.

Corner Oak Manor ¢ &
53 Saint Dunstans Road, 28803

Tel: 704–253–3525

Handstitchery and handicrafts are a special focus at the Corner Oak Manor, an English Tudor-style cottage with a curved roof reminiscent of a thatched cottage. Owners Karen and Andy Spradley have highlighted the decor with the work of local artisans, including that of Karen and her sister Kathie. The house is furnished in soft tones of ivory, rose, blue, and green; guest rooms have antique or reproduction brass or iron beds. Breakfast recipes utilize herbs, vegetables, and berries from Karen's garden, and include homemade breads (maybe apple streusel muffins and cranberry lemon bread); fresh or poached fruit; and an entrée—savory baked eggs with cheddar, dill, chives, and mustard; or pumpkin pancakes with apple cider syrup and sausage.

"Andy and Karen suggested great area activities and restaurants. Extra touches in my room included fresh flowers and candy, bath salts, books, handmade quilts and afghans." *(PD)* "Cats and cat memorabilia adorn each room. Andy works in the Biltmore Estates Vineyard and knows all about Asheville's greatest attraction." *(David & Amy Greer)* "We were given our own house key which made us feel much more comfortable about coming and going. Perfect location; convenient yet removed from the hub-bub of town. Andy and Karen's flexibility is endless." *(Kelly Ann Gunther)* "Quiet neighborhood with lots of birds and squirrels. We relaxed in the hot tub, smelling the flowers and the enjoying scenery." *(Mary & Steven Mortimer)* "Though not large, our room had a comfortable queen-size bed, settee, dresser, private bath, and an effective, quiet, ceiling fan. Breakfast was served in a bright sunroom at group tables, graced by attractive blue pottery, and consisted of delicious breads with molded butter, fresh-squeezed orange juice, crustless quiche, and sausage." *(Jack & Esther Magathan)*

Minor niggle: "Our room had hooks but no closet."

Open All year.
Rooms 3 doubles, 1 cottage—all with private shower and/or tub, ceiling fan. Cottage with radio, air-conditioning, refrigerator.
Facilities Living room with fireplace, piano, stereo; reading/game room; dining room. Deck with hot tub.
Location 2 m from downtown. From I-40, take exit 50 or 50B. Stay in right lane until Biltmore Ave., then move left & turn left on St. Dunstans Rd. Follow St. Dunstans Rd. 2 blocks to Grindstaff; turn right to inn, 1st driveway on right.
Restrictions No smoking. Children under 12 in cottage only.
Credit cards Amex, Discover, MC, Visa.
Rates B&B, $100 cottage, $85–90 double, $65 single. Extra person, $20. Children under 5 free. 2-night holiday weekend minimum. Mystery weekend packages.
Extras Limited wheelchair access in cottage.

Flint Street Inns ¢
100 and 116 Flint Street, 28801

Tel: 704–253–6723

Lynne and Rick Vogel restored their circa-1915 home in 1981 and opened it as Asheville's first bed and breakfast, expanding to include the English Tudor next door in 1985.

"Inviting living room, with its easy chairs and couch, its cut-glass windows and shelves of period bric-a-brac. If we arrive on a cold, drizzly day we know there will be a fire in the fireplace and hot cider waiting. If we return to the inn on a warm afternoon, they will offer us a glass of iced tea or lemonade while we sit on the porch. The Vogels spend enough time with each guest to get to know their preferences, directing one to the crafts, baskets, and quilts, and another to the best hiking trails." *(Norman & Katherine Kowal)* "The Garden Room has a sitting area, vintage magazines to read, and a large front porch for sitting and relaxing." *(Marianne & Ronald Cohn)*

"Lynne has decorated with lots of 1920s memorabilia. Our room had a queen-sized bed, with her grandmother's hat collection hung on the wall behind it. The attached bath was a converted back porch with its own sofa, privacy screen around the toilet, and half-sized tub and a shower. Special touches included candy in our room, tea, lemonade or iced tea at any time of day, restaurant suggestions and reservations, tickets to the Biltmore Estate, lovely gardens, and breakfasts of grits, biscuits, blueberry pancakes or eggs. Lynn ran after us with an umbrella when she thought it might rain; Rick greets guests in the parking lot and helps unload the car." *(Julia & Dennis Mallach)* "Great lemon poppyseed muffins." *(Jo-Ann Johnsen)* Comments welcome.

Open All year.
Rooms 8 doubles—all with full private bath, radio, air-conditioning, fan. 2 with desk, some with fireplace. Inn occupies 2 adjacent buildings.
Facilities Dining rooms, 2 parlors. 1 acre with flower gardens, fish ponds. Off-street parking.
Location Montford Historic District. 3 blocks from Civic Center/downtown.

Restrictions No children under 12. No smoking in dining room.
Credit cards Amex, Discover, MC, Visa.
Rates B&B, $85 double, $65 single, plus tax. Extra person, $25. 2-night minimum peak weekends.

Haywood Park Hotel 🛏 ✕ ♿

One Battery Park Avenue, 28801

Tel: 704–252–2522
800–228–2522
Fax: 704–253–0481

Asheville's once decaying downtown area is experiencing a renaissance, as its lovely Art Deco buildings are slowly restored or refurbished. The Haywood Park, built as a department store, has been completely renovated, and is now connected to a sunlit atrium, with a variety of shops and restaurants. Guest rooms are exceptionally spacious, elegantly decorated with contemporary decor in shades of pearl gray and soft mauve, and supplied with enough amenities to earn the hotel a four-diamond rating from AAA. We heard from a great number of the hotel's guests; the majority were delighted with the spacious accommodations, relaxing atmosphere, service, convenient if uninspired continental breakfast, turndown service, as well as the lighting, plumbing, parking and location. Several reports also commented on the fine food and service at the hotel restaurant, 23 Page. "A very expensively renovated small hotel with huge rooms, a striking ultra-modern decor and magnificent bathrooms. The staff is friendly, the restaurant is first class." *(Judith Brannen)*

Open All year.
Rooms 33 suites—all with full private bath and/or shower, telephone, radio, TV, desk, air-conditioning, wet bar, computer hook-ups. Some with whirlpool tub.
Facilities Restaurant, bar, atrium with shops, fitness center, parking garage. Limousine service. In-room massage.
Location Downtown. Take I-240 to Exit 4C. Continue on Haywood St. to Battery Park Ave. on right.
Restrictions No smoking on some guest floors. Traffic noise in some rooms. Some windows face brick walls.
Credit cards Amex, DC, Discover, MC, Visa.
Rates B&B, $120–280 suite, $98–120 single. Extra person, $15. Children under 12 free in parents' room. 10% AARP discount. Alc lunch, $5; alc dinner, $25.
Extras Wheelchair access; some rooms equipped for disabled. Airport/station pickup. Crib, babysitting.

The Inn on Montford

296 Montford Avenue, 28801

Tel: 704–254–9569
Fax: 704–254–9518

Designed in 1900 by Richard Sharp Smith, Biltmore's supervising architect, the Inn on Montford is an English cottage interpreted in the Victorian Arts and Crafts style. It was restored as a B&B in 1992 by innkeepers Owen Sullivan and Ripley Hotch, who previously owned an inn in West Virginia. Broad porches span the front of the house, with original woodwork inside. Attention to detail is evidenced by plenty of plush towels, good lighting, extra pillows, queen-sized beds, and comfortable chairs. Their collections of art and antiques highlight the decor. The living room is accented with Owen's Imari china while the den features marine paintings and blue-and-white porcelain. Breakfast, served family-style at 9 A.M., includes such specialties as Bavarian puffed pancakes, raspberry-filled French toast, or frittatas, plus homemade muffins and breads, fresh fruit, cinnamon coffee, and teas. Afternoon tea is accompanied by freshly made cookies, brownies, or scones.

"Warmth, hospitality, and pampering from our welcome to the helpful directions at departure. Relaxing, comfortable atmosphere; quality information and conversation." *(Linda & Charles Hunter)* "Creative breakfasts are served in the formal dining room. One morning we were served baked grapefruit followed by delicious croissants baked with oranges and custard. Rooms are spotless with comfortable chairs, antique dressers, and lots of personal touches. Bathrooms are supplied with lovely scented soap and brightly colored towels. Owen and Rip love to talk with guests and are always open to suggestions." *(Judith & Terry Marre)* "We never would have discovered Biltmore Forest without our hosts' advice, a place not to be missed." *(MNS)* Comments welcome.

Open All year.
Rooms 4 doubles—all with full private bath, radio, clock, desk, air-conditioning, fireplace. 3 with whirlpool tub, 1 with TV.
Facilities Dining room, living room, library—all with fireplace; foyer, garden room, porch. 1/2 acre with gazebo, lawn games.
Location 3/4 m from downtown. From I-240, take Exit 4C (Montford Ave.). Go N 3/4 m to inn on left.
Restrictions No smoking.
Credit cards Amex, Discover, MC, Visa.
Rates B&B, $90–120 double. 2-night weekend minimum (April-Dec.).
Extras Airport pickups. French spoken.

Richmond Hill Inn ✕ &.
87 Richmond Hill Drive, 28806

Tel: 704–252–7313
800–545–9238
Fax: 704–252–8726

Considering the broken windows, peeling paint, and collapsing porches of Richmond Hill in the 1970s, even a starry-eyed visionary would have been hard put to imagine the extraordinary restoration of this historic mansion. The road to preservation was a long and bumpy one, both literally and figuratively—involving major fundraising efforts by the Buncombe County Preservation Society and moving the 1 1/2-million-pound building 600 feet. A happy ending—or perhaps a new beginning—began in 1987 when Greensboro publishers, Dr. Albert and Marge Michel, bought Richmond Hill and began its renovation as a country inn and restaurant.

This grand Queen Anne-style mansion overlooks the French Broad River from its hilltop location. Built in 1889 by former congressman and ambassador Richmond Pearson, the guest rooms are named for family members or other prominent figures and authors from Asheville history. Much of the inn's original woodwork was saved, including the native oak of the entrance hall, the cherry-paneled dining room, and the fireplaces with neoclassical revival mantels. Guest rooms are decorated with draped canopy beds or four-posters, Victorian antiques, and Oriental rugs. Some retain original claw-footed bathtubs and fireplaces. Completed in 1991 were five neo-Victorian cottages housing nine guest rooms. Named for

North Carolina trees, they overlook the croquet courtyard and have large bathrooms, pencil-post beds with down comforters, and fireplaces. The inn's restaurant, Gabrielle's, was named for Pearson's wife, and it occupies the formal dining room and the enclosed sun porch.

"Delicious dinner and breakfast, with a pleasing variety of choices." *(Carol & Donald Purcell)* "The F. Scott Fitzgerald Room has a wicker queen-sized bed, window seat, skylights, and such extras as bathrobes, hair dryer, and chocolates. Breakfast was filling and delicious; we chose from crêpes, omelets or waffles." *(Deanna Yen)* "The Gail Godwin room was quiet, pleasingly bright, and small but not cramped. A choice of feather or foam pillows was accompanied by extra towels." *(JPS)* "Our cottage bedroom was large enough to comfortably house a queen-size bed, two overstuffed chairs, a cocktail table, a stocked refrigerator, and plenty of built-in luggage and counter space. Great bedside reading lights. Spacious, spotless bath with a separate tub and shower and an oversized vanity." *(Ben & Peg Bedini)* "Afternoon tea was delicious with wonderful pastries. Beautiful woodwork in the restored house." *(Nancy Bernard)* "Done in soothing hues of taupe and cream, our cottage was spotlessly clean, uncluttered and perfectly appointed. Thoughtful, sincere hospitality from the initial telephone reservation call through our reluctant departure." *(Nancy & Bob Benson)*

Open All year.

Rooms 2 suites, 19 doubles—all with private bath and/or shower, telephone, radio, TV, heat/air-conditioning control; most with fireplace. Suite with fireplace, wet bar, whirlpool tub. 9 rooms in 5 cottages; all with porch, gas fireplace.

Facilities Restaurant, piano entertainment Wed–Sun; lobby, drawing room, 2 parlors, library, all with fireplace; ballroom, porch with rockers. Meeting facilities. 47 acres with croquet lawn, hiking trails.

Location 3 m from downtown. From I-240, take North Weaverville exit at Rtes. 19/23. Continue on Rtes. 19/23 to Exit 251/UNC-Asheville. At bottom of ramp, turn left. At 1st stoplight, turn left on Riverside Dr.; turn right on Pearson Bridge Rd. & cross the bridge. At sharp curve, turn right on Richmond Hill Dr. to inn at top of hill. "A bit tricky to find, so follow directions and watch turns carefully."

Restrictions No smoking.

Credit cards Amex, MC, Visa.

Rates B&B, $275–295 suite, $125–215 double. Extra person, $15. Alc dinner, $30–50.

Extras Limited wheelchair access, one room equipped for disabled. Crib.

BALSAM

Balsam Mountain Inn ✕ ♿
Balsam Mountain Inn Road, P.O. Box 40, 28707

Tel: 704–456–9498
800–224–9498
Fax: 704–452–1405

"If you are coming to the mountains come all the way up," read the advertising slogan of the Balsam Mountain Inn when this Colonial Revival structure opened in 1908. In those days, visitors traveled via the Southern Railway to the old Balsam Depot—once the highest railway station east of the Rockies, at an elevation of 3500 feet. Over the years, the inn experienced only minor changes, until an extensive restoration was undertaken in 1990 by owner Merrily Teasley. Restored hardwood floors, beaded board walls, original art, and Victorian furnishings are among the interior accents. The spacious dining room and kitchen have also been refurbished, while guest rooms are simply decorated with an eclectic assortment of period pieces, brightly patterned fabrics, and walls painted in pastels. Breakfast might include eggs strata or cheese soufflé, poppyseed muffins, bacon, fresh fruit, and orange juice. "Beautiful restoration job, with great use of color and fabrics. My room, #200, had pale teal-green beaded board walls, dark green floral fabric at the windows and on the king-size bed, coordinating linens and plush towels. Rustic twig furniture created a comfortable seating area. While tiny, the bathroom had good lighting (even a nightlight), a new stall shower, hooks where I wanted them to be, and a shelf next to the antique corner sink. Early morning coffee is available in the game room, one of several comfortable and welcoming common areas." (NB, also Sheila & Joe Schmidt) "Two wonderful porches run clear across the front of the inn, with inviting wicker rocking chairs and inspiring mountain views. While the main lobby is large, Merrily has arranged a number of inviting furniture groupings to create an intimate feel. Top quality mattresses and springs; circulating pumps produce hot water at the turn of a faucet. Some bathrooms have clawfoot tubs, others have modern showers. Best is the whole-hearted welcome from the entire staff, including Quintas, the inn dog. The food is delicious; the kitchen staff is delighted to prepare special entreés to meet the needs of individual guests, given a few hours notice." (Maurice & Jean Feldman, also James & Pamela Burr)

Open All year.
Rooms 3 suites, 31 doubles—all with private bath and/or shower; some with desk, 1 with fan.
Facilities Dining room with piano, living room with fireplaces, library, game room, guest refrigerator, porches. Dinner music some weekends. 26 acres with trails, creek, springs, pond, lawn games. Tennis, golf, whitewater rafting, fishing nearby.
Location W NC. 35 m SW of Asheville; 100 m E of Knoxville, TN. From Rtes. 74/23, exit ¼ m S of Parkway overpass at green sign marking town limits. Make immediate right, crossing train tracks; continue ⅓ m, cross more tracks before turning into inn's driveway at top of hill.
Restrictions Some non-smoking guest rooms. BYOB.
Credit cards MC, Visa.
Rates B&B, $120–150 suite; $75–85 double; $70–80 single. 10% extended stay, senior discount. 2-night high-season holiday minimum. Alc lunch, $8; dinner, $14.
Extras Wheelchair access, some rooms equipped for disabled. Airport/station pickups. Crib. French spoken.

BANNER ELK

Also recommended: The **Archers Mountain Inn** (Beech Mountain Parkway, Route 2, Box 56A, 28604; 704–898–9004) is a rustic contemporary lodge, with 14 guest rooms are paneled in pine, some with four-poster beds, others with brass and iron headboards. Guests enjoy relaxing on the old-fashioned porch rockers, with lovely views of the mountains beyond, or in the comfortable living room with equally beautiful views. Rates include a full breakfast, with family-style dinners served nightly at 6:30 P.M. "We prefer the spacious, pine-paneled rooms in the annex, equipped with a cozy eating area with refrigerator and microwave, small sitting area with a large stone fireplace, two four-poster beds, and pine-paneled bathroom. Indescribable views, especially in the early morning fog. All rooms have a fireplace, with wood boxes replenished nightly. Tasty breakfasts with wonderful birds to watch at the feeders." *(Marcia Hostetter)*

Banner Elk Inn   *Tel: 704–898–6223*
Highway Route 194N, Route 3, Box 1134, 28604

Built in the 1920s, the renovated Banner Elk offers guest rooms furnished with an eclectic assortment of country antiques, handmade crafts and artifacts from around the world. Breakfast consists of whole wheat bread, fruit breads, and an egg dish or casserole. Owner Beverly Lait is a portrait artist and tapestry maker; her 17 years' experience hosting official governmental functions abroad made innkeeping seem a natural choice when she bought the inn in 1990.

"A cozy, inviting inn where one can feel comfortable meeting other guests without being overwhelmed. Beverly is helpful and informative, yet never intrusive. The rooms are charming, comfortable, and immaculate. Beverly is always available to answer questions and solve problems. Convenient location, yet quiet and serene. Restaurants, shops, and ski areas readily accessible, even in bad weather." *(Andrea League)* "Her 'Fun Map' of local attractions is better than any guidebook." *(F. Seillier)* "Beverly's delicious breakfasts feature homemade breads and creative dishes served on elegant fine china; my favorite is cottage cheese pancakes." *(Carol Perry)* "Lovely flower beds; it's delightful to sit on the side porch and relax." *(Evelyn Johnston)*

Open All year.
Rooms 4 doubles—2 with full private bath, 2 with maximum of 4 people sharing bath. All with fan, 1 with desk, telephone.
Facilities Dining room, breakfast/living room with fireplace, TV, stereo, books. Garden with fountain. Off-street parking. 2 m to downhill, cross-country skiing.
Location NW NC. 123 m NW of Charlotte, 19 m NW of Boone, NC. 6 m from Blue Ridge Parkway on Hwy 194 N.
Restrictions No smoking. Children over 4 preferred.
Credit cards MC, Visa.
Rates B&B, $70–95 double, $60–85 single. Extra person, $10. 2-3 night weekend/holiday minimum.
Extras Pets by arrangement. German, Spanish spoken.

BEAUFORT

Pronounced BO-fort (in contrast to BEW-fort, South Carolina), Beaufort is North Carolina's third oldest town, and is located in the south coastal area, 45 miles south of New Bern, 100 miles north of Wilmington, and 150 miles southeast of Raleigh. There's ample opportunity for tennis and golf, plus fishing, swimming, and boating.

Reader tips: "A charming village; everything is within walking distance." *(Donna Bocks, also Gail Owings)* "Originally a whaling village, founded in 1709, with beautiful old houses, their dates posted outside. Lovely gardens, narrow streets, interesting shops, all right on the water. Fascinating water traffic. Beaches close by." *(Betty Sadler)* "We were delighted with dinner at the Net House, a five-minute walk from the Beaufort Inn." *(Brian Donaldson)* "North Carolina Maritime Museum is well worth seeing. Plenty of mosquitoes; bring insect repellent." *(Bill Novak)*

Beaufort Inn ¢ &.   Tel: 919–728–2600
101 Ann Street, 28516

"Although a new structure, the inn blends in beautifully with Beaufort's 18th and 19th century architecture. Its location right on the banks of the Beaufort Channel makes it delightful to pull up a rocker on one's private porch and watch the fishing boats, sailboats, yachts, seagulls and pelicans, especially at sunset. The guest rooms are comfortable, furnished with quality reproductions, and overlook the water or the quaint town. The delicious breakfast includes juice, homemade cheese and sausage pie, croissants, muffins, cereals, fruits, and coffee." *(Betty Sadler)* "Request a waterfront room, where you can watch the changing action in the harbor." *(Duane Roller)* "At night you can watch the lights of the incoming fishing trawlers as the shrimp boats are unloaded across the way." *(Donna Bocks)*

"Don't be put off by the fact that the road to the inn passes a working waterfront. Rooms are restful, clean, comfortable—not spacious, but more than adequate; my private balcony overlooked a waterway teeming with working fishing boats. A good breakfast, promptly served, started a morning of touring off in a fine way." *(John E. King, also Brian Donaldson)*

Minor niggle: "We called two months ahead to reserve a room, but were told that they couldn't guarantee us a room with a water view."

Open All year.
Rooms 41 doubles—all with full private bath, telephone, TV, air-conditioning, balcony.
Facilities Lobby, dining room, conference room. Bicycle, boat slip rentals.
Location E end of Graydon St. Bridge (U.S. Rte. 70). From bridge, go 2 blocks S on Moore, 1 block W on Ann. 2 blocks from Maritime Museum.
Restrictions No smoking in common areas.
Credit cards Amex, DC, Discover, MC, Visa.
Rates B&B, $49–99 double. Extra person, $10. AAA, AARP discount.
Extras Wheelchair accessible rooms on 1st floor.

Delamar Inn ¢   Tel: 919–728–4300
217 Turner Street, 28516

Built in 1866, the Delamar Inn is a Greek Revival home restored as a B&B in 1989 by Mabel and Tom Steepy. Rates include breakfast and complimentary wine, soda, and cookies. "A charming and a gracious hostess, Mabel Steepy offers guests a unique blend of southern and Scottish hospitality. Mornings begin with a good breakfast of homemade breads and muffins, yogurt, fresh fruit, coffee, and herbal tea." *(Bill Novak)* "Immaculate B&B, close to waterfront shops, museums, marina, and restaurants. Comfortable bed, beautiful furnishings, modern bath." *(R. Reach)* "Beautifully restored and furnished with period antiques, family heirlooms, and heart pine floors. But the best part was the warm welcome we received, and the way the Steepys accommodated our needs." *(Jeff Krueck)*

Open All year.
Rooms 3 doubles—all with private bath and/or shower, radio, clock, desk, air-conditioning, ceiling fan. Some with deck.
Facilities Dining room, living room with books, fireplace, stereo; family room with TV; deck, screened porch. Garden, off-street parking. 2 blks. from ocean.
Location Historic district. 1 blk. off I-70, on Turner St.
Restrictions No smoking. Children over 10.
Credit cards MC, Visa.
Rates B&B, $58–88 double. Extra person, $12. Senior, AAA discounts.
Extras Babysitting.

Langdon House ¢
135 Craven Street, 28516

Tel: 919–728–5499

In 1983 Jimm Prest restored and opened the Langdon House in one of Beaufort's oldest homes. He prides himself on meeting the individual needs of his guests: "This is my home, so we're here to fix you a cup of tea to accompany an evening rock on the porch or supply an antacid if those wonderful hush puppies from dinner are still barking in the night."

"Jimm Prest did the restoration work himself, and showed me the original attic frame, the addition line of the floorboards, the 18th-century stone chimney, and the many knickknacks that make the ambience genuine." *(Jonathan Mudd)* "Brandy on the mantel, beds turned down, hot coffee in the morning, followed by fresh OJ, gingerbread waffles, and country ham. When I wanted a rowboat to get to Carrot Island, there it was. It's just a short walk to the working waterfront—the restoration of old sailboats, salty dogs living upon the water, and many shops are fun to watch and visit. A beautiful display of fruit breads, fresh fruit, pastries, cheeses, and coffee is served in the sunny parlor." *(Sally Thomas Kutz)* "Jimm Prest is a man who puts his heart and soul into everything he does. He goes out of his way to make your stay special, without intruding on your privacy. Immaculate housekeeping." *(Marla Potter)* "Quiet garden setting, yet right in the middle of this little town." *(AJ)*

Open All year.
Rooms 4 doubles—all with queen-size beds, private bath and/or shower, radio, air-conditioning.
Facilities Dining room; parlor for reading, games, breakfast; porch; gardens. Bicycles, fishing rods, beach baskets, beach towels, small coolers. 1 block to boardwalk, shops, restaurants.
Location Historic district, corner Craven & Ann Sts. From Hwy. 70, turn at light onto Turner St., then left on Ann St. 1 block to inn at corner.
Restrictions No smoking. No children under 12.
Credit cards None accepted.
Rates Room only (midweek), $69–79 double. B&B, $79–115 double, $73–115

single. Extra person, $15. 10% discount for 6-day stays or equivalent. 2-night minimum some weekends. Packages.
Extras Airport/station pickup.

Pecan Tree Inn
Tel: 919–728–6733
116 Queen Street, 28516

Those of us getting on in years may be comforted to know that pecan trees do not reach their prime until they're over 75 years old. Named for the 200-year-old pecan trees that grace the property, the Pecan Tree Inn was built in 1866, with Victorian porches and ornamentation added in the 1890s. Restored as an inn by Susan and Joseph Johnson in 1991, the rates include a breakfast of fresh fruit and juice, cereal, with homemade breakfast breads, cakes, and buns.

"Easy walking distance to shops, restaurants, and the waterfront." *(Mr. & Mrs. Jim Garriss)* "Susan and Joe made us feel right at home, from the homemade peanut brittle to the fresh-baked morning pastries. After a day of sun, sightseeing, and shopping, we sipped drinks on the wonderful covered porch, catching the afternoon breeze. The Blue Room was done in a blue floral print with wicker chairs, a lovely antique dresser, and many windows. The other guest rooms and common areas were equally lovely and spotlessly clean. A small refrigerator in the sitting room was filled with an assortment of soft drinks." *(Ellen & Mike Daly)* "The Bridal Suite had a huge lace canopy bed and double Jacuzzi, terry robes, private balcony and entrance. Ample hot water for post-beach showers, plenty of parking. Although the bustling boardwalk is nearby, the inn is always quiet. Susan and Joe help with dinner reservations and provide good information about the area." *(Erin Donnelly & Rick Heeren)* "The English garden is for strolling and bird watching." *(Suzanne Mackey)*

Open All year.
Rooms 1 suite, 6 doubles—all with private bath, radio, clock, air-conditioning, fan. 1 with whirlpool tub, desk; 2 with balcony/deck.
Facilities Dining room, living room, library with books; guest refrigerator, porch. Garden, with pond, fountain, parking.
Location Historic district, ½ block from waterfront. From I-70 and Hwy. 101, go left onto Queen St.
Restrictions No smoking. Children over 12 preferred.
Credit cards MC, Visa.
Rates B&B, $95–120 suite, $65–105 double, $55–100 single. Extra person, $15. 5th day free.
Extras Local airport pickup. Spanish spoken.

BELHAVEN

Information please: Current reports are needed on **River Forest Manor** (600 East Main Street, Belhaven, 27810; 919–943–2151), a popular restaurant and inn on the inland waterway. The original mansion dates to 1899, and has hand-carved ceilings, oak mantels for the eleven fireplaces, sparkling cut glass leaded into the windows, crystal chandeliers, and dining room tapestries. In 1947 it was purchased by Axson Smith, whose widow and sons still operate the hotel today. The famous 65-dish buffet smorgasbord is served daily from 6–9 P.M., with brunch on Sundays from 10 A.M. to 2 P.M. B&B double rates for the ten guest rooms range from $65–80. Comments welcome.

BLACK MOUNTAIN

The Red Rocker Inn ¢ ✕ ੬.
136 N. Dougherty Street, 28711

Tel: 704–669–5991

"The Red Rocker Inn is located in a small, friendly mountain town. The innkeepers, Fred and Pat Eshleman, are warm, efficient, and hospitable. The inn is an old-fashioned, three-story beige house with wraparound porch, all sizes of red rockers, and a red swing. The walkway is lined with red and white impatients and geraniums. Each guest room has a name reflecting its decor—the Music Room has old musical instruments and wallpaper with a musical theme; the Preacher's Room has a stained glass window and a prayer bench. You are welcomed as you are seated for dinner, then the innkeeper blesses the meal, served by the courteous and youthful staff." *(Ruth Fox & Alice Johnson)* "A quiet inn located at the end of a secluded street, surrounded by huge shade trees." *(Frank Campbell)* "Each immaculate room is decorated with an eclectic, comfortable mix of furnishings. We dined on the enclosed porch with views of the garden and mountains beyond." *(Victoria & Henry Barnes)*

"Interesting gift and antique shops a few blocks down the hill in Black Mountain; the lake with walking paths and ducks are in the other direction." *(Jane Thomas)* "From Pat's Belgium waffles to Fred's eggs and grits, breakfasts are a treat, as are the dinners of mountain trout with almond butter, meatloaf, country fried steak, barbecued ribs, grilled chicken, and pork tenderloin. Be careful not to fill up on homemade zucchini muffins, fresh vegetables, salads and soups, or you'll have no room for desserts like Mud Pie, Pea-pickin' cake, homemade cobblers, strawberry shortcake, or spice cake. House guests get priority on dinner reservations, but guests should be sure to tell Fred if they plan to eat in." *(Beth & Jay Childress)*

Minor niggles: "We think it's part of the charm of an older home, but floors slant in some rooms; a few bathrooms are quite small." Also: "Our room could have used brighter lighting."

Open May 1–Oct. 31.
Rooms 18 doubles—all with private bath and/or shower, fan. 1 with fireplace.
Facilities Restaurant, game room with piano; living room with library, fireplace; sun room with games, puzzles, cards; porch. 1 1/2 acres with flower garden, swings. Swimming pool, tennis, golf, fishing, hiking nearby.
Location W NC, 17 m E of Asheville. 2 blocks from center. Take Exit 64 off I-40 to center of town, turn left and go 2 blocks, then right on Dougherty St. to inn on top of hill.
Restrictions No smoking, no alcohol in public rooms. Parking limited. Children must be well supervised.
Credit cards None accepted.

Rates Room only, $40–70 double, $35–65 single, plus 17% service. Extra person, $12.50. Full breakfast, $7.50. Alc dinner, $16. Children's menu ½ price.
Extras Limited wheelchair access.

BLOWING ROCK

Blowing Rock is a resort town along the Blue Ridge Parkway, named for a unique rock formation, where air currents from the Johns River Gorge return light objects thrown toward the rock. The town has many attractive craft shops. It's located in northwestern North Carolina's High Country, approximately 7 miles south of Boone, and 110 miles northwest of Charlotte. Blowing Rock is known as the "ski capital of the south." With an elevation of almost 4,000 feet, it also offers cool summers and beautiful fall foliage; one reader warned that summer fog and mist can result in days when you never see the mountain peaks.

For additional area entries, see **Boone**, below.

Gideon Ridge Inn   *Tel: 704–295–3644*
6148 Gideon Ridge Road, P.O. Box 1929, 28605

The Gideon Ridge Inn was built in 1939 as an elegant yet rustic stone mansion, and offers beautiful views of the Blue Ridge Mountains. In 1983 Cobb and Jane Milner converted this house to an inn, and have furnished the rooms with antiques. Jane says that "our guests leaf through our art books and listen to Mozart and Bach at breakfast; they hike, play bridge, shop for crafts and antiques." For breakfast, enjoy a choice of Jane's muesli and fresh fruit, or one of her hot entrées. Rates also include afternoon tea—perhaps cream scones, shortbread cookies, and assorted tea sandwiches.

"We entered to find a roaring fire in the library and an equally warm greeting from our hosts and their cat." *(Linda Stanley)* "The easy charm of Cobb and Jane Milner complements their immaculate and beautifully maintained inn. The bedrooms are spacious, comfortable; the baths are thoughtfully provided with ample storage space for cosmetics." *(Elizabeth Rupp)* "The stone terrace that wraps around the inn is a perfect place to watch a perfect harvest moon rise over the mountains, serenaded by the frogs, crickets, and owls." *(Jane & Luther Manners)* "Cobb and Jane have been joined by their son and his wife Cindy, adding vigor to a wonderful place." *(Dr. & Mrs. Paul Tolmie)* "Furnishings and bedding were beautiful, bath towels were nice and thick, and there were big, warm comforters on the beds. The owners were friendly and helpful but respected your privacy." *(Debbie Murray)* "The Victorian Room has period antiques, a comfortable bed, working fireplace, chairs with reading lamps, windows that opened, and a door onto the terrace. Blowing Rock is a delightful, scenic town with a variety of great restaurants." *(Judith Brannen)*

Open All year.
Rooms 9 doubles—all with private bath and/or shower, desk, fan; some with gas fireplace, 1 with double whirlpool.
Facilities Dining room, library with TV, fireplace, terraces. 5 acres with wooded paths, formal gardens. Golf, horseback riding, hiking, biking, skiing nearby.

Location 1½ m to town, ¼ m W of Rte. 321; 3 m S of Blue Ridge Parkway. Call for exact directions.
Restrictions No smoking. No children under 12.
Credit cards Amex, MC, Visa.
Rates B&B, $100–140 double. Single mid-week corporate rate. 2-night weekend minimum summer/fall.

BOONE

Named for Daniel Boone, this little town high in the Blue Ridge Mountains is home to Appalachian State University and the Appalachian Cultural Museum. In the summer, get tickets for the *Horn in the West*, a musical recounting of Boone's story. Area attractions include hiking, bicycling, fishing, swimming, boating and hunting; in winter, five downhill ski areas are within a 20-minute drive. Boone is located in western North Carolina, roughly 100 miles north of Charlotte, and 80 miles west of Winston-Salem.

Also recommended: A mile from downtown Boone is **The Gragg House** (Kalmia Acres, 210 Ridge Point Drive, 28607; 704–264–7289), a contemporary home in the woods, with mountain views. The two guest rooms share a bath, and the B&B double rate of $65 includes breakfasts of apple cobbler, home-baked breads, and a ham and egg casserole. "Clean, comfortable, and quiet, with terrific breakfasts and helpful owners." *(Anne & Wade Barber, and others)*

A good choice for budget travelers is **Grandma Jean's B&B** (209 Meadowview Drive, 28607; 704–262–3670), offering three guest rooms at a double rate of $50–60, including continental breakfast. "A widely traveled former teacher, Grandma Jean is a delightful hostess. The rooms are small, clean, and share a bath." *(Joe Schmidt)*

For additional area entries, see **Blowing Rock,** above.

Lovill House Inn ♿
404 Old Bristol Road, 28607

Tel: 704–264–4204
800–849–9466

The Lovill House was built in 1875 by Captain Edward Lovill, a decorated Confederate officer, who helped to draft the founding papers of what is now Appalachian State University. Home to the Lovill family for nearly a century, the building was restored as an inn by Lori and Tim Shahen in 1993. During the renovation, the Shahens preserved the old—rebuilding three of the original fireplaces, and refinishing the floors—while taking care to provide modern comfort. To assure privacy, they double-insulated the guest room walls.

Coffee and just-baked muffins are set outside guest rooms at 7:30, followed by breakfast served from 8–9:30, with fresh squeezed juice; baked apples or broiled fruit compote; Belgian waffles, vegetable strata, or eggs Benedict; and sausage, served on fine china at tables for four and six. Rates also include an afternoon social hour with complimentary beverages and appetizers, offered from 5:30–6:30 P.M.

"We were warmly welcomed by Tim and Lori, and were given a tour of the inn; much care was taken to preserve the unusual woodwork during the renovation. Although convenient to Boone's business district, the inn's location at the edge of the city is private, and the woods behind the inn are ideal for a peaceful walk." *(Cynthia Miller)* "Lovely porch for enjoying your first cup of morning coffee or for unwinding at the end of the day." *(Ann O'Quinn)* "The furnishings are a pleasing blend of antique and reproduction; our room had a king-size bed, fireplace, and beamed ceiling. Baked apples, waffles with fresh fruit, broiled grapefruit, and egg strata were among our favorite breakfast dishes. Menus of all the Shahen's favorite restaurants were available, and reservations made with pleasure; we loved 'Sam & Stu's' restaurant. Turn-down service, daily fresh towels, and wonderful soaps, too." *(Robert & Pamela Kreigh)* "When the weather turned cool one afternoon, we returned to find a goose down comforter atop our bed." *(Mike & Ginny Denmark)* "The guest rooms have a television discretely hidden in a cabinet, designer comforters or handmade quilts, and fresh flowers. " *(Maria Santomasso-Hyde)*

Open All year. Closed March & mid-Sept.
Rooms 5 doubles—all with full private bath, TV, telephone, clock, desk, fan, radio. 1 with fireplace. 5 add'l. rooms planned in barn for 1995.
Facilities Dining room, living room with fireplace, stereo; country kitchen with fireplace, guest refrigerator, laundry, wraparound porch with rockers. 11 acres with hammock, gardens, lawn games, off-street parking, stream, waterfall, berry patches, mt. bicycles.
Location 1 m from old downtown Boone, ASU campus. Hwy. 321/421 becomes W King St. in Boone. Going W, turn right on Old Bristol Rd. to inn on right. Going E, turn left on Old Bristol Rd. to inn immediately on left.
Restrictions No smoking. Children over 12.
Credit cards MC, Visa.
Rates B&B, $68–115 double. Extra person, $20. 2-night minimum holiday weekends.
Extras Wheelchair access planned in 1995.

BREVARD

Brevard is located in the Blue Ridge Mountains, 30 miles south of Asheville.

Information please: A block from Main Street is **The Red House Inn** (412 West Probart Street, 28712; 704–884–9349), built in 1851, and restored in 1984 as a B&B by Lynne Ong. Breakfast includes eggs, homemade biscuits and muffins, jams, and bacon or sausage, with plenty of coffee and tea. Area attractions include the Brevard Music Center, Flat Rock Playhouse, and numerous hiking trails and waterfalls. The six guest rooms are furnished with antiques; the B&B double rates are $45–80.

About two miles from Brevard is the **Key Falls Inn** (151 Everett Road, Pisgah Forest, 28768; 704–884–7559), a Victorian farmhouse built in 1862, and furnished with antiques. The five guest rooms are air-conditioned with private baths; B&B double rates range from $55–85 and include afternoon tea. The inn's 35 acres include a tennis court and fishing pond; the trail to the falls begins at the inn. Built between 1860 and 1868, the inn is a large Victorian furnished with antiques. "Delightful B&B; excellent full breakfast; historic, rustic charm." *(Jim Clayton)*

BRYSON CITY

Located just two miles from the entrance to the Great Smoky Mountains National Park entrance, Bryson City is a center for visitors coming to enjoy hiking, rafting, canoeing, fishing, swimming, horseback riding, and skiing in the Smokies. For a relaxing, scenic excursion, ride the Great Smoky Mountains Railway west from Bryson City, across Fontana Lake, to the Nantahala Gorge. The town is 60 miles west of Asheville, in western North Carolina.

Reader tip: "As you drift down the wonderful Blue Ridge Parkway you tend to assume that in the Smoky Mountains, the highest part of the range will be the most beautiful part of all, which is indeed true of the mountains and the road itself. *But*, at either end of the road, and impossible to avoid, are Gatlinburg [Tennessee] and Cherokee. Gatlinburg is merely unbridled development. Cherokee, on the other hand, is truly dreadful. Uncontrolled shabby ribbon development is patrolled by Indians in hopelessly unauthentic dress, waiting to be humiliated by tourists with their cameras at the ready." *(Richard Gollin)* To minimize such horrors, we'd suggest seeking out two valid experiences, the Oconaluftee Indian Village, and "Unto these Hills," a dramatic presentation of Cherokee history.

Pat Borysiwiecz reports that "it was well worth the 17-mile drive from Bryson City for dinner at Relia's Garden Restaurant."

For additional area recommendations, see listings under **Dillsboro** and **Whittier.**

Information please: The **Hemlock Inn** (P.O. Drawer EE, 28713; 704–488–2885) is situated on top of a small mountain (elevation 2300 feet) on the edge of the Great Smoky Mountains National Park. Rooms and cabins are furnished in country antiques and pieces made by mountain craftspeople; guests can enjoy rafting, tubing, and hiking in the surrounding mountains, or just admiring the mountain views from a porch rocker. Double rates are a reasonable $120–135, including breakfast, dinner, and gratuities.

The **Randolph House** (Fryemont Road, P.O. Box 816, 28713; 704–488–3472 or off-season, 404–938–2268), built in 1895 and now owned by Ruth and Bill Adams, is extensively furnished with period antiques, some dating back to the 1850s, with many original to the inn. Although Ruth is a descendant of Amos Frye, who built this mountain mansion, she is best known today for her talents in the kitchen. Rates include a full country breakfast and dinner; favorite entrées include veal Marsala and local mountain trout, with homemade fruit cobblers and key lime pie among the dessert specialties.

Folkestone Inn ¢   *Tel:* 704–488–2730
101 Folkestone Lane, 28713   *Fax:* 704–488–8689

Owners Norma and Peter Joyce note that "our inn attracts people who love the outdoors—mountains, streams, rivers, and waterfalls." A farmhouse built in the 1920s and renovated in 1988, the inn has stone floors and pressed tin ceilings in the ground floor guest rooms, a mix of antiques throughout the house, and a claw foot tub in every bathroom. Porches on both levels of the house provide a quiet spot for relaxing. Rates include an English/Southern breakfast of meat, eggs or another hot dish, freshly baked breads, and fruit.

"Norma Joyce is from Chattanooga, and Peter is from England; we shared delicious tea with fresh baked scones, and then toured the inn. My favorites were the delightfully cool rooms built into the stone foundation. A babbling brook meanders just below the inn at the edge of the Great Smoky Mountains National Park." *(Jonathan Douglas)* "Different areas of the inn evoke varying moods, from English pub, to Victorian, to country. The front porch offers lots of books, magazines, and rockers. The location is delightful, within walking distance of the park entrance, and 15 minutes to Nantahala River rafting." *(Susan Boehlke)*

"Norma agreeably prepared low cholesterol breakfasts for us. Our bed was turned down at night and brandy and a rose was left on the nightstand." *(Donna Sites)* "Wonderful advice on local trips, a chorus of bird songs around you, and total quiet at night." *(Gerhard Bedding)* "Special touches—scented bath oil by the tub, coffee and freshly baked cake on the porch, or hot cider on a cool evening." *(Dan & Barbara Nichols)* "We thought the Honeymoon suite well worth the price with its large bath and expanse of glass in the bedroom." *(Gordon Sutherland)* "We were greeted with iced tea and freshly baked spinach squares. The grounds are lovely, with a wonderful herb garden. Outstanding stuffed French toast and herbed scrambled eggs. Norma never seemed rushed or too busy to answer our questions, even though the inn was fully booked." *(Pat Borysiewicz, also Anne Boucherd)*

Open All year.

Rooms 10 doubles—all with private bath with hand-held shower, fan. 6 with private balcony/deck.

Facilities Dining room, living room with woodstove, piano, stereo; library with books, porch. 3 1/2 acres with croquet. Children's play equipment available. Fishing, tubing, white water rafting, boating, swimming nearby.

Location Swain County. 60 m W of Asheville. 150 m NE of Atlanta. 2 m from center of town.

Restrictions No smoking. "Well-behaved children welcome."

Credit cards None accepted.

Rates B&B, $59–84 double, $51–78 single. Extra adult, $20; extra child, $10. 2-night weekend minimum April–Nov., also & holidays. 3-night minimum Thanksgiving.

Extras Asheville airport pickup, $30.

BURNSVILLE

Information please: A rustic mountain lodge, the **Celo Inn** (1 Seven Mile Ridge Road, 28714; 704–675–5132) is owned by Randy and Nancy Raskin. This simple but homey inn is set by a river for swimming and fishing; the area is great for hiking or bicycling. "A meticulously crafted gem in the cottage style. Surrounded by lovely gardens, the inn includes a large main building and an outlying cottage. Much of the post and beam construction is hand-pegged, and the gables feature charming but unorthodox framing. Guest rooms are small but adequate (no phone or TV). Our twin-bedded room had a chest of drawers with mirror, rocker, floor lamp, bedside table and shared reading lamp. The private bathroom across the hall was immaculate. Breakfast on weekends is a casual help-yourself affair in the dining room, featuring fresh fruit, warm scones with butter and jam, homemade granola with raisins, yogurt and coffee. On weekdays, Nancy cooks breakfast to order at reasonable prices." *(Esther Magathan)* Double rates are a modest $25–35 double.

Nu Wray Inn ✗ ஃ

Town Square, P.O. Box 156, 28714

Tel: 704–682–2329
800–368–9729

Owned by the Wray families for four generations, the Nu-Wray was bought by Chris and Pam Strickland in 1993. In operation as an inn since 1830, it is best known for its family-style breakfasts and dinners, both open to the public. Guests are seated family-style at several large tables; a full breakfast is served at 8:30, while the dinner bell rings at 6:30, except on Sunday when it's served at 1:00. Dinner consists of two meats (fried chicken, roast beef, roast turkey, chicken pot pie, baked ham, or barbecue ribs), plus five vegetables, salad, biscuits, beverage and dessert.

"Fresh, seasonal, local produce used to prepare wonderful country-style meals. We relaxed on the front porch in the comfortable rockers, talking quietly and watching cars go around this small town square." *(Sue Ann Spears)* "Outstandingly friendly staff from the owners to the waitresses. Exceptional fried chicken. Beautiful antiques throughout." *(Angela Ard)* "We love to sit by the open fireplace in the big den. Breakfast includes country ham, hash browns, grits, sausage, eggs, hot apple sauce, apple butter, honey and biscuits that melt in your mouth, juice, and coffee. Within walking distance are appealing antique shops, art galleries, and craft studios" *(Joyce Wilhelm)* Reports welcome.

Open All year. No dinner Mon.–Wed., Nov.–April.

Rooms 1 cottage, 6 suites, 20 doubles—all with private bath and/or shower, radio, clock, TV, desk, fan.

Facilities Restaurant, lobby with fireplace, games, books; upstairs parlor, guest refrigerator, piano room with baby grand, player piano; upstairs parlor, verandas. 1/2 acre with lawn games. Swimming pool, tennis, golf, hiking nearby. 30 mins. to fishing, canoeing, Whitewater rafting.

Location 30 m NE of Asheville. Blue Ridge Mountains. Historic district, on Town Square. From I-40, take Rte. 226 N to Spruce Pine. Go left onto US Rte. 19E. Go 15 m to Burnsville. Go right at 3rd light. 1/2 block to town square.

Restrictions No smoking.

Credit cards Amex, MC, Visa.

Rates B&B, $110 cottage, $90–110 suite, $70–110 double, $60–100 single. Extra person, $10. AAA discount. 2-night minimum Oct., some holidays, special weekends. Alc dinner, $15, Sunday dinner, $16. Special offers, Jan.–April. Picnic lunches. Breakfast, $6

Extras Wheelchair access; public rooms, 1 guest room fully accessible. Crib, $5.

CASHIERS

A popular resort town since the 19th century, Cashiers is located in southwest North Carolina, 60 miles southwest of Asheville, and 155 miles north of Atlanta, Georgia, at an elevation of 3500 feet. The name of the town is pronounced CASH'-ers, not like the people who take your money at the supermarket. The Nantahala National Forest offers 1.3 million acres for hiking, fishing, and rafting; Whitewater Falls is a special favorite.

Information please: Surrounded by dogwood trees, rhododendron, and mountain laurel, the **Millstone Inn** (Highway 64 West, P.O. Box 949, 28717; 704–743–2737) has burnished pine-paneled walls and gleaming rock maple floors, with antique and contemporary furnishings. A millstone, one of several found on the property, is embedded in the granite stones of the living room fireplace. Double B&B rates range from $90–130.

With a dramatic location on a wooded hillside overlooking Lake Glenville, the **Innisfree Inn** (Highway 107 North, P.O. Box 469, Glenville 28736; 704–743–2946 or 800–782–1290) is a neo-Victorian B&B just four miles north of Cashiers. "Exuberantly furnished with crystal, gilt, cherubs, Oriental rugs, and rich colors. The guest rooms have every amenity you'd want—firm mattresses, fine linens, plush towels, and good lighting. Exuberant, warm, hospitable hosts." *(NB)* Accommodations are available in eight guest rooms and cottages, at B&B double rates of $100–130, including a full breakfast.

High Hampton Inn   🏃 ✕ 🎾 ♿   *Tel:* 704–743–2411
Highway 107 South, P.O. Box 338, 28717   800–334–2551

At an elevation of 3,600 feet, High Hampton was built as the private summer home of the Hamptons of South Carolina. It was purchased by the McKee family in 1922, who have retained its traditional atmosphere. Accommodations are plain and rustic, with walls of sawmill-finished pine and sturdy, mountain-crafted furniture. The food is good, plain Southern country cooking, with homemade breads and pastries and home-grown vegetables.

"Many of the guests are the third generation to enjoy High Hampton; its popularity is due to the personal attention each guests receives." *(Mr. & Mrs. Charles Rawls)* "Beauty, charm, friendliness, good food, and excellent management. A person traveling alone would find it informal and friendly. Cashiers is a lovely little village with lots of gift shops." *(Mrs. Theodore Palmer)* "The cottages and rooms are rustic, basic, comfortable but not elaborate. The lodge is charming, with a huge four-sided fireplace, where guests gather to play games and to visit. The food is home-cooked Southern. The grounds are magnificent, with a huge dahlia garden where guests are invited to cut a bouquet for their room." *(Betty Sadler)* "A warm, friendly, casual, family-oriented resort where all find friends, food, and fun. The bountiful buffet offers scrumptious hot and cold choices three times daily, and the college students who serve as waitresses, bellhops, and activity leaders couldn't be more accommodating. This is a dry county so liquor is not served, but set-ups are provided between 6–8 P.M. *(Louise & Richard Weithas)* "Fully endorse existing write-up. During my May visit, the azalea and wildflower hiking trails were a profusion of blooms." *(NB)*

Open April through Nov.

Rooms 7 suites, 123 doubles—all with private bath, desk, fan, deck. Some with fireplace. Some cottages available. 98 rooms in annex.

Facilities Dining rooms, living/game/TV room, piano/organ entertainment in lounge. 1,200 acres with gardens, lake, paddleboats, tennis, 18-hole golf course, archery, canoeing, fishing, hiking, waterfalls, teen center, children's program, play equipment, games.

Location 2 m S of Cashiers on Hwy. 107.

Restrictions Coats, ties required at dinner. BYOB.

Credit cards Amex, MC, Visa.

Rates Full board, $69–88 per person, double; $80–92 single. Extra person, $49–56. No tipping, no service charge. Reduced rates for children. Tennis, golf packages. Modest extra charges for facilities use, excluding packages. Weekly discounts.

Extras Wheelchair access. Airport/station pickup, $35–50. Kennel for pets. Cribs, babysitting.

CHAPEL HILL

Located in central North Carolina, Chapel Hill is best known as the home of the main campus of the University of North Carolina.

Also recommended: Built in 1924 in the Colonial Revival style and donated to the University of North Carolina, the **Carolina Inn** (211 Pittsboro Street, P.O. Box 1110, 27514; 919–933–2001 or 800–962–8519) projects an image of the genteel, formal Old South in its handsome lobby and 140 traditional guest rooms. Readers are pleased with its key on-campus location (where parking spaces are nearly impossible to find), friendly and accommodating staff, efficient management, small but reasonably priced and well-kept guest rooms. A $13.5 million renovation of the hotel began in November, 1994, resulting in its temporary closing. Re-opening is anticipated for September, 1995, with an updated heating/cooling system, and refurbished decor.

For luxury hotel amenities, including marble-lined baths, health spa, and limousine service, plus a continental breakfast, *Melissa Robin* recommends **The Siena** (1505 East Franklin Street, P.O. Box 2561, 27514; 919–929–4000 or 800–223–7379). "I had a spacious, well-lighted room done in antique reproductions, overlooking the woods. Unfailingly friendly and helpful staff." This 80-room hotel was built in the 1920s, and has a decor of stone and stucco, columns and arches, with contemporary Italian designer fabrics and furniture. Its restaurant, Il Palio, has an excellent reputation for Northern Italian cuisine. Rates range from $99–135, with AAA and senior discounts; children under 12 stay free.

Information please: Listed in past editions, we need current reports on the **The Inn at Bingham School** (Mebane-Oaks Road, P.O. Box 267, 27515; 919–563–5583) long owned by Jane Kelly, and listed as being for sale when we went to press. A combination of Greek Revival and Federalist styles, the inn provides elegant accommodation in rooms in the main house, as well as in a 1791 log cabin. "Rich in architectural detail and Southern hospitality, the inn is set amid rolling farmland. Exceptional breakfast of homemade heart-shaped biscuits, grits, fresh country eggs, baked apples, sausage or bacon, and a variety of fruit." *(Nancy Harrison & Nelson Ormsby)* Six guest rooms are available, at B&B double rates of $75–85.

For an additional area entry, see **Pittsboro,** for a description of **Fearrington House**.

CHARLOTTE

Located in the southwestern part of the state, Charlotte is one of North Carolina's largest cities, as well as a major textile-producing center, with hundreds of factories in the surrounding area. The city is home to a number of museums and parks of interest, as well as the University of North Carolina at Charlotte.

Also recommended: In the downtown historic district is **The Dunhill Hotel** (237 North Tryon Street, 28202; 704–332–4141 or 800–354–4141), a local historic landmark. The 60 guest rooms are furnished in Chippendale reproductions, plus all expected modern amenities and luxuries. "Our exquisitely furnished corner room had a double Jacuzzi." *(Judilynn Niedercorn)* "Lovely room, though a little small. Service was friendly and courteous. The attached restaurant, Monticello, was outstanding. Convenient downtown location." *(KM)* Double rates are $110 weekdays, $70 weekends.

The Homeplace ¢   *Tel: 704–365–1936*
5901 Sardis Road, 28270

Peggy and Frank Dearien had never stayed in a B&B, let alone run one, when they decided to buy The Homeplace in 1984. A turn-of-the-century Victorian, the inn has been completely renovated, from the foundation to the widow's walk. Windows, insulation, wiring, plumbing, heating and air-conditioning—even the roof was redone, while the house's original hand-crafted staircase, ten-foot-high ceilings, and heart-of-pine floors were preserved. Peggy decorated the house with Victorian and country-style furnishings; the guest rooms are done in shades of blue, rose, and green, and many are highlighted by the primitive paintings done by Peggy's father. A 1930s "dog trot" log barn is used for Peggy's workshop on flower and herb drying and arranging.

"The Homeplace has airy porches, plenty of rocking chairs, and cross-stitchings everywhere." *(John Hill)* "Spotless housekeeping; exceptional hospitality. Food was graciously served with flexible serving times. A bonus was a plate of homemade cookies in the evening. The grounds were lovely, the front porch inviting, the bath immaculate, the warmth pervasive." *(Lynn Grisard Fullman,)* "Although it's located on the corner of a busy intersection, once you're in the driveway of the Homeplace, it's easy to feel as though the city is miles away. Nicely wooded, beautifully landscaped. A gazebo and the rocking chairs on the wraparound porch contribute to its charms. Breakfast began with baked apples, followed by scrambled eggs flavored with dill and wrapped in a crepe, asparagus spears, and bagels toasted with parmesan cheese. Frank kept our water, juice, and coffee cups filled to the brim." *(Tawnya & Henry Fabian)* "The bathrooms are well stocked, with plenty of towels, shampoos, lotions, razors, and such; lots of extra hangers in the closet." *(Dianne Crawford)* "Just as wonderful on a return visit." *(Lynn Edge)*

Open All year.
Room 4 doubles—2 with full private bath, 2 with a maximum of 4 people sharing bath. All with air-conditioning.
Facilities Dining room, parlor with TV, books, meeting room; wraparound porch. 2½ acres with gazebo, gardens.
Location Mecklenburg County. 2 m from Rte. 74. 15 min. from center. SE Charlotte at corner of Sardis and Rama Rds. 15 min from I-77 and I-85.
Restrictions No smoking. No children under 10.
Credit cards Amex, MC, Visa.
Rates B&B, $78–88 double. Extra person, $20. 2-night holiday weekend minimum.

The Inn on Providence

Tel: 704–366–6700

6700 Providence Road, 28226

Shaded by tall cedars, this gracious Federal-style brick Colonial with white trim and black shutters, built in 1934, has been owned by Dan and Darlene McNeill since 1985. Decorating with Darlene's collection of 19th century furniture, antique quilts, and family heirlooms, they've transformed a handsome home into a lovely B&B. In good weather, guests breakfast together on the screened veranda, furnished in white wicker, overlooking the lawn and swimming pool. The meal includes fresh fruit and juice; home-baked breads, muffins, or coffee cake; and an egg dish, pancakes, or baked French toast.

"Dan and Darlene McNeill were gracious hosts, making us feel instantly welcome and giving us several helpful suggestions for dinner and sightseeing. Our two bedrooms were comfortable and attractive, as were the dining and sitting rooms; several rooms are done in a lovely Wedgwood blue and cream color scheme. Darlene fixed us a delicious breakfast of juice, coffee, muffins, cheese grits, and individual ramekins of a tasty egg, ham and tomato dish, served hot from the oven." *(Robert Boas)*

Open All year.
Rooms 2 suites, 3 doubles—3 with private bath and/or shower, 2 with maximum of 4 people sharing bath. All with radio, clock, air-conditioning. 4 with fan, 2 with desk, 1 with fireplace, balcony/deck.
Facilities Dining room, living room, library, screened veranda with fans. 1.3 acres with off-street parking, swimming pool. Golf, lakes nearby.
Location 10 m S of downtown. 6 m to historic district. On Hwy. 16 (Providence Rd.), approx. 1 m N of Hwy. 51.
Restrictions Traffic noise in some rooms. No smoking. Children over 10.
Credit cards Amex, MC, Visa.
Rates B&B, $79–100 suite, $59–100 double. 2-night minimum weekends, holidays.

Still Waters ¢ 👫   *Tel: 704–399–6299*
6221 Amos Smith Road, 28214

Built in the 1930s, this cozy log home right on Lake Wylie has been owned by Rob and Janet Dyer since 1989. Guests can bring their own boat, and use the inn's boat ramp and dock, or just sit and enjoy the wooded surroundings, just minutes from the bustle of Charlotte. The family room has contemporary and country-style oak furniture; a wall of windows provides views of the lake through the trees. Breakfast includes orange juice, mixed fruits, sweet rolls, and breakfast steaks, buttermilk pancakes, or herb omelets.

"The hospitable Dyer family made us feel right at home." *(Mr. & Mrs. Daniel Page)* "Convenient to dining, recreation, theatre and more." *(Edward Bennett)* "Grandma Shue's Room is done in 1930s furnishings, and has a great view of the grounds and the beautiful lake. Breakfast was served on the porch, with a view of the lake and dozens of birds to watch at the feeder, and consisted of homemade biscuits, eggs, grits, sausage, coffee and juice, cinnamon apple pancakes, and ham. Their two outside dogs, Buddy and Kelly, bark when you first approach, but are friendly once you are properly introduced." *(Ann Christoffersen)* "Appreciated choice of breakfast time." *(Robert Nadler)* "Simple Scandinavian feel to the decor; good lighting, comfortable bed." *(Elisabeth McLaughlin)*

Open All year.
Rooms One suite, two doubles—all with private bath and/or shower, radio, air-conditioning, refrigerator. Some with telephone, TV, desk, deck.
Facilities Living room with TV/VCR, fireplace. Family room, sun porch, deck. 2 acres with sport court. Dock, boat ramp. Golf nearby.
Location 3 m W of town; 10 min. from airport. Convenient to I-85, Rte. 74, & Billy Graham Parkway. Construction has made area road signage confusing; call for directions.
Restrictions No smoking.
Credit cards DC, MC, Visa.
Rates B&B, $65–85 suite, $50–75 double. Extra person, $5. 2-night weekend minimum during peak season. Reduced rates for children.
Extras Airport pickup. Crib.

CLYDE

Windsong: A Mountain Inn 🦙   *Tel: 704–627–6111*
120 Ferguson Ridge, 28721   *Fax: 704–627–8080*

Gale and Donna Livengood built their "dream inn" in 1988; they had planned to escape Chicago for a warm sunny island, but were entranced by the mountains of western North Carolina. The rooms are large, bright and airy, with cathedral-beamed ceilings, light pine logs, and Mexican Saltillo tiled floors throughout; large windows and skylights let in the mountain and woodland views. The Livengoods have artfully decorated the rooms with their collection of Native American art, artifacts, and rugs; each guest room has a different theme—African safari, country, Alaska, and Santa Fe. They have a small herd of llamas which they breed and use for wilderness trekking. Breakfast includes fruit and juice, homemade breads and muffins, and a hot entrée, perhaps buckwheat banana pancakes or egg-sausage-mushroom strata. Coffee is offered after guests return from dinner.

"The Santa Fe room is a charming mix of Native American, Southwest and Mexican furnishings." *(Sandra Scragg)* "To us, Windsong stands for rejuvenation, peace and pampering. Thoughtful touches include bubble bath and terry robes. The delicious breakfasts are a good time to plan the day and make new friends. Guests can enjoy a shopping spree to nearby Waynesville or Asheville, a picnic and llama trek through the Smokies, or a lazy day on the deck with a good book. Donna and Gale are enthusiastic, flexible, and eager to please." *(Paul & Patrice Phelps)* "With its mountaintop setting, luxurious amenities, and gracious hosts, Windsong is an exceptional experience. Where else can you have your photograph taken with a llama herd?" *(Sheila & Joe Schmitt)*

Open Feb. 1–Dec. 31.

Rooms 5 doubles—all with full private bath (shower & double soaking tub), fan, fireplace, VCR, patio or deck. Telephone on request. 2-bedroom cabin: living room with wood stove, 2 bedrooms, private bath with double-size tub, deck.

Facilities Dining room, common room with wet bar, VCR, videotape library, pool table, books, games, piano. 25 acres with heated swimming pool, tennis court, hiking trails. 20 min. to downhill skiing. 30 min to Great Smoky Mts. National Park, Biltmore Estate. 40 min. to whitewater rafting. Golf nearby.

Location W NC, Great Smoky Mts. region. 30 m W of Asheville. From I-40 take Exit 24. Go N on Rte. 209 for 2½ m, & turn left on Riverside Dr. Go 2 m & turn right on Ferguson Cove Loop. 1 m to inn.

Restrictions No smoking. Children over 8; any age in cabin.

Credit cards MC, Visa.

Rates B&B, $120–140 cabin, $85–95 double, $76–85 single. Extra person, $20. 10% discount for 5-night stay. Dinner llama treks.

DILLSBORO

Squire Watkins Inn ¢   *Tel:* 704–586–5244
Haywood Road, P.O. Box 430, 28725   800–586–2429

J.C. and Flora Watkins were among Dillsboro's first settlers when they built their home in the 1880s. Unfortunately, J.C. died quite young, leaving Flora with a heavily mortgaged house and business, and a large family to raise. The sheriff arrived with foreclosure papers and the house was to be sold at auction. Flora and her son wrote letters to 150 Masonic Lodges, explaining the situation, and enough money arrived to hold off the sale and save the family home. Flora opened the house to boarders, but when she found some of them drinking and gambling up on the widow's walk, she had the railing (and the boarders) removed. The inn stayed in the Watkins family until it was purchased and restored (including the railing) in 1983 by the Wertenberger family.

"Convenient location, just off the highway to Cherokee. Dillsboro has quality arts and crafts shops, unlike the over-commercialized town of Cherokee. Tom and Emma Wertenberger are easy people to talk with, and adept at including everyone in the conversation. My room was quiet, sunny, sparkling clean, with lovely furnishings—just like the rest of the inn." *(Patricia Harrington)* "The grounds are lovely with flower and herb gardens—it was a treat to find black-eyed Susans on the nightstand and lemon mint in the fruit cup at breakfast. Lulu's Cafe in nearby Sylva was perfect for a fine lunch or dinner in a casual setting." *(Pat Borysiewicz)* "Tom and Emma really love what they're doing and it shows. Attractive flower bouquets throughout the house. While Tom maintains that gardening is Emma's passion, after savoring a breakfast of sausage strudel and herbed scrambled eggs, I think that she is equally devoted to cooking." *(NB)* Comments welcome.

Open All year.
Rooms 2 suites, 3 doubles—all with private bath, desk. 1 cottage with private bath, kitchen, fireplace.
Facilities Parlor; game room; living room with piano, books; sun porch with books, magazines, games; gift shop. 3½ acres with gardens, pond. Stream, lake fishing, horseback riding, white-water rafting, canoeing, hiking, steam train excursions nearby.
Location W NC, 50 m W of Asheville. 2 blocks from town. At intersection of U.S. 441 and Haywood Rd.
Restrictions Smoking limited. Children over 11 in inn; any age in cottage.
Credit cards None accepted.
Rates Room only, $64 cottage. B&B, $78–82 suite, $68–72 double. Extra person, $7–12.50. Weekly rates in cottages.
Extras Crib for cottages only. Airport/station pickup.

DUCK

Sanderling Inn 🛏 ✗ 🎏 ♿   *Tel: 919–261–4111*
1461 Duck Road, 27949   *Fax: 919–261–1638*

As much as we love historic old inns, we are equally delighted when readers enthuse about contemporary inns built with style and distinction. The Sanderling is just such a place. Traditional beach front architecture is blended with a modern sense of space, and the decor combines natural oak with wicker and soft pastel colors. The inn's restaurant is housed in a restored turn-of-the-century lifesaving station; the lunch entrées include pizza topped with smoked shrimp and blue crab, or grilled tuna salad. A dinner selection might be crab and scallop cake appetizer, followed by corn bread and country ham-crusted salmon and red bliss potatoes. Rates include a continental breakfast, afternoon tea and health club use.

"Luxurious common rooms with working fireplaces, current magazines and best sellers. Most rooms have an outstanding view of the ocean or Currituck Sound." *(Lana Alukonis)* "An extensive collection of bird carvings and Audubon prints highlight the public areas." *(DLG)* "In a relatively unspoiled part of the Outer Banks, the inn overlooks a beautiful, vast private beach." *(JM)* "Our room was huge and spotless. We spent relaxing days going from the private beach to the pool to the private deck off our room to the rocking chairs on the front porch to the whirlpool." *(Rebecca*

Anderson) "Bottomless cups of early morning coffee in the common areas. Immaculate rooms. Endless sea, sand, and sky reminded me of Nantucket." *(Angela Foote)* "We chose the Sanderling based on your write-up. Our expectations were met and indeed exceeded. Everything about the inn epitomizes comfort, care, and graciousness, from the handsome rooms, the greeting treats, bathrobes, and coffee/tea service. The adjacent nature trails are an added treat for wildlife viewing." *(James Burr)*

Worth noting: Some first floor rooms lack water views.

Open All year.

Rooms 11 suites, 76 doubles—all with full private bath, telephone, TV, radio, desk, air-conditioning, fan, coffee maker, kitchenette or wet bar, porch. 44 rooms in South Inn; 32 rooms in North Inn. Presidential suite in conference center with Jacuzzi bath, steam shower, decks.

Facilities Restaurant, bar, library with fireplace; living room with TV/VCR, games; meeting facilities; gallery. Health club with indoor swimming pool. Outdoor swimming pool, hot tub, tennis courts, private beach, jogging trails; 3400 nature preserve adjacent. Golf, indoor tennis, birdwatching nearby.

Location NE NC, Outer Banks. 80 m SE of Norfolk, VA. 5 m N of Duck. Take Rte. 158 or 64 onto Outer Banks. From Kitty Hawk, go N approx. 12 m to Sanderling.

Restrictions Some non-smoking rooms; no cigar or pipe smoking in restaurant.

Credit cards Discover, MC, Visa.

Rates B&B, $205–350 suite, $110–205 double. Extra person, $30. Presidential suite, $800 double. 2-night weekend minimum. Discount for 7-night stay or 5-night Sun.–Fri. Corporate rates. New Year's Eve, July 3 Birthday, romance, tennis packages. Alc breakfast, $2–5; alc lunch, $3–7; alc dinner, $15–25.

Extras Wheelchair access; some rooms equipped for disabled. Station pickup, fee charged. Crib, $10; babysitting.

DURHAM

Located in the Piedmont region of central North Carolina, Durham is the home of Duke University, and is a center for medical education. South of town is an area known as the Research Triangle, a center industrial research, supported by the area's three major universities—Duke, UNC, and NC State.

Arrowhead Inn 👫 ♿
106 Mason Road, 27712

Tel: 919–477–8430
Fax: 919–477–8430

The Arrowhead dates from 1775, when it was a large slave-holding property. Owners Jerry and Barbara Ryan have preserved the inn's Colonial architecture, and have decorated the rooms in a homey and comfortable style, ranging from Colonial through Victorian. A five-foot stone arrowhead stands on the lawn; erected sixty years ago, it marks the Great Trading Path to the Smokies, which carried Indians, and then white settlers, to the West. Rates include afternoon refreshments and a full country breakfast.

"Carefully restored and charmingly furnished in period. The bathrooms are modern and spotless. The Ryans provided us with maps, brochures, and discount coupons for area attractions." *(John & Kris Driessen)* "Our carriage house room had beautiful country-style furnishings and primitive quilts." *(Rachel Gorlin)* "The Ryans are personable hosts, ready for conversation when guests wish, but otherwise busy behind the scenes." *(James & Janice Utt)* "Our rough-hewn log cabin had a large bath, a good bed, and an inviting sitting room with a working fireplace." *(Cecily Sharp-Whitehill)* "The delicious breakfasts included poached pears with French toast and herbed tomatoes with scrambled eggs. Coffee, tea, and hot chocolate, plus delicious cookies are available in the sitting room." *(Sue & Harvey Goldberg)* "All business conveniences in a family atmosphere." *(Natalie Chanin)* "Barbara greeted us at the door and showed us around the inn. Service, cleanliness, parking, quiet, location were all outstanding; best of all were the food and the Ryan's hospitality." *(Nancy Stevens)*

Open All year.

Rooms 1 cabin with private bath, fireplace; 1 suite with private bath, fireplace; 6 doubles—4 with full private bath, 2 with maximum of 4 people sharing bath. All with air-conditioning, radio, desk. Some with telephone, TV. 2 rooms in carriage house.

Facilities Dining room, family room with TV/VCR, games, stereo, fireplace, books; living room with fireplace, guest refrigerator. 4 acres with gardens, picnic area, swings, fish pond, children's play equipment. Tennis, golf, boating, fishing nearby.

Location 8 m N of Durham. 7 m N of I-85. Take Rte. 501 (Duke St./Roxboro Rd.) N; look for West Point on the Eno Park. Go 3 m further N to traffic light at intersection of Rte. 501 and Mason/Snow Hill Rd. to inn on left.

Restrictions No smoking in guest rooms.

Credit cards Amex, DC, MC, Visa.

Rates B&B, $150 cabin, $125 suite, $70–95 double, $65–85 single. Extra person, $15. Discount for extended stays.

Extras Cabin has wheelchair access. Crib. French spoken.

Old North Durham Inn ¢ 👫   Tel: 919–683–1885
922 North Mangum Street, 27701

The Old North Durham Inn is a B&B&B—bed & breakfast & baseball. In addition to food and lodging, guests receive free tickets to all the Durham Bulls' home games. The inn is located just across the street from the residence filmed in the movie, *Bull Durham*, and is five minutes from the ballpark. A Colonial Revival home built in 1906, the inn was Durham's first B&B when Debbie and Jim Vickery opened it in 1990. Guest rooms have ten-foot ceilings, queen-size beds, and period wall coverings and furnishings. Breakfasts of juice, coffee or tea, fresh fruit, muffins, egg dishes, fruit-filled pancakes, or perhaps apple cheddar quiche, with sausage, ham or bacon, are served at guests' convenience; rates also include afternoon refreshments, served in the parlor or on the rocking chairs of the wraparound porch.

"Lovely old home with lots of books and games; elegant breakfast accompanied by interesting conversation. Lots of menus and area information, and a big front porch for sitting." *(Celia McCullough)* "Welcoming hospitality, careful attention to detail." *(GR)*

Open All year.

Rooms 1 suite, 3 doubles—all with full private bath, radio, clock, desk, air-conditioning. 3 with ceiling fan, 2 with fireplace, 1 with TV, whirlpool tub.

Facilities Dining room, living room with fireplace, piano, TV, stereo; sitting room with books; game room with pool table; porch. $1/2$ acre with off-street parking.
Location $1/2$ m to downtown, historic district. From I-85, take "Durham Downtown" exit. Road bears right, then left onto N. Mangum St. to inn on left after 1 traffic light. 5 min. to Duck, baseball park, convention center, theater.
Restrictions No smoking.
Credit cards MC, Visa.
Rates B&B, $120 suite, $70–85 double, $70–80 single. Extra person, $20. Children under 3, free.
Extras Crib.

EDENTON

Edenton is filled with tree-lined streets of 18th- and 19th-century houses. It's located in northern coastal North Carolina on the Albemarle Sound, 70 miles south of Norfolk, 125 miles south of Richmond, VA, and 150 miles east of Raleigh.

Reader tips: "Edenton is a lovely town off the beaten track. The oldest courthouse in the nation is there, and I would particularly recommend a visit to the charming St. Paul's Episcopal Church (1736)." *(Harrison Gardner)* "We took the worthwhile walking tour originating at the Visitors' Center, with a gracious volunteer guide. Spring and summer are noted for azaleas and crape myrtle displays." *(Peg Bedini)*

Information please: Current reports are requested for the **Granville Queen Inn** (108 South Granville Street, 27932; 919–482–5296), best known for its unusual decor. Each of the guest rooms is named and decorated for a different "Queen," from the Queen of Egypt room with imported bronze 600-pound sphinxes and tented seating area, to the Peaches and Queen room with ornate Victorian furniture and lacy accents. The five-course breakfast, served from 8–10 A.M., includes apple crunch muffins, fresh fruit cup, yogurt with granola, filet mignon or chicken, served with eggs and rosemary potatoes, and a soufflé or blueberry cream cheese crepe. B&B double rates range from $85–95 on weekends, including a full breakfast and evening wine tastings; corporate rates midweek. Comments please.

Captain's Quarters Inn ¢ ♿
202 West Queen Street, 27932

Tel: 919–482–8945

Sailors and landlubbers alike will enjoy a stay at the Captain's Quarters, a Colonial Revival home built in 1907, and restored as an inn by Bill and Phyllis Pepper in 1993. Guest rooms are furnished with period reproductions; the nautical motif is carried throughout the inn. The Captain Perk's room has a massive queen-size four-poster bed, with matching floral comforter and curtains and an Oriental rug, while the Captain Anne Bonney room is done in crisp forest green and white, with coordinating stripes and florals and white wicker furniture.

Continental breakfast is served weekdays at 7:30 A.M. to accommodate business travelers; full breakfasts are served from 8–9:30 A.M., and on Sunday, a multi-course buffet is set out at 9 A.M. Four-course dinners are served by reservation, or you can take the dinner cruise at 6 P.M. with Captain Bill.

"A short walk to downtown Edenton or the waterfront; quiet neighborhood." *(Margaret Orndorff)* "Afternoon snacks included brownies, cheese and crackers, and tea, soda, beer, and wine. Hot water was ample, the pressure good; good lighting throughout the inn." *(Alexandra Hoseet)* "Amenities included candies, shampoo, toothpaste, and bubble bath." *(Kevin & Kris Ross)* "Hearty breakfast of freshly squeezed orange juice, a choice of buttermilk pancakes with sausage, a seafood souffle omelet, or Southern casserole of cornmeal grits, eggs, cheese, and ham. The lovely wraparound porch with wicker furniture is inviting whether you want to sit and read, talk or swing." *(Jack & Fran Fuchs)* "The owners were pleasant and outgoing, knowledgeable about local attractions and history. Our room was immaculate and fully stocked; the whirlpool tub was a real treat." *(Walt Jenkins)* "Firm, comfortable beds. We were treated to wine and munchies upon arrival, and to afternoon tea on our second day." *(Tom & Loretta Beaumont)*

From the Nothing's Perfect Department: "The contemporary living room furnishings didn't quite seem in period."

Open All year.

Rooms 1 suite, 7 doubles—all with private bath and/or shower, telephone, clock, TV, air-conditioning, fan. 2 with desk. Suite with whirlpool tub.

Facilities Dining room with fireplace, living room with fireplace, books, TV/VCR; lobby, porch. Off-street parking, garden, bicycles. 3 blocks to Albermarle Sound for sailing. Golf nearby.

Location On Rte. 17, in historic district, 1 block from town. From Norfolk VA, take Rte. 17 S to last Edenton exit (5th one). Turn left onto Rte. 17 Bus. (W. Queen St.). Just past Moseley St. (at 3.3 m), look for inn sign on left. Inn is 1 house before 1st traffic light.

Restrictions No traffic noise at night. No smoking. Children over 7.

Credit cards MC, Visa.

Rates B&B, $85 suite, $65–75 double, $55–65 single. Extra person, $10. 2-night minimum holiday weekends. Tips appreciated. Sailing, dinner cruises; 10% discount for overnight guests. Prix fixe dinner, $18. Mystery, Sail & Snooze weekends.

Extras Wheelchair access; 1 room specially equipped.

The Lords Proprietors' Inn 🏃 ♿

300 North Broad Street, 27932

Tel: 919–482–3641
800–348–8933
Fax: 919–482–2432

Since they first opened The Lords Proprietors' Inn in 1981, Arch and Jane Edwards have renovated three adjacent Victorian buildings. Rooms are furnished with antiques, and beds have been specially constructed by local cabinetmakers. Chef Kevin Yokley now prepares dinners at the inn; a recent meal included smoked salmon; green salad; veal stuffed with goat cheese and sundried tomatoes; and chocolate pecan pie.

"A lovely old inn, tastefully decorated with quality period antiques, supplemented by overstuffed reading chairs in the parlors. Early risers will find the parlors an inviting place for reading." *(John Blewer)* "We breakfasted in a separate one-story dining house, where we enjoyed fresh fruit, orange juice, coffee, and eggs." *(Bruce Campbell)* "I enjoyed canoeing in a nearby mill pond, exploring the world of cypress swamps and beaver dams under a canopy of Spanish moss, then returning at the end of the day to a room in the Pack House. Simple rag rugs from North Carolina's mountains contrast with handsome antiques and fit perfectly with the wide floor boards. The rooms are wonderfully spacious, with high ceilings, skylights, and original windows; the bathroom was a pleasure, with a large shower and a separate bathtub." *(Rick Larson)* "Furnished in an eclectic country Victorian manner, our room was comfortable and quiet, even though it is on the main street. Lovely back garden; delicious breakfast of sour cream waffles and sausage. Iced tea and homemade cookies available all day in the sitting room." *(Julia & Dennis Mallach)* "Delicious French toast with blueberry sauce." *(D.J. Farrington)* "I appreciated the privacy afforded by a larger inn, although travelers who enjoy lots of owner contact might disagree." *(BK)* Reports needed.

Open All year.
Rooms 20 doubles—all with full private bath, telephone, TV, air-conditioning. Most with desk. Rooms in 3 adjacent buildings.
Facilities 4 parlors, all with fireplace, 1 dining/meeting room, gift shop, patios, 2 guest kitchens. 1.5 acres. Docks, marinas, golf, tennis, river for fishing, swimming nearby. 1 hr. to Outer Banks beaches.
Location Center of Historic District. Follow Hwy 17 until it becomes Broad St. Inn is 6 blocks N of waterfront at corner of Albemarle & Broad Sts.
Restrictions No smoking in dining room or guest rooms. "Well-behaved children welcome." Central AC; most windows don't open.
Credit cards None accepted.
Rates B&B, $80–120 double, $60–70 single. Extra person, $20. MAP, (Tues.–Sat.) $140–180 double. Winter weekend package.
Extras 1 room has wheelchair access and equipped for disabled. Airport/station pickup. Portable crib, babysitting.

ELIZABETH CITY

Information please: Elizabeth City is located 45 miles south of Norfolk, on the Pasquotank River in the Albemarle area. **The Culpepper Inn** (609 West Main Street, Elizabeth City, 27909; 919–335–1993) is a Colonial Revival home, built in the 1930s, with a large swimming pool added in the 1980s. Some of the 11 guest rooms have king-sized beds, soaking tubs, and fireplaces. A sample breakfast menu includes fruit with lemon yogurt sauce, apple puff pastry, sausages, scrambled eggs with mushrooms and Brie, cranberry muffins, orange juice, coffee and teas. B&B double rates ranges from $85–95. Reports needed.

FLAT ROCK

Highland Lake Inn 🧍 🚫 ♿
Highland Lake Drive, P.O. Box 1026, 28731

Tel: 704–693–6812
800–762–1376
Fax: 704–696–8951

Founded as a private club in 1910, Highland Lake was for many years a military school, then a summer camp, and was restored as an inn and conference center in 1985 by Kerry Lindsey. Kerry's brother Larc is in charge of the kitchen, and menus balance Southern favorites with creative dishes that use produce from the inn's extensive gardens. For breakfast, guests might enjoy poached eggs on black bean cakes with yellow grits or apple-lemon pancakes with cider syrup. A typical dinner might consist of carrot tarragon soup, lettuce with raspberry vinaigrette, lamb chops with lime sauce, grilled vegetables with sesame sauce, and walnut pie with whipped cream.

"A wonderful family place. Our kids loved the many cats, dogs, peacocks, goats, cows, horses, ducks, and geese. Nice swimming pool, lake for canoeing and fishing, big vegetable garden which contributed to the delicious meals, and rocking chairs on the porches of the rustic but comfortable cabins. The all-inclusive rates ensure that you're not charged extra for every activity. Nice people, pretty area, and interesting things around to see. Live piano music in the dining room, and hammocks all around the grounds. Very safe, fun, and relaxing." *(Celia McCullough)*

Open All year.

Rooms 15 cottages, 10 suites, 39 doubles—all with full private bath, radio, clock, air-conditioning. Most with telephone, fan. Some with TV, desk, balcony, fireplace, refrigerator. Rooms in 12 buildings.

Facilities Restaurant, dining room, living room, family room, guest kitchen, laundry facilities, porch. Weekend piano in restaurant. 180 acres with organic gardens, farm animals, swimming pool, tennis, rope swing, tree swing, lawn games, Ping Pong, walking trails, high elements ropes course, bicycles, lake with canoes, fishing, paddle boats, swimming. 9-hole golf course across street.

Location W NC, Blue Ridge Mts. 45 min. S of Asheville, 50 min. N of Greenville, SC, 2 m S of Hendersonville. 2 min. to historic district. Take I-40 or I-85 to I-26, Exit 22. Follow Upward Rd. SW. After crossing Rte. 176, name changes to Highland Lake Rd. Watch for inn on left at waterfall. From Hendersonville, take Rte. 25 S to Flat Rock. Continue to Pinecrest Presbyterian Church on left & turn left on Highland Lake Rd. to inn on right.

Restrictions No smoking.

Credit cards Amex, Discover, MC, Visa.

Rates All-inclusive rates. Room only, $140–185 suite, $65–109 double, $59–99 single. Extra person, $10. B&B, $158–203 suite, $83–127 double, $68–108 single. Extra person, $19. MAP, $208–253 suite, $133–177 double, $93–133 single. Extra person, $44. Children under 5, free. 2-night minimum weekends. Prix fixe lunch, $12, prix fixe dinner, $24.

Extras Wheelchair access; 1 cottage, 8 guest rooms specially equipped. Crib.

GERMANTOWN

Meadowhaven Bed & Breakfast   *Tel:* 910–593–3996
N.C. Highway 8, P.O. Box 222, 27019-0222

A contemporary home built in 1976, Meadowhaven was purchased by Darlene and Sam Fain in 1992; in 1994 four cottages were completed. Guests in the main house are served a breakfast of banana-walnut pancakes, waffles, or quiches, with fruit, and freshly baked goods; cottage guests have a continental breakfast delivered to their door. Rates also include afternoon refreshments and turndown service.

"Great hosts: Darlene is friendly and efficient; Sam is entertaining and an excellent cook." *(Deborah & David Scharf)* "The grounds are welcoming and well kept. The handsome indoor swimming pool is home to several pet birds, one of whom welcomes you saying, 'Hi, sweety!' The guest pantry is stocked with snacks, sodas, and herbal teas. Decks at the back of the house face a private pond and the mountains." *(J. Gillease)* "The Loft Room is the inn's smallest, but it was comfortable and cozy. We relaxed in the hot tub outside on the huge deck. Breakfast was served at 8:30 A.M. to 10:00 A.M., and included eggs, bacon, zucchini bread, and biscuits." *(Sue & Steve Johnson)* "Attention to guests' comfort extends from the welcoming snacks to evening turndown service and the large fluffy robes." *(Richard Blockley)* "Special touches include popcorn and hot chocolate before bed." *(Bob & Sally Glenn)*

Area for improvement: "A restaurant close by for lunch or dinner."

Open All year.
Rooms 4 cabins, 3 doubles—all with private bath and/or shower, radio, clock, TV/VCR, desk, air-conditioning, fan. Most with balcony/deck. Cabins with kitchen, fireplace, heart-shaped Jacuzzi. 3 with telephone.
Facilities Dining room, living room with fireplace, TV, game room with TV, books, magazines, movie library; deck with hot tub. Fax, copy service. 25 acres with indoor swimming pool, gazebo, lawn games, fishing pond (equipment available). Tennis, golf, fly-fishing, hiking, rock climbing, canoeing, tubing nearby.
Location Piedmont foothills. 16 m N of Winston-Salem. Take US 52 N to Germantown Rd. Exit at NC Hwy. 8N. Go left, drive 7.6 m. Go left on NC Hwy. 8 again at Germantown Texaco. Go N for 8.5 m. Sign on left.
Restrictions No smoking in main house. Children over 12.
Credit cards Amex, MC, Visa.
Rates B&B, $125–225 cabins, $65–95 double. Extra person, $25. 2-night minimum holiday, special events, Thur.–Sun. in cabins.
Extras Contained or outside pets allowed. Spanish spoken.

GRASSY CREEK

Also recommended: In the northwest corner of North Carolina, near the Virginia border, is the **River House** (1896 Old Field Creek Road, 28631; 910–982–2109), on the North Fork of the New River. Just off Route 16, the inn has nearly a mile of riverfront for wading, tubing, canoeing and fishing. "While the furnishings are simple, the welcome is warm and the food is elegant. The hosts mingle with their guests, and you have the feel of being entertained at a private party. The large porches are good for conversation." *(Sibyl Nestor, also Chris Wise)* B&B double rates for the nine guest rooms, some with whirlpool tubs, range from $75–110. The inn's restaurant has an excellent reputation.

HENDERSONVILLE

Nestled between the Great Smoky and Blue Ridge Mountains, Hendersonville is both a popular resort and an active farming community.

Throughout the 19th century, wealthy southerners took refuge from the summer heat in the fresh mountain air, building summer homes and hotels. Today's visitors enjoy hiking in nearby Chimney Rock Park, as well as the town's many summer festivals, highlighted by the North Carolina Apple Festival, a ten-day event held through Labor Day. There's an excellent theater in neighboring Flat Rock, and on Monday nights, Hendersonville closes sections of Main Street for two hours of clogging and square dancing. The home of Carl Sandburg, also in Flat Rock, is worth seeing.

Hendersonville is in western North Carolina, 20 miles south of Asheville via I-26.

Information please: Under the ownership of experienced innkeepers Frank and Karen Kovacik is the **Echo Mountain Inn** (2849 Laurel Park Highway, 28739; 704–693–9626), a century-old stone and wood structure atop Echo Mountain. The inn has a full-service restaurant with views of Hendersonville below; 32 guest rooms are in the original structure and a newer addition. If you're in the area, stop by and let us know how they're doing.

For an additional area entry, see **Flat Rock**, five minutes away.

Waverly Inn ¢ 👫	*Tel:* 704–693–9193
783 North Main Street, 28792	800–537–8195
	Fax: 704–692–1010

Built as a boarding house in 1898, the Waverly Inn is the oldest surviving inn in Hendersonville, and it is listed on the National Register of Historic Places. The inn offers spacious porches—upstairs and down—for rocking, a striking Eastlake staircase in the foyer, and guest rooms comfortably decorated with king- and queen-sized lace-canopied rice beds, spindle beds, and white wicker, along with some dressers from its boarding house days. John and Diane Sheiry bought the inn in 1988, and came to it in an interesting way: both had worked in the hotel and restaurant business on the corporate level, and when John went back to school for his MBA, his thesis was on the operation and marketing of country inns. By the time he graduated, the Sheirys were ready to start a new life as innkeepers.

"John and Diane made every effort to see to our needs: they made dinner reservations, suggested places to visit, and had our wine chilled for us at the end of the day." *(G. Kemp Liles)* "Spectacular whole grain blueberry pancakes; the menu choices enable you to eat like a bird or a beast." *(Charles & Martha Jean Liberto)* "The upstairs sitting room was convenient for watching TV; hot and cold soft drinks were available all day." *(Carol Guidi)* "This old house on a tree-lined street has charming rooms decorated with floral themes. The Dogwood room had a canopied bed, with wicker chairs out on the porch." *(Theresa Boyd)* "Every evening at 5:00 P.M., guests gather on the front porch for wine, cheese and crackers. The Waverly is located in downtown Hendersonville across the street from a beautiful church. We sat on the front porch, sipping hot chocolate and watching the Christmas parade." *(Michael & Donna Smith)*

Open All year.
Rooms 1 suite, 14 doubles—all with private bath and shower, telephone, radio, desk, fan, air-conditioning. Some with TV.

Facilities Dining room, living room, library, 3 TV rooms, porches. ⅓ acre with lawn. Tennis, golf, horseback riding, nearby.

Location 20 m S of Asheville. 2 blocks from Historic District. On Main St. between 7th and 8th Aves.

Restrictions No smoking in dining room. Midweek traffic at 8:00 A.M. & 5:00 P.M.

Credit cards Amex, Discover, MC, Visa.

Rates B&B, $110–145 suite, $75–89 double, $50–65 single. Extra person, $10; no charge for children under 12. Senior, AAA discount. Weekend theme packages.

Extras Station pickup. Crib, highchair.

HICKORY

Hickory B&B ¢   *Tel:* 704–324–0548
464 Seventh Street SW, 28602   800–654–0548
                                           Fax: 704–345–1112

Known for its many area furniture manufacturers and discount retailers, Hickory is located about halfway between Winston-Salem and Asheville. A Georgian-style home built in 1908, the Hickory B&B has been owned by Bob and Suzanne Ellis since 1991, and is highlighted by the original high ceilings, wainscotting, crown moldings, bevelled windows, and oak and heart pine floors. Breakfast includes juice, fresh fruit, freshly baked muffins and bread, breakfast meats, coffee and tea, plus puffed pancakes topped with fresh fruits, or baked French toast. Afternoon refreshments include homemade pecan pie, lemon meringue pie, blueberry or peach cobbler.

"Bob and Suzanne Ellis are a delightful couple who welcome you into their Christian home. Huge, delicious breakfasts. The inn is shaded by huge old trees; lots of songbirds." *(Dianna Lewis)* "Guest rooms are decorated with pretty pastel colors, dhurri rugs, some antiques, and country decor." *(Ann Higgs)* "Spacious rooms with large beds, new mattresses, modern bathrooms." *(SB)* "Bob and Suzanne Ellis were gracious and helpful with information and directions. In the afternoon, iced tea and lemonade are served with warm treats from the oven." *(Janet & Rob Patterson, also Sammy Estridge)*

Open All year.

Rooms 1 suite, 3 doubles—all with private bath and/or shower, clock, fan. 2 with fireplace, 1 with radio, desk.

Facilities Dining room, parlor with piano, TV/VCR; library with fireplace, books; family room. 1¼ acres with off-street parking, swimming pool. Golf, lake with swimming, fishing, boating, nearby.

Location 1 hr. N of Charlotte, 1½ hr. E of Asheville, 1 hr. W of Winston-Salem. 5–10 mins. from town. From Hwy. 70, go right onto 4th St. Go left onto 6th Ave. SW. Go right onto Seventh St. SW.

Restrictions No smoking. No alcohol. Children over 11.

Credit cards None accepted.

Rates B&B, $60–70, $55 double. 2-night minimum stay.

Extras Local airport pickup.

HIGHLANDS

Highlands is in western North Carolina, 125 miles north of Atlanta, and 60 miles southwest of Asheville. The town has auction galleries, antique shops, and summer theater, along with hiking, tennis, swimming, horseback riding, fishing, white-water rafting, an 18-hole Arnold Palmer golf course, and skiing. Surrounded by national forest lands, it has little of the commercialism found in other tourist areas. Because of its 4000-foot elevation in the Blue Ridge mountains, the mean temperature is around 75°, making for comfortable days and cool nights.

Reader tips: "One of the prettiest towns of the Blue Ridge Mountains. Highlands is a marvelous place in summer—cool, fresh, and with lots of charming little shops. There are many hiking trails nearby, and the people in the hiking store will advise you on the level of difficulty." *(SN)* "This is waterfall country, and Smoky Mountains National Park is just a one-hour drive away." *(ML)* "We were surprised at the high quality of Highlands' restaurants—for such a small town, they were very good and surprisingly sophisticated." *(MS)*

Colonial Pines Inn ¢
Hickory Street, Route 1, Box 22B, 28741

Tel: 704–526–2060

Chris and Donna Alley moved from Atlanta in 1984 and renovated this old farmhouse, adding modern baths and furnishing it with antique and modern country furnishings.

"Donna maintains just the right balance between helping her guests and staying out of the way until needed. We relaxed on the spotless porch swing, gazing out at the mountains." *(Antonia Bernstein)* "Donna's attention to detail makes the difference between adequate and special." *(Sibyl Nestor)* "The inn is set back from the road on a hillside, offering beautiful mountain views from a three-sided porch. Donna's little extras made our stay delightful—from the constant aroma of cinnamon and fresh-baked bread, to local directions and advice. Comfortable beds; great breakfasts of fresh fruits, homemade breads, delicious sausage or ham, eggs, and excellent coffee." *(Mark Lampe)* "Friendly, knowledgeable innkeepers; excellent breakfast served with a smile; ample parking; and wonderful mountain views from nearly all rooms." *(James & Christy Collins, also BB)* Comments please.

Open All year.
Rooms 1 suite, 4 doubles, 1 single—all with private bath and/or shower. Suite with TV. 3-bedroom guest house with fireplace, kitchen, patio, TV, telephone.
Facilities Dining room, living room with TV, grand piano, books; porches. 2 acres with picnic table, berry picking.
Location ½ m from town. From Main St. take Hwy. 64 E. Go 6 blocks and turn right on Hickory St. to inn at corner.
Restrictions No smoking. Children over 12 in inn.
Credit cards MC, Visa.
Rates B&B, $125–200 guest house (sleeps 6), $85–95 suite, $65–75 double, $50–65 single. Extra person, $10. 2-night minimum holidays, peak weekends. Off-season specials.

Long House B&B
Highway 64E; Route 2, Box 638
P.O. Box 2078, 28741

Tel: 704–526–4394
800–833–0020

Built in the 1920s, Lynn and Valerie Long restored this log home as a B&B in 1986. "Lynn and Valerie are congenial hosts, furnishing us with restaurant menus and information about area hikes and waterfalls. Lynn cooked a hearty, delicious family-style breakfast of apple pancakes with cinnamon sauce, eggs, sausage, bowls of fresh fruit, plus fresh orange juice blended with fruit. Valerie's quilts and needlework grace this beautiful cabin. Our room had a large deck overlooking a forest of blooming rhododendrons." *(Caroline Heider)* "Our charming country-style room was clean and roomy with a rabbit motif. Outstanding breakfasts served on beautiful, locally hand-made pottery." *(Jean & Jack Shelling)* "Friendly, down-home comfortable atmosphere." *(Judy Rosser)* "No air-conditioning, but it cools off nicely at night. Great breakfast and warm, welcoming people." *(Susan Doucet)*

Open All year.
Rooms 4 doubles—all with private bath and/or shower, clock, fan. 3 with deck, 2 with desk.
Facilities Dining room, living room with fireplace, TV/VCR, stereo; porch. 2 acres with off-street parking. Hiking nearby.
Location 1.5 m to town. On Hwy. 64.
Restrictions No smoking.
Credit cards MC, Visa.
Rates B&B, $55–95. Extra person, $15. 2-night weekend minimum. Midweek off-season discounts.
Extras Crib. Babysitting possible.

Old Edwards Inn & Highlands Inn ¢ ✗ ♠ ♿
Main Street, P.O. Box 1030, 28741

Tel: 704–526–5036
704–526–9380
Off-season: 912–638–8892

Rip and Pat Benton renovated the Central House Restaurant, in the original part of the Old Edwards Inn (over 100 years old), then the guest rooms, and finally the Highlands Inn across the road. The decor is primarily Victorian, with antique furnishings, hand-stenciling, and period wall-coverings in every guest room.

"Our hand-stenciled room had a fresh nosegay of flowers, little candies and a selection of bath amenities." *(Leah Fleenor)* "Delicious food served piping hot. I had baked scallops in dill sauce, and the inn's justly famous bread pudding in rum sauce. The breakfast buffet is perfect for those who like to rise and eat at their own pace. We enjoyed coffee on the porch as we watched the town wake up." *(Carol Guidi)* "We were pleased with the service and food, especially the locally caught trout." *(Teresa Hall)* "The hotel is right in the middle of this attractive town with its delightful old buildings and upscale shops. Guest rooms are beautifully decorated and very welcoming, most with four-poster beds, well-chosen drapes and antique furniture; many have delightful views of the streets of the town. The large sitting room has a huge carved stone fireplace with a roaring log fire. Guests gather for good conversation and delicious snacks, left there to attract those (like me) with no self control. A large moose head stands guard over the fireplace. Breakfast is taken across the road at the Highlands Hotel. The main dining room in the inn is equally welcoming, and the food is freshly cooked and imaginatively prepared. The house trademark is the hush puppy—not, as a Brit might think, an old shoe, but a deep fried doughy bun with a delicious cinnamon taste." *(Richard Gollin)* "Most rooms have beautiful footed tubs, and only a few have a shower; washing your hair in an antique tub can be quite an experience!" *(CG)* "Our spacious room overlooking Main Street had a sitting area, and a separate bathroom and shower room. Friendly, helpful staff; delicious buffet breakfasts." *(Jo-Ann Johnson)*

Open April through Nov.
Rooms 50 suites and doubles—all with private tub or shower. Some with ceiling fan, balcony. Rooms in 2 buildings.
Facilities Restaurant. Golf nearby.
Location About 40 m SW of Asheville. In town.
Restrictions Light sleepers should request rooms away from street. Children welcome at Highlands.
Credit cards Amex, MC, Visa for payment, not reservations.
Rates B&B, $79–89 suite, $69–89 double. Weekly, rates available.
Extras Highlands Inn with wheelchair access. Crib, babysitting.

HILLSBOROUGH

Hillsborough House Inn
209 East Tryon Street, P.O. Box 880, 27278

Tel: 919–644–1600

The Hillsborough House has been in Bev and Katherine Webb's family for all but one year of the last 140, and was known as the Webb-Matheson mansion until they restored it as an inn in 1989. Katherine utilized her training as an artist to design a new gallery entryway to keep the splendid front porch free for quiet sitting and rocking; the new space displays contemporary art and treasures salvaged from another family home. She constructed the canopy and four-poster beds so that they would conceal trundle beds beneath and draped the frames with coordinating fabrics; the bathroom floors are painted to look like marble. The Webbs have also converted the brick summer kitchen, built in 1790, into a romantic cottage, with a queen-size bed set in a bower of white branches.

Katherine's creative streak also appears at breakfast, when the menu might include puff pastry filled with sweetened cream cheese, raisins, and nuts; a breakfast pizza topped with custard and fruit; or granola in cookie form with oatmeal, raisins, nuts, carrots, and pumpkins seeds; accompanied by mango and kiwi, homemade muffins and breads (maybe molasses oatmeal or an egg braid), a Havarti or farmer's cheese, and a selection of coffees and teas.

"Bev and Katherine are the perfect host and hostess. Katherine's artistic talents add an eclectic air to this old-fashioned home." *(Ada Lea Dew)* "A peaceful, comfortable haven with impeccable, unobtrusive service. Children will love the period-style playhouse under the trees in the garden. Comfortable bed; housekeeping, plumbing, and lighting were all fine.

Delicious homemade jams, preserves, and cheese served for breakfast." *(Judith Marshall)* "Our room was glorious with a canopied bed, fresh flowers, beautiful linens, and tons of magazines. Super breakfast. Katherine is exceptionally attentive to her guests' wishes. When she learned that we enjoy an early morning cup of coffee, Katherine had put out a tray with two mugs and the fixings. Great coffee." *(Bernard Cohen)*

Open All year.
Rooms 1 cottage, 5 doubles—all with private bath and/or shower, clock radio, desk, air-conditioning, ceiling fan. Some with gas fireplace, porch. Cottage with Jacuzzi tub, TV, wet bar with refrigerator.
Facilities Dining room, living room/library with fireplace, den with TV/VCR, games; guest kitchen. 7 acres with swimming pool, volleyball, basketball, croquet. Golf nearby.
Location From I-85, take Exit 164 (or from I-40, take Exit 261). Follow Hillsborough signs to Churton St. At 6th stop light, turn right onto East Tryon St. At the second stop sign, turn left into driveway.
Restrictions No smoking. Children over 9.
Credit cards MC, Visa.
Rates B&B, $165 suite, $95–105 double. Extra person, $25.
Extras Some French spoken.

HOT SPRINGS

Also recommended: About 20 miles north of Asheville is the **Duckett House** (P.O. Box 441, Hot Springs, 28743; 704–622–7621). Set in the Unaka Mountains, the inn is close to the Appalachian Trail for hiking, as well as white water rafting, swimming and the Hot Springs Mineral Baths. "A real find. The rooms were very nicely decorated, and the inn was spotless." *(Joe Schmidt)* Double rates are $60 a night and include a full breakfast.

LAKE LURE

Also recommended: The Blue Ridge Mountains and Lake Lure offer such activities as hiking, boating, water sports, golf or tennis. The **Lake Lure Inn** (P.O. Box 10, 28746; 704–625–2525 or 800–277–5873) is a 50-room inn decorated with a Euro-Mediterranean touch, plus a swimming pool, gardens and solariums to enjoy. "An excellent dining room and pleasant pool." *(Celia McCullough)* B&B double rates range from $59–109; children under 12 stay free.

Lodge on Lake Lure   *Tel:* 704–625–2789
Charlotte Drive, Route 1, P.O. Box 529A, 28746   800–733–2785
                                                        Fax: 704–625–2421

Originally built in 1932 as a refuge for (not from) the North Carolina Highway Patrol, the Lodge at Lake Lure offers rest and relaxation amid spectacular scenery on the shores of this 27-mile-long crystal clear lake; it's owned by Jack and Robin Stanier.

"Set off the main road in a quiet setting with spectacular mountains and lake views from the delightfully cheerful breakfast room. We enjoyed a breakfast of fresh fruit, juice, eggs and bacon, home-baked breads, preserves, and coffee. The spacious great room has a stone fireplace that can hold eight-foot logs, with a millstone set in the stone chimney. Equally relaxing is the deck at the lake's edge." *(Betty Norman)* "Rooms are attractive, clean and cozy. Robin and Jack are the perfect hosts to preside over a lodge of this type—you're on your own, but if you want their friendly conversation and hospitality, it's there." *(Janet Lorentz)* "Instead of the pontoon boat, we usually opt for one of the canoes to paddle out on the lake for a private lunch. The innkeepers help us out with basket, napkins—whatever we need." *(Cynthia Bettridge)* "Delicious breakfasts are served in an enclosed porch with magnificent views of the lake and the mountains beyond. Three huge, yet charming public rooms; one has a large fireplace that became a focal point on chilly evenings." *(Phyllis Salesky)*

Open All year.
Rooms 1 suite, 10 doubles—all with private bath and/or shower, fan.
Facilities Living room with fireplace, piano; breakfast room; game room with TV; porch, deck. 3 acres with trails, lake swimming, pontoon boat, canoes, boats for fishing. Tennis, 12 golf courses nearby.
Location Blue Ridge Mts. foothills. 25 m SE of Asheville, 90 m W of Charlotte. From Hwy. 64/74, turn at Lake Lure fire station opposite the golf course. Follow signs to lodge.
Restrictions Smoking restricted to den. One child per room.
Credit cards Amex, Discover, MC, Visa.
Rates B&B, $95–105 suite, $80–90 double. Extra person, $15. 10% Senior discount. 2-3 night weekend/holiday minimum. Weekly discount.
Extras Crib. Spanish spoken.

LAKE TOXAWAY

Greystone Inn 🛏 ✕ 🦆
Greystone Lane, 28747

Tel: 704–966–4700
800–824–5766
Fax: 704–862–5689

The Greystone is one of North Carolina's most expensive inns, but if you're looking for a truly extravagant mountain getaway, you may find it the perfect choice. Offering luxurious country inn atmosphere in a modern resort setting, the Greystone was established in 1985 by Timothy Lovelace. The inn includes a 1915 Swiss Revival summer mansion, a second building, the Hillmont, a modern structure built to blend in with the style of the original mansion, and the Cottage, a lakeside home adjacent to Hillmont with two suites. The area is being developed for home sites with a private club, and only homeowners and inn guests can use the facilities. Rates include a full breakfast, afternoon tea, and dinner, served in the newly built restaurant, just ten yards from the lake with lovely views from its numerous windows. There's no extra charge for use of any of the sports facilities except for peak season golf; a highlight is

253

the lake cruise which leaves every day at 5 P.M., with a skipper to recount tales of the lake's history.

"The enormous Astor Room, an upper-level corner room in the Hillmont, has a cathedral-ceilinged room, a sitting area with sofa and chairs in front of a large fireplace, a king-sized bed, a huge bathroom with Jacuzzi, and a wet bar complete with coffee maker. The furnishings were of excellent quality. French doors opened out onto a spacious covered private deck with wicker furniture, which looks out through the trees onto the lake. Standard-size rooms in the mansion were smaller, although ample." *(Barry Gardner, also DLG)* "Not only did we enjoy breakfast and dinner, we played tennis, golf, and went canoeing. The common rooms were particularly delightful. Afternoon tea and coffee were served on the covered porch furnished with white wicker, and there was always a fire roaring in the reception area. Soft drinks and ice were available in the library/game room." *(Deborah Ross)*

Open May through Nov.
Rooms 1 2-bedroom cottage, 2 suites, 30 doubles—all with full private bath, telephone, radio, TV, fan. 17 with air-conditioning, 16 with Jacuzzi, fireplace; 13 with wet bar. Some with private entrance, terrace or balcony; 19 rooms in main house, 12 rooms in annex.
Facilities Restaurant with fireplace, lounge with piano entertainment nightly, living room with fireplace, piano; library. 5,000 acres with 640-acre lake, heated swimming pool, 6 tennis courts, 18-hole golf course, croquet, all water sports, children's program, horseback riding.
Location W NC. 50 m SW of Asheville, between Brevard and Cashiers. 2½ hrs. NW of Atlanta, GA. Turn off Rte. 64 onto Greystone La. & go 3.3 m N to inn.
Restrictions Dry county; BYOB.
Credit cards Amex, MC, Visa.
Rates MAP, $270–460 suite (for two persons), $220–425 double. Child rates. 15% service. 2-night weekend minimum. Weekly, off-season, mid-week discounts. Off-season golf packages.
Extras Airport pickup, $40 round trip. Crib, babysitting.

LINVILLE

Eseeola Lodge
Linville, 28646

Tel: 704–733–4311
800–742–6717

Listed on the National Register of Historic Places, the Eseeola Lodge is an old-time mountain retreat, built in 1926 in the shadow of Grandfather Mountain; its name is Cherokee for "cliffy or craggy river." Guest rooms are furnished with handmade quilts and antiques, and the rates include nightly turndown service, fresh flowers, and bathrobes. Breakfasts offer everything from fresh berries to hearty omelets and waffles; dinner choices include both French and regional dishes. John Blackburn is the long-time general manager.

"An unspoiled area with a minimum of fast-food joints or chain motels." *(WL)* "Many guests come here for the golf or the fall foliage. Old-fashioned Southern atmosphere. Popular seafood buffet on Thursday nights. Flexible serving times: 7–9:30 A.M. for breakfast, 7–9 P.M. for dinner. If you have room for lunch, it's available at the golf club, one block from the lodge. Our first-floor room was cool and comfortable." *(Trina Welin)*

Open Mid-May–mid-Oct.
Rooms 1 cottage, 26 doubles, 3 singles—all with private bath, telephone, radio, TV, desk, hair dryer; most with private porch.
Facilities Restaurant with fireplace, lobby. 18-hole Donald Ross golf course, croquet court, tennis courts, heated swimming pool, fishing, hiking trails, playground. Children's program, mid-June–mid-Aug.
Location NW NC, Blue Ridge Mts., High Country. 70 m NE of Asheville, 100 m NW of Charlotte, 100 m W of Winston-Salem.
Restrictions Traffic noise in some rooms. Dress code at dinner. BYOB.
Credit cards MC, Visa.
Rates MAP, $300–375 cottage, $200–270 double, $140–250 single. Extra person, $40. 15% service. June, Sept, Oct. mid-week golf package.
Extras Cribs, babysitting. Airport/station pickups.

LITTLE SWITZERLAND

Big Lynn Lodge ¢ ♁ &
Highway 226A, P.O. Box 459, 28749–0459

Tel: 704–765–6771
800–654–5232

Set at an altitude of 3,100 feet, Big Lynn is known for its beautiful views, fine food, comfortable accommodations, and reasonable rates. Named for the 600-year-old Linden tree that once shaded the main lodge, Big Lynn was bought by Gale and Carol Armstrong in 1989. Gale reports that "our elevation keeps us cool and mosquito-free all summer. Our primary market is retired people, but families with pre-teen children also enjoy it here. We take pride in our food service, and extra helpings are offered." While the Armstrongs have upgraded and refurbished a number of the rooms, and have built four spacious condos, most accommodations here are more a "view with a room" than the reverse.

Breakfast includes your choice of juice, fruit, coffee or tea, cereal, eggs to order with toast, grits, pancakes, or waffles. A typical fixed-menu dinner might include broiled trout or chicken, red-skinned potatoes, steamed broccoli and baby carrots, cole slaw, honey wheat rolls, and double chocolate cake with ice cream.

"The fresh trout from a local hatchery was delicious and we were surprised when the owner and chef came to our table to see if we would like seconds." *(Betty Norman)* "Big Lynn is not for those looking for historic buildings, meticulously restored and laden with antiques. My room was plain but comfortable and immaculate. The food is good, old-fashioned, wholesome home cooking. Breads are homemade, and desserts were difficult to refuse; the apple pie had a light, flaky, golden crust, with tart and well seasoned apples. But the best part of our stay was the friendly folks we met. The common rooms and grounds offer many places for spontaneous and spirited conversation." *(Linda Nelson)* "The entire staff is efficient, friendly, and genuinely dedicated to giving excellent service. Our clean, comfortable room was above average in size, comfortably furnished with two rocking chairs, good lighting, with good cross ventilation. Rest and relax, or use the inn as a base for interesting day trips." *(Sam Beckley)*

Open Mid-April–Nov. 1.

Rooms 4 suites, 21 doubles, 5 singles, 12 cabins—all with private bath and/or shower, telephone, radio, desk, fan. Most with porch. Condos with TV, air-conditioning, balcony, kitchen. Rooms in 13 buildings.

Facilities Restaurant, library with player piano, game room with fireplace, TV lounge, gift shop, porch, laundry. 22 acres with lawn games, hiking. Fishing, golf nearby.

Location W NC. 50 m NE of Asheville, on Blue Ridge Parkway; 5 m SW of Spruce Pine.

Restrictions No smoking in dining room; several non-smoking guest rooms.

Credit cards Discover, MC, Visa.

Rates MAP, $105 suite, $77 double, $68 single. Extra person, $22. No charge for children under 5. Alc breakfast, $6. Weekly, monthly rates.

Extras Limited wheelchair access. Crib. German spoken.

MAGGIE VALLEY

Also recommended: The 75-room **Maggie Valley Golf Resort** (Box 99, Maggie Valley, 28751; 704–926–1616 or 800–438–3861) is set in the Blue Ridge Mountains. "Excellent value. King-size bed, lovely room, fantastic mountain view overlooking the first tee. With a golf tournament in progress, we enjoyed the activity from our deck. Excellent restaurant on the premises. Gorgeous grounds with flower beds everywhere." *(Pat Borysiewisz)* Another good choice is the **Pioneer Village Resort** (Route 1, Box 405, Campbell Creek Road, 28751; 704–926–1881): "Welcoming owners. Twelve log cabins on 14 acres, some with several bedrooms, set in a large circle with a grassy area and picnic tables in the middle; some have mountain views, others overlook a mountain brook. Our cabin had a deck in back with two rocking chairs so we could sit with a cup of coffee and watch the water. The cabin was very clean, with country furnishings. Interesting display of antique farming equipment; enjoyed watching the horses graze. At night, we went to the Maggie Valley Stompin' Grounds to watch championship cloggers and Western dancing. A good place to eat is J. Arthur's Restaurant." *(PB)*

Information please: You don't have to go out West for a quality riding vacation—just mosey over to the **Cataloochee Ranch** (Route 1, Box 500F, Maggie Valley, 28751; 704–926–1401 or 800–868–1401). Owned by the same family since 1934, rustic accommodations are available in the historic main lodge, a newer lodge, and in seven two- and three-bedroom cabins. Many have wood-burning fireplaces, and are furnished with quilts and primitive or classic antiques. Hearty meals are served family style, using produce from the ranch gardens. The ranch is open from May 1–October 31; double rates of $115–340 include breakfast and dinner, while rides cost $27 for a half-day ride, $60 for full day. You'll explore the ranch's 1,000 acres, plus the 500,000 acres of the adjoining Great Smoky Mountains National Park. Additional activities include tennis, hiking, trout fishing, or soaking in the oversize hot tub. Cinnamon puffed toast is a breakfast classic, and dinners typically include a choice of trout or steak, turkey or pork, accompanied by just-baked bread, salad and vegetables with a fruit cobbler for dessert. Reports welcome.

MANTEO

Manteo is located on Roanoke Island of the Outer Banks, 90 miles south of Norfolk, Virginia, and is the long-time mercantile hub and government center of the Outer Banks. Travelers will want to visit the *Elizabeth II* (a reproduction of Sir Walter Raleigh's ship), the Fort Raleigh National Historic Site, and the Elizabethan Gardens; in summer, get tickets for the *Lost Colony*, an outdoor musical drama playing since 1937. Outdoor sports include tennis, golf, swimming, boating, fishing, and windsurfing.

Information please: Just opened in 1995 is the newly renovated **The White Doe Inn** (319 Sir Walter Raleigh Street, Box 1029, 27954; 919–473–9851), a Victorian home with eight guest rooms, each with private bath and a gas fireplace.

For additional area entries, see **Nag's Head**.

The Roanoke Island Inn   *Tel:* 919–473–5511
305 Fernando Street, 27954

Originally a small, simple island house built in the 1860s for owner John Wilson's great-great grandmother, the Roanoke has been expanded many times over the years, most recently in 1990, when it was restored and renovated as an inn; Ada Hadley is the longtime manager. Rates include a breakfast of juice, coffee, tea, cereal, muffins, and pastries, plus access to the innkeeper's pantry for beverages and light snacks.

"The inn provides guests with the privacy of outside entrances and a comfortable common room. Guests can enjoy breakfast or cocktails on a second-floor porch overlooking the waterfront. Our spacious, well-appointed, quiet room was furnished with a canopy bed, and had a view of the bay. The friendly, knowledgeable innkeepers were helpful with restaurant recommendations." *(Susan Hedeler)* "Immaculately maintained; warm, friendly, unobtrusive service. A wonderful frog pond and garden." *(Wade & Melissa Register)* "The front rooms have a boardwalk and harbor view; the back ones overlook a quaint yard with a pond." *(Daisy Glaus)*

Open Open Easter–"until we're tired."
Rooms 2 suites, 6 doubles—all with full private bath, telephone, radio, TV, desk, air-conditioning, fan. 2 with fireplace.
Facilities Living room with fireplace, books; innkeeper's pantry, porch. 1 acre with garden, frog/goldfish pond, off-street parking, harbor front; bicycles. 5-min. walk to sound swimming; 5-min. drive to Nag's Head ocean beaches.

Location In historic center, facing Shallowbag Bay. Take Hwy. 64 from W, or Hwy 158 from N to Outer Banks. Follow sign for *Elizabeth II* State Historic Site to Manteo. On waterfront at S end of boardwalk.

Restrictions Smoking permitted. Children welcome in family suites.

Credit cards MC, Visa.

Rates B&B, $78–108 suite, double. Extra person, $20. 2-night minimum most rooms; 3-night holiday weekends.

Extras Airport pickups. Some French spoken.

Tranquil House Inn 👪 ✕ ♿

Queen Elizabeth Street, P.O. Box 2045, 27954

Tel: 919–473–1404
800–458–7069
Fax: 919–473–1526

The Tranquil House was built in the style of its namesake 19th century inn, yet it is enhanced by the amenities 20th-century travelers expect and enjoy. The spacious rooms are decorated with reproduction lace-canopied, brass and four-poster beds, Oriental or Berber carpets, and handsome wallpapers; the bathrooms are all hand-tiled. Rates include a continental breakfast, plus evening wine and cheese. After a day of exploring, guests relax in the Adirondack chairs on the inn's ample verandas overlooking Shallowbag Bay. Don and Lauri just bought the inn in 1993; in 1994 they opened the 1587 Restaurant, offering water view tables and a creative menu; recent entrées included sesame-crusted tuna with wasabi vinaigrette; jerk pork with mango rum salsa; veal with chanterelle mushrooms; and pepper pasta with sun-dried tomatoes, mozzarella, and basil pesto. Appetizers and desserts are no less tempting.

"Relaxed atmosphere and beautifully decorated rooms. Location is ideal for access to the Outer Banks beaches, but close enough to Virginia for an easy trip to the city." *(Steven Lawson)* "Exceptionally clean and fresh; relaxing, quiet atmosphere; polite, helpful staff." *(Mr. & Mrs. Kenneth Wagner)* "Our room was beautifully decorated, spacious, and comfortable. The wine and cheese evenings were a plus. Breakfast on the deck was glorious." *(Lyn & Chip McNees)* "Good sunset views of the *Elizabeth II* from the second floor deck. Tasty breakfast of orange juice, fresh fruit, granola or wonderful homemade scones, served from 7:30–10:00 A.M." *(DLG)*

Open All year.

Rooms 2 suites, 23 doubles—all with full private bath, telephone, TV, desk, air-conditioning.

Facilities Lobby/living room with books; lookout room; porches. Bicycles, barbecue grill.

Location Coming from the north, take Rte. 158 to Whalebone Junction in Nags Head. Follow signs to Manteo, bearing right onto Rte. 64/264 W. Turn right at first traffic light on Sir Walter Raleigh St. to inn at harborfront.

Restrictions No smoking in lobby, some guest rooms.

Credit cards Amex, Discover, MC, Visa.

Rates B&B, $99–149 suite, $79–149 double. Extra person, $10. Children under 16 free in parents' room. 10% senior discount. Special packages. 2-night minimum weekends in season. Alc dinner, $20–30.

Extras Wheelchair access; some rooms equipped for disabled. Airport pickup. Crib, $10.

MARS HILL

Baird House ¢ 👫
Tel: 704–689–5722
41 South Main Street, P.O. Box 749, 28754

Innkeeper Yvette Wessel moved to North Carolina after years in the New York metropolitan area. She notes that "aside from parents of Mars Hill College students, winter skiers, and Appalachian Trail hikers, my guests are primarily those looking for a beautiful mountain getaway, and who like the rural quality of tiny Mars Hill, with cows and sheep grazing just yards from the house. Many also enjoy the summer repertory theater at Mars Hill College." Baird House was built in 1898 by Dr. John Baird; at that time it was the grandest house in the area, with servants' quarters, a 225-foot well with the "sweetest water in the world," and two kitchen gardens. This brick house has 18-inch-thick walls and is furnished with colorful antiques.

"A fine example of 19th-century architecture, combining period with modern convenience. Mrs. Wessel is a warm and gracious hostess, and an interesting, cosmopolitan individual." *(Dr. & Mrs. Robert McKiernan)* "The marvelous breakfasts are served at a mutually agreeable time and include homemade breads and granola, custards, fresh fruit, coffee, and tea. The decor is a beautiful mixture of traditional and antique furnishings." *(Nancy & Jack O'Connor)* "Ms. Wessel has gone out of her way to accommodate us when working hours have been unusual. Modern plumbing, lighting adequate. Guests are introduced at breakfast and interesting conversation always follows." *(Kelly Coleman)* "The old-fashioned garden is a joy and the owner will share cuttings with you." *(J. Preston Maynard)*

Open Jan. through Nov.
Rooms 1 suite, 4 doubles—2 with private bath or shower, 3 with maximum of 6 people sharing bath. 3 with desks, fan; 1 with TV, 2 with fireplace.
Facilities Dining room, living room both with fireplace; library, porch with rockers. 1/3 acre with patio. Tennis, swimming, fishing nearby. 10 m to downhill skiing.
Location W NC. 18 m N of Asheville. In center of town.
Credit cards Amex.
Rates B&B, $75 suite, $42–53 double. Extra person, $10 (must bring own sleeping bag). No charge for children under 12 in parents' room. Weekly rates.
Extras Crib. French spoken.

MOUNT AIRY

If you remember Andy Griffith's old sitcom, *Mayberry RFD*, you'll be interested to know that Mount Airy was Griffith's hometown and served as the inspiration for the show. Mount Airy is located about 35 miles northwest of Winston-Salem, a few miles south of the Virginia border, in the foothills of Blue Ridge Mountains.

Information please: For an escape to the woods, consider the **Pilot Knob Inn** (P.O. Box 1280, Pilot Mountain 27041; 910–325–2502), on the eastern slope of Pilot Mountain, about 8 miles southeast of Mount Airy.

Jim Rouse has painstakingly restored five century-old tobacco barns for overnight accommodations, combining rustic charm with antique furnishings, double Jacuzzi tubs, and a swimming pool. "Individual cabins, spaced for privacy, have a downstairs living area with a large stone fireplace; in winter, the porches are stocked with firewood. The main house holds a breakfast room and library. The deck is built into the trees, blending with the forest. Jim is well traveled and interesting to talk to. His parents help run the place and also work to make your stay comfortable." *(Sue Johnson)* B&B double rates are $100 midweek, $150 weekends.

Merritt House B&B ¢
618 North Main Street, 27030

Tel: 910–786–2174
800–290–6290
Fax: 910–786–2174

In 1901 William Merritt built a twelve-room, two-story red brick house meant to last for generations—complete with a steep hipped roof with bracketed eaves, tall paneled chimneys, wraparound porch, and a tower-like projecting bay. Restored by Rich and Pat Mangels and opened as a B&B in 1993, guest rooms are furnished with antiques and queen- or twin-size beds. One room is done in muted brick red and hunter green, with a rich paisley pattern accenting the walls and windows, and has a handsome four-poster bed, while another room is more feminine with a white iron bed, lace swags, and a pink, white, and soft green floral color scheme. Guests are welcomed with refreshments; in the morning, Pat and Rich serve a breakfast of fresh fruit and juice, perhaps quiche and sausage, fresh-baked muffins or bread, tea and coffee.

"Pleasant, extremely clean, comfortable, quiet and private. The gracious owners showed me around the whole house, with its lovely antiques." *(Laura Stiles)* "Informative, witty hosts; good conversations sitting on the front porch." *(George McCauley)* "Spacious rooms; we enjoyed the family memorabilia throughout the house. Magnificent breakfast." *(Dyanne & Robert Snyder)*

Open All year.
Rooms 4 doubles—2 with full private bath, 2 with maximum of 4 sharing bath. All with clock, air-conditioning, fan.
Facilities Dining room, living room with fireplace, TV, VCR, stereo; porch. ³/₄ acre with gardens, croquet, hot tub, smokehouse gift shop.
Location Downtown Mt. Airy Historic District. From I-77 take W Pine St. Go left onto Renfro St. Go left onto N Main St. to inn on corner.
Restrictions No smoking. No alcoholic beverages. Children over 12 preferred.
Credit cards MC, Visa.
Rates B&B, $55–75 double, $40–65 single. Extra person, $5. 10% senior discount. 15% midweek business discount.
Extras Airport/station pickup, $20 roundtrip.

Pine Ridge Inn ¢ 👫 ✕ ✈
2893 West Pine Street, 27030

Tel: 910–789–5034
Fax: 910–786–9039

Pine Ridge is a sprawling mansion built in 1948 and luxuriously decorated with antique and traditional furnishings. Ellen and Manford Haxton bought the inn in 1985; their son and his wife now help run the inn. The dinner menu includes such classics as prime rib, chicken Kiev, veal Marsala, and shrimp scampi.

"The Pine Ridge feels like a southern plantation mansion, complete with great white pillars and circular drive. The back of the house looks over a swimming pool and the beautiful North Carolina hills. The entrance foyer is highlighted with a circular stairway, while the main living room has a fireplace and Steinway grand piano; the paneled library beckons with soft velvet-covered couches, and antiques and fresh flowers are everywhere." *(Mr. & Mrs. Arthur Heitmann)* "The owners' son greeted us warmly, and gave us a tour of the house and its spacious rooms. Ours had an antique brass bed, polished and inviting, with crisp, fluffy linens and comforter, lots of windows, comfortable chairs, and current issues of great magazines. After checking in, we had a soak in the indoor hot tub." *(KFR)*

"Baths are huge, with terry robes and lots of hot water; wonderfully fluffy towels. We really enjoyed the varied art work throughout the inn." *(Perri & Mike Rappel)* "Gracious hospitality; good breakfast of soufflé with sausage, homemade blueberry muffins, and fresh fruit." *(Bill Novak, also Katherine Bradley)*

Open All year. Closed week of Christmas. Restaurant closed off-season.
Rooms 2 suites, 4 doubles—all with private bath and/or shower. All rooms with telephone, radio, TV, air-conditioning. Some with desk.
Facilities Living room with piano, fireplace, library with fireplace, TV, VCR, stereo, books, dining room with fireplace, play room, exercise room. 8 acres with hot tub, swimming pool, tennis court, bike paths. Golf nearby.
Location On Rte. 89; 5 m to town, 2 m from Exit 100 off I-77.
Restrictions Light sleepers should request rooms away from highway. Smoking in library only.
Credit cards Amex, Visa, MC.
Rates B&B, $60–100 double. Extra person, $10. 10% family, senior, AAA discount. Alc lunch, $12; alc dinner, $18. Weekly rates, weekend packages.
Extras Crib, $10.

MURPHY

Huntington Hall B&B ¢ 🚢
500 Valley River Avenue, 28906

Tel: 704–837–9567
800–824–6189
Fax: 704–837–2527

Bob and Katie Delong purchased Huntington Hall, a restored 1880s clapboard house, in 1990, and report that "our comfortable inn is decorated in the tradition of an English country garden home; recent improvements include new carpeting or restoration of the heart pine floors, as well as exterior and interior painting to keep the inn fresh. We are avid backpackers and can advise guests on hiking trips in the Great Smoky Mountains, or white-water rafting on the Ocoee River, chosen for the 1996 Olympics in kayaking and canoeing."

"Highlights were innkeepers Kate and Bob and their young daughter Lizzie, and the delicious breakfasts." *(Mike Glerum)* "Restful living room with Oriental rugs; pleasant, sunny breakfast room. My favorite guest room is the Avalon, with a peach and blue color scheme, heart pine floor, Oriental rug, comfortable queen-size bed, reading chairs, and a large, functional 1950s-era bathroom." *(Suzanne Carmichael)* "We had a glass of wine before bedtime, and a delicious breakfast of fresh orange juice and coffee, miniature raisin bran muffins, peach crepes with apricot topping, and bacon." *(Becky Hopkins)* "Our favorite breakfast consisted of French toast made with French bread, topped with butterscotch sauce, whipped cream, and sliced pecans." *(William & Heidi Rhyne)* "Our privacy was respected yet we felt comfortable asking for anything we might need." *(Carolyn & Leonard Carroll)* "Without being cluttered, each cheerful room is artfully accented with art and antiques. The in-town location was extremely quiet with adequate parking. Plenty of hot water, fresh towels and linens, herb soaps, and good lighting; truffles on our turned-down beds." *(Mr. & Mrs. Otto Clariyio)* "Table settings were elegant. Although service was efficient, we never felt hurried." *(Carol Durham)* "The Crantock room is beautifully decorated, as is the spacious bathroom with its clawfoot tub and shower attachment." *(Pat Momich)* "The rooms are well lit—each with several lamps, overhead lights and good lighting around the mirror." *(Shelby Watson)* "I was surprised at how little noise could be heard from the rest of the inn was when I was in my room." *(Virginia & Dwight Johnson)*

Open All year.
Rooms 5 doubles—all with full private bath, TV, desk, air-conditioning, fan.
Facilities Dining room with fireplace, library; living room with TV, breakfast room, screened porch. Swimming pool, tennis, golf nearby. Lakes, rivers nearby for swimming, kayaking, canoeing. Theatre, whitewater rafting, mystery weekend packages.
Location W NC. 90 m E of Chattanooga TN, 90 m W of Asheville, 100 m N of Atlanta. 2 blocks from downtown. From U.S. 64, take Hwy. 19 to downtown area. Turn onto Peachtree St. Then right onto Valley River Ave. Pass Presbyterian Church; inn is on right.
Credit cards Amex, DC, Discover, MC, Visa.
Rates B&B, $65 double, $49 single. Extra person, $10. Murder mystery weekends.
Extras Airport/station pickups. Crib.

NAGS HEAD

Reader tip: "Don't be disappointed if the sand dunes block your view of the ocean when you're staying in the Outer Banks. Buildings unprotected by sand dunes are soon *in* the ocean." *(DLG)*

For additional area entries, see **Manteo**.

First Colony Inn 🏃 ♿.   *Tel:* 919–441–2343
6720 South Virginia Dare Trail, 27959   800–368–9390
                                              Fax: 919–441–9234

Innkeeping is a moving experience, and in the case of the Lawrence family, longtime Outer Banks residents, it's been true literally as well as figuratively. The last surviving Nag's Head oceanfront hotel, built in 1932, the

First Colony Inn was rescued by the Lawrence family and moved 3 1/2 miles to a safer location. Now listed on the National Register of Historic Places, the inn re-opened in 1991 after a three-year renovation, which preserved the inn's historic charms while adding up-to-date plumbing, heating, and cooling systems. Guest rooms are decorated with English antiques, traditional furnishings, old photographs and prints, and king, queen, or extra-long twin beds.

The buffet breakfast changes daily, but might offer croissants, ham and cheese bread, hard rolls, lemon poppy seed cake, raspberry Danish, corn muffins, and assorted fresh fruits, assorted hot and cold cereals, yogurt, coffee, tea, and juices; rates also include afternoon tea, cookies, cheese and crackers.

"The wide wraparound porches (on both the first and second floors) are great for morning coffee or afternoon tea. The private baths include heated towel racks with an individual hot water heater. Each room has its own climate system with remote control." *(Bill & VR Claypoole)* "The exterior looks like an old-fashioned Nantucket cottage, complete with weathered shingles, brass fixtures and a lovely garden. We stayed in room 11, facing the ocean, and decorated with natural oak, wicker, and nautical prints; rocking chairs awaited on the porch, directly outside." *(Marie & Tom Gigot)*

"Although the character and atmosphere of the original hotel have been preserved, its tiny rooms have been combined into spacious ones with modern amenities. Camille Lawrence is a great character, with lots of knowledge and stories. Fascinating documentation of the moving of the inn." *(Barry & Kathy Kean)* "We stayed in a third floor corner room facing the ocean, with a side view up the coast and toward Albermarle Sound; it was spacious and comfortable. The staff are courteous and genuinely eager to please, offering detailed restaurant reviews when I asked their advice, and accommodating our special requests. The four-poster bed was enormous, warm, and comfy, with elegant white eyelet sheets topped with a puffy down comforter." *(Johanna Hewlett Brown)* "The long, private walkway ends in a gazebo which overlooks the beach and the ocean." *(Carolyn Kulisheck)*

Open All year.
Rooms 6 suites, 20 doubles—all with full private bath and/or shower, telephone, radio, clock, TV, air-conditioning, kitchenette. Most with desk, 2 with whirlpool tub, screened porch. 8 with VCR.
Facilities Dining room, library with fireplace, organ, books, games; sundeck. Secure bicycle/windsurfer storage. 5 acres with off-street parking, swimming pool; plus 2 1/2 acres on beach side of street with boardwalk, gazebo, swimming, surfing, windsurfing, sailing. Complimentary beach chairs, beach towels, grills, picnic tables. Tennis, golf nearby. Rental boats, party boats, hunting or fishing guides.
Location Outer banks of NC. 80 m SE of Norfolk, VA. Parking E side of US 158 at mile post 16.
Restrictions Smoking only in two guest rooms.
Credit cards Discover, MC, Visa.
Rates B&B, $80–200 suite, $60–200 double. Extra person, $30. Babies, $10. 2–3-night weekend, holiday minimum.
Extras Wheelchair access. Crib, babysitting service. Minimal French, Spanish, German spoken.

NEW BERN

New Bern is located in mid-coastal North Carolina, 2 hours east of Raleigh, at the confluence of the Trent and Neuse rivers. It's a 45-minute drive to the Atlantic Ocean beaches. The town was founded in 1710 by German and Swiss colonists searching for political and religious freedom. New Bern prospered from the production of tar, pitch, and turpentine. When the royal governor of the Carolinas, William Tryon, saw the need for a permanent capital, New Bern was selected as the site. Tryon Palace, completed in 1770, was the Colonial capitol and the first state capitol of North Carolina. New Bern's prosperity continued through much of the 19th century, and many of its finest buildings date from the early 1800s. A number of historic buildings have been restored and are open to the public as museums. On a more commercial note, Pepsi-Cola (known originally as "Brad's Drink") was invented here in the 1890s by a local pharmacist, C.D. Bradham.

Information please: Two of New Bern's best-known B&Bs changed hands as we were going to press, and current reports are welcome on both: **The Aerie** (509 Pollock Street, 28562; 919–636–5553 or 800–849–5553) was built in 1882, and remained in the same family for almost 100 years. Refurbished as a B&B in 1985, it's decorated in Williamsburg colors, with early American-style furnishings. Located in the historic district just one block from Tryon Palace, The Aerie offers seven guest rooms, all with private bath and TV, at B&B rates of $80–95 double. Close by is the **Harmony House Inn** (215 Pollock Street, 28560; 919–636–3810 or 800–636–3113), built in the 1850s. Around 1900, two of the builder's sons sawed the house in half to enable the addition of another hallway, front door, staircase and four more rooms. Each brother lived in his own half for the next 20 years. Today Harmony House is furnished with antiques and reproductions, many of the latter made by local craftspeople. The B&B double rate for the nine doubles is $85; each has a private bath, TV, and air-conditioning.

King's Arms Colonial Inn
212 Pollack Street, 28560

Tel: 919–638–4409
800–872–9306

Built in 1848, the King's Arms was restored as an inn in 1980, and was purchased by Richard and Patricia Gulley in 1992. Breakfast, delivered to your room, includes cinnamon coffee or tea, orange juice and fresh fruit, and such baked treats as ham biscuits, banana bread, or perhaps lemon ginger muffins, along with the morning paper; you can also breakfast on the wicker rockers on the back porch. "We had a delightful stay with Richard and Pat Gulley. Our room was attractively appointed and quiet, the bath spacious, and our hosts were dedicated to making our stay comfortable and enjoyable." *(Lou Moriconi)*

Area for improvement: "An inside common area for guests to gather."

Open All year.
Rooms 10 doubles—8 with full private bath, 2 with maximum of 4 sharing bath. All with telephone, TV, air-conditioning. 8 with fireplace, 2 with fan.

Facilities Refrigerator, porch, off-street parking. Golf, rivers, boating, fishing nearby.

Location In historic district. From US Rte. 17 N, go left onto E. Front St. Go right onto Pollack St. to inn on corner of E. Front St. & Pollack St.

Restrictions No smoking.

Credit cards Amex, MC, Visa.

Rates B&B, $85 double, $65 single. Extra person, $10. Senior, AAA discount.

Extras Crib.

OCRACOKE

Ocracoke is on the Outer Banks of coastal North Carolina, about 1½ hours south of Nags Head, and 40 minutes by ferry from Hatteras village.

Reader tip: "Come to Ocracoke to heighten your awareness of the incredible forces of nature. Violent summer storms sweep through in minutes, and the pounding of ocean waves never ceases. The island is mercifully undeveloped, since most of it is part of the Cape Hatteras National Seashore. There's little to do but relax and enjoy the beautiful uncrowded beaches, fish and swim, rent a bicycle, and explore. The seafood is delicious; some of it familiar, some unusual to Yankee tastebuds." *(MS)*

Also recommended: Although not really suitable for a full entry, readers are pleased with the **Pirate's Quay Hotel** (P.O. Box 526, Ocracoke 27960; 919–928–1921) is a five-unit condominium overlooking Silver Lake, in the village of Ocracoke. Each unit has two bedrooms, a kitchen, 1½ baths, and a balcony. Limited covered parking and a private dock are available.

Information please: Owned by Ocracoke native, Alton Ballance, and managed by Mary Hollowell, the **Crews Inn B&B** (P.O. Box 460, 27960; 919–928–7011) was built in 1908. The inn is decorated with pictures taken from Alton's book about the island and its people. Abundant porches offer views of the surrounding oaks, cedars and pines, and provide a place for breakfast in warm weather. The simply furnished rooms are not air-conditioned, but have fans, multiple windows, and ocean breezes. B&B double rates range from $40–60 (no credit cards).

Listed in past editions, we need current reports on the **Berkley Center Country Inn** (On the Harbor, P.O. Box 220, 27960; 919–928–5911) long owned by Ruth and Wes Egan. Rooms are highlighted by fir, cypress, and cedar-paneled walls and ceilings, with overstuffed Queen Anne wing chairs and sofas, quilts, baskets, and the work of local artists. B&B double rates for the nine guest rooms, most with private bath, are $65–85, including a breakfast of coffee, juice, and cereal, with muffins, biscuits, or bagels.

PITTSBORO

Information please: About 15 miles west of Pittsboro is **Bed & Breakfast at Laurel Ridge** (Siler Mill Road, Rt. 1, Box 116, Siler City, 27344;

919–742–6049 or 800–742–6049), set on a 26-acre site bordering the Rocky River, with hiking trails and an English country garden. Owned by David Simmons and Lisa Reynolds, breakfasts includes fresh-squeezed juice, home-baked breads, and such dishes as poppy seed pancakes, omelets, or frittata. Two guest rooms share a bath, at rates of $30–50; the suite ($85), has a queen-sized canopy bed and Jacuzzi bath.

The Fearrington House ✕   *Tel:* 919–542–2121
2000 Fearrington Village Center, 27312

Fearrington Village is a small complex consisting of a well-established first-class restaurant and cafe, a number of small quality shops, and a luxurious country inn. Owned by R.B. and Jenny Fitch, and managed by Richard Delany, The Fearrington House features rooms richly decorated with English pine antiques and carefully matched Laura Ashley wallpapers and fabrics. The Fearrington House restaurant is known for its innovative Southern cuisine; a recent dinner included braised rabbit over homemade sage pasta, seared pork tenderloin with apricot glaze, and warm apple tarts, custard sauce, and caramel ice cream.

"Our second floor room was lush and beautiful with a separate sitting room overlooking the beautiful flower gardens and fountains. It was decorated in colorful floral fabrics with a comfortable window seat and two plush soft chairs. The bedroom was done in white pine and florals and was equally lovely. The beds were wonderfully firm with soft comfortable pillows and baby soft sheets. The huge bright spotless bathroom was filled with every possible bath product from soap to lotions, bath salts, hair dryer, and loads of thick soft towels. There were small vases of fresh cut flowers throughout the room and bathroom, as well as chilled bottled water waiting our arrival. Off the front courtyard is a sitting room where guests are welcome to browse through the shelves of books, sip complimentary sodas, nibble fruit and cookies, or just sit and relax. Part of this complex is a working farm with a rare breed of cattle called Belted Galloways, as well as horses and sheep. The cafe serves good food in a casual setting, while the restaurant serves exceptional food in an elegant setting. Breakfast was served on fine china, with fresh flowers and impeccable service; it consisted of eggs, bacon, potatoes, juice, fresh fruit, muffins and bread, coffee and more." *(Perri & Michael Rappel, also Kevin Sellers)* "White exterior with Southern-style pillars, surrounded by beautifully appointed gardens. The restaurant is elegant and sophisticated with excellent nouvelle cuisine." *(Carole Vesely)*

Open All year.
Rooms 9 suites, 4 doubles—all with private bath and/or shower, telephone, radio, TV, desk, air-conditioning.
Facilities Living room, restaurant, bar/lounge, wine bar, cafe, specialty shops. 60 acres with bike trails, swimming pool. 8 m to Lake Jordan for swimming, boating, fishing. 15 min. to golf, tennis.
Location Central NC. 8 m SW of Chapel Hill, 20 m to Research Triangle Park. From Chapel Hill, go S on Rte. 15/501 toward Pittsboro & Sanford.
Restrictions Smoking permitted in lounge only. No children under 12. Lobby noise in 1 room.
Credit cards MC, Visa.

Rates B&B, $250 suite; $150–200 double. Alc lunch, $5–10; prix fixe dinner, $45.
Extras Wheelchair access; some rooms equipped for disabled. Airport/station pickup, $30. Spanish, French, German spoken. Member, Relais et Chateaux.

RALEIGH

The Oakwood Inn ¢   *Tel:* 919–832–9712
411 North Bloodworth Street, 27604   *Fax:* 919–836–9263

Pressured business travelers with appointments in North Carolina's capital city will find a welcome respite at The Oakwood Inn, opened in 1984. Built in 1871 as the Raynor Stronach House, the inn is listed on the National Register of Historic Places, and is located in the historic Oakwood District, home to twenty blocks of Victorian buildings, ranging in style from Greek Revival to Steamboat Gothic. In 1993, the inn was purchased by Lisa, Jim, and Vara Cox. In addition to juice, fresh or cooked fruit, just-baked biscuits and muffins, breakfast entrées might include gingerbread pancakes with lemon syrup, stuffed French toast with orange sauce, or a mushroom and cheese omelet.

"The exquisite Polk Room, on the ground floor, has a large private porch and an ample sitting area within the bedroom." *(PD)* "A lovely area for a late afternoon walk." *(Ron Simblist)* "Complimentary soft drinks, cheese and crackers; excellent full breakfast." *(KM)* "I travel on business and this is the only place I'd stay in Raleigh. Lovely, quiet, safe neighborhood. Spectacular breakfasts, served in a friendly manner. Lots of thoughtful touches, from jelly beans by my bed, to wine in the refrigerator." *(Roxanne Kenny)* Comments welcome.

Open All year. Closed Christmas.
Rooms 6 doubles, 1 single—all with private bath and/or shower, telephone, air-conditioning. Many with fireplace. TV on request.
Facilities Dining room, parlor with fireplace, porches. ½ acre with rose garden. Fax, copier service.
Location In historic district. Between Oakwood and Polk Sts.
Restrictions Smoking in designated areas only. "Small children may find us boring."
Credit cards Amex, DC, Discover, MC, Visa.
Rates B&B, $75–110 double, $65–90 single. Weekday rates.
Extras Limited wheelchair access.

ROBBINSVILLE

Information please: Listed in many past editions, we need current reports on the **Snowbird Mountain Lodge** (275 Santeetlah Road, 28771; 704–479–3433), in the Joyce Kilmer National Forest, set atop a low mountain at 2,880 feet, and built of chestnut logs and native stone. In 1994, the original owners, Bob and Connie Rhudy, re-purchased the lodge from Jim and Eleanor Burbank. Although most readers are delighted with Snowbird's isolated setting, it's not for everyone. Accommodations are clean and comfortable but basic, and lighting and soundproofing could be improved; windows are not sealed and you can expect that the odd bug or two will find your room inviting. Come here for the fabulous views, glorious mountains, and beautiful woods, for the beautiful hiking, canoeing, fishing, and rafting—not mounds of thick towels or bedtime mints. Double rates for the 21 guest rooms ranges from $115–133, including three meals daily. Robbinsville is 100 miles west of Asheville, 80 miles south of Knoxville, Tennessee.

SALISBURY

Salisbury is located in central North Carolina, 42 miles north of Charlotte, and 39 miles south of Winston-Salem. Founded in 1753, it was the site of one of the Confederacy's largest prison camps, and about 5,000 Union soldiers are buried in the National Cemetery here. Pick up information on walking tours of the historic district from the local visitor center, and visit the town's antique shops.

Reader tip: "We were unable to find a local restaurant serving food of any quality."

Rowan Oak House ⊄   *Tel: 704–633–2086*
208 South Fulton Street, 28144   800–786–0437

A Scottish-Celtic legend tells of a magical tree that symbolized beauty, hospitality, privacy, peace, and sanctuary—the Rowan Oak. So, when Bill and Ruth Ann Coffey sold their house in Texas and moved to Salisbury to start their retirement career as innkeepers, they decided the Rowan Oak symbolized everything they hoped to achieve with their inn. Built in 1901, this blue-gray and cream house was constructed in the Queen Anne style and has been furnished by the Coffeys in high Victorian decor. The breakfast menu changes daily, but might include baked grapefruit, baked eggs with salsa and cheese, accompanied by home-baked apple bran muffins, whole wheat sourdough bread, and poppyseed cake. Afternoon refreshments are served in the living room, and fresh fruit and flowers are placed in each guest room.

"Beautiful, comfortable furnishings which matched the inn's Victorian atmosphere. A delicious breakfast was served on fine china and crystal." *(Franklin Bryan)* "Huge bathrooms, all furnished beautifully." *(Elisabeth McLaughlin, also Phyllis Salesky)* "Our well-traveled hosts pampered us but also respected our privacy. Fine antiques throughout; the atmosphere is congenial, not stuffy." *(Janet Beck)* "Lots of reading material of general and local interest. Nice common room upstairs. The Coffeys' experience as guests at other B&Bs have given them insight into what makes a good one." *(Margaret Stanley, also Phil & Karen Neely)* "Much of the pleasure of our visit was derived from Bill and Ruth Ann Coffey." *(James & Pamela Burr)*

Note: At press time, we learned that the inn was for sale; inquire further when booking.

Open All year.

Rooms 4 doubles—2 with private bath and/or shower, 2 with maximum of 4 sharing bath. All with telephone, radio, desk, air-conditioning, fan. 1 with whirlpool bath, fireplace; 1 with private porch.

Facilities Dining room, parlor with fireplace, game room with TV, wraparound porches. $\frac{1}{2}$ acre with gardens. Tennis, golf nearby.

Location 3 blocks to center of town. In historic district. From I-85 take Exit 76B. Go W on Innes St. Turn left on Fulton St. Inn on right.

Restrictions Smoking in living room, lounge only. No children under 10.

Credit cards Discover, MC, Visa.

Rates B&B, $65–95 double, $55–85 single. Extra person, $15. No tipping. Reduced rates for extended stays. 10% senior, AAA discount. 2-night minimum stay some weekends.

Extras Local airport/station pickups. Crib. Some Spanish spoken.

SALUDA

Saluda is a quiet, small town in the foothills of the Blue Ridge Mountains of western North Carolina, 30 miles south of Asheville, near the South Carolina border. There are many antique and craft shops in the area, along with restaurants serving good mountain cooking, and lots of good hiking trails. The Carl Sandburg National Historic Site is also nearby.

Information please: We need current reports on **The Orchard Inn** (Highway 176, P.O. Box 725, 28773; 704–749–5471 or 800–581–3800), listed in past editions. In the early 1900s, the Southern Railway Company built a summer mountain retreat for railroad clerks and their families; Kenneth and Ann Hough renovated it as the Orchard Inn in 1982, and have decorated the rooms with antiques and casual country charm, including brass/iron and four-poster beds, rag and Oriental rugs, and baskets and other craftwork. B&B rates for the nine double rooms ranges from $75–120. The intimate dinners are served at 7 P.M. by candlelight, and include a choice of entrée—perhaps prime rib, chicken, or trout.

Another possibility is the **Ivy Terrace** (Main Street, P.O. Box 639, 28773; 704–749–9542 or 800–749–9542), built in the 1890s, and renovated as an eight guest-room B&B in 1993. Furnished with country antiques and period decor, the B&B double rate of $85–125 includes a full breakfast.

SOUTHERN PINES

Located in the Sandhills of south central North Carolina, Southern Pines is known for its mild winters and exceptional area golf courses (31 within a 20-mile drive) in both Southern Pines and neighboring Pinehurst.

Information please: The **Jefferson Inn** (150 West New Hampshire Avenue, 28387; 910–692–8300) was re-opened in 1992 under new owners, who've worked hard to renovate this 1902 hotel, starting with the restaurant and common areas, working gradually to upgrade the 20 guest rooms. Two of the four partners are professionally trained chefs, one from the Culinary Institute of America in Hyde Park, New York, the other from Switzerland, and the reasonably priced menu includes both European and American specialities. All guest rooms are air-conditioned, with private baths, and the double rate of $65–75 includes a continental breakfast; golf packages are available. "Energetic young owners are working hard to renovate this lovely old hotel. Although we didn't see the guest rooms, if the gleaming, beautifully carved wooden staircase and blue flowered wallpaper is any indication, the bedrooms must be charming. The dining room has been decorated with the feel of a Viennese tea room—white painted tin ceiling, flowered wallpaper with white background, and airy white lace curtain. Our dinner included fork-tender sauerbraten with red cabbage, spaetzle, and hot-from-the-oven rolls to sop up every last bit of the delicious gravy." *(Mary Rafferty)* Reports welcome.

We need current reports on the reasonably priced **Inn at the Bryant House** (214 North Poplar Street, Aberdeen 28315; 919–944–3300 or 800–453–4019), just south of Southern Pines. "Graciously renovated 1913 home. The rooms are large and comfortable and the breakfast features fresh-baked breads and muffins with homemade jellies and jams. Picnic facilities under the pecan trees, and flower and vegetable gardens add to the southern charm of this historic community." *(Ann Milton)*

Knollwood House

1495 West Connecticut Avenue, 28387

Tel: 910–692–9390
Fax: 910–692–0609

Golf can be the most elegant of sports, and a stay at Knollwood House will certainly supply that quality—even if it is lacking in your swing. Built in 1925, and restored as a B&B in 1992 by Mimi and Dick Beatty, Knollwood is handsomely decorated with late 18th and early 19th century family antiques, soft colors, warm chintzes, tapestry and needlepoint work. Attention to detail includes the starched white eyelet cotton sheets, terry robes, and towels—changed as often as three times daily. The back lawn extends 100 feet to Mid-Pines, a golf course designed by Donald Ross. Dick is knowledgeable about area courses, and can assist guests in obtaining tee times. A typical breakfast might include juice, fresh fruit with yogurt and sour cream sauce, Viennese bread pudding with raspberry purée, baked Canadian bacon, and cranberry coffee cake. Hors d'oeuvres are served at 6 P.M., giving guests the opportunity to get to know each other and the Beattys.

"The Beattys allow guests to feel totally at home in their beautiful inn. Careful attention to detail, family heirloom furnishings, delicious breakfasts, and lovely surroundings make for a most comfortable visit. The evening cocktail hour provided us with an opportunity to become better acquainted with our hosts and the other guests." *(Philip Miller)* "Elegant yet comfortable, with livable antiques. Spacious common areas with several conversational groupings; gorgeous fabrics and wallpapers. Wonderful beds; quiet, unpretentious service." *(Kittie Jones)*

Open All year.
Rooms 2 suites, 2 doubles—all with private bath, telephone, clock, air-conditioning. Some with desk, TV; 1 with fireplace.
Facilities Dining room with fireplace, living room with fireplace, TV/VCR, books,

stereo; solarium. 5 acres with gazebo, lawn games. Overlooks Mid-Pines golf course.

Location 3 min. to downtown, in historic district. From I-95, take US 1. Take Midland Rd. exit. Go left on Pee Dee Rd. Bear left onto West Connecticut Ave. Inn on left.

Restrictions Smoking on 1st floor only. Children over 10.

Credit cards Visa.

Rates B&B, $105–135 suite, $90–100 double, $80–90 single. Extra person $20. No tipping.

Extras Airport/station pickups.

SPRUCE PINE

Spruce Pine is located in western North Carolina, in the Blue Ridge Mountains, 60 miles east of Asheville, 100 miles northwest of Charlotte, and 45 miles west Boone. Within a 30-minute drive are a number of High Country attractions, offering everything from hiking to caving, skiing to rockhounding.

The Fairway Inn ¢ 🏃   *Tel: 704–765–4917*
110 Henry Lane, 28777   Off-season: 904–724–7379

Pierce and Margaret Stevens, owners of the Fairway since 1985, welcome guests to their comfortable mountain home, overlooking an 18-hole golf course. The spacious white clapboard house is decorated eclectically with traditional and contemporary decor; one guest room is done in rattan, another with iron beds. Breakfast features such entrées as baked cheese blintzes, sausage and egg casserole, or French toast made with homemade bread.

"Worth visiting for the breakfasts alone. If Pierce and Margaret go out for the evening, an inn sitter is on duty to help guests; ours was a delightful high school student." *(Joe Schmidt)* "The suite was ideal for our family of four. Delicious blueberry pancakes for breakfast. When we talked about handmade quilts, the owners suggested a wonderful shop in a nearby town." *(Stephen & Rebecca Vargha)* "John and Margaret greeted us warmly, and helped us choose a restaurant for dinner." *(Ron & Dottie Kight)* "Our spacious room had a sun porch, private entrance, pretty bathroom, good closet, plenty of chairs, a good-sized table, large chest of drawers, good lamps and bedside tables, ample pillows, and fresh flowers; the color scheme was quiet and tasteful, and everything was spotless. Every day we had delicious, imaginative breakfasts, served around the dining room table, accompanied by friendly conversation. Close by is the Blue Ridge Parkway, which led us to many interesting spots. There are dozens of gem stores nearby and some antique shops, but the area is unsophisticated. We loved the quiet beauty of the grounds and giant spruces, the birds and rabbits." *(Janet & Clifford Nelson)* "They put a piece of candy on your pillow every night and make the beds promptly in the morning. They also have an evening happy hour with crackers, home-made spreads, and wine or spiked cider." *(Virginia Henke)* "Margaret easily accommodated my need for a sugar-free breakfast." *(ES)*

Open April through Dec.

Rooms 1 apartment, 2 suites with fireplace, 2 doubles—all with private bath and/or shower, desk, fan. 1 with kitchen, whirlpool tub.

Facilities Dining room, living room with TV, fireplace, library with games, porch. 1½ acres with lawn. Golf, tennis nearby, $2 discount on greens fee. 30 min. to lake for fishing, boating.

Location 1 m from town. From Blue Ridge Pkwy. take Rte. 226 N to Spruce Pine Shopping Ctr., then turn left on Fairway Ln., which becomes Henry Ln., to inn on left.

Restrictions Smoking permitted only in living room during cold weather.

Credit cards MC, Visa.

Rates B&B, $120 suite, $65–85 double. Room only, $60. Extra person, $12. Weekly rates for apartment. Reduced rates for families.

Extras Babysitting.

Richmond Inn ¢ ♈   Tel: 704–765–6993
101 Pine Avenue, 28777   Fax: 704–765–6993

Built in 1939, the Richmond Inn has been owned by Bill Ansley and Lenore Boucher since 1989. Shaded by white pine, the inn's grounds are landscaped with dogwood, mountain laurel, and rhododendron; the terrace overlooks the valley of the North Toe River. Breakfast is served family-style, and consists of eggs, bacon or sausage, grits, juice, toast, muffins, butter, jelly, coffee, tea, and milk; the bottomless cookie jar is also a guest favorite.

"Large, attractive house, with spacious rooms. I had a chance to see most of the guest rooms, and each has individual appeal, from the hand-carved antique dresser and lovely photography in the Rowan Room to the huge turned-wood queen-size four-poster and hand-drawn map of the Southern Highlands in the Ferguson Room. The pretty Steven room has a queen-size bed with a handmade quilt, two comfortable wing chairs, a pink and blue color scheme, and a large full bath. The guest pantry has mugs made by local craftspeople, and is stocked so that you can get coffee and tea at your convenience. Bill, a former Miami area police officer, is very friendly. He is knowledgeable about area crafts and can tell you how to find the local studios. The dining room is light and airy, with a bay window at one end; a generous and tasty breakfast of pancakes, eggs, bacon, warm spiced apples, and orange juice was served at the mahogany table." (SC)

Open All year.

Rooms 1 cottage, 7 doubles—all with private bath and/or shower, clock, radio, fan, desk.

Facilities Dining room, living room with fireplace, wide-screen TV/VCR; guest pantry. 1½ acres with off-street parking, covered patio.

Location 3 blocks from historic district. From Blue Ridge Parkway, go N on Hwy. 226. In Spruce Pine, turn right onto Oak Ave., then left on Walnut Ave. at NCNB. Take 2nd left, then left again on Pine Ave. to inn on left.

Restrictions Smoking only on covered patio.

Credit cards MC, Visa.

Rates B&B, $45–70 double, $45–60 single. Extra person, $10; Children under 12, free. Senior, AAA discount. Winter, commercial rates.

STATESVILLE

Also recommended: At the 150-year-old **Cedar Hill Farm B&B** (Elmwood Road, Route 1, Box 492, 28677; 704–873–4332 or 800–484–8457 ext. 1254) owners Brenda and Jim Vernon raise sheep for hand-spinning wool. Fresh eggs, ham and sausage come from a nearby neighbor and their own garden provides herbs and vegetables for breakfast, while fruits from the orchard go into preserves. Guests can stay in the one guest room in the farmhouse ($55) or in the renovated granary ($70); both are furnished with country antiques. "The scenery is gorgeous, and the farmyard is full of geese, sheep and a playful dog." *(Ken Letner)* "Gracious Southern hospitality. Our children were warmly welcomed. Flexible breakfast menu and serving time." *(Shelley Gallup)* "Nice place, fine people, terrific porch swing." *(Celia McCullough)* "Their stories about farm life have you roaring. We kept busy with the trampoline, horseshoes, badminton, swimming, swinging, and the hammock." *(Anita & Foy Taff)*

Madelyn's ¢   *Tel:* 704–872–3973
514 Carroll Street, 28677

Madelyn and John Hill opened their long-time home, built in 1949, to B&B guests in 1989. Madelyn reports that "our location at the crossroads of two major interstates makes our location conducive to both business and vacation travelers. I love birds and we have feeders for guests to watch while eating breakfast, which might include baked grapefruit, gingerbread pancakes with butter pecan ice cream or sliced strawberries, crispy bacon and juice or coffee; another morning might bring a fresh fruit salad, followed by eggs Benedict with country ham, lemon peppered potatoes, and buttermilk biscuits."

"A bowl of fresh fruit, raisins, homemade cookies, and candy kisses, were set next to our king-size bed; our bathroom had a basket of toiletries, including Madelyn's homemade soap." *(Joon & Arnold Kerzner)* "Warm and friendly atmosphere. We were welcomed with lemonade and hot spiced tea. Quiet location, good for walking or jogging. The delicious breakfast was served on fine china, with crystal goblets, sterling silver flatware, and fresh pansies at each place." *(Rebecca Smith)* "The house was spotless. Madelyn provided plates of homemade cookies, extra towels, and turned down the beds at night." *(WO)*

Open All year.
Rooms 3 doubles—all with private bath and/or shower, radio, air-conditioning, fan.
Facilities Dining room, breakfast room with fireplace, piano; sun room with TV/VCR, stereo; porch, laundry facilities. Garden with berry bushes, lily pond. Tennis, golf nearby. 20 min. to Lake Norman.
Location W central NC. 45 m N of Charlotte, SW of Winston-Salem, near intersection of I-40 & I-77. 4 blocks from center. From I-40, take exit 150 to N. Center St.; go 0.3 m, turn right (S) onto Race St. Carroll St. is 1.1 m on left.
Restrictions No smoking. No children under 10.
Credit cards MC, Visa.

Rates B&B, $55–65 double. 10% discount for 4-night stay. 10% senior discount.
Extras Airport/station pickups.

TRYON

Tryon is in the heart of Carolina fox-hunting country; the climate is mild, with golf and horseback riding available year-round. Just a mile from the South Carolina border, Tryon is located in western North Carolina, 100 miles west of Charlotte, 150 miles north of Atlanta, halfway between Asheville and Spartanburg, South Carolina.

Pine Crest Inn ¢ 🏃 ✕
200 Pine Crest Lane, 28782

Tel: 704–859–9135
800–633–3001
Fax: 704–859–9135

Established by Michigan equestrian Carter Brown in 1917, and listed on the National Register of Historic Places, the Pine Crest was purchased by Jeremy and Jennifer Wainwright in 1990. Originally from Great Britain, the Wainwrights have renovated the main building to evoke the feeling of an English country inn, with leather chairs and richly upholstered furnishings, and a traditional hunt and steeplechase decor. The restaurant is open to the public, serving two meals daily; sample entrées might include lamb with mustard and Madeira sauce, filet mignon with three peppercorn sauce, and mountain trout with lemon parsley.

"The atmosphere is posh, but practical, with Ralph Lauren decor supplementing the antiques. The dining room is evocative of Colonial Williamsburg, with small dining rooms of just four to six tables. My favorite selections are the classically prepared lamb and the crabcakes. The wonderful breakfast includes entrées such as eggs Benedict or Florentine. The Front Pine room has a half-tester paisley canopy, down duvet, and a hunting print over the bed, accenting the dark paneling and shutters and the hunt green and red color scheme. All rooms have thick towels and robes, English soaps and gels in generous portions." *(SHW)*

"Secluded setting, yet close to the center of a lovely small town just at the edge of the Blue Ridge Mountains." *(Sandra & Berge Heede)* "Though it's not for tall people, we were delighted with our accommodations in the Swayback cabin, down the hill from the main buildings, with a queen-sized bed and alcove sitting area." *(Deborah Ross)* "Gorgeous surroundings, beautifully decorated rooms, and incredible staff—warm, friendly, and genuinely interested in our comfort. Sumptuous dining." *(Diane & Wes Drexler)* Reports appreciated.

Open All year.
Rooms 5 cabins, 2 2-bedroom suites, 16 doubles—all with private bath and/or shower, telephone, TV, desk, air-conditioning. Rooms in 10 buildings and cabins, most with fireplace.
Facilities Restaurant, lobby, den with fireplaces, TV, books, games, puzzles, piano, Ping-Pong; porches. Conference center with fax, copier, computer. 3 acres. Swimming pool, golf, tennis, hiking nearby.
Location ½ m to town; 4 m from I-26.

Credit cards MC, Visa.
Rates B&B, $100–495 cottage, $140 suite, $100–140 double. 17% service. Extra adult, $35; extra child age 6–17, $15; children under 6 free in parents' room. Alc dinner, $20–35.

Stone Hedge Inn ¢ ✕
Tel: 704–859–9114
P.O. Box 366, 28782–0366

All the stone needed to built this mansion in 1934 was brought from a local quarry by horse and wagon. Restored as an inn in 1977, the Stone Hedge is owned by Ray and Anneliese Weingartner. The Weingartner's German background is reflected in their restaurant menu, which always includes a German dish in addition to such specials as fresh seafood and Black Angus steak. Guest rooms have mountain views, and are decorated with some antiques. "Excellent food, hospitable owners, beautiful fireplace." *(Mrs. William Downer)* "Lovely stone house and cottage. Nice views, comfortable rooms, and delicious breakfast of fruit and French toast." *(Celia McCullough)*

Open All year.
Rooms 1 cottage, 6 doubles—all with private bath and/or shower, telephone, radio, clock, TV, air-conditioning. Some with kitchenette, fireplace, desk, deck. Guest rooms in 3 buildings.
Facilities Restaurant, guest laundry, patio. 28 acres with unheated pool, horseshoes. Tennis, golf, hiking nearby.
Location 2 m from downtown. Take I-26 to Tryon-Columbus. Exit 36. Take NC 108 toward Tryon. 2 1/2 m. Turn right on Howard Gap Rd. Inn is 1 1/2 m on right.
Restrictions Smoking permitted. Children 12 or over.
Credit cards Visa, MC.
Rates B&B, $65–85 double, $55–75 single. Extra person, $10. Alc dinner, $20–25.
Extras German spoken.

VALLE CRUCIS

Named for the three streams that cross in this high mountain valley, Valle Crucis is the home of the Mast General Store, dating back to 1883, and several interesting craft stores; it was founded by Scottish Highlanders, and hosts the largest gathering of the clans in the U.S. each summer. The village has been designated a National Historic District, the first rural one in North Carolina, and it encompasses 1,000 acres. Valle Crucis is located in the High Country of northwest North Carolina, midway between Boone and Banner Elk, 100 miles north of Charlotte, and 93 miles west of Winston-Salem. Within a short drive are such activities as golf, tennis, horseback riding, hiking, fishing, canoeing, downhill and cross-country skiing.

The Inn at the Taylor House 🏠
Tel: 704–963–5581
Highway 194, P.O. Box 713, 28691

Describing an inn is easiest when we can clearly label the decor as Victorian, Williamsburg Colonial, Arts & Crafts style, or perhaps contemporary—and is hardest in the case of an inn like this one, where phrases like "elegant good taste" are more than empty adjectives. In the case of the Inn at the Taylor House, Chip and Roland Schwab, who opened the inn in 1988, have done an exceptional job of renovating and decorating their 1911 home. The living room is done with Oriental carpets and lamps, period antiques and reproductions, and lots of overstuffed chairs and couches. Each bedroom is different, one done in soft flowered corals and white wicker, another crisp with striped wallpaper and soft green fabrics. Imported duvets combine handsome appearance with real comfort. Guests enjoy relaxing on the plant-filled porch, looking out on a field of cattle, or assembling in the dining room for one of the Schwabs' hearty breakfasts. Roland is Swiss, and a fifth-generation innkeeper; his specialties include Birchermuesli—a Swiss cereal of local fruits and berries combined with oats, nuts, and yogurt—followed by omelets, corned beef hash, or blueberry pancakes.

"Chip and Roland Schwab made us feel at home from the moment we arrived. Each morning of our stay was something to look forward to. Coffee is put out early, and we couldn't resist strolling through the herb and flower gardens with a steaming fresh cup. The colors used in our room were striking—a deep forest-green carpet with terra-cotta walls and complementing drapes." *(Valerie Vogler-Stipe)* "Blends sophisticated elegance with genuine concern for guest comfort." *(Henry & Val Egem)* "The luxury suite on the top floor has a cathedral ceiling and a view of the treetops; sliding glass doors opened onto our miniature balcony. The bathroom was new and spotless." *(Pauline Anderson, also Sibyl Nestor)*

Open April 15–Dec. 15.
Rooms 2 suites, 5 doubles—all with private bath and/or shower, desk, fan. 1 suite with air-conditioning, balcony.
Facilities Breakfast room, living room with fireplace, wraparound porch. 2 acres with gazebo, herb garden.
Location 5 m W of Boone. On Hwy. 194 between Banner Elk and Valle Crucis.
Restrictions No smoking. Children by arrangement.
Credit cards MC, Visa.
Rates B&B, $145 suite, $110 double. Extra person, $25. 2-night weekend minimum.
Extras Airport/station pickup. Crib, babysitting. German, Italian, French, Spanish spoken.

Mast Farm Inn ✕ &.
P.O. Box 704, 28691

Tel: 704–963–5857
Fax: 704–963–6404

The Mast Farm began as a log cabin in 1812, and grew to include a blacksmith shop, meat house, spring house, wash house, apple house, and barn. The main house was completed in 1885 and served as a thirteen-bedroom, one-bath (!) country inn through the first half of this century. Francis and Sibyl Pressly left careers in Washington, DC, and bought and restored the inn in 1985.

"The rooms are airy, large, and clean, with adequate lighting, at least one easy chair, comfortable beds and appropriate decorative touches. Service is mostly provided by the Presslys themselves (except at meals), and is unfailingly gracious. Sibyl Pressly oversees the kitchen, house, and cutting garden. Her recipes form the basis of memorable meals, served family-style in two dining rooms. Breakfast is simple—juice and coffee, fresh fruit and home-baked muffins, breads, honey-pecan rolls, pancakes, homemade apple butter, and locally made preserves. Dinner is a major event, with a set menu for every day of the week. Thursday is chicken and dumplings, Friday is sautéed trout with vegetable strudel, and Sunday brings fried chicken and country ham with biscuits and gravy. The entrées are accompanied by home-style vegetables (corn, beans, potatoes, black-eyed peas, carrots, and more), fresh salad, and savories. No alcoholic beverages are served, but the staff is happy to chill and serve your wine." *(Beth & Vaughn Morrison)* "The Presslys make an effort to seat guests in compatible groups at meals. Our favorite times to visit are for the wild-flower and birding weekend in May, and again in July or August when the produce from the garden is served in the dining room." *(Sibyl Nestor)*

"Our spacious room was furnished with country antiques, with fresh-cut flowers." *(Robert Folger)* "The baths have old-fashioned tubs, painted to go with the color scheme of the room." *(Chuck & Linda Shore)* "Guests are encouraged to come back to the kitchen for coffee anytime after dinner. Most gather on the large wraparound front porch to rock, sip their coffee, chat, and watch the cars go by." *(Mrs. Carolyn Hemric)* "Our room was squeaky clean and extremely comfortable; we liked the lemon soap in the bathroom." *(Mrs. Louis Haynes)* "An ideal mountain retreat for just relaxing or skiing at several nearby areas." *(Mary Catherine & Neb Rodgers, also PB)*

Minor niggles: Parking is tight when the inn is busy with outside and resident dinner guests; the third floor can be hot in summer, despite plenty of fans.

Open May–Nov., Jan.–Feb. Restaurant closed to public on Mondays.
Rooms 1 suite, 10 doubles, 1 cottage—10 with private bath, 2 with a maximum of 4 people sharing bath. All with radio, fan. 5 rooms with desk. 3 rooms in out-buildings.
Facilities Restaurant, parlor with fireplace, sun porch, library/game room. 18 acres with river for trout fishing; pond for fishing, swimming. Downhill, cross-country skiing nearby.
Location On SR 1112, 3 m from NC 105.
Restrictions No smoking. No children under 12. Some traffic noise in front rooms.
Credit cards MC, Visa.
Rates B&B, $125 cottage, $145 suite, $110 double. Extra person, $25. MAP, $165 cottage, $120–155 suite, $90–155 double. Children 12–18, $23. Extra person, $35. Sunday prix fixe lunch, $14; prix fixe dinner, $14. 2-night weekend minimum.
Extras First-floor bedroom equipped for disabled. Portuguese spoken.

WASHINGTON

Pamlico House Bed & Breakfast ¢   *Tel: 919–946–7184*
400 East Main Street, 27889

A Colonial Revival house built in 1906 as an Episcopal rectory, Pamlico House was restored as an inn by Jeanne and Larry Hervey in 1988. Guest rooms are individually decorated with antiques and good lighting, one with a queen-size lace canopy bed, another in white wicker, and a third with a hand-painted Victorian cottage set and a beautifully appliqued pink and white floral quilt. Breakfast includes fresh fruit and juice, bacon or sausage, home-baked goods, and such entrées as pancakes, waffles, or French toast.

"A rose theme carries throughout, with lace and rose placemats, a rose pattern on the china, and fresh roses on the table." *(Cynthia Nordstrom)* "Although on the same floor, the rooms are spaced apart from each other for privacy. Snacks and soft drinks are readily available. Potpourri, bathroom soaps and creams, and complimentary postcards are among the little extras that make this place special." *(Don & Michelle Carll)* "The red brick walkway led up to a wraparound porch where I relaxed in the hammock and my husband dozed in a cushioned rocker. Later, Jeanne and Larry chatted with us in the cozy parlor, pointing out the area's historic sites. Smooth, silky sheets; four soft pillows. We had our own well-lit reading nook by the fireplace complete with current magazines." *(Lena Fratz)* "Despite our late arrival the first night and car trouble the next, our hosts could not have been nicer or more accommodating." *(Maxine Fraade)*

Open All year.
Rooms 4 doubles—all with private shower bath, telephone, radio, clock, TV, desk, air-conditioning, ceiling fan.
Facilities Dining room, living room with piano, books, stereo; porch. ½ acre with off-street parking. Two blocks to river, marina.
Location E NC. 20 m E of Greenville. Historic district. Corner of Main & Academy Sts.
Restrictions No smoking. Children over 5.
Credit cards Visa, MC, AMEX, Discover.
Rates B&B, $65–75 double, $55–65 single. Extra person, $10. 5% senior discount.
Extras Airport/bus pickup.

WAYNESVILLE

Waynesville is a popular mountain resort, set between the Great Smoky Mountains National Park and the Pisgah National Forest. Summer activities include hiking, fishing, horseback riding, white-water rafting, golf, and tennis, while downhill and cross-country skiing are available nearby in the winter. Waynesville is 25 miles west of Asheville, 130 miles southeast of Knoxville, and 190 miles north of Atlanta.

Information please: The **Mt. Pisgah Inn** (Milepost 408.6, Blue Ridge Parkway, P.O. Drawer 749, Waynesville 28786; 704–235–8228), a motel-like structure, set on a mountaintop a mile high, with 360° panoramic views and cool nighttime temperatures. Rooms are plain but clean, with contemporary decor, and a balcony or deck to take in the vistas. Be sure to eat in the restaurant if you'd like the view; the cafeteria is fine if it's foggy or you're on a tight budget. "Ask for a room on the second floor with sliding glass doors; they have magnificent views." *(Joe Schmidt)*

Hallcrest Inn ¢ 👭 ✗
299 Halltop Circle, 28786

Tel: 704–456–6457
800–334–6457

Built as a private home in 1880, the Hallcrest sits atop Hall Mountain with views of Waynesville and the Balsam Mountains, in a quiet setting at the end of a gravel road. Martin and Tesa Burson, and David and Catherine Mitchell are the long-time innkeepers. Guest rooms are simply furnished, highlighted by family antiques; four rooms are in a motel-type annex called the Side Porch. The extremely reasonable rates include a breakfast of eggs, grits, juice, fruit, biscuits, breakfast meat, and beverage. A typical dinner might include roast beef, brown rice, squash casserole, lima beans with herbs, marinated cucumbers and tomatoes, home baked rolls with strawberry preserves and apple butter, and homemade ice cream. Apples in some form are served at each meal.

"Come to the Hallcrest to slow down and relax, make new friends, and eat excellent food. The food is placed on lazy Susans in the center of each table, enabling one to select (again and again) all the different dishes. Our room on the second floor of the main building was clean and comfortable with good reading lights." *(April Burwell)* "Although guests are welcomed into this extended family circle, one's need for privacy is equally respected. The front porch has a row of rockers inviting friendly conversation, overlooking the Blue Ridge Mountains and the town below. Hot homemade biscuits and rolls, tasty in themselves, are doubly scrumptious when topped with a touch of butter and a generous dollop of strawberry preserves." *(Ken Horn)* "The food remains plentiful and tasty as ever. Our favorites are the four bright upstairs rooms in the farmhouse." *(Joe Schmidt)* "We agree with your description. Lovely Appalachian views. We enjoyed our meals most when the dining room wasn't full." *(MR)*

Open May 1–Nov. 30.
Rooms 12 doubles—all with private bath and/or shower, fan. Some with fireplace. 4 rooms in motel-style annex.
Facilities Dining room, living room with TV, sitting room with TV, games, library; porches with rockers. 4 acres with lawns, woodland, children's play equipment.
Location W NC. 25 m W of Asheville. 2 m from town. Take Rte. 276 N from Waynesville, then turn left on Mauney Cove Rd. Follow signs to inn.
Restrictions No smoking in dining room. No alcohol at mealtimes.
Credit cards Discover, MC, Visa.
Rates MAP, $70–80 double, $50–60 single. Extra person, $30. Tipping of housekeeper, dining room staff appreciated. Children under 12, half-price; under 2, free. Weekly rates.
Extras Airport pickup, $15; station pickup. Crib.

Heath Lodge ¢ 👭 ✗ ♿
900 Dolan Road, 28786

Tel: 704–456–3333
800–432–8499

Set at 3,200 feet, Heath Lodge offers pure mountain air, to be enjoyed on wide porches with high-backed rockers. The buildings are constructed of native poplar and stone, and rooms are rustic but comfortable, many with wood-paneled walls and patchwork comforters. Bob and Cindy Zinser, who bought the inn in 1992, note that Heath Lodge attracts golfers, hikers, rafters, sightseers, and those whose only desire is to rock or lie in the hammock between meals. Breakfast is a hearty affair with fresh fruit, juice and such specialties as Red River pie, and banana nut pancakes, along with bacon, sausage, freshly baked muffins and biscuits. If preferred, the staff will deliver a continental breakfast to your room.

"The outdoor hot tub lets you admire the mountain, sky and trees, while soothing your muscles after a day of hiking or white water rafting." *(Pauline Feltner)* "Convenient location, yet a relaxing country-like setting." *(D. Bennett)* "Delicious four-course dinners are served in handsome dining room, with a crackling fire, rough stone walls, and beautiful quilts hung on the walls." *(Ruth Hoke)* "Spotless rooms with scented soap, shampoo, and lotion. Cindy Zinser produces splendid meals which are creative, imaginative, delicious, and healthy. Our waitress was a delightful college girl whose cheery disposition and charming mountain accent did much to enliven our meals. The lodge is a rustic, restful getaway, cooled by enormous trees. We enjoyed the lodge cats, especially Fred, who visited our room. The Zinsers bend over backward to be solicitous of guests' needs." *(Helen Barranger)*

Open All year.

Rooms 2 suites, 20 doubles—all with private bath and/or shower, TV, desk, fan. 2 rooms in main lodge, 20 in 7 outlying buildings.

Facilities Dining room; great room with card tables, TV, piano; library. 6 wooded acres with hot tub, gazebo, stream. Golf, fishing nearby.

Location 1 m to town. From I-40, take Exit 27, Hwy. 19/23. Go 6 m to Waynesville exit and take Hwy. 276 S. Go about 1/4 m to Kentucky Fried Chicken (opposite Pizza Hut), turn right onto Love Lane. Turn right again onto Dolan to inn on left.

Credit cards MC, Visa.

Rates MAP, $105–130 double, $75–100 single. Extra person, $50–75. Reduced rates for children. Prix fixe dinner, $20.

Extras Wheelchair access. Crib.

The Swag 👤 ♿

Route 2, Box 280-A, Hemphill Road, 28786

Tel: 704–926–0430
Fax: 704–926–2036

Innkeeper Deener Matthews reports that a " 'swag' is a dip between two knolls on a high mountain ridge. It is the traditional term used by our mountain neighbors for as long as anyone can recall to designate our particular site." Perched at 5,000 feet, the inn is made of hand-hewn logs from original Appalachian structures dating back hundreds of years, with a massive stone fireplace in the living room and original North Carolina art work. Each guest room is individually decorated with handmade quilts and woven rugs. Regional cuisine is presented in a healthy, imaginative and innovative style. The dinner menu might include clam chowder, baby greens with tomato dressing, grilled rainbow trout with saffron angel hair pasta, garlic sautéed vegetables, cheesy corn muffins, and chocolate mousse with brandy snaps.

"Our room, high under the eaves, was cozy, comfortable, with a remarkable view. The luxurious bathroom was equipped with soft terry cloth robes. For recreation you can step out the door and hike in the Great Smoky Mountains National Park, engage in activities from racquetball to croquet, or sit by the fire and enjoy a book from the extensive library.

Several times during the summer naturalists, musicians, and other experts offer programs for the guests." *(Sheila & Joe Schmidt)* "Deener is a warm, gracious hostess; the food is excellent, the grounds beautiful, and the company good." *(Sibyl Nestor)* "Individual log cabins are most private; for conviviality and conversation, there's a high-ceilinged common room and cheerful, all-at-one-table service for the three spectacular meals a day. Views, hiking trails (including a marked one that introduces the local wildflowers, trees, and shrubs), and kind, intelligent, interesting innkeepers, make this a special place." *(Crescent Dragonwagon)*

Worth noting: "Don't forget your toothbrush—it's miles to town."

Open Mid-May through Oct.

Rooms 2 cabins, 12 doubles—all with private bath and/or shower. Many with balcony, refrigerator. 7 with steam shower, 9 with woodstove or fireplace, coffee maker. 1 cabin with whirlpool tub, refrigerator, wet bar, fireplace.

Facilities Dining room, living room with fireplace, player piano, games, library; porch. 250 acres with woodland, wildflowers, hammock, swing, hiking trails, badminton, croquet, underground racquetball court, sauna, private entrance to Great Smoky Mt. National Park. Golf nearby.

Location W NC. 12 m from Waynesville, 5 m from Maggie Valley, 30 m W of Asheville. From Waynesville, take I-276 N toward Knoxville. Go 2.3 m past intersection with Rte. 19 to Hemphill Rd. Turn left on Hemphill Rd. to inn.

Restrictions No smoking. No children under 7. Dry county, BYOB.

Credit cards MC, Visa.

Rates Full board (for 2 people), $250–325 cabin, $175–285 double. Extra person, $60–70. Prix fixe lunch, $10; prix fixe dinner $30. 15% service. Box lunches. Nature, hiking, special workshops. 2-night minimum.

Extras Wheelchair access; some rooms equipped for the disabled.

WHITTIER

Information please: The **Chalet Inn** (Nations Creek Road, Route 2, Box 99, 28789; 704–586–0251) offers the feel of an Alpine guest house set against the backdrop of the Blue Ridge mountains. Twenty acres of forested land offer several trail options for hikers, while children can enjoy the play equipment.

The Fisher House B&B ¢   *Tel: 704–497–5921*
Camp Creek & Beck Branch Roads
Mailing address: P.O. Box 108, Bryson City, 28713

The Fisher House, an 1881 farmhouse, was home to five generations of the Fisher/Kinsland family before it was purchased in 1985 by Beverly and Gary Means.

"Hospitable, welcoming innkeepers. The decor is largely contemporary, with an emphasis on wood and the work of local artisans. The cozy den with overstuffed sofa and stone fireplace is especially inviting. Each guest room has its own temperature controls and large fluffy towels. Gary was also helpful in arranging dinner reservations on a busy evening. Breakfast is served in the dining room around 8:30 A.M., with everyone generally eating together, but the Meanses are flexible. We had an excellent egg, sausage, and cheese casserole, parsley potatoes, outstanding homemade biscuits, plus preserves, orange juice and fresh fruit. There's a big porch out front with a good view of the rolling hills and neighboring farms. An excellent base for touring the area." *(Virginia Henke)* "Our room was sunny and cozy, with a comfortable queen-size bed!" *(Joan Williamson)* "Lovely country decor and soft colors throughout; outstanding breakfasts." *(Kathleen Ferguson)* Comments appreciated.

Open All year.
Rooms 3 doubles—all with full private bath, fan, hairdryer. 1 with fireplace.
Facilities Dining room, den with fireplace, piano, TV, stereo, books; porch with swing, rockers. 2 acres with deck, hot tub, barbecue, picnic area. Swimming, boating, fishing, rafting, hiking, bicycling nearby.
Location W NC, 50 m W of Asheville. Midway between Cherokee, Bryson City, & Dillsboro; 5 min. to entrance to Great Smoky Mts. National Park & S terminus of Blue Ridge Pkwy. Just off Rte. 441 at intersection of Camp Creek & Beck Branch Rds. From I-40, take Exit 27 & follow Rte. 74W past Sylva. Take Rte. 441N to Cherokee exit and go $1/2$ m to Camp Creek Road & turn right.
Restrictions No smoking. Children by prior arrangement.
Credit cards None accepted.
Rates B&B, $50–70 double, $40–60 single. Extra adult, $20; extra child, $10. 2-night holiday/weekend minimum peak season. 10% discount for 4-night stays.
Extras Airport/station pickups, $.22/mile.

WILMINGTON

Located in southeastern North Carolina, on the Cape Fear River, 125 miles south of Raleigh, Wilmington is the state's largest port and a major trading center. Its historic district has been restored in recent years, and is now home to several B&Bs. The city has plenty of charm and several museums of interest, including the U.S.S. *North Carolina* Battleship Memorial; it's just a short drive to the ocean beaches and to several restored plantation homes.

Information please: Listed in past editions, we need current reports on **Catherine's Inn on Orange** (1410 South Front Street, 28401; 910–251–0863 or 800–476–0723), located on the Cape Fear River in Wilmington's historic downtown. Each of the three guest rooms has a private bath, and the B&B double rate of $60–80 includes a full breakfast, afternoon refreshments, bedtime liqueur, and terry-cloth robes.

In the residential Mansion District, a short drive from the Historic District and the beach, is the **Market Street B&B** (1704 Market Street, U.S. Highway 17–74, 28403; 910–763–5442 or 800–242–5442), offering three guest rooms at B&B double rates of $60–75. This handsome Colonial Revival-style home was built in 1917, and is listed on the National Register of Historic Places.

The Inn at St. Thomas Court ♿   *Tel:* 910–343–1800
101 South Second Street, 28401   800–525–0909
                                   Fax: 910–251–1149

Reconstructed from turn-of-the-century commercial buildings, The Inn at St. Thomas Court combines the privacy and independence of a hotel with some of the ambiance of an inn. Situated in the heart of historic Wilmington, the area is rich with antique and gift shops, museums and galleries.

"The main building is a Charleston-style two-story building with wide porches and wicker chairs. Our spotless one-bedroom suite had wide plank floors. Suites are individually decorated, with furnishings ranging from country French to Southwestern to antebellum, though the layout is the same in each. A pleasant surprise was the abundant lighting, large mirrors and shelf space in the bathroom. Terrific location, two blocks down to the Riverwalk to stroll and shop, with quite a few restaurants in walking distance. This is not a 'home-style' inn, although we found the office staff to be pleasant and helpful. There is a small bar for guests. Breakfast, which consists of a choice of juice, cereal, pastry or muffins, is ordered at check-in, then delivered to your door in a basket with the newspaper. You prepare your own coffee or tea in your suite. Linen napkins and real china are a nice addition." *(Ben & Peg Bedini)*

Open All year.
Rooms 34 1-2 bedroom suites—all with private bath, telephone, radio, clock, TV, desk, air-conditioning, fan, refrigerator, deck/balcony. Some with kitchenette, washer/dryer, whirlpool tub, fireplace. Rooms in 4 buildings.
Facilities Bar/lounge, guest laundry, books. Conference room, fax, copier, business services. Garden, courtyard, gazebo, off-street parking. Golf, tennis, sailing packages.
Location In downtown historic area. 15 min. to I-40, airport, beaches. On 2nd St. at Orange, 2 blocks from river. Call for directions.
Restrictions Smoking permitted in some suites.
Credit cards Amex, DC, MC, Visa.
Rates B&B, $90–100 suite. Extra person, $10. 2-night minimum holidays/special events. Weekly rates.
Extras Wheelchair access; 1 unit specially equipped. Cribs. German spoken.

Stemmerman's Inn ♦ᵢ

130 South Front Street, 28401

Tel: 910–763–7776
Fax: 910–763–7776

One of Wilmington's few riverfront inns, Stemmerman's was built as a warehouse in 1886, and restored as an inn in 1988. Owned by Joseph and Rita Khoury since 1987, it's managed by Debi Bohler. The guest rooms are on the second floor; a cocktail lounge occupies the first floor. "A restored turn-of-the-century warehouse with tall windows, nice river views, and convenient location. Comfortable room. Breakfast was muffins, coffee, and fruit left in the room that you prepared yourself." *(Celia McCullough)* Comments appreciated.

Open All year.
Rooms 7 suites—all with full private bath, telephone, clock, TV, desk, air-conditioning, fan, kitchenette, washer/dryer. Answering machine, microwave oven on request.
Facilities Bar/lounge with evening entertainment, terrace. Fax, copier service. Off-street parking.
Location In historic district. Take Market St. to downtown. Go left on Front St. for 1¾ blocks to inn on right (green awning).
Restrictions Traffic noise in some rooms. Smoking permitted.
Credit cards Amex, DC, Discover, MC, Visa.

Rates B&B, $59–179 suite. Extra person, $10. Children under 12 free. 10% corporate discount midweek. Senior discount. 20% weekly discount. 2-night weekend minimum. Tipping encouraged.
Extras Crib. Arabic spoken.

Taylor House Inn ¢
14 North Seventh Street, 28401

Tel: 910–763–7581
800–382–9982

The Taylor House Inn (formerly the Five Star Guest House) was built as a private residence in 1908, with golden oak fireplaces and an elaborate staircase, inlaid parquet and heart pine floors, stained glass and leaded windows, and 12 foot ceilings. Purchased in 1993 by Ray Higgins and Jim Long, the decor of guest rooms vary from Jacobean to antebellum. Furnishings are antique throughout, and most rooms have Oriental rugs, individual sitting areas, queen-size beds, and original clawfoot tubs. Breakfast includes juice, cereal, fresh fruit, and such daily entrées as eggs Benedict, blueberry pancakes, French toast, or quiche, served in the dining room by candlelight with china, silver, Waterford crystal and linen napkins. Also included is an early evening social hour with wine and hors d'oeuvres.

"Accommodating, hospitable innkeepers. A delightful Victorian home, decorated appropriately and highlighted by loving touches. Breakfast was a treat to linger over. Thoughtful touches: a decanter of sherry, homemade mints at bedside, wine and cheese at six, and a little gift at departure." *(Mrs. Richard Smith)*

Open All year.
Rooms 1 suite, 3 doubles—all with private bath and/or shower, telephone, radio, clock, air-conditioning, fan, fireplace.
Facilities Dining room, living room, family room with books, fireplace; library with piano, stereo; porch with swings. Walled garden, off-street parking.
Location Historic district. ½ blk from Market at N 7th St. 8 blks E of river.
Restrictions No smoking. Children over 12.
Credit cards AMEX, MC, Visa.
Rates B&B, $90 suite, $75 double, $65 single. Extra person, $15. 2-night weekend minimum, May–Oct. & holidays. 10% discount on 3-night stays.
Extras Airport/station pickup.

WILSON

Miss Betty's B&B Inn ¢ &
600 West Nash Street, 27893

Tel: 919–243–4447
800–258–2058

"Wilson," reports Fred Spitz, co-owner of Miss Betty's B&B inn, "is the antiques and tobacco capital of North Carolina, in the heart of swine country where 'Eastern Carolina' barbecue is king. Wilson is not a tourist town; we cater to the needs of the business community. Halfway between New England and Florida, and close to I-95, we offer a welcome resting point for the north/south traveler. My wife—Miss Betty—is a purist, an interior decorator, an antiques dealer, an excellent cook, and a natural personality for a bed and breakfast inn."

The inn occupies four buildings, dating from 1858 to 1943; two are listed on the National Register of Historic Places, and all are furnished with Victorian antiques and reproductions. Breakfast includes fresh juice, eggs, hot cakes, grits, bacon or locally made sausage, English muffins, and homemade pastries.

"Wonderful recommendations for area restaurants and entertainment. Spotless rooms with comfortable beds and beautiful antiques; quiet, homey atmosphere. Betty dresses in period costume and sets the breakfast table with antique china." *(Charlene Petrone)* "The honeymoon suite was private, immaculate, with extra treats of chocolates, crackers, and nuts. Lovely grounds with large shade trees and flowering shrubs." *(Barry Fetzer)* "Breakfast is excellent and ample for the most hearty appetite." *(Gail Webb Owings)* Reports needed.

Open All year.
Rooms 5 suites, 6 doubles—all with private bath and/or shower, telephone, TV, air-conditioning. Most with fireplace, ceiling fan. Some with desk. Rooms in 4 buildings.
Facilities Dining room, 4 parlors with fireplace, TV/VCR, laundry facility. 1½ acres with lawn games, off-street parking. Swimming, golf, tennis nearby.
Location E NC, 60 m E of Raleigh, 5 m E of I-95, ½ m from town center. From I-95, take Exit 116 to Rte. 42 E into Wilson. Turn left on Nash St. to inn on right.
Restrictions No children.
Credit cards AMEX, Discover, MC, Visa, DC, CB
Rates B&B, $70 suite, $60–70 double, $50–60 single.
Extras Wheelchair access; 1 room equipped for disabled.

WINSTON-SALEM

Winston-Salem is known for its attention to the arts, and is the home of Old Salem, a restored 18th-century Moravian village. Other sites of interest include Reynolds House, the estate of the late R.J. Reynolds, founder of the tobacco firm that bears his name. The residence and gardens are open to the public; the house has an excellent collection of American art. If all that culture makes you thirsty, we suggest a free tour of the Joseph Schlitz Brewing Company; their Winston-Salem facility produces 4 million barrels of beer annually.

Winston-Salem is in central North Carolina, 144 miles east of Asheville, 80 miles north of Charlotte, and 104 miles west of Raleigh.

Also recommended: About 12 miles west of Winston-Salem is the **Tanglewood Manor House** (Highway 158, P.O. Box 1040, Clemmons 27012; 910–766–0591). Once the private estate of William and Kate Reynolds, Tanglewood is now operated by Forsyth County as an 1150-acre park. Reasonably priced accommodations are available in the Manor house, a motel lodge, and cabins; a restaurant is also available. Recreation facilities include 3 golf courses, 9 tennis courts, a swimming pool and lake, horseback riding, and more. "Our room in the manor house overlooking the rose garden was super—spotless and well decorated. We enjoyed the porch with a beautiful view of the park. The park trails and gardens were an added treat." *(Cheryl Hill, also KJ)*

The **Wachovia B&B** (513 Wachovia Street, 27101; 910–777–0332) is a rose-and-white Victorian cottage with wraparound porch and white wicker rockers. The reasonable rates include a breakfast of fresh fruit and juice, yogurt, and home-baked breads and pastries, plus afternoon wine and cheese, and evening tea. "Clean and comfortable; friendly, low-key owner; great breakfast and snacks." *(Linda Phillips)*

For an additional area entry, see **Germantown**, 16 miles north of Winston-Salem.

Brookstown Inn 🏃

200 Brookstown Avenue, 27101

Tel: 910–725–1120
800–845–4262

The Brookstown Inn is based in an old cotton mill complex dating back to 1836. After a century of industrial operation, the mill had become obsolete, and was scheduled for demolition in the 1970s, when historians identified it as the city's first factory. The mill was placed on the National Register of Historic Places, and was restored as an inn.

Many guest rooms are exceptionally large, with loft ceilings, exposed, handmade brick walls, and rough-hewn beams. The decor is an eclectic mixture of Appalachian handmade quilts, traditional pieces, and antiques. Rates include the morning paper and a breakfast of coffee, orange juice, fresh fruit, cereal, and Moravian buns; early evening wine and cheese; and bed-time cookies and milk; evening turndown service. The Brookstown is located between Winston's commercial center and the restored Colonial village of Old Salem.

"Furnishings reflect its history: the cotton mill, the countryside, and the Moravian crafts." *(William MacGowan)* "Wine and cheese in the early evening and a fine continental-plus breakfast." *(Betty Norman)* "Walking distance to the best Winston-Salem has to offer." *(Carey Sutton)* "The staff is extremely courteous, helpful, and efficient. Some rooms are more charming than others, but that is strictly a matter of taste." *(Jeanne Smith)*

Open All year.
Rooms 71 suites—all with private bath, telephone, radio, TV, air-conditioning. Some with whirlpool bath, fireplace, microwave, coffee maker, or wet bar.
Facilities Parlor, dining room, meeting rooms. Courtyard, off-street parking.
Location Central NC. 4 blocks to downtown. From Business I-40, take Cherry St. Exit to Marshall Ave. Follow signs to Brookstown Ave.
Credit cards Amex, CB, DC, MC, Visa.
Rates B&B, $105–125 suite, $95–115 double. Extra person, $20. Children under 12 free in parent's room.
Extras Wheelchair access; some rooms equipped for disabled. Crib.
Rates B&B, $60–50 double, $40 single. 2-night minimum in cottage.

Henry F. Shaffner House

150 South Marshall Street, 27101

Tel: 910–777–0052
Fax: 910–777–1188

Built in 1907, the Henry F. Shaffner House is a handsome Tudor-style Queen Anne mansion restored as an inn by Henry Falls, Jr. in 1993; David Regnery is the manager. The original tiger oak and marbleized woodwork, brass fixtures, and hand-stenciled hardwood floors have been restored, and are complemented by elegant antique and reproduction decor. The guest room furnishings range from the cherry French country garden decor of the Reynolda room to the sophisticated neoclassic style of the Piedmont Room. Rates include a breakfast of fresh fruit, cereal, granola, muffins, Danish, fresh-squeezed orange juice, and yogurt, plus evening wine and cheese. "An elegant, charming place, close to area restaurants and the charm of Old Salem. Convenient to Business I-40." *(Lee Milton, also Earl Tonkin)*

Open All year.

Rooms 4 suites, 4 doubles—all with private bath and/or shower, telephone radio, clock, TV, air-conditioning, fan. 2 with whirlpool tub, 6 with desk, 2 with wet bar/refrigerator.

Facilities Dining room, living room with piano, library area, sun room, tea room. Off-street parking, hot tub planned for 1995. Free health club membership with tennis, swimming pool.

Location Border of downtown & Old Salem. 6 blocks to downtown; 3 blocks to Old Salem. 20 min. from airport. From Bus. I-40 E, take Cherry St./Convention Ctr. exit & go left on High St. 2nd left is Marshall; inn is at corner of Marshall & High Sts. From I-40 W, take Cherry St. Exit & go left on 1st St. Left again on Marshall to inn on right.

Restrictions Smoking only on 3rd floor veranda, front porch.

Credit cards Amex, MC, Visa.

Rates B&B, $119–250 suite, $89–140 double. Extra person, $15. Children under 12 free. 10% senior discount.

Extras Airport/station pickup. Crib.

Free copy of *INNroads* newsletter

Want to stay up-to-date on our latest finds? Send a business-size, self-addressed, stamped envelope with 52 cents postage and we'll send you the latest issue, *free!* While you're at it, why not enclose a report on any inns you've recently visited? Use the forms at the back of the book or your own stationery.

South Carolina

TwoSuns Inn B&B, Beaufort

South Carolina's major area of tourist interest is the Low Country, extending from Charleston down along the coast from Beaufort and Hilton Head to Savannah. This area's original wealth came from shipping and rice plantations, and later from cotton. For an interesting side trip, take Route 17 north from Charleston to Mt. Pleasant. A highlight of this drive is the stands lining the highway where sweetgrass baskets are sold. Using skills brought from Africa on slave ships, the local basketmakers create intricate pieces from simple trivets to large lacy baskets.

Inland, visitors will find deep forests, the foothills of the Blue Ridge mountains, and the Santee Cooper Lakes. In Aiken, visit Hopeland Gardens' flower-lined paths; in Abbeville, see a play in the restored Opera House; or snap photos of the colorful fields at Greenwood's Park Seed Company gardens.

AIKEN

Also recommended: About five miles southeast of Aiken is **Annie's Inn B&B** (Highway 78, P.O. Box 300, Montmorenci 29839; 803–649–6836). Built in the 1830s on a 2000-acre cotton plantation, it was later used by a country doctor as a home and a hospital. Scottie Peck opened Annie's as a B&B in 1984, decorating the rooms individually in country antiques. Though several common rooms are available, the large old-fashioned kitchen often serves as a gathering place for guests. "The rooms each have a private bath, heart-of-pine floors, fireplaces, and beds with handmade quilts and feather pillows. Scottie is a delightful, hospitable woman with a nice little dog, Annie Lou. Rural atmosphere with cotton fields out back and a pecan grove." *(Ann Christoffersen)* Annie's Inn has a wraparound porch, a swimming pool, and a practice green, while nearby Aiken offers golfing, polo grounds and tennis. B&B double rates for the eleven guest rooms range from $45–75 a night.

ANDERSON

River Inn ¢   *Tel:* 803–226–1431
612 East River Street, Route 76, 29624   *Fax:* 803–296–2203

Constructed in 1914 of heart-pine, the River Inn was restored as a B&B in 1990 by Patricia Clark, and features walnut-stained woodwork, beamed ceilings, and crown moldings. Breakfast is served at guests' convenience, and includes grits (whether you eat them or not), meat, eggs, fruit, juice, hot bread, coffee, and tea. "We had breakfast in our room, and enjoyed the artichoke quiche. Relaxing hot tub." *(Tracey Gelinas)* "Great food; friendly, helpful owners." *(Regina Smith)* Comments welcome.

Open All year.
Rooms 3 doubles—all with private tub and/or shower, radio, clock, TV, air-conditioning, fireplace. One with desk, balcony.
Facilities Dining room with fireplace, living room with stereo, fireplace, TV, books, fireplace; porch with swing. 6 acres with off-street parking, hot tub. Lakes nearby.
Location NW SC. Halfway between Atlanta, GA & Charlotte, NC. 50 m SW of Greenville. Historic district, 1½ m from town. From I-85 take Rte. 76 S. At fork, go left onto Main St. Go left onto River St. to Inn on right.
Restrictions No smoking. Children 5 and over.
Credit cards Amex, MC, Visa.
Rates B&B, $65 double, $55 single. Extra person, $10. AARP discount. 2-night minimum Clemson football season.

BEAUFORT

The second oldest town in the state, Beaufort (pronounced BUE-fort) was founded in 1711. Overlooking the Intracoastal Waterway, this historic port town has beautifully restored 18th and 19th century antebellum homes shaded by century-old trees. Beaufort is located in the Low Country of coastal South Carolina, 50 miles northeast of Savannah, Georgia, and 62 miles southwest of Charleston. It's 15 miles to the beaches of Hunting Island State Park on the Atlantic for swimming, fishing, and boating.

    Reader tip: "Our favorite restaurant, just short drive from town, was the Gullah House." *(Steve Holman)*

    Information please: Listed in many past editions is the well-known **Rhett House Inn** (1009 Craven Street, 29902; 803–524–9030), a handsome antebellum mansion, with a beautiful, flower-bedecked veranda. Although readers continue to report on the charm of some of the upper-floor guest rooms, the general perception is apparently that attention to detail has declined as prices (B&B, $125–195 double) have increased.

Facing the Intracoastal Waterway is the Greek Revival-style **Bay Street Inn** (601 Bay Street, 29902; 803–522–0050), on a quiet residential street convenient to downtown. Purchased in 1992 by Jeffrey, Leslee, and Haley Peth, the $95–125 B&B double rates includes a full breakfast.

Also recommended: Just opened in 1994 is the **Beaufort Inn** (809 Port Republic Street, 29902; 803–521–9000), built in 1920. Located one block from the water, it offers 13 luxurious guest rooms, combing period decor with such modern conveniences as in-room telephone with voice mail and computer hookups, soundproofed walls, and individually controlled thermostats. The $110–175 rates include a full breakfast and afternoon tea.

TwoSuns Inn B&B ♿
1705 Bay Street, 29902

Tel: 803–522–1122
800–532–4244
Fax: 803–522–1122

This 1917 Neoclassic Revival building, complete with veranda, was built as a private home. From 1943 until the mid-60s, it was used as the "teacherage," providing housing for Beaufort's female teachers. When purchased by Carrol and Ron Kay in 1990, it had been virtually abandoned. After extensive renovation and restoration, the inn opened in 1990. Oriental rugs accent the inlaid oak floors in the living and dining rooms, and Carrol's weaving loom resides in the adjoining parlor.

"Magnificent view of the bay from most rooms. We stayed in Chamber B, with access to a semi-private second floor porch furnished with white wicker. The inn is immaculate and parking is ample. The hospitable Kays made us feel right at home, providing maps, and ideas for things to do. Breakfast was served in the sunny and inviting dining room; we had a fresh fruit compote, homemade muffins and rolls, juice, cereal, and crepes filled with cheese, mushrooms, and turkey." (*Mr. & Mrs. Jerry Hammel*) "Our large bathroom had the original 'body' shower, with brass piping in a semi-circle to produce spray all around, set in new tiles." (*Patricia Swift*) "Rooms are fresh and cheery, some with interesting color combinations." (*SWS*) "My downstairs room had a private entrance from the porch. Breakfast was good and plentiful consisting of fresh fruit and juice, home-made muffins, and banana pancakes." (*William Novack*) "Welcoming, friendly host, who organized a croquet and horseshoes competition on the front lawn." (*Steve Holman*)

Open All year.
Rooms 5 doubles—all with private bath and/or shower, radio, telephone air-conditioning, telephone, fan. Cable TV on request. 3 with balcony/deck.
Facilities Dining room, living room with fireplace, books, games; parlor with TV/VCR, porch. Bay-front city lot with croquet; bicycles. Boating, fishing, swimming nearby.
Location Beaufort County SC. 45 m N of Savannah, GA. 65 m S of Charleston, SC. 5 short blocks from downtown.

Restrictions No smoking except on veranda, 2nd floor porch. No children under 12.
Credit cards Amex, MC, Visa.
Rates B&B, $108–120 double, $96–108 single. Extra person, $20. No tipping. AARP, AAA discounts. 10% discount for 4-day stay. Murder mystery weekends. 25% discount off-season.
Extras Wheelchair access; 1 room equipped for disabled.

CHARLESTON

Charleston, founded in 1670, was at one point the wealthiest city in Colonial America; many think that it is still the most beautiful. The Civil War brought major devastation and poverty to the city and halted development. Efforts to preserve the city's priceless heritage began in the 1920s. Restoration work progressed slowly until around 1975, when the American Bicentennial, followed by the founding of Spoleto Festival U.S.A., sparked the restoration and conversion of numerous homes and commercial properties into bed & breakfast inns and restaurants.

Sights of interest in Charleston and the surrounding area include the many restored houses and museums, antique shops, the city market, tours of the river and harbor, the public beaches and resorts (with full golf and tennis facilities) at Folly Beach, Seabrook Island, and Kiawah Island, and last but far from least, the beautiful gardens of Middleton Place, Magnolia Gardens, and Cypress Gardens. Although all three gardens bloom year-round, many think that they are at their most magnificent from late March to early April, when the azaleas are in full bloom.

The peak season in Charleston runs from March to mid-June, and from September through October. The times of highest demand are in late March and early April for the azaleas, and in late May and early June for the Spoleto Festival. Charleston is located midway along the South Carolina coast, at the confluence of the Ashley, Cooper, and Wando rivers and Intracoastal Waterway. It's 106 miles northeast of Savannah, GA, 113 miles southeast of Columbia, SC, and 94 miles southwest of Myrtle Beach.

Budget tip: If you're traveling along the coast, and Charlestown prices are tough on your wallet, consider spending a night or two in **Georgetown,** about an hour away, where prices are about 50% less. See listings for details.

Reader tip: "We parked our car on the street overnight with no problem, but another guest at the inn where we stayed had left some packages on the seat, and their car was broken into." And: "In most of Charleston's B&Bs, breakfast is served in your room or in the courtyard; if you prefer a communal breakfast, be sure to inquire."

Also recommended: The three suites at **Thirty-Six Meeting Street** (36 Meeting Street, 29401; 803–722–1034) are an excellent choice if you enjoy privacy plus B&B ambiance. Elegantly furnished with queen-sized rice beds and private baths, rates include breakfast and use of the inn's bicycles; the walled garden is available for relaxing. Owners Anne and Vic Brandt are Charleston natives. "Perfect location, just a short walk to the Battery, shops, churches, and markets of the historic district. Beautiful

Georgian detailing on this 1740 Charleston 'single house.' Our ground-floor suite had two bedrooms, private bath, sitting area, and several fireplaces. Lots of books, antiques, and fresh flowers. The kitchenette was supplied with fresh fruit, juice, homemade muffins and breads, gourmet coffee and eggs for a make-your-own breakfast." *(Betty Sadler)*

Information please: We need current reports on **The Anchorage Inn** (26 Vendue Range, 29401; 803–723–8300 or 800–421–2952), originally a 19th century brick waterfront warehouse. Renovated in 1990 in the English Tudor style, it has common areas accented with leaded glass windows, dark woodwork and paneling against ivory-colored walls, and Oriental rugs on parquet floors. Most of the 19 well equipped guest rooms face an interior courtyard, although those at the back of the inn look onto the street. The B&B double rate of $100–175 includes a full breakfast and afternoon tea; the inn is located just steps from Waterfront Park.

The Battery Carriage House (20 South Battery, 29401; 803–727–3100 or 800–775–5575) has been repaired, renovated, and redecorated under the ownership of Katherine and Drayton Hastie. Overlooking the waterfront and White Point Gardens, the inn offers eleven luxurious guest rooms, all with private baths, at B&B rates of $99–199. A continental breakfast is delivered to your room on a silver tray, or can be enjoyed in the garden. Built in 1790s, **The Brasington House** (328 East Bay Street, 29401; 803–722–1274) is a Charleston "single" house, meaning it's one room wide, two rooms deep, and three stories high, with a corresponding three-story piazza (Charlestonian for porch). Four guest rooms are available, and the $89–109 B&B double rates include a continental breakfast, afternoon wine, and liqueurs served in the evening; the bedrooms have either king/twin or queen-size beds. **The Elliott House Inn** (78 Queen Street, 29401; 803–723–1855 or 800–729–1855) has 26 guest rooms with period decor and Oriental rugs; guests gather in the garden courtyard for iced tea, afternoon wine and cheese, or to relax in the hot tub. The $89–130 rates also include continental breakfast, delivered to guests' rooms, and evening turndown service.

For a taste of Low Country plantation life, an easy drive from Charleston, see listings in **Edisto Island** and **McClellanville**).

Ashley Inn/Cannonboro Inn ¢

201/184 Ashley Avenue; 29403

Tel: 803–723–1848 (Ashley)
803–723–8572 (Cannonboro)
Fax: 803–723–9080

The Ashley and Cannonboro Inns were built in 1832 and 1853, respectively, and have been owned by Bud and Sally Allen since 1990. Rates include both breakfast and afternoon refreshments. A typical morning menu includes grits, cheese and sausage casserole, and buttermilk biscuits, or lemon poppyseed pancakes served with bacon, plus fresh fruit, juice, and coffee.

Ashley: "Elegant yet warm and homey feeling. Bud and Sally are warm and friendly innkeepers. Comfortable common areas for reading and conversation; tea, coffee, cookies, and sherry were always available." *(Solomon Levine)* "The owners and staff always made time to visit with us and answer questions, make reservations, and recommend attractions and restaurants. Delicious breakfasts; special diet requests accommodated. Our top-floor room was clean, attractive, and quiet." *(Caroline Pierson)* "The inn was exquisitely restored in period." *(Robert & Helen Buggert)*

Cannonboro: 'Delightful breakfast of almond crepes with lemon sauce served on the veranda alongside a narrow garden. Nicely appointed with antiques and matching fabrics. The helpful innkeepers have menus from almost every restaurant in town." *(Brad & Babs Rymer)* "Wonderful breakfast strawberries laced with Grand Marnier. Impeccably clean. Bud is an experienced builder, and Sally's interior decorating skills are evident from the moment one steps in the door." *(Keith Lay)*

Open All year.
Rooms 2 suites, 11 doubles—all with private bath, telephone, clock, TV, desk, air-conditioning, fan. Some with balcony/deck, fireplace, refrigerator.
Facilities Dining rooms, living rooms with fireplace, TV, stereo, books, guest refrigerator; porches, terrace. Bicycles, off-street parking.
Location Historic district; 15 min. walk from downtown; approx. 1 m to waterfront. From I-26, follow last exit sign, "Meeting St. Visitor Info" onto Meeting St. Go right onto Calhoun St. Go right onto Ashley Ave. Across from USC medical center. On trolley bus route.
Restrictions Street noise possible in front rooms. No smoking. Children over 11.
Credit cards Amex, Discover, MC, Visa (5% surcharge)
Rates B&B, $105–130 suite, $79–95 double. Extra person, $20.
Extras Spanish spoken.

John Rutledge House Inn   🏃 &.
116 Broad Street, 29401

Tel: 803–723–7999
800–476–9741
Fax: 803–720–2615

The John Rutledge House Inn was built in 1763 by one of the fifty-five signers of the U.S. Constitution, John Rutledge, later Chief Justice of the U.S. Supreme Court. Much of the history of South Carolina and the U.S. can be traced to meetings and writings which took place in the ballroom and library here; reminders of Rutledge's service is visible in the Federal eagle and South Carolina's emblem, the palmetto tree, forged in the antebellum ironwork. Of equal significance to some is the fact that Charleston's famous she-crab soup was supposedly invented here.

Meticulously restored and stylishly updated in 1989 by Rick Widman, rooms are furnished in antiques and period reproductions. Readers should be aware that one of the two carriage houses is a new building, constructed to duplicate the original; rooms in the main house have the most historic feel. Rates include continental breakfast brought to your room or served in the courtyard between 7 and 10 A.M. weekdays, until 11 A.M. on weekends, plus brandy and chocolates at your bedside each evening.

"We stayed in Mrs. Rutledge's Room, and were impressed by its beauty, spaciousness, and comfort." *(Donna Jacobson)* "Excellent location; friendly helpful staff. A good compromise between a true B&B and a big hotel." *(SK)* "Iced tea and cookies, or sherry, are served in the large, lovely parlor each afternoon. Extremely efficient service." *(Robert Freidus)* "Graciousness and quality. Our room, number 11, had a spacious bedroom with a sitting area, lounge chair with ottoman, and a gorgeous four-poster bed with handsome king-size canopy bed. Large dressing room area and bathroom with both tub and separate shower." *(Lee Todd)* "Our room in Cooper House (one of the carriage houses) was large and comfortable; the bathroom was exceptional." *(Judith Brannen)* "Our room in the original carriage house was immaculate with two canopied queen-size beds and a modern bathroom. Delightful breakfast in the courtyard." *(Jo-Ann & David Purser)*

Open All year.
Rooms 3 suites, 16 doubles—all with full private bath, telephone, radio, TV, desk, air-conditioning, fan, mini-refrigerator. Some with fireplace, deck. Rooms in inn and 2 carriage houses.
Facilities Parlor with fireplace, ballroom with fireplace, games, library. Off-street parking.
Location Historic district. From King St. turn right on Broad St. to inn.
Restrictions Smoking restricted in some guest rooms.
Credit cards Amex, MC, Visa.
Rates B&B, $235–285 suite, $130–225 double, $115–180 single. Extra person, $15. Children under 12 free in parents' room. 10% senior, AAA discount. Minimum stay requirements. Full breakfast, $5–10 plus 15% service.
Extras Limited wheelchair access; some rooms equipped for disabled. Crib, babysitting. Spanish, French spoken.

Lodge Alley Inn 🏃 ✕
195 East Bay Street, 29401

Tel: 803–722–1611
Inside SC: 800–821–2791
Outside SC: 800–845–1004
Fax: 803–722–1611

Originally built as a series of warehouses, the Lodge Alley offers the amenities of a small luxury hotel, and the feel of an historic inn. Rooms have the exposed brick walls and pine flooring of the original warehouses, and are decorated with Oriental rugs and elegant period reproduction furniture.

"Our one-bedroom suite had a small sitting room with comfortable couch and chairs, and overlooked a charming courtyard. Good breakfast." *(Ruth Tilsley)* "A small elegant hotel with a perfect location right next to the market. Our attractive, spacious room overlooked the courtyard. Our dinner here easily equalled the food served in some of the city's more celebrated restaurants." *(Brian Donaldson)*

Minor niggle: "Better reading lights."

Open All year.
Rooms 60 1–2 bedroom suites, 34 doubles—all with full private bath, refrigerator, telephone, radio, TV, air-conditioning, gas fireplace. Most with kitchenette; 8 with whirlpool tub, some with fireplace. 12 rooms in annex.
Facilities Restaurant, lounge, parlor with fireplace, meeting rooms, courtyard. Valet parking.
Location In historic district. On East Bay St., between Cumberland St. & Vendue Range.
Credit cards Amex, MC, Visa.
Rates Room only, $125–299 suite, $105–139 double. Extra person, $15. Children under 13 free in parents' room. Full breakfast, $5–7; alc lunch, $10–14; alc dinner, $37–40.
Extras Crib, babysitting. French, Italian spoken.

Middleton Inn ♦ ✕ 🕱

Ashley River Road, 29414

Tel: 803–556–0500
800–543–4774
Fax: 803–556–0500

Now a National Historic Landmark, Middleton Place was the plantation home of Henry Middletown, President of the First Continental Congress, and his son Arthur, a signer of the Declaration of Independence. Laid out in 1741, its formal, landscaped gardens were the first in America, with sweeping terraces and vast plantings of camellias, magnolias, and roses. Constructed on the grounds in 1986, the Middleton Inn has won architectural awards for its vine-covered concrete, glass, and wood design. Rates include breakfast and a tour of the plantation; there's an additional fee to tour the house itself. A short walk from the inn is the Restaurant at Middleton Place, which specializes in Southern plantation cooking. A buffet breakfast of cereals, fruits, muffins, Danish, juice, tea, and coffee is served from 7:30–10:00 A.M. in the inn's central lodge.

"A strikingly unusual sight as you approach. Nordic interior design; bright and comfortable guest rooms, each with floor-to-ceiling windows and views of the Ashley River. Wonderful for bird-watching. Enjoyed the swimming pool overlooking the river, the wildlife, and the beautiful gardens. The front desk staff was helpful with dinner recommendations and directions. Penachio's, an excellent Italian restaurant, is just down the road toward town." *(Celia McCullough)* "We drove into Charleston at night for dinner." *(Kate Sexton)* "During breakfast, a fox appeared for his morning snack from the hospitable desk clerk." *(Naomi Moschitta)* "Baths are fabulous in concrete, tile, and marble; all is fresh and spotless. Unlimited access to the magnificent gardens is a real plus." *(Carl Lundgren)* "The blond wood furniture seems hand-crafted; the large sofa facing a great fireplace is most inviting. The first sight of the severe concrete buildings in this peaceful and tranquil setting is somewhat startling. The interiors soon refute that impression; gradually the angular harshness of the buildings assumes a rugged, graceful air." *(John E. King)*

Open All year. Restaurant open for lunch daily; dinner on weekends.
Rooms 50 suites, doubles in 4 adjacent buildings—all with full private bath, telephone, radio, TV, air-conditioning, refrigerator, fireplace.
Facilities Lobby/living room with fireplace, breakfast cafe, restaurant, conference rooms. 100 acres with heated swimming pool, lawn games, 2 clay tennis courts, hiking trails, stableyard with farm animals. Golf nearby.
Location 14 m N of Charleston on Rte. 61.
Credit cards Amex, MC, Visa.
Rates B&B, $159 suite, $109 double. Dinner/museum package, $159.
Extras Pets by arrangement. Cribs, babysitting.

Two Meeting Street Inn

2 Meeting Street, 29401

Tel: 803–723–7322

Built 1892 as a father's wedding present to his daughter, this Victorian mansion has been run by the Spell family since 1946; Karen Spell is the innkeeper. Rates include afternoon tea and sherry, and a breakfast of home-baked muffins, fresh fruit, four kinds of juice, coffee, and a selection of teas, served in the dining room or on the veranda. This inn is deservedly popular; advance reservations (4–6 months ahead in season) are essential.

"An excellent location with beautiful views; staying among the historic houses gives you a real Charleston feel. Beautiful English oak paneling on the main floor. The living room and dining room have Victorian furnishings, built-in cabinets, and stained glass windows, installed by Louis Comfort Tiffany himself. Family silver, crystal, and mementos are tastefully displayed. Although guests share the breakfast table, they come and go at will and are served individually on china and silver. Guests compare dining experiences to the benefit of all." *(Susan Waller Schwemm)*

"Delightful breakfast served in the garden; friendly innkeeper, too." *(Pat Borysiewicz)* "The intimate atmosphere which makes each guest feel special and welcome." *(Sammy Feehrer)* "The wraparound piazzas are wonderful for morning coffee and evening sherry, with their Battery and harbor views." *(Janet Cyester)* "Unbeatable combination of marvelous architecture, beautiful decor, and attentive, friendly service. The staff also helped us plan other B&B stays in the Low Country." *(James & Pamela Burr)*

The Spell family also owns the **Belvedere** (40 Rutledge Avenue, 29401; 803–722–0973), an imposing, turn-of-the-century Colonial Revival home with early Adam-style woodwork brought from the old Belvedere Plantation (circa 1800), hence the name. Beautifully refurbished by David Spell, the house also has a real "Charleston feel" with period antiques and reproductions—rice beds, ceiling fans, even sweet grass baskets. "Quiet location a ten-minute walk from the market area. Efficiently managed by Rick Zenger, the Belvedere serves an 8:30 A.M. continental breakfast on individual trays in the second floor sitting room or on the circular porch overlooking Colonial Lake. Sherry, candy, chocolates and assorted munchies are left out for guests. The video, 'Dear Charleston,' which can be seen downtown for a fee, is available here for viewing anytime." *(Marty Wall & Kip Goldman)* "Attentive service, relaxed atmosphere encourages socializing among the guests." *(John & Mary Jenkins)* "Colonial Lake provides a cool breeze even on the hottest days, and is perfect for strolling or jogging." *(Donna Bocks)* "Comfortable and enjoyable; an excellent value." *(James Burr)*

Open All year. Closed Dec. 24, 25, 26.
Rooms Two Meeting Street: 9 doubles—all with private bath and/or shower, TV, air-conditioning, ceiling fan. Some with fireplace, balcony/deck. Belvedere B&B: 3 doubles—all with private bath and/or shower, TV, air-conditioning.
Facilities Two Meeting Street: dining room with fireplace, breakfast room, lobby with fireplace, parlor with fireplace, piazzas, formal garden. Belvedere: Parlor, dining room, porch; on-street parking. Tennis, golf, picnic area, beaches nearby.
Location Two Meeting Street: historic district, opposite Battery Park. Exit I-26 or Rte. 17 onto Meeting St. Inn is at end of Meeting St., the corner house at the Battery, near Battery Park. Call for directions to Belvedere.
Restrictions No smoking. No children under 9.
Credit cards None accepted.
Rates Two Meeting Street: B&B, $130–275 double. Extra person, $20. Belvedere: B&B, $95 double. Suggested tip: $5 per day. 2-3 night weekend/holiday minimum.
Extras German spoken at Two Meeting Street.

COLUMBIA

Capital of South Carolina for over 200 years, Columbia is located in the center of the state, and is home to the University of South Carolina. Children will enjoy visiting the Riverbanks Zoo and the Criminal Justice Hall of Fame, while history and architecture buffs will enjoy seeing the Hampton-Preston Mansion, a restored antebellum home, and the State House.

Information please: Recently renovated and ideal for longer stays is **The Whitney** (700 Woodrow Street at Devine, 29205; 803–252–0845 or 800–637–4008), about a 1/4 mile from the Five Points intersection, in a quiet residential neighborhood. The 74 handsome spacious rooms are furnished traditionally with American and English antique reproductions, and are equipped with private baths, TV, telephone, air-conditioning, kitchen with microwave, and a washer dryer. One- and two-bedroom suites are available at rates of $105 and $125 respectively, including a breakfast of juice and coffee, sweet rolls and biscuits, served in the inviting living room; children under 18 stay free in their parents' room.

Thirty miles northeast of Columbia is the **The Greenleaf Inn** (1310 North Broad Street, Camden 29020; 803–425–1806 or 800–437–5874), composed of two houses, the Colonial-style Reynolds House, built in 1840, and the Victorian-era McLean House. Rooms are furnished with antiques and period reproductions; its restaurant, McLean's, offers a creative Southern menu. "Although the inn's exterior needed sprucing up when we visited, we were delighted with our comfortable, spacious, and immaculate Reynolds House suite with modern private bath, cable TV, and telephone. Continental breakfast was delivered each morning at the requested time. We had an exceptional dinner at the Mill Pond restaurant, eight miles away." *(Peggy Bedini)* B&B double rates are $65–75.

Claussen's Inn at Five Points 🚸 ♿ *Tel:* 803–765–0440
2003 Greene Street, 29205 800–622–3382
Fax: 803–799–7924

Originally constructed in 1928 as Claussen's Bakery, the structure was rebuilt in 1986 as a small luxury inn by Richard T. Widman (owner of John Rutledge House in Charleston); Dan Vance is the general manager. Rates include a breakfast of coffee, juice, muffins and croissants; afternoon fruit and sherry, and turndown service with chocolates. Many of the building's original architectural features were preserved in the renovation, while skylights and terra-cotta tiling were added. Rooms are decorated with lots of plants, overstuffed furniture, four-poster or iron and brass beds, and traditional furnishings.

"The inn is interesting architecturally and ideally located within easy walking distance of the University of South Carolina. The Five Points area is a mixture of sidewalk cafés, small shops, and good restaurants." *(Pam Harpootlian)* "Quiet, good service, friendly staff; good area for a morning run." *(William Webster)* "Our room was on two levels, with a large living room and bathroom on the lower, and a sleeping alcove (and second bathroom and TV) on the upper level." *(Robert Freidus)* "As described. My two-level room was huge, with a modern bathroom." *(KM)* Reports welcome.

Open All year.
Rooms 8 suites, 21 doubles—all with full private bath, telephone, radio, TV, desk, air-conditioning. Some with fan, balcony, or loft.
Facilities Lobby with breakfast area, bar, fountain. Hot tub. Off-street parking.
Location Five Points section, near intersection of Saluda, Greene, and Harden Sts., in SE section of city. 4 blocks to center.
Restrictions No smoking in some guest rooms.
Credit cards Amex, MC, Visa.
Rates B&B, $115 suite, $85–105 double, $90–95 single. Extra person, $10. Children under 12 free. 10% AAA, AARP discount. Corporate rate, $75–105.
Extras Wheelchair access; some rooms equipped for disabled. Crib. Spanish spoken.

Richland Street B&B
1425 Richland Street, 29201

Tel: 803–799–7001

A neo-Victorian home built as a B&B in 1992, the Richland Street B&B showcases the design talents of owner Naomi Perryman, and offers the high ceilings, spacious rooms, and grand staircase typical of a Victorian home. The guest rooms are named for South Carolina governors, and have queen- or king-size beds with antique or reproduction decor; color schemes range from the soft peach and green of the Campbell room to the dark wood and deep red of the Hollings room. Breakfast menus include home-baked breads and muffins, with Belgian waffles or an egg and cheese casserole; rates also include afternoon refreshments.

"Naomi and Jim Perryman were friendly and helpful. The inn was built to blend with the architecture of this historic area. The spotless guest rooms are large with lovely furnishings. Delicious breakfast of waffles with bananas. Lemonade is served in summer on the front veranda. Though the inn is on a busy street, we were not aware of any traffic noise. Well-lit off-street parking." *(Susanne Ventura)* Additional comments welcome.

Open All year.
Rooms 1 suite, 6 doubles—all with private bath and/or shower, telephone, TV, air-conditioning. 2 with double whirlpool tub.
Facilities Dining room, living room with fireplace, verandas. Off-street parking.
Location Historic Preservation District. On Richland, between Bull & Assembly Sts. Walking distance to USC, Sidney Park, Roger Center.
Restrictions No smoking. Children 12 and over.
Credit cards MC, Visa.
Rates B&B, $120 suite, $80–100 double.

EDISTO ISLAND

Cassina Point Plantation
1642 Clark Road, 29438

Tel: 803–869–2535

If you need a break from busy Charleston, head south to sleepy Edisto Island and the historic Cassina Point Plantation. This 1847 plantation home was bought and restored by Bruce and Tecla Earnshaw in 1988. A typical breakfast might include juice and coffee, strawberries and cream, French toast with maple syrup, and sausage-stuffed mushrooms; the rates also include afternoon refreshments.

"During the Civil War, this house was occupied by Union troops after the island was evacuated, and much of their graffiti remains on the basement walls. The Earnshaws' careful restoration and exquisite furnishings allow one to clearly imagine 19th century plantation life. Molly, their well-mannered Labrador retriever, will accompany you on enjoyable nature walks along the creek and marsh. The innkeepers arranged a fascinating tour of local historical sites." *(James & Pamela Burr)* "Warm and welcoming innkeepers; clean, attractive rooms; delicious meals, beautifully presented." *(Carmella Bosile)* "After evening wine and cheese, we had an excellent dinner at the Old Post Office Restaurant." *(Perry Morehouse)* "Good lighting, plumbing and plenty of parking." *(Ethelyn Owen)* "Remote setting with a grove of huge oak and pecan trees, grazing horses and a beautiful marsh view." *(Thomas Russell)* "After a morning of walking and birdwatching, we relaxed on the covered deck by the river." *(Bob & Barbara Armstrong)* A word to the wise: "Finding the inn can be a challenge. Listen carefully if you receive directions on the phone."

Open All year. Weekends only Jan., Feb. Closed Mon., Tues.
Rooms 4 doubles—all with private sink/toilet, sharing 2 full baths. All with clock, air-conditioning, fan, fireplace.
Facilities Dining room with fireplace, living room with fireplace, family room with TV/VCR, library; 2 porches. 145 acres with parking, creek house, lawn games, dock. 100 feet to creek, salt marsh for boating, fishing, crabbing, shrimp. Golf nearby. 6 m to Edisto Beach for swimming, shelling.
Location SE SC. 45 m S of Charleston. From Rte. 17 take Rte. 174 onto Edisto Island. Go left onto Indigo Hill Rd. At end of road, go left onto Clark Rd. At end of Clark Rd. you will come to three dirt roads. Turn right on the dirt road that looks the most travelled. At red-roofed barn, go through the gates to inn.
Restrictions No smoking. Children over 5 preferred.
Credit cards None accepted.
Rates B&B, $95 double, $75 single. Extra person, $20.
Extras Boat moorings; horses boarded.

GEORGETOWN

Originally settled in the early 1700s by indigo and rice planters, Georgetown has long been a major port. A variety of tours is available to explore the town: walking, horse and carriage, tram, and water tours cover the historic district, area plantations, the port, and other sights of interest. Beautiful beaches are nearby at Huntington State Park and Pawley's Island, while most of the rice plantations, the area's original source of prosperity, have largely been replaced with golf courses. Georgetown is located on the South Carolina coast, about 10 minutes from the beach, about 30 minutes south of Myrtle Beach and one hour north of Charleston.

Also recommended: Received just as we were going to press was an enthusiastic report on the **King's Inn at Georgetown** (230 Broad Street, 29440; 803–527–6937) "A restored 1825 Federal mansion, handsomely decorated with many interesting touches in the public rooms and guest rooms. Breakfast is worth forgetting your diet for. Charming owners Marilyn and Jerry Burkhardt make you feel glad you've come." *(Jean Burbage)* B&B double rates for the seven guest rooms are $75–115.

For an additional area entry, see **McClellanville**.

1790 House ¢ ♿   *Tel: 803–546–4821*
630 Highmarket Street, 29440

Built in 1790 in the West Indies style, when Georgetown's rice planter culture was at its peak, the 1790 House was bought by Patricia and John Wiley in 1992. Breakfast is served in dining room or on the veranda, and might include fresh strawberries, chicken quiche, cheddar potatoes, fried green tomatoes, and home-baked pumpkin ginger muffins. Soda and iced tea are always available, and evening wine is served.

"John Wiley was a most hospitable host, who graciously recommended restaurants for dinner, and described a recent archaeological excavation made on the property. The spacious Indigo Room has a sitting area, twin-size pencil post beds, and a fireplace. The bath was decorated in shades of red and had a modern shower." *(William Novack)* "Rooms are well appointed and sensibly priced. John is knowledgeable about area attractions. Delightful breakfast." *(Jerry & Barbara Ryan)*

Open All year.
Rooms 1 cottage, 1 suite, 5 doubles—all with private bath and/or shower, radio, clock, air-conditioning. Some with desk, fan, fireplace. Telephone, TV on request. Cottage with whirlpool tub, refrigerator, patio.
Facilities Dining room with fireplace, living room with fireplace, piano; family room with fireplace, books; porch; bicycles.
Location Historic district. From Hwy. 17 S, go left onto Screven St. Go left onto Highmarket St. to inn on left.
Restrictions No smoking. Children 12 & over.
Credit cards Amex, MC, Visa.
Rates B&B, $115 cottage, $85–95 suite, $65–75 double. Extra person, $25. Child, senior, AAA discount. Corporate, midweek rates off-season.
Extras Limited wheelchair access. Airport pickup.

The Shaw House ¢ 🧍   *Tel: 803–546–9663*
8 Cyprus Court, 29440

Mary Shaw describes her B&B as "a recently built two-story Colonial with a large front porch and rocking chairs. Rooms are spacious, furnished with antiques, and our location is ideal—close to town yet very quiet. We serve refreshments on arrival, and a home-cooked Southern breakfast each morning. We turn back beds at night, and always send guests on their way with 'a little something'—perhaps a recipe, a Christian prayer, or a little jar of jam or jelly."

"We ate breakfast in the den, overlooking the beautiful Willowbank salt marsh." *(Leslie & Pat Rowell)* "Located in a picturesque part of Georgetown, a delightful area for bird lovers." *(Betty Norman)* "Mary and Joe made us feel at home instantly. Mary's breakfasts were delicious; her enthusiasm for the area left us with wonderful memories." *(Bob & Kathy Van Dyne)* "My lovely ground floor room had a four-poster bed, lots of pillows, and a good reading light. Mary Shaw is friendly and personable." *(Robin Clarke)*

Open All year.
Rooms 3 doubles—all with full private bath, telephone, radio, TV, air-conditioning.
Facilities Living room with piano, den with TV, games; kitchen, porch. Golf, tennis, marinas nearby.
Location Coastal SC. 30 m SW of Myrtle Beach, 10 m S of Pawley's Island, 60 m NE of Charleston. 4 blocks from center of town. From Hwy. 17, turn W on Orange St. and continue to Cyprus Ct. Turn left on Cyprus to inn.
Credit cards None accepted.
Rates B&B, $45–55 double. Extra person, $10. 10% senior discount.
Extras Airport/station pickups. Crib, babysitting.

GREENVILLE

Pettigru Place B&B
302 Pettigru Street, 29601

Tel: 803–242–4529
Fax: 803–242–1231

While many people think of B&Bs only for vacation travel, there's no better way to perk up your spirits on a tough business trip than a stay at a welcoming inn. A classic Georgian Federalist home built in the 1920s, Pettigru Place was restored as a B&B in 1993 by Gloria Hendershot and Janice Beatty, who took care to accommodate the needs of business travelers. Breakfast is served at guests' convenience, and includes fresh fruit and juice, homemade breads, muffins, or coffee cake, and a hot entrée—an egg casserole, waffles, or French toast with breakfast meat. Rates also include evening turndown service with a pillow sweet. The simple but elegant guest rooms have queen- or king-size beds, antiques, period reproductions, fresh flowers, and featherbeds. "Careful attention to detail. Charming innkeepers; first-rate breakfast; excellent location. Have dinner at the magnificent Seven Oaks restaurant, two blocks away." *(Ina Gartenberg)*

Open All year.
Rooms 1 2-bedroom suite, 3 doubles, 1 single—all with private bath and/or shower, telephone, radio, clock, TV, desk, air-conditioning, ceiling fan. 1 with fireplace, double whirlpool tub, balcony.
Facilities Dining room, living room with fireplace, books; conference room, guest kitchen, porch. Fax, copier service. English garden, off-street parking. Golf nearby.
Location NW SC. 1 hr. S of Asheville, 1½ hrs. NW of Columbia. Downtown historic district; 3 blocks to center. Easy access from I-385, I-85, I-26; call for directions. On Pettigru between Toy & Williams Sts.
Restrictions No smoking. Children over 12.
Credit cards Amex, MC, Visa.
Rates B&B, $145 suite (triple), $79–130 double, $69 single. Corporate rate.

GREENWOOD

Inn on the Square ¢ ✕   *Tel:* 803–223–4488
104 Court Street, 29646   800–231–9109
                                      Fax: 803–223–7067

The Inn on the Square includes two commercial buildings dating back to the early 1900s; after use as everything from a car dealership to a dance hall, they were rebuilt in 1986 as a part of Greenwood's Uptown Square revitalization project. Tom Fischer owns the inn; Ellyn McKenna is the manager. The inn's dining room specializes in such entrées as prime rib, rack of lamb with rosemary, and grilled salmon with lemon caper sauce. "Charming restoration. Guest rooms are pleasant, medium in size, and furnished with period reproductions. The restaurant has a fine French chef, but we were looking for vegetarian dishes, so we opted for Dini's, a nearby Italian restaurant. The Park Seed Company demonstration gardens are worthwhile to visit." *(Celia McCullough)* More reports welcome.

Open All year. Closed Christmas.
Rooms 48 doubles—all with full private bath, telephone, radio, clock, TV, desk, air-conditioning. Refrigerator on request.
Facilities Restaurant, dining room, atrium lobby; bar/lounge with TV, jukebox, live blues/jazz Mon., Wed. Off-street parking, swimming pool. Lake Greenwood nearby.
Location NW SC. 53 m S of Greenville. In town, historic district.
Restrictions Street noise in some rooms. No smoking on second floor.
Credit cards Amex, DC, Discover, MC, Visa.
Rates Room only, $73–85 double. Alc breakfast, $3–5; alc lunch, $8; alc dinner, $25–30.
Extras Wheelchair access; some rooms specially equipped. Crib, babysitting with notice. French, Spanish spoken.

MCCLELLANVILLE

Laurel Hill Plantation ¢   *Tel:* 803–887–3708
8913 North Highway 17, P.O. Box 190, 29458

Lee Morrison's family goes back four generations in the McClellanville area; in the early 1980s, he and his wife Jackie moved the 140-year-old family home, Laurel Hill, from Route 17 to a more scenic spot overlooking the water. Destroyed by Hurricane Hugo in 1989 (along with much of McClellanville), the Morrisons rebuilt the home, retaining its historic charm but adding effective insulation and modern conveniences. Breakfast is served at 8:30 A.M., and might include a grits casserole or artichoke strata with Canadian bacon, fruit salad, home-baked Amish bread with herb butter, plus preserves, juice, coffee, and tea. "We love to sit out with a cup of coffee on the inviting wraparound porch; one of the inn's five outdoor pet cats will probably join you for a snooze. The inn is furnished with simple country antiques, handmade quilts, canopy and spindle beds, and primitive designs. The Gator Gaze room has two antique three-quarter beds and overlooks a fresh-water pond where several alligators (not pets) live. The area abounds with birds and wildlife, and the porch binoculars bring them into close range. The owners are warm and hospitable, knowledgeable about the area, its customs and events." *(Phyllis Cline)* "Outstanding food, attractively served. When the tides and weather are cooperative, guests are taken for a pontoon boat ride. The antique shop has reasonable prices, superb quality. A few restaurants in town, with a larger selection in Georgetown, Mt. Pleasant, and Charleston. Magnificent views of Jeremy Creek, the marsh, the inland waterway, islands, and a distant lighthouse. Extremely clean and well lit; beautiful, well maintained grounds." *(Douglas Macfie)* "Charming but non-intrusive hosts. Spectacular sunrises and sunsets." *(Sandra Buck)*

Open All year.
Rooms 4 doubles—all with full private bath, air-conditioning, clock, desk, fan.
Facilities Dining room, living room, common room with piano, fireplace, TV; sunporch, porch with swing, hammock; gift shop. 80 acres with parking, lawn games, swings, freshwater pond, saltwater creek with dock for fishing, boating, crabbing. Cape Romain National Wildlife Refuge.
Location Low Country; 30 m N of Charleston, 25 m S of Georgetown. 5 m to village. From Hwy. 17S, go left onto dirt road across from St. James Santee School. Go approx. $7/10$ m to Inn. From Hwy. 17N, go right onto dirt road after fire station (across from St. James School).
Restrictions No smoking. Children over 5.
Credit cards MC, Visa.
Rates B&B, $65–85 double, $55–65 single. Extra person, $15. No tipping. AAA discount.
Extras Crib.

MYRTLE BEACH

The largest city on South Carolina's 60-mile-long Grand Strand, Myrtle Beach is a popular tourist destination with the usual complement of boardwalk entertainment, plus water and amusement parks. In addition to swimming, fishing and boating in the Atlantic, the area is home to over 70 golf courses, most popular in spring and fall. On rainy days, you can sample innumerable shopping outlets, country music, and variety theaters. Myrtle Beach is about 90 miles north of Charleston, and about 20 miles south of the North Carolina border.

Brustman House ¢
400 25th Avenue South; 29577

Tel: 803–448–7699
800–448–7699
Fax: 803–626–2478

Owned by Mina and Wendell Brustman and their daughters Brandy and May since 1992, The Brustman House offers a welcome change from the busy boardwalk area. A Colonial-style home built in 1968, it is furnished throughout with contemporary Scandinavian decor; low-fat, heart-healthy breakfasts are a speciality. Breakfast is served at guests' convenience and might include 10-grain buttermilk pancakes, fritatta with fresh garden herbs, or eggs scrambled with low-fat cream cheese, and fresh fruit. Early morning coffee and the newspaper awaits guests in the garden room.

"The quiet, inviting wooded setting as well as the spacious and comfortable suite would be a most welcome refuge after a day on the beach." *(Betty Norman)* "The Brustmans helped us make golf plans. Nice, clean accommodations. Afternoon tea and brownies, or wine, cookies, nuts and more, were available daily. Comfortable, well located, well managed. Interesting hosts." *(Nancy Hodge)*

Open All year.
Rooms 1 suite, 4 doubles—all with private bath, telephone, radio, clock, desk, air-conditioning, fan. Suite with TV/VCR, refrigerator.
Facilities Dining room, living room with books, video library, games, piano; guest kitchen, laundry facilities, porch. 1½ acres with off-street parking, gazebo, lawn games, walking paths, bicycles. 300 yards from ocean beach.
Location S end of Myrtle Beach. From N or Hwy 501, take Business 17S through downtown Myrtle Beach; turn left onto 25th Ave S. From S take Business 17 when it splits from Bypass 17. 4 blocks after golf course (on right), turn right after sign for Kingsway Pentecoastal Church.
Restrictions No smoking. Children over 10 preferred.
Credit cards MC, Visa to hold reservations only.
Rates B&B, $80 suite, $38–75 double, $35–70 single. Extra person, $10. Reduced rates for children. 10% senior, AAA, or 4-night discount. 2-3 night weekend/summer holiday minimum. Alc dinner by advance reservation, $25.
Extras Airport, station pickup. Pets at management discretion. Crib. Limited French, German spoken.

Serendipity, An Inn ¢

Tel: 803–449–5268

407 71st Avenue North, 29572

Serendipity is a Spanish mission–style inn purchased by Terry and Sheila Johnson in 1994; they offer comfortable motel-style accommodations, just 300 yards from the beach. A breakfast of juice, fruit salad, cereal, hard-boiled eggs, and home-baked bread and muffins is served in the breakfast room, decorated with white wicker.

"Our room was done in country prints and antique furniture. Terry, Sheila, and their daughter Deborah were always around and never seemed too busy to give directions, offer recommendations, or just chat. Clean and neat swimming pool area with lots of flowers." *(Suzanne Zill)* "Excellent lighting, spotless housekeeping, satisfactory plumbing, ample parking, quiet setting, comfortable room, food fresh and healthy, and delightful owners, who treated us like old friends." *(Paul Whittington)*

Open All year.
Rooms 3 suites, 12 doubles—all with private bath and/or shower, TV, desk, refrigerator, air-conditioning. Some with radio, fan, balcony, kitchen. 8 rooms in annex.
Facilities Living room with TV/VCR, fireplace, books; garden room, patio with fountain. Heated swimming pool, Jacuzzi, gas grill, shuffleboard, garden, Ping-Pong. 300 yds. to ocean beaches, fishing, water-skiing.
Location N coastal SC, Horry County. 90 m NE of Charleston, SC; 40 m NE of Georgetown, SC; 60 m SW of Wilmington, NC. Center of town. Take Hwy. 17 Bus. to 71st Ave. N. Turn E toward ocean; inn is just off Hwy. 17.
Restrictions No smoking in common rooms.

Credit cards Amex, MC, Visa.
Rates B&B, $73–115 suite, $52–95 double. Extra person, $10. Tipping encouraged.
Extras Crib.

Free copy of *INNroads* newsletter

Want to stay up-to-date on our latest finds? Send a business-size, self-addressed, stamped envelope with 52 cents postage and we'll send you the latest issue, *free!* While you're at it, why not enclose a report on any inns you've recently visited? Use the forms at the back of the book or your own stationery.

Key to Abbreviations and Symbols

For complete information and explanations, please see the Introduction.

¢ Especially good value for overnight accommodation.
♦ Families welcome. Most (but not all) have cribs, baby-sitting, games, play equipment, and reduced rates for children.
✗ Meals served to public; reservations recommended or required.
✗ Tennis court and swimming pool and/or lake on grounds. Golf usually on grounds or nearby.
♿ Limited or full wheelchair access; call for details.
Rates: Range from least expensive room in low season to most expensive room in peak season.
Room only: No meals included; European Plan (EP).
B&B: Bed and breakfast; includes breakfast, sometimes afternoon/evening refreshment.
MAP: Modified American Plan; includes breakfast and dinner.
Full board: Three meals daily.
Alc lunch: À la carte lunch; average price of entrée plus nonalcoholic drink, tax, tip.
Alc dinner: Average price of three-course dinner, including half bottle of house wine, tax, tip.
Prix fixe dinner: Three- to five-course set dinner, excluding wine, tax, tip unless otherwise noted.
Extras: Noted if available. Always confirm in advance. Pets are not permitted unless specified; if you are allergic, ask for details; *most innkeepers have pets.*

Tennessee

Blue Mountain Mist Country Inn, Sevierville

Music (from country to bluegrass to rock 'n' roll), whiskey, horses, Davy Crockett, and Appalachian mountain crafts are sounds and images evoked by the name of this state. A major attraction (perhaps too much so) is the Great Smoky Mountains National Park, the most visited national park in the country. Although we think of Tennessee as a rural state, its major cities—Nashville, Memphis, Knoxville, and Chattanooga—are key manufacturing centers, while Oak Ridge is home to National Laboratory and other high-tech industries. The key to Tennessee's development dates to the 1930s. At that time Tennessee Valley Authority built huge dams all over the state, creating inexpensive electricity for homes and business.

Worth noting: Many of Tennessee's inns are in dry counties; if you enjoy having a glass of wine with your dinner, call ahead or come prepared.

ASHLAND CITY

Bird Song Country Inn   *Tel:* 615–792–4005
1306 Highway 49 East at Sycamore Hill, 37015   *Fax:* 615–329–0134

In interior design, artful juxtaposition can make the most distinctive statement. At Birdsong, chinked cedar log walls contrast with a contemporary art collection by Salvador Dali, Paul Harmon, Red Grooms, Peter Max, Andy Warhol, R.C. Gorman, and Ouray Meyers; beautiful antiques and Persian rugs are set off by hand-stitched quilts and a rough stone fireplace. Built as a summer house in 1910 by the Cheek family of Maxwell

House coffee fame, Birdsong was restored as an inn in 1990 by Anne and Brooks Parker. "The friendly hosts welcomed me with delicious refreshments." *(Anne Alexander)* "One can snuggle in bed under a soft down quilt with a good book, or join other guests in front of the great room fireplace and share stimulating conversation and a glass of wine. After an afternoon of horseback riding through acres of wooded forest, you can relax in the patio hot tub, surrounded by an herb garden. Breakfast starts with fresh coffee, fresh-squeezed orange juice or apple cider, scones, sweet rolls, or pastry baked by Anne and served by Brooks, followed by homemade granola, mini-quiches, and berries in cream." *(Sue & John Catching)* "Beautifully furnished; unobtrusive attention to detail, from the fresh flowers to the carafe of spring water in our room." *(Nancy Polk)*

Open All year.

Rooms 1 suite, 3 doubles—all with private bath and/or shower only. All with clock, desk, air-conditioning. 2 with fan. 1 bedroom in guest cottage.

Facilities Living/dining room with stereo, fireplace; library with TV/VCR; porch with swing, patio with grill, hot tub. 10 acres with off-street parking, hammocks, gazebo, gardens, lawn games. River with picnic area, swimming, canoeing, fishing. Hiking, horseback riding, golf, tennis; massage by reservation.

Location N central TN. 20 m NW of Nashville. 4 m N of town. From I-24 W take Exit 24, Ashland City, Hwy 49. Go S to inn on left.

Restrictions No smoking in living room, dining room.

Credit cards Amex, Discover, MC, Visa.

Rates B&B, $80–100 suite, double. Extra person, $15. Senior, AAA discount.

Extras Airport, station pickup, $20. Pets by arrangement. Cribs. Spanish spoken.

CHATTANOOGA

Chattanooga is located on the Tennessee River, in southeastern Tennessee, at the Georgia border. For an overview of the city, drive or take the incline railway to the top of 2,100-foot high Lookout Mountain, just south of the city. Of particular interest is the Tennessee Aquarium, and the Chickamauga and Chattanooga National Military Park, commemorating several Civil War battles.

Also recommended: While too large at 300 rooms for a full entry, the **Chattanooga Choo-Choo Holiday Inn** (1400 Market Street, 37402; 615–266–5000 or 800–TRACK–29) is really enjoyed by readers. Located in the depot of that memorable railway and listed on the National Register of Historic Places, the lobby offers seating beneath the soaring dome of the vestibule. "Most of the rooms are in three different motel sections, but the antique-filled rooms in the old railroad cars are charming, spacious, and romantic; ask for one facing the attractive gardens." *(Ruth & Derek Tilsley)* "Our railroad car had Victorian style furnishings, a queen-size bed, firm mattress, marble stands on each side with hanging lamps, and two comfortable chairs with a marble top table in between, and more. A trolley connects this large complex; parking is tight." *(HJB)*

The **Radisson Read House Hotel** (827 Broad Street, 37401; 615–266–4121 or 800–333–3333) is listed on the National Historic Register, and has 250 guest rooms, a swimming pool and restaurant. Double rates range from \$86–112; children under 18 stay free, and appealing packages are available. "Historic downtown hotel, completely renovated. Furnished in the usual period reproductions; pleasant experience, convenient location." *(KM)*

Bluff View Inn ✕ ⅋

412 East Second Street; 37403

Tel: 615–265–5033
Fax: 615–265–5944

Overlooking the Tennessee River, the Bluff View Inn is a Colonial Revival mansion built in 1928, and restored as a restaurant and inn by Charles and Mary Portera in 1991; Doug Schumaker is the manager. Nearby are the River Gallery and Sculpture Garden, Anna Houston Museum, Hunter Museum of Art, and the Tennessee Riverwalk, leading to the Tennessee Aquarium. A typical dinner at the inn's restaurant might include grilled scallops with pepper coulis, followed by lamb chops with pesto gratin, concluded with chocolate fritters; casual meals are served at the Back Inn Café. Breakfasts, which might consist of fruit salad with mango-raspberry sauce, and frittata with sausage, avocado, and salsa, are served at individual tables between 8–9 A.M.

"Beautiful outdoor sculpture garden overlooking the river. Mary Portera also owns the art gallery next door." *(Lynn Edge)* "Staff is friendly and efficient; rooms are clean and tidy. Good water pressure and adequate heat control. Enjoyed the Back Inn Café's vegetarian selections. Phenomenal breakfast." *(Becki Carroll)* "The inn is shaded by immense magnolia trees." *(Vanessa Young)* "Wonderful warm Brie with herbs. The C.G. Martin room had a spectacular 180° view of the river and surrounding hills." *(Gunter Rauh)*

Areas for improvement: "Low-fat breakfast choices; afternoon tea or wine so the guests could get acquainted."

Open All year. Restaurant closed on Sundays.
Rooms 3 doubles—all with full private bath (jetted tubs), telephone, clock, TV, air-conditioning, gas fireplace. 1 with balcony.
Facilities Restaurant, café, living room, library with fireplace, books; sitting room with fireplace, bar/lounge, unscreened porch. 1 acre with parking.
Location Downtown Chattanooga, arts district. From I-24, take Hwy 24 N. Turn right onto 4th Street. Turn left onto High St. Go left on East Second St. Inn on right.
Restrictions No smoking.
Credit cards Discover, MC, Visa.
Rates B&B, \$125–175 double. Corporate rate Mon.–Thurs., \$115–135. Alc lunch, \$8; alc dinner, \$45.
Extras Wheelchair access to restaurant, public bathroom.

The Milton House B&B ¢

504 Fort Wood Place, 37403

Tel: 615–265–2800

Built in 1915, and restored as a B&B in 1993 by Susan Mehlen, Milton House is a red brick Greek Revival home with Ionic white columns, handsome stonework, and a slate roof. The interior is no less imposing with 12-foot ceilings, maple and heart pine floors, and ornate trim. Breakfast, served at 8 or 9 A.M., includes home-baked muffins, cereal, yogurt, milk, orange juice, fresh fruit and such entrées as quiche, scrambled eggs, or pancakes and bacon.

"An imposing structure, beautifully furnished with antiques and fine linens. Tasty breakfast of eggs, pancakes, bacon, juice, and coffee. Gracious hospitality." *(Ina Gartenberg)* "Susan is delightful, enthusiastic, bubbly, loquacious, and entertaining. Attractive, individually decorated guest rooms." *(Mr. & Mrs. J. Thaddeus May)*

Open All year.

Rooms 1 suite, 3 doubles—2 with full private bath, 2 with maximum of 4 people sharing bath. All with clock, air-conditioning. Some with whirlpool tub, TV, fan, fireplace, balcony.

Facilities Dining room, living room with fireplace, books; family room with piano, TV/VCR, stereo; billiard room, laundry facilities. Off-street parking. Massage therapist; health club passes.

Location Fort Wood Historic District. 1–2 m to river, downtown; walking distance to aquarium. Take Hwy. 27 to 4th St. Exit. Follow 4th St. to Palmetto St. (approx. 1 1/2 m). Go right on Palmetto St. 2 blocks to Ft. Wood Pl. Go left on Ft. Wood Pl. 1 block to inn on right.

Restrictions No smoking. Children over 6 preferred; all welcome.

Credit cards None accepted.

Rates B&B, $135–150 suite, $65–95 double. Extra child, $25. Discount for 2-night stay.

Extras Airport pickup, $25.

DANDRIDGE

Located 30 miles east of Knoxville, Dandridge is the second oldest town in East Tennessee and has the distinction of being the only town in the U.S. named for George's wife, Martha Dandridge Washington. A walking tour of historic Dandridge includes 29 historic homes, shops, and taverns, most dating to the mid-1800s or earlier.

Information please: Magnificent lake and mountain views are offered by the **Mountain Harbor Inn** (1199 Highway 139, 37725; 615–397–3345), overlooking Douglas Lake and owned by the McEwan and Steinaway families. The 12 guest rooms are decorated with antiques and quilts, and most have a private porch where you can "set a spell" on a locally crafted rocking chair; rooms also have private baths, refrigerators, coffee makers, and microwave ovens. The lake offers excellent bass and crappie fishing, but if you'd rather sleep in, the breakfast buffet (juice, fruit, bagels and muffins, and a daily hot entrée) is kept fresh for three hours each morning. The inn's restaurant is open for lunch and dinner, with sandwiches and salads at lunch, beef, pork and chicken entrées at dinner. B&B double rates are $60–75; MAP, $80–95.

The **Sugarfork Bed & Breakfast** (743 Garrett Road, 37725; 615–397–7327 or 800–487–5634) is a contemporary two-story home overlooking Douglas Lake, with a view of the mountains in the distance. Rooms are decorated with many personal touches, from the wild bird pillows mounded on one of the beds to the oversize watch on the wall of one of the bathrooms. Southern breakfasts, served from 8–10 A.M., include country ham and eggs, or quiche with bacon. B&B double rates for the three guest rooms range from $60–70. "Delicious food, exceptional hospitality." (Jane Zenger)

ELIZABETHTON

Information please: Just across from Tennessee's oldest covered bridge (still in use) is the **Hunter Cottage B&B** (213 South Riverside, 37643; 615–542–9268), a restored 1902 Victorian home decorated with period antiques. The owners, John and Lisa Bunn, spent four years redecorating and remodeling their two guest-room B&B. B&B double rates range from $65–85.

FRANKLIN

Lyric Springs Country Inn *Tel:* 615–329–3385
7306 South Harpeth Road, 37064 800–621–7824
P.O. Box 120428, Nashville; 37212 *Fax:* 615–329–3381

The Lyric Springs Country Inn originated a century ago as a log cabin, and was updated many times over the years without losing its rustic country flavor. Patsy Bruce bought and expanded the house in 1974, opening it as a B&B in 1990; Pam Matthews is the manager. Patsy's collection of beautiful quilts is used to drape tables and upholster chairs; a grouping of antique wrought iron is artistically displayed on one wall. The inviting "saloon" is filled with memorabilia from Patsy Bruce's music and film career; she co-wrote such country hits as *Mammas Don't Let Your Babies Grow to be Cowboys* and *Texas When I Die* here at Lyric Springs. Breakfast is served at guests' convenience, and includes fresh fruit and juice, hot muffins, just-baked bread, and such entrées as vegetable frittata or Belgian waffles.

"Set in beautiful rolling hills beside a small river. Owner and innkeeper are fantastic. Large rambling house decorated with great flair." (*Laura Patterson*)

Open All year. Closed Dec. 20–Jan. 2.
Rooms 3 doubles—all with private bath and/or shower, radio, clock, desk, air-conditioning, fan. 1 with balcony.
Facilities Dining room, living room, family room with TV/VCR, fireplace, books; saloon with pool table, piano; sun porch. 50 acres with swimming pool, barn. Golf, fishing, hiking nearby.
Location 23 m SW of downtown Nashville; 18 m W of downtown Franklin. From I-65, exit at Hwy. 96 & go E 13.9 m to Old Harding Rd. & turn left (SW). Continue to stop sign at Fernvale Grocery. Continue to S. Harpeth Rd. & inn on right.
Restrictions No smoking. Adults.
Credit cards Amex, MC, Visa.
Rates B&B, $100 double. Prix fixe lunch, $10; dinner, $18.
Extras Airport, station pickup, $12. Horses boarded.

GATLINBURG

People come to Gatlinburg because it is a convenient starting point for exploring the Great Smoky Mountains National Park. Unfortunately, the road from Knoxville to Gatlinburg is littered with one tourist trap after the next. Gatlinburg itself is no better, with dozens of tacky souvenir shops, no-go traffic, and non-stop people, and precious few parking spaces. Leave the town, and then your car, behind as soon as possible. Spend your time exploring the beauty and peace of the park—easily accessible hiking trails ensure that you won't have to go far on foot to leave the crowds behind.

Gatlinburg is located in southeastern Tennessee, 50 miles southeast of Knoxville.

Information please: Adventurous inngoers will enjoy **LeConte Lodge** (250 Apple Valley Road, Sevierville 37862; 615–429–5704). Five hiking trails lead to the lodge, ranging in length from 5½ to 8 miles. Set in a sheltering saddle near the 6,593-foot summit of Mt. LeConte, the lodge was built four years before the Great Smoky Mountains National Park was created in 1930. The LeConte is self-sufficient, with propane gas for cooking, and kerosene for heating and lighting. Accommodations are provided in little cabins, each with a bunk bed and daybed with wool blankets, a basic table and chair, and a kerosene lamp. Reservations for each spring opening begin on Oct. 1; per person daily rates, including breakfast and dinner, are approximately $60.

Breath-taking mountain views are yours from the many porches of the Victorian-style **Hippensteal's Mountain View Inn** (Grassy Branch Road, P.O. Box 707, 37738; 615–436–5761 or 800–527–8110), about five miles from town. Built as an inn in 1990, each of the eight guest rooms has a queen-sized bed, reading chairs, full private bath with whirlpool tub, TV, air-conditioning, ceiling fan, and gas fireplace. Vern Hippensteal is a leading area watercolorist, and his works highlight the inn's eclectic decor. There's a spacious wicker-filled living room for guests to relax in, and a dining room where a full breakfast is served each morning. B&B double rates ranges from $100–115.

About a mile from Gatlinburg is **The Colonel's Lady** (1120 Tanrac Trail, 37738; 615–436–5432) with eight luxurious guest rooms, most with hot tubs or whirlpool baths and fireplaces, ideal for a honeymoon or anniversary. The $100–135 rates include a full breakfast and afternoon tea.

Buckhorn Inn ✕ ♿   Tel: 615–436–4668
2140 Tudor Mountain Road, 37738

The Buckhorn's white-columned porch overlooks a panorama of Mount LeConte and the blue-gray Smoky Mountains. The spacious living room and dining area are decorated with antiques and country-comfortable sofas. Guest rooms in the inn are furnished simply, with spindle beds and some antiques. Breakfast is served from 8–9:30 A.M. and might include a choice of blueberry pancakes or broccoli-mushroom-Havarti omelets with fresh-squeezed orange juice, fresh fruit, homemade hash browns, biscuits, and home-mixed mueslix. Dinner is served promptly at 7 P.M. by reservation only; a typical menu might include corn and tasso chowder; mixed green salad; mountain trout meuniere, mixed vegetable sauté, and gnocchi with feta cheese; and raspberry cake. The Buckhorn has been owned by the Young family since 1979, and is managed by John and Connie Burns. John is the grandson of the inn's architect, and great-nephew to the original owner.

"The atmosphere is homey, relaxed, and friendly, reflecting the hosts' nature." *(Betty & Ed Sternberg)* "The grounds are lovely, with ducks and geese to feed. Our room was comfortable, but best of all was the excellent food and service provided by the attentive, energetic innkeepers." *(Robert Ziek)* "We stayed in one of the newer cottages, with 60s decor, and a nice view from the back windows." *(Celia McCullough)* "Very close to my Platonic ideal of an inn. Enjoyed the nature trail." *(EA)*

Minor niggle: "Perhaps the chef was having a bad day, but dinner didn't seem quite as wonderful as on previous visits."

Open All year. Closed Dec. 24, 25. No dinners Sun.
Rooms 2 2-bedroom guest houses, 4 cottages, 6 doubles—all with private bath and/or shower, air-conditioning. Cottages with TV, fireplace, porch, refrigerator.
Facilities Dining/living room with fireplace, piano, books. 35 acres for hiking, fishing; nature trail. 1 m to swimming, trout fishing. 8 m to downhill skiing.
Location 5 m from town. From Gatlinburg, take Hwy. 321 N 5 m; turn left at Buckhorn Rd. Go 1 m and turn right on Tudor Mt. Rd. to inn. Call for backroads directions.
Restrictions Smoking only in 2 cottages; covered patio. Children 6–10 in cottages; no children under 10 at dinner.
Credit cards MC, Visa.
Rates B&B, $175–275 guest house, $125–135 cottage, $95–115 double; includes tax. Extra person, $20. 5% service. 2-night weekend minimum. Prix fixe dinner, $26 for inn guests, $29 for public. Sack lunch, $6.

Butcher House ¢   *Tel: 615–436–9457*
1520 Garrett Lane, 37738

The Butcher House is a stone and cedar "Swiss chalet-style" home with views extending for miles around; it is elaborately decorated with period antiques and reproductions. Former corporate executives Hugh and Gloria Butcher opened a B&B after choosing early retirement from years of travel throughout the U.S. and abroad. Breakfast consists of French roast coffee, mini-muffins, fresh fruit, almond granola, and fruit yogurt, crêpes, or an egg dish, served on the mountain-view deck, or in the dining room.

"The Butchers assisted us with area information, and in getting reservations for shows. We breakfasted on eggs Florentine, croissants, and fruit compote, served on a linen tablecloth with napkins and crystal water glasses." *(Lorraine Koenig)* "When I phoned for reservations, Gloria treated me with great courtesy and kindness; the welcome when we arrived was equally warm. The inn is immaculate, with an ample well-lit parking area. We enjoyed getting to know the Butchers and the other guests. Each day, they suggested different walking trails; in the evening, we returned from dinner to find goodies left out for the guests in the kitchen." *(Gayle Beckner)* "We arose early and were greeted by a beautiful sunrise, as the sun lit the valley below." *(Ralph Conn)*

Open All year.
Rooms 1 suite, 4 doubles—all with private bath and/or shower, TV, air-conditioning.
Facilities Dining room, living room with fireplace, family room with fireplace, TV, books. Guest kitchen, deck. 2 m to cross-country, downhill skiing.
Location 3 m NW of Gatlinburg. From US-441 go S to Gatlinburg, turn right at traffic light #10 on Ski Mtn. Rd. Turn right on Wiley Oakley Rd. At 4-way stop turn left on Ski View Rd., then right on Wiley Oakley Rd. Go N to Garret Dr., turn left. Turn right on gravel road to inn on right.
Restrictions No smoking. No children under 10.
Credit cards MC, Visa.
Rates B&B, $69–90 double, $69–75 single. 2-night minimum stay.
Extras Italian, some French, Spanish spoken.

GREENEVILLE

Big Spring Inn ¢   *Tel: 615–638–2917*
315 North Main Street, 37743

The historic town of Greeneville, birthplace of Davy Crockett and President Andrew Johnson, is also home to a delightful B&B. This well-shaded, turn-of-the-century brick manor house was purchased in 1993 by Marshall and Nancy Ricker. The guest rooms are bright and cheery, with antiques and reproduction furnishings, soft floral papers and pastel trim, and such extra touches as fresh flowers, snacks, and terry-cloth robes. Early morning coffee is left outside your door, and breakfast might include fresh fruit and juice, muffins or bread, and puffed pancakes with sautéed apples.

"Wraparound porch lead to a spacious foyer with a wide staircase rising to the spacious guest rooms. The inn is an easy walk to historic buildings and a short drive to mountain trails. Nancy served us a fine breakfast of fresh fruit, breads and pastries, local jams, steaming hot coffee, eggs to order, and cheese-stuffed French toast with apricot sauce. Our room was furnished with comfortable chairs, a writing desk, large closet, dresser, and a comfortable king-size bed; the large bathroom had thick towels and ample hot water. The common areas are good places to gather with the hosts and other guests, or to find a quiet spot to read about the region's history and ecology. Through the large windows we watched a wide range of songbirds in the surrounding boxwoods and evergreens. Nancy has wonderful gardening ideas, and Marshall is an architect with exciting plans for the inn's further renovation and redesign." *(Hal & Cheryl Baker)*
"Gracious Greek Revival house on a street lined with antebellum homes. Pleasant, accommodating owners." *(Robert Austin)*

Open All year.
Rooms 6 doubles—all with private shower and/or bath, telephone, radio, clock, TV, desk, air-conditioning. 2 with fireplace. 1 room in carriage house.
Facilities Dining room, living room with fireplace; sitting room with games, TV, books, library. 2 acres with swimming pool, gardens, lawn games. Swimming, whitewater rafting, hiking, golf, tennis nearby; Cherokee Nat'l. Forest.
Location E TN. 75 m E of Knoxville. From I-81 N, take Exit 23 (Greeneville-Bulls Gap) & turn right. Follow Bus. Rte. 11-E to Main St. & turn left. Go 3 stoplights. Inn is 7th house on left after 3rd light. From I-91 S, take Exit 36 (Baileytown Rd.),

turn left & go 14 m to light. Go right onto N. Main St. Continue to Nelson & turn right.

Restrictions Occasional train noise. No smoking. Children over 4.
Credit cards Amex, MC, Visa.
Rates B&B, $75 double, $60 single. Extra person, $10. Prix fixe dinner, $15–20.

HAMPSHIRE

Ridgetop Bed & Breakfast ¢ ♿
Highway 412 West, P.O. Box 193, 38461

Tel: 615–285–2777
800–377–2770

A contemporary-style cedar home built in 1979, the Ridgetop was opened as a B&B in 1992 by Bill and Kay Jones. Breakfast includes fruit, blueberry muffins, bacon, and such entreés as scrambled eggs, pancakes with blueberry sauce, or pecan waffles. "Charming hosts who made us feel at home. Our spacious room looked out over the forest ridge. Delightful living room; beautiful porch with a fountain and water garden made by Bill. Kay is a good source of information on the beautiful Natchez Trace National Parkway." *(Sibyl Nestor)* "Comfortable, antique-filled surroundings; wonderful breakfast." *(Perry Craft)*

Open All year.
Rooms 1 two-bedroom cottage, 1 double—all with private shower bath, air-conditioning, clock, fan. Cottage with refrigerator, patio.
Facilities Dining room, living room with fireplace, TV, stereo, books; guest kitchen, deck with swing. 170 acres with hiking, woods, creeks. Bicycling on Natchez Trace; Buffalo River for canoeing, fishing nearby.
Location Central TN. 75 m SW of Nashville; 4 m to Natchez Trace. 4 m from town. From I-65 take Hwy 412 W to inn.
Restrictions No smoking.
Credit cards MC, Visa.
Rates B&B, $80 cottage, $60 double, $55 single. Extra person, $10.
Extras Limited wheelchair access. Airport/station pickups. Pets with approval.

JACKSON

Also recommended: An easy drive from I-40, about 75 miles east of Memphis, and approximately 100 miles west of Nashville is the **Moss Rose Inn & Café** (586 East Main Street, Jackson 38301; 901–423–4777), an 1857 Greek Revival home, restored as a restaurant and B&B by Anne Stamps. Although too small for a full entry with only two guest rooms, it is highly recommended by frequent contributor *Ann Christofferson:* "Located in the impressive East Main Street Historic District, the inn has a warm and inviting atmosphere. Amenities appreciated by business travelers include the availability of complimentary beverages at all hours, private in-room telephones, and use of the inn's copier and fax machine. Private baths and TVs are also a big plus. Wonderful breakfasts of juice, fruit salad with yogurt, and pancakes with sausage. Delightful meals in the popular café. B&B rates are $65 a night.

JONESBOROUGH

In the mountains of northeast Tennessee, Jonesborough is the state's oldest town, founded in 1779, with many historic buildings. Every October, it sponsors a famous storytelling festival.

Information please: The **Jonesborough B&B** (Woodrow & Cherokee Streets, P.O. Box 722, 37659; 615–753–9223) offers five guest rooms with high beds, antique furnishings, and fireplaces, at B&B rates of $69–100. A secluded terrace and a large porch with rocking chairs are adjacent to the house, while the famous Parson's Table Restaurant is across the street.

KNOXVILLE

Once an outpost of the western frontier, Knoxville is today a manufacturing center and home of the University of Tennessee. Its location in eastern Tennessee, about 50 miles northwest of Gatlinburg, makes it a common starting point for visits to the Smokies.

Reader tip: About 15 miles north of Knoxville is the fascinating Museum of Appalachia (P.O. Box 0318, Norris, 37828; 615–494–0514), where you can observe nearly every Appalachian skill, craft, art, and music—except for the making of moonshine.

We're sorry to note that we have *no* Knoxville recommendations. Readers are urgently requested to report in with any suggestions. Fortunately, a number of appealing B&Bs can be found in nearby towns.

Information please: About ten minutes south of Knoxville, I-40, and I-75 is the **Wayside Manor B&B** (4009 Old Knoxville Highway, Rockford 37853; 615–981–1890 or 800–675–4823), offering six guest rooms, most with private baths, in a handsome, red brick, turn-of-the-century country estate. Guest rooms have antique and modern furnishings, while the grounds offer a tennis court, swimming pool, and more. The $85–95 double rates include a full breakfast and afternoon refreshments. Reports?

For an additional area entries, see **Loudon** and **Sevierville.**

LEBANON

Lebanon is located about 20 miles east of downtown Nashville, via I-40, and makes a good choice if you'd like to combine a visit to the "Music City" with rural relaxation.

Also recommended: A Greek Revival home built in 1842, the **Campbell Country Inn** (2344 Lebanon Road, Highway 70 West, 37087; 615–449–7713) has been home to the Campbell family for five generations. This B&B offers five guest rooms, including a Jacuzzi suite ($135); B&B

double rates are $75. "Mrs. McFarland was a charming hostess; her patio, gardens, and swimming pool are lovely. Great breakfast with fresh tomato pie." *(BJ Hensley)*

Equally delightful are the two romantic suites (B&B, $65–95) at **Rockhaven Bed & Breakfast** (126 Timber Trail, Lebanon 37087; 615–443–2327 or 800–647–4144), owned by Rhonda Anthamatten. "Our magnificent bedroom had beautiful antiques, a king-size bed, and fresh flowers. Our bathroom was breathtaking with a shower, huge double vanity, floor-to-ceiling solid wood cabinets, stained glass window, and a double Jacuzzi tub. Delightful full breakfast with homemade biscuits, fresh jellies, and more. Rhonda was exceptionally kind, helpful with all our travel plans." *(William & Bonita Agee)*

LOUDON

The Mason Place B&B
600 Commerce Street, 37774

Tel: 615–458–3921

When riverboat Captain Thomas Jefferson Mason began construction of this Greek Revival mansion in 1861, 250,000 bricks were made for the house. "The War" intervened and the bricks were confiscated. General Longstreet crossed the Tennessee River here with 30,000 troops, and both sides camped on the grounds (bullets and artifacts are still being found on the property today). When the Civil War ended, the house was completed in 1865 with heart of pine boards. The Mason family moved in, and their descendants occupied the mansion for the next five generations. In 1986, Robert and Donna Siewert bought the house at auction, and restored it extensively, opening as a B&B in 1991. Now listed on the National Register of Historic Places, each spacious (18' by 17') guest room is furnished with comfortable period antiques, and a featherbed.

"Victorian decor with a huge ornate bed with lace coverlet, flowered Louis Nicole wallpaper, and little books of prose at bedside." *(Susan & Mike Peck)* "The spacious gathering room is a sunken solarium with wood planked walls and a brick floor. Our candlelit breakfast was served in the Victorian dining room on the fine china. Fresh fruit was followed by thick slices of banana-coconut French toast with whipped butter and homemade syrup. Bacon, juice and steaming mugs of coffee completed the meal. When we came back after dinner, Donna served us homemade apple pie." *(Tom & Betty Bishop)* "Guests can choose complete privacy or join warm conversations." *(Susan Cameron)* "Tempting chocolates were set out on tiny china plates. The grounds are lush and quiet, with a beautiful pool, porch swings, and flowers everywhere. Delicious strawberry crepes for breakfast. Best of all are Bob and Donna, who attended to our every need. Convenient location for escaping to the Smoky or Cherokee mountains." *(Sarah & Bill Wainscott)*

Open All year.
Rooms 5 doubles—all with private shower bath, radio, desk, air-conditioning, gas fireplace.

Facilities Dining room, parlor with piano, keeping room with TV/VCR, books; all with fireplace; garden room with TV, deck, 3 porches. 3 acres with garden, lawn games, swimming pool, gazebo, fish pond, waterfall. Tennis, golf, boating, fishing nearby.

Location E TN. 25 m SW of Knoxville. 3 m from I-75, Exit 76. Turn E to Hwy. 11. Turn right into Loudon. Right at 1st light. Go 2 blocks, right onto Commerce.

Restrictions No smoking. No children.

Credit cards MC, Visa.

Rates B&B, $88–96 double. 2-night minimum some holiday weekends. Tips not expected. Corporate rates.

Extras Airport/station pickups.

MCMINNVILLE

Falcon Manor Bed & Breakfast ¢ &.   *Tel: 615–668–4444*
2645 Faulkner Springs Road; 37110

From "the finest house in Warren County" to a hospital and rest home, and back to turn-of-the-century elegance is the history of Falcon Manor in a nutshell. Built in 1896, it was bought by George and Charlien McGlothin in 1989, and opened as an inn four years later after extensive renovation. Lowered ceilings and dividing walls were removed; porches and gables reconstructed. Now returned to its original elegance, the decor includes deep, rich Victorian colors, 12-foot ceilings, ornate woodwork, a sweeping staircase, and authentic Victorian antiques throughout, including beautiful hand-carved wooden double beds. Breakfast is served in the dining room at 8 A.M., and includes country ham and biscuits, fresh fruit, beignets (French donuts), cereal, milk, juice, coffee and tea; every evening at 8 P.M., George and Charlien gather with their guests for refreshments and conversation.

"George and Charlien shared the fascinating history of the house and its restoration. We toured the inn, then gathered for coffee and cake." *(Sue Gatlin)* "Delightful get-together with the owners and other guests each evening. Fascinating collection of both modern and antique books." *(Edmund Wilt)* Comments welcome.

Open All year.

Rooms 5 doubles—1 with private bath (tub), 4 rooms with maximum of 4 people sharing bath. All with air-conditioning, ceiling fan. 2 with desk, 1 with clock.

Facilities Dining room, parlor with fireplace, sitting room with books, verandas. 3 acres with parking. Creek across the street for wading. State parks nearby for swimming, boating, fishing, hiking, caving.

Location Central TN. 100 m SW of Knoxville, 71 m SE of Nashville, 71 m Ne of Chattanooga. 2½ m from town. In historic district. From I-24, turn E at Exit 111, (Manchester/McMinnville) onto Hwy. 55. In McMinnville, stay on 4-lane highway.; will become 70S bypass towards Sparta. Go left at 4th traffic light to inn at end of Faulkner Springs Rd.

Restrictions Smoking permitted only in smokehouse (no pun intended). Children over 11 preferred.

Credit cards MC, Visa.

Rates B&B, $75 double. Extra person, $10.

Extras Limited wheelchair access.

MEMPHIS

Information please: More listings are desperately needed. At present, your best bet for a B&B is to call **B&B in Memphis** (P.O. Box 41621, 38174; 901–726–5920). Owner Helen Denton reports that they specialize in one or two-room B&Bs in private homes, "in the best neighborhoods," as well as unhosted furnished apartments. Reader reports on Helen's placements are excellent.

The city's best-known hotel is the 450-room **Peabody** (149 Union Avenue, 38103; 800–PEABODY). Although everybody loves the ducks (stop by at either 11 A.M. or 5 P.M. to see them march through the lobby), readers were less amused by ordinary rooms at high prices, inept service, and noise from elevators and conventioneers.

MONTEAGLE

Monteagle is an ideal escape from Tennessee's many high-decibel attractions. Listed on the National Register of Historic Places, its Chautauqua Assembly was founded in 1882 and remains active with lectures, concerts, and movies for eight weeks each summer; it was inspired by the original Chautauqua in western New York state. The South Cumberland State Recreation Area is nearby, with wonderful hiking trails in the Cumberland Mountains, as well as trout fishing and canoeing. Natural attractions include the Great Stone Door, Lost Cove Cave, Cathedral Falls, Fiery Gizard Trail, and Sewanee Natural Bridge. Monteagle is 45 miles northwest of Chattanooga, and 85 miles southeast of Nashville. The University of the South is 6 miles away in Sewanee.

Adams Edgeworth Inn ¢   *Tel:* 615–924–2669
Monteagle Assembly, 37356   *Fax:* 615–924–2669

Wendy and David Adams, owners of the Adams Edgeworth Inn since 1990, report that "our inn is enjoyed by those who love to hike the surrounding mountain trails and enjoy quiet calm of the mountains." Strolling the picturesque grounds filled with similar gingerbread Victorian cottages, sitting and rocking on the wraparound porch, or gathering by the library fireplace to chat or read a book are delightful options year-round.

The entrance parlor has light poplar walls and white wicker furnishings with flowered cushions. The 1000-book library has comfortable antique chairs and lots of well-read books. Guest rooms are simply furnished with brass or iron beds, country Victorian fabrics, period dressers and chairs. The country-style dining room has two long tables where guests can help themselves to homemade sourdough bread, fresh fruit and juice, coffee cake, homemade muffins, coffee, tea, and hot chocolate. A recent dinner menu (by reservation) listed smoked salmon, salad and raspberry sorbet; filet mignon with gingered carrots and potatoes in pesto; topped off by chocolate chunk cookies and strawberries. "Wonderful sound of rain on the tin roof. David served us cereal with fresh blueberries and hot biscuits and ham; spoonbread and homemade dill bread were a treat on the second day." *(Camille Williams)* "In addition to the Monteagle Assembly program, I enjoyed the many concerts at the nearby University of the South." *(Vivian Scott)* "Delightful guests provided good conversation and company." *(Ann Smith)* "Lovely restoration. Welcoming spirit, inviting setting." *(Kerri McQuiddy)*

Open All year.
Rooms 1 suite, 13 doubles—all with private bath and/or shower, fan. Some with desk, air-conditioning, fireplace, refrigerator, microwave, porch. 1 with Jacuzzi tub.
Facilities Dining room, living room, library with fireplace; sun room, steam room, guest kitchen. Wraparound porches with hammock. Golf cart for touring Assembly. ½ acre surrounded by 93-acre Victorian village grounds, with walking trails, tennis. Golf, swimming, hiking, fishing nearby.
Location S central TN, 45 m NW of Chattanooga. From I-24 take Exit 134 to Monteagle. Turn left through gate into Monteagle Assembly. Follow East Circle Drive to #23.
Restrictions No smoking. Children by prior arrangement.
Credit cards MC, Visa.
Rates B&B, $100–135 suite, $65–95 double, plus $8 daily gate fee mid June–mid Aug. Extra person, $25. 2-night weekend minimum on weekends. Weekly rate. Midweek off-season discount. Prix fixe dinner by reservation.

NASHVILLE

Nashville is both the capital and the commercial center of Tennessee, and, as everyone knows, it's the country music capital of the world. It's also home to seventeen colleges and universities and to tourist attractions ranging from the sublime to the ridiculous, starting and ending, of course, with Opryland.

Information please: Reports are needed for **Union Station** (1001 Broadway, 37203; 615–726–1001 or 800–331–2123), a Romanesque-style fortress built in 1900 as a showpiece for the Louisville & Nashville Railroad, and renovated as a hotel, complete with a clock tower, lofty gables, a barrel-vaulted coffered ceiling, stained glass windows, massive columns, hand-carved oak railings, and wrought iron balconies. Guest rooms are furnished with period reproductions; some look into the lobby through huge arched windows, others overlook the street. The hotel is just blocks from the convention center, Music Row, and Vanderbilt University. Double rates for the 125 rooms range from $115–145. While readers are delighted with the hotel's decor and location, recent reports on the service have been less positive.

The **Hermitage Hotel** (231 Sixth Avenue North, 37219; 615–244–3121 or 800–251–1908) was built in 1910 at a cost of $1,000,000, with all possible luxuries and amenities. In 1986 the hotel was restored to its early elegance, after years of decay; its original 250 rooms were redone as 112 suites. Many of the rooms were refurbished in 1994. Double rates of $110 weekday, $79 weekend include turndown service, luxury soaps, and the morning paper. The hotel restaurant offers continental cuisine in an elegant atmosphere. "Spacious, comfortable, soundproof suite. Impressive lobby when the sun shined. Good dinner in the restaurant." *(KLH)*

For additional area entries, see listings under **Ashland City**, **Franklin**, and **Lebanon**, all within a 20–30 mile drive.

PIGEON FORGE

Pigeon Forge has so much going on that the ratio of motel rooms to permanent residents is now two to one. Both the eponymous carrier pigeons and the forge are long gone, but what you will find here are "six miles of action-packed entertainment" in the form of innumerable discount shopping outlets, and attractions ranging from Dollywood to the Dixie Stampede, with water parks thrown in for good measure. If you're traveling with kids, either pass through in the dead of night when they're fast asleep, or put your brain on hold and enjoy the fun. As always, avoid visiting in July and August (especially weekends) unless you're nostalgic for rush-hour conditions.

Day Dreams Country Inn ¢ 🏃 ♿   Tel: 615–428–0370
2720 Colonial Drive, 37863

The Day Dreams Country Inn is a contemporary cedar log home with a quiet setting amid weeping willow trees and a babbling creek. Owners Yvonne and Mark Trombley offer a quiet base for exploring the Great Smokies but are also within walking distance of the Pigeon Forge trolley which takes you into town for all activities. They have furnished their home with antiques and reproduction pieces, comfortable couches, and country accents. Breakfast includes eggs, biscuits and gravy, breakfast meats, fruit, juice, and coffee.

"The charm of an older home with the conveniences of a modern one; scrupulously clean and beautifully decorated." *(Erin Lotherington)* "Ample breakfasts are served family-style with Mark and Yvonne making sure that each guest was satisfied and happy." *(Fred & Beverly Holweger)* "The owners are young, energetic, and cheerful. Parking is excellent and it's nice to walk to town without worrying about traffic." *(Mr. & Mrs. Arthur Douglas)* "We love to relax on the screened porch, sipping iced tea on the two-seater swing." *(Dave Gorden)* "Awaken to the smell of bacon and sausage frying, the aroma of coffee brewing." *(Donald Millsap)* "We were free to fix hot or cold drinks and make ourselves at home. Although we were less than two blocks from the noisy 'strip,' it was amazingly quiet." *(Bonnie Schwartzkopf)*

Open All year.
Rooms 2 suites, 4 doubles—all with private bath and/or shower, radio, desk, air-conditioning. 2 with TV.
Facilities Dining room, living room with fireplace, TV/VCR, books; screened porch with swing. 3 wooded acres with creek, picnic area, children's play equipment. 5 m to downhill, cross-country skiing.
Location E TN, 35 m E of Knoxville. ¼ m from town center. From I-40, take exit

for Rte. 66 S. Go S 13 m to Rte. 441, turn right into Pigeon Forge. Turn right on Wears Valley Rd. Go 1 block, turn left on Florence Dr. Take 3rd right onto Colonial Dr. to inn on right.
Restrictions No smoking.
Credit cards MC, Visa.
Rates B&B, $99 suite, $79 double. Extra person, $15. Family rate. 2-night minimum Oct. 10% discount for 4-night stay.
Extras Limited wheelchair access. Crib, babysitting available.

PIKEVILLE

Fall Creek B&B Inn ¢   *Tel:* 615–881–5494
Highway 284, Route 3, Box 298B, 37367   *Fax:* 615–881–5040

Fall Creek is a country manor home built by Rita and Doug Pruett in 1981, and opened as a B&B in 1991; the decor combines Victorian and country elements. Breakfast is served at individual tables with a different menu each day; perhaps pecan waffles with maple butter, sausage and fresh fruit cup; or an egg, cheese, sausage, and potato casserole with drop biscuits and home-baked cinnamon rolls.

"The beautiful Sweetheart Room has Victorian decor and a bathroom with a red heart-shaped whirlpool tub. Doug and Rita are gracious hosts who made us feel at home." *(Margaret & Robert O'Leary)* "Immaculately clean, with careful attention to detail, including scented soaps, lotions, bubble baths, and body shampoos. Wonderful breakfasts of homemade preserves, eggs Benedict, hot coffee and fresh squeezed orange juice." *(Wanda Walden)* Comments welcome.

Open All year.
Rooms 8 doubles—6 with full private bath, 2 with maximum of 4 people sharing bath, 1 with whirlpool tub. All with radio, clock, air-conditioning, fan.
Facilities Dining room, living room with TV/VCR; family room with TV, books, games; guest kitchen, porch. 40 acres with heated swimming pool, tennis courts, golf, lawn games. 1 m to Fall Creek Falls State Park; 3 m to golf, swimming, hiking, horseback riding, tennis, fishing.
Location 50 m N of Chattanooga. 15 m NW of Pikeville. From Rte. 30 or Rte. 111, take Hwy. 284 & call for directions. Inn is off Hwy 284 just S of Rte. 30.
Restrictions No smoking. Children 8 & over.
Credit cards MC, Visa.
Rates B&B, $50–93 double, $50–57 single. Extra person, $10. 2-night minimum holidays, Oct. weekends.

ROGERSVILLE

Hale Springs Inn ¢ ✕   *Tel:* 615–272–5171
110 West Main Street, Town Square, 37857

Rogersville is one of Tennessee's oldest towns, founded in 1786 when this area was still the western frontier. The Hale Springs Inn was built in 1824 and is the oldest continuously running inn or hotel in Tennessee. Presidents Jackson, Polk, and (Andrew) Johnson all stayed here. Originally called McKinney's Tavern, the inn was used as Union headquarters during the Civil War. Confederate headquarters were across the street, in Kyle House. In 1982, Captain Carl Netherland-Brown purchased the inn and began its restoration. Many of the original furnishings are still intact, including several Victorian settees, side chairs, and claw-foot bathtubs. The decor also includes comfortable velvet-covered wing chairs, handsome brass chandeliers, canopied four-poster beds, Oriental carpets, and handmade quilts. Dinner entrées include prime rib, stuffed pork chops, chicken Creole, and shrimp scampi.

"The inn is located right downtown in a pleasant area; appealing gift and specialty shops are nearby." *(Larry & LaDonna Swain)* "The inn's self-guided walking tour was a highlight of our stay. The restaurant is attractively decorated in period, with good service and food." *(Dana Abdella)* "Cordial welcome and assistance with baggage." *(Helen Hamilton)* "Immaculate housekeeping, personal attention. When I made my reservation, the staff described the spacious rooms in detail so I could make just the right choice." *(Mrs. B. R. Wilson)* "Well maintained and beautifully furnished with genuine antiques. Excellent value. Enjoyed breakfast of juice, cereal, fruit, pastries, and coffee in a sun parlor overlooking the scenic square." *(Betty Norman)*

Worth noting: Three guest rooms have thermostats which control temperature for all.

Open All year. Restaurant closed Sun.

Rooms 4 suites, 5 doubles—all with private shower and/or bath, TV, air-conditioning. Most with desk, wood-burning fireplace.

Facilities Restaurant, sitting room with fireplace, library; lobby, balcony with rocking chairs. Formal garden with gazebo. Swimming, boating, fishing, tennis, golf nearby.

Location Upper E TN. 65 m E of Knoxville; 30 m W of Kingsport. 16 m NW of I-81 on Rte 11W. In center of town.

Restrictions Traffic, pedestrian noise in front rooms. Dry county; BYOB. No children under 7.

Credit cards MC, Visa.

Rates B&B, $65–90 suite, $45–70 double. Alc lunch, $7.50; alc dinner, $16.

RUGBY

When English author *(Tom Brown's School Days)* and social reformer Thomas Hughes launched his Utopian colony in 1880, he wrote: "For we are about to . . . create a new center of human life . . . in this strangely beautiful solitude." Unfortunately, his words were more accurate than he had perhaps intended; after reaching a peak population of 450 in 1884, the community foundered, as did most such noble 19th century experiments. A small farming community did survive, and in 1966, Historic Rugby, Inc. was founded to restore the surviving buildings and to encourage historically compatible enterprise. Located on the Cumberland Plateau, the town sits at the southern border of the Big South Fork National River and Recreation Area—a wilderness of high plateaus and rugged river gorges.

Contact the Superintendent (Big South Fork National River and Recreation Area, Route 3, Box 401, Oneida 37841; 615–879–3625) for information about recreational opportunities.

Reader tip: "Big South Fork is an undiscovered treasure with high cliffs, natural bridges, deep gorges, and magnificent views. Adults and children will enjoy visiting the wonderfully restored Blue Heron coal mine, best reached by the Big South Fork Scenic Railway. Food prices in the area are very reasonable and the many outdoor activities make it an ideal family vacation spot. " *(Joe & Sheila Schmidt)*

Information please: Though not appropriate for a full entry, for a nearby wilderness experience, hike to **Charit Creek Lodge** (mailing address: 250 Apple Valley Road, Sevierville 37862; 615–429–5704), in Big South Fork National River and Recreation Area of the Cumberland Plateau. You can get to the lodge only on foot or horseback; the shortest trail is less than a mile. You'll need to bring your own towel, but everything else is provided, including a hearty breakfast and dinner, bed linens, kerosene lamps, and even flush toilet and showers. There's a library stocked with books, indoor and outdoor games, and a stable and pastures for your horse. Summer is hot here, so visit in spring or fall for excellent hiking and riding trails, and rivers for canoeing, kayaking, fishing, whitewater rafting, and swimming. "Once a homestead, complete with ghost, Charit Lodge offers a beautiful valley location. You sleep in communal bunkrooms; there is no electricity and the restroom facilities are a bit primitive. The menu is basic but the quality is high." *(Joe & Sheila Schmidt)*

Grey Gables (Hwy 52, P.O. Box 5252, Rugby 37733; 615–628–5252) is owned by Linda and Bill Jones, closely involved in Rugby's restoration. The $90 double rate includes a hearty country breakfast and an evening meal. Guest rooms are individually decorated with Victorian antiques and American country pieces. An 80-foot veranda encircles the inn, welcoming guests to enjoy the wicker furniture and rustic Tennessee-crafted rockers. Reports welcome.

Newbury House at Historic Rugby ¢ ✕ ⅋.   Tel: 615–628–2430
P.O. Box 8, 37733

Newbury House, Rugby's first boarding house, was built in 1880 and has been restored as a guest house, decorated with lace curtains and Victorian antiques; additional accommodation is available in the restored Pioneer Cottage. Three meals a day are served at the Harrow Road Cafe, which serves both traditional English dishes and Tennessee favorites—from shepherd's pie to deep-fried catfish. Room rates include a full breakfast. Take a walking tour of the restored buildings, and browse through the crafts and books at the Rugby Commissary and the Board of Aid Bookshop.

"The area is quiet, a haven for all kinds of birds. Nature trails take you along the river; interesting rock formations." *(Melanie McKeever)* "Small, modest guest rooms; inviting parlor and porch; friendly staff. We visited in July when the waterlilies were blooming in the pond out back, and the bushes were full of ripe blackberries. We took a leisurely walk to the swimming hole for a refreshing dip in the hot humid weather; bring bug spray. We also enjoyed a visit to Tennessee's oldest winery, about 15 miles away." *(Suzie Tolmie)* "The cottage was a comfortable lodging experience for a reasonable price." *(Bill Novack)*

Open All year. Restaurant closed Thanksgiving, Christmas Eve, Day; no dinner served midweek.
Rooms 1 3-bedroom cottage, 5 doubles—3 with private bath, 2 with maximum of 4 people sharing 1 bath. All with air-conditioning, fan. Some with desk, 1 with radio. Cottage with screened porch, fully-equipped kitchen.
Facilities Parlor with books. Hiking trails. Canoeing, fishing, swimming nearby.
Location NE TN, 70 m NW of Knoxville. From I-40, take exit for Rte. 27. Go N approx. 32 m to Elgin. Turn left on Rte. 52, go W 7 m to Rugby.
Restrictions No smoking. No children under 12 in inn. Any age fine for cottage. Light sleepers may wish to request a room at the inn instead of in cottage.
Credit cards MC, Visa.
Rates Inn: B&B, $59–69 double, $49–59 single. Extra person, $10. Cottage: room only, $59 double. Extra person, $10. Extended stay discounts in cottage. Alc breakfast, $3–4, alc lunch $4–6, alc dinner $8–15.
Extras Wheelchair access to restaurant.

SEVIERVILLE

Sevierville, along with Pigeon Forge three miles down the road, has very much become part of the strip of "attractions" lining the route from Knoxville to Gatlinburg. In Sevierville you'll find the Forbidden Caverns (once inhabited by Native Americans, more recently by moonshiners).

Located in east Tennessee, Sevierville is situated 30 miles southeast of Knoxville, and 5 miles north of Gatlinburg and the Great Smoky Mountains National Park.

Blue Mountain Mist Country Inn ♿   *Tel:* 615–428–2335
1811 Pullen Road, 37862   800–497–2335

The Blue Mountain Mist Inn, set on a hilltop overlooking meadows and rolling hills with the Smokies as a backdrop, is a delightful country retreat built in 1987 by Norman and Sarah Ball. Guest rooms are furnished with country antiques and collectibles, including beautiful old quilts on the walls and beds. Early risers can take a cup of coffee out to one of the porch rockers and watch the sun rise over the misty valleys and mountains beyond. Breakfast is served at 8:30 A.M. and typically includes biscuits and gravy, eggs, sausage, bacon, grits, fresh fruit, and coffee cake. Rates also include evening tea or coffee and one of Sarah's special desserts. "Gracious hosts, comfortable rooms, charming decor, lovely setting. Frequently Sarah's father or another family member is available to share stories and area information." *(Sibyl Nestor)* "The wide porch's rocking chairs were occupied by guests chatting like cousins at a family reunion when I arrived. There was orange cake for the taking in the kitchen. Breakfast included stuffed French toast, eggs and bacon, accompanied by plenty of conversation among the contented guests."

(Millie Ball) "Our well-equipped cabin had a queen-size bed, and a porch with beautiful mountain views." *(Wayne Cook)* "Cheerful dining room walled with windows overlooks the mountains. Guests can have as much privacy or companionship as they wish. Minutes from outlet shops and Dollywood." *(Nancy Cornell)*

Open All year.
Rooms 5 cottages, 1 suite, 12 doubles—all with full private bath, clock, air-conditioning, fan. 2 with whirlpool bath, 3 with balcony/deck, 4 with desk. Cottages with whirlpool tub, telephones, TV/VCR, books, fireplace, kitchenette, porch.
Facilities Dining room, living room with fireplace, family room with TV/VCR, books, videotapes; porch with hammock. Occasional musical entertainment. 60 acres with gazebo, lawn games. Lake, mountain stream nearby. 12 miles to skiing, 10 miles to hiking.
Location 4 m to town. From I-40 take Rte. 66S. Take U.S. 411E to Rte. 416S. Go right onto Jay Ell Rd. Go right onto Pullen Rd. Inn on right.
Restrictions No smoking. Children 12 and over.
Credit cards MC, Visa.
Rates B&B, $95 suite, $79–125 double, $69–115 single. Extra person, $15. Senior discount. 2-night minimum holiday, weekends in October. 25% midweek discount off-season.
Extras Limited wheelchair access.

Von Bryan Inn
2402 Hatcher Mountain Road, 37862

Tel: 615–453–9832
800–633–1459

The Von Bryan Inn, owned by D.J. and Jo Ann Vaughn since 1988, is a magnificent log home with beautiful mountain views from its windows, porches, decks, and patio. The cathedral-ceilinged living room has a stacked stone fireplace; guests can socialize and relax in the 11-person outdoor hot tub after a day of hiking or shopping. Guest rooms offer a blend of traditional and antique furnishings, with handmade quilts. A typical breakfast might include fresh fruit and juice, cereal, biscuits or popovers, and sausage-egg casserole or rice-asparagus casserole; rates also include afternoon refreshments.

"The inn sits on top of a 2,000-foot mountain, with panoramic views of the Wears Valley, farmland and grazing cows below, and the mountains beyond. The spacious guest rooms are spotlessly clean, comfortably furnished with queen- or king-sized beds, nice sitting areas, and ample closet and drawer space." *(Doris Waters)* "Helpful innkeepers who allowed us our privacy. Spent evenings rocking on the porch, relaxing in the hammock swing, or soaking in the hot tub. Most nights the innkeepers sit with a group of guests in the parlor or on the porch to chat in a relaxed, homey atmosphere. Breakfast favorites included stuffed French toast and sausage casserole." *(Mark & Jennifer Gragg)* "Magnificent sunrises and sunsets. Jo Ann, D.J., and their sons David and Patrick, are gracious and skilled hosts." *(Stephanie Reith)* "Gets our vote for the best views anywhere." *(Sibyl Nestor)*

Open All year.
Rooms 6 doubles—all with private bath and/or shower, telephone, radio, air-conditioning. 2 with whirlpool tub, 1 with steam shower. 3-bedroom, 2-bath cottage with living room with fireplace, kitchen, wraparound porch, TV, hot tub.

Facilities Dining room, living room with fireplace, piano, books, games, TV, stereo; sitting room, hot tub. 6 acres with swimming pool, swings, hammock, English garden. Hiking, skiing, fishing, rafting, tubing, boating, canoeing nearby.
Location From N and E: From I-40 take Exit 407 to Pigeon Forge. Go right onto 321S & 7.2 m to Hatcher Mt. Rd. Turn right & go to top of mountain. From S and W: Exit I-40 at #364 or I-75 at #81 onto 321N. Go through Maryville to Townsend, where 321N turns left. Stay on 321N for 8 more m. Turn left on Hatcher Mt. Rd.
Restrictions No smoking. No children under 11 in main house; any age welcome in cottage.
Credit cards Amex, Discover, MC, Visa.
Rates B&B, $160 cottage, $80–125 double. Extra person, $15. 10% discount for 2 or more nights midweek. 2-night minimum in cottage. Prix fixe lunch, $11; prix fixe dinner, $17.

SHELBYVILLE

Information please: The **Bottle Hollow Lodge** (111 Gobbler Ridge Road, P.O. Box 92, Shelbyville 37160; 615–695–5253) was built in 1990 of brick and fieldstone. Floral wallpapers decorate the spacious guest rooms; the decor includes cherry, walnut, and maple furnishings— both family antiques and hand-crafted period pieces. Breakfast typically includes country ham, biscuits, eggs, preserves, gravy, grits, and fruit. The inn's location on top of a high ridge provides handsome views and a peaceful, quiet setting. B&B double rates for the five guest rooms are $85.

About eight miles east of Shelbyville is the **Parish Patch Farm & Inn** (625 Cortner Road, Normandy 37360; 615–857–3018 or 800–289–3017), a 150-acre working farm, inn, and conference center on the banks of the Duck River. Guests can relax in the spacious living room or by the swimming pool, and dine at the nearby Cortner Mill Restaurant. Double rates range from $96–110, including a full breakfast. "Peaceful, serene, private. Stroll the riverbanks and eat at the old mill or at Our House Restaurant." *(Laura Patterson)*

TOWNSEND

Dubbed "the peaceful side of the mountain," Townsend occupies a scenic valley at the entrance to the Cades Cove loop of the Great Smoky Mountains National Park.

Information please: Owned by Jim and Bobbie Webb, the **Old Smoky Mountain Inn & Cabins** (238 Webb Road; Highway 321, Box 437, 37882; 615–448–2388) is comprised of the Mountain View Inn, with a deck and swimming pool, and a ten-person hot tub. Nearby, in the woods, are both "honeymoon" and regular family cabins. "Our cabin had a king-size water bed with mirrored canopy, a fireplace, hot tub, complete kitchen, back deck with grill and front porch with mountain views." *(Lynn Fullman)* Rates for the 24 units range from $55–125. Comments?

Richmont Inn   *Tel:* 615–448–6751
220 Winterberry Lane, 37882

Without exception, guests rave about the distinctive decor and architecture, gracious hospitality, exceptional comfort, attention to detail, beautiful mountain views, outstanding food, and romantic atmosphere of the Richmont Inn, built in 1991 by Jim and Susan Hind. Built in the unusual architectural style of the Appalachian cantilevered barn, with planked wood and slate floors, mortar-chinked log walls, and 13-foot high beamed ceilings, the inn offers pastoral views of the rolling green pastures of Laurel Valley and Rich Mountain. The elegant but comfortable decor includes 18th century American-English antiques, accented with American-French paintings and prints. Breakfast is served at tables for two in the panoramic dining area where you can watch the morning mist rise from the valley floor; a typical menu might consist of fresh-squeezed orange juice, granola, French baked eggs, apple oatmeal cinnamon pancakes, and home-baked sourdough bread. After dinner, guests return to the inn for such desserts as Grand Marnier soufflé, crème brulé Kahlua, and bourbon pecan cake, accompanied by flavored decaf coffees and herbal tea.

"Scenic views of the mountains, the scent of mountain heather, the relaxing sounds of romantic music." *(Kathy & Joe Mullin)* "Guest rooms are decorated after influential people in the history of the Smokies—a stained glass church window in the circuit rider's room; Native American designs in the rooms honoring Cherokee Indians." *(Linda Smalley)* "Tempting evening desserts, followed by weekend presentations by musicians, magicians, or mountain folk." *(Ronald & Leila-Anne Pass)* "Richmont is a 'second honeymoon' every time you visit." *(Charles Torrey)* "Wonderful hiking recommendations." *(Mary Rita & Ann Schwartz)* "Susan takes pride in her 200-ply cotton sheets and thick towels. Memorable granola, French baked eggs, and sugared bacon." *(Kathy Huncilman, and many others)*

Open All year.
Rooms 1 suite, 9 doubles—all with full private bath, air-conditioning, stereo. Most with double whirlpool tub, desk, fireplace, balcony/deck. 1 with refrigerator.
Facilities Dining room, living room with fireplace, piano, books; library with VCR; gift shop, deck. 11 acres with patio, lawn games, nature path, waterfall, pond. Golf, mountain river with fishing, kayaking, canoeing, hiking, skiing nearby.
Location E TN. 35 m E of Knoxville. 3 m to town. Enter Townsend city limits from Maryville on U.S. 321 N. Go right on Old Tuckaleecheee Rd. Follow signs to Laurel Valley. Take 1st paved rd. on right, Laurel Valley Rd. Go $^8/_{10}$ m, bear right through stone entrance to Laurel Valley. Stay on paved road to crest of hill. Turn left into inn.
Restrictions No smoking. Children over 12.
Credit cards None accepted.
Rates B&B, $135–140 suite, $85–125 double. Extra person, $25. 2-night minimum holidays & Oct. weekends. Prix fixe dinner, $25 for two. Picnic lunches.
Extras Wheelchair access; 1 bathroom specially equipped.

WALLAND

Blackberry Farm ♿
1471 West Millers Cove, 37886

Tel: 615–984–8166
800–862–7610
Fax: 615–983–5708

If an inn called Blackberry Farm, set in the Smokies, makes you think of country bumpkins and corncob pipes, think again. Built in 1930 of mountain stone, shingles, and slate, Blackberry Farm is undoubtedly the most elegant—and most expensive—inn in Tennessee. Owned by Kreis and Sandy Beall since 1976, and managed by Barry Marshall, its handsome rooms are richly appointed with Oriental rugs, flowered chintzes and other fine fabrics, and English and American antiques.

Famous for its fine food, prepared under the watchful eye of chef John Fleer, the inn's breakfasts always include fresh fruit and just-baked breads, with a choice of thick sliced bacon and blueberry cornmeal pancakes, or perhaps scrambled eggs, homemade sausage, buttermilk biscuits, and sawmill gravy. A typical lunch choice might consist of a leek and ricotta tart served with a salad of hearty greens and citrus, and lentil soup. At dinner, try the potato-horseradish crusted catfish or hickory-smoked loin of pork. The long list of desserts is no less tempting. Comments required.

Open All year.
Rooms 1 suite, 2 cottages, 28 doubles—all with full private bath, desk, air-conditioning. 1 with fireplace. Telephone, TV on request. Rooms in 2 buildings.
Facilities Dining room, lounge, breakfast room, living room, family room with TV/VCR, stereo, books; guest pantry. Most with fireplace. 1,100 acres with meeting facilities, heated swimming pool, 4 tennis courts, outdoor pavilion, stocked bass lake & trout pond; trout stream. Hiking trails; 3 m paved nature trail for jogging, bicycling; basketball court, lawn games. Bicycles, fly-fishing equipment, spin casting equipment, tennis racquets, basketballs. Golf, skiing nearby.
Location E TN. 40 min. S of Knoxville, 20 min. from Knoxville Airport. Halfway between Maryville and Townsend. From downtown Knoxville, take I-40 to Airport exit (Hwy. 129 S). Go 12.5 m to McGee Tyson airport. Past airport follow Hwy. 321 N 16 m to West Mills Cove Road ($\frac{1}{2}$ m past Foothills Pkwy.). Turn right & go 3/5 m to inn.
Restrictions No smoking in guest rooms, dining room. Children under 10 welcome only at Thanksgiving, Christmas. BYOB. Jackets required at dinner.
Credit cards Amex, MC, Visa.
Rates Full board (all-inclusive rates), $350–450 double, 15% service. 2-night weekend minimum.
Extras Limited wheelchair access. Member, Relais et Chateaux.

Appendix

STATE TOURIST OFFICES

Listed here are the addresses and telephone numbers for the tourist offices of the Southern states covered in this book. When you write or call one of these offices, be sure to request a map of the state and a calendar of events. If you will be visiting a particular city or region, or if you have any special interests, be sure to specify this as well.

Alabama Bureau of Tourism and
   Travel
401 Adams Avenue, P.O. Box 4309
Montgomery, Alabama 36103
205–242–4169 or 800–ALABAMA

Arkansas Department of Parks and
   Tourism
1 Capitol Mall
Little Rock, Arkansas 72201
501–682–7777 or 800–NATURAL

Florida Division of Tourism
Collins Building
107 West Gaines Street
Tallahassee, Florida 32399-2000
904–487–1462

Georgia Tourist Division
285 Peachtree Center Avenue NE,
Suite 1000, Box 1776,
Atlanta, Georgia 30303–1232
404–656–3590 or 800–847–4842

Kentucky Department of Travel
   Development
P.O. Box 2011
Frankfort, Kentucky 40602
800–225–TRIP

Louisiana Office of Tourism
P.O. Box 94291
Baton Rouge, Louisiana 70804–9291
504–342–8119 or 800–633–6970 (out
   of state)

Mississippi Division of Tourism
   Development
P.O. Box 1705
Ocean Springs, Mississippi 39564
800–WARMEST

North Carolina Travel and Tourism
   Division
430 North Salisbury Street
Raleigh, North Carolina 27611
919–733–4171 or 800–VISIT NC (out
   of state)

South Carolina Parks, Recreation and
   Tourism
1205 Pendleton Street
Columbia, South Carolina 29201
803–734–0122

Tennessee Tourist Development
P.O. Box 23170
Nashville, Tennessee 37202
615–741–2158

MAPS

MO

TN

Eureka Springs
Johnson
Hardy
Mountain View
Heber Springs

Altus

Little Rock
Brinkley
Corinth
Decatur

Hot Springs
Helena
Langley
ARKANSAS

Tupelo

ALA

Pine Bluff

Birmingham

MISSISSIPPI

Jemison
Shreveport
Monroe
Eutaw
Pra

Vicksburg
Greensboro
Sel

Natchitoches
Jackson

LOUISIANA
Natchez

TX
Lecompte

St. Francisville
Jackson
Eunice
New Roads
Baton Rouge
Slidell
Mobile
Lafayette
Fairhope
White Castle
De

St. Martinville
Darrow
New Orleans
Pass Christian
Orange Beach
S

Napoleonville
Pensacola
B

Lafitte

Gulf of Mexico

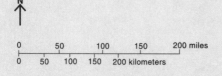

N

| 0 | 50 | 100 | 150 | 200 miles |
| 0 | 50 | 100 | 150 | 200 kilometers |

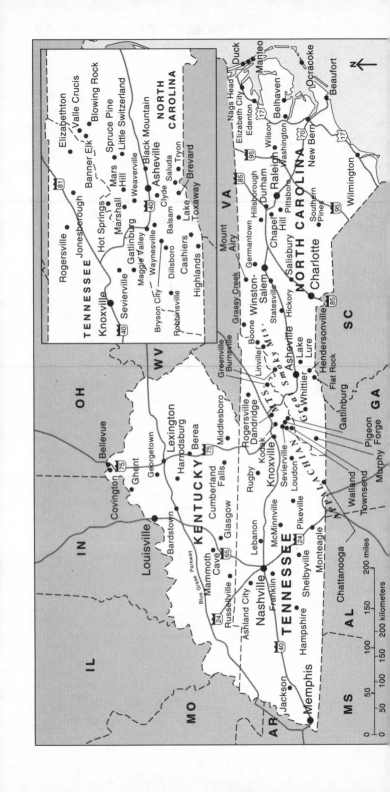

Index of Accommodations

Hotel/Inn Report Forms

The report forms on the following pages may be used to endorse or critique an existing entry or to nominate a hotel or inn that you feel deserves inclusion in next year's edition. Whichever you wish to do, don't feel you have to use our forms, or, if you do use them, don't feel you must restrict yourself to the space provided. All nominations (each on a separate piece of paper, if possible) should include your name and address, the name and location of the hotel or inn, when you have stayed there, and for how long. A copy of the establishment's brochure is also helpful. Please report only on establishments you have visited in the last eighteen months, unless you are sure that standards have not dropped since your stay. Please be as specific as possible, and critical where appropriate, about the character of the building, the public rooms, the accommodations, the meals, the service, the nightlife, the grounds, and the general atmosphere of the inn and the attitude of its owners. Any comments you have about area restaurants and sights would also be most appreciated.

Don't feel you need to write at length. A report that merely verifies the accuracy of existing listings is extremely helpful, i.e.: "Visited XYZ Inn and found it just as described." There is no need to bother with prices or with routine information about the number of rooms and facilities, although a sample brochure is very helpful for new recommendations. We obtain such details directly from the hotels selected. What we are eager to get from readers is information that is not accessible elsewhere.

On the other hand, don't apologize for writing a long report. Although space does not permit us to quote them in total, the small details provided about furnishings, atmosphere, and cuisine can really make a description come alive, illuminating the special flavor of a particular inn or hotel. Remember that we will again be awarding free copies to our most helpful respondents—last year we mailed over 500 books.

Please note that we print only the names of respondents, never addresses. Those making negative observations are not identified. Although we must always have your full name and address, we will be happy to print your initials, or a pseudonym, if you prefer.

These report forms may also be used, if you wish, to recommend good hotels in Europe to our equivalent publication, *Europe's Wonderful Little Hotels & Inns* (published in Europe as *The Good Hotel Guide*). Reports should be sent to *Europe's Wonderful Little Hotels & Inns*, St. Martin's Press, 175 Fifth Avenue, New York, NY 10010; to P.O. Box 150, Riverside, CT 06878; or directly to *The Good Hotel Guide*, 61 Clarendon Road, London W11. Readers in the UK can send their letters postage-free to *The Good Hotel Guide*, Freepost, London W11 4 BR.

To: *America's Wonderful Little Hotels & Inns,*
    P.O. Box 150, Riverside, CT 06878.

Name of hotel_____

Address_____

Telephone_____

Date of most recent visit_____ Duration of visit_____

☐ New recommendation   ☐ Comment on existing entry

Please be as specific as possible about furnishings, atmosphere, service, and cuisine. If reporting on an existing entry, please tell us whether you thought it accurate. Unless you tell us not to, we shall assume that we may publish your name in the next edition. Thank you very much for writing; use your own stationery if preferred:

I am not connected with the management/owners.
I would stay here again if returning to the area.   ☐ yes   ☐ no

Have you written to us before?   ☐ yes   ☐ no

Signed_____

Name_____
                        (Please print)

Address_____
                        (Please print)

_____

SO95/6

To: *America's Wonderful Little Hotels & Inns,*
  P.O. Box 150, Riverside, CT 06878.

Name of hotel_____

Address_____

Telephone_____

Date of most recent visit_____ Duration of visit_____

☐ New recommendation   ☐ Comment on existing entry

Please be as specific as possible about furnishings, atmosphere, service, and cuisine. If reporting on an existing entry, please tell us whether you thought it accurate. Unless you tell us not to, we shall assume that we may publish your name in the next edition. Thank you very much for writing; use your own stationery if preferred:

I am not connected with the management/owners.
I would stay here again if returning to the area.   ☐ yes   ☐ no
Have you written to us before?   ☐ yes   ☐ no

Signed_____

Name_____
                    (Please print)

Address_____
                    (Please print)

SO95/6